JAZZ
TALK

ROBERT S. GOLD

THE BOBBS-MERRILL COMPANY, INC.

Indianapolis / New York

FINE ARTS AND RECREATION

Copyright © 1975 by Robert S. Gold

Published by the Bobbs-Merrill Company, Inc.
Indianapolis/New York

ISBN 0-672-52093-1 hardcover
ISBN 0-672-52106-7 paperback
Library of Congress catalog card number 74-17642
Designed by Irving Perkins
Manufactured in the United States of America

First printing

FOR
Josh
(MY MAIN MAN)

PREFACE

There are literally hundreds of slang terms that reside in that gray area between two specialized slang vocabularies: jazz and black; jazz and rock; jazz and junkie; jazz and underworld; etc. I've included such "overlap" terms only when I've judged them to have an especial currency in the jazz world over and above their use in the general slang-using population.

I've excluded terms that have a too-restricted currency: Cab Calloway, Slim Gaillard, Mezz Mezzrow and other linguistically inventive jazz personalities have used terms that never gained much acceptance outside of their own immediate circles.

I've also excluded all kinds of spurious press-agent neologisms: "lip-splitter" for horn player; "box of teeth" for accordion; "gas pipe" for trombone; "belly fiddle" for guitar; and a hundred more terms that have seen the ink of print but not the vapors of speech (unless the columnist mouthed as he typed).

The credit for authenticating my text must go to all of those generous musicians, writers and jazz buffs who clarified so much for me. Thanks again to those who helped with the original *A Jazz Lexicon* (New York: Knopf, 1964): Danny Barker, Emmett Berry, Eubie Blake, Harold Flakser, Ira Gitler, Gigi Gryce, Allan F. Hubbell, Leon James, Dick Katz, Jan Kindler, Paul Knopf, Eddie Locke, S. P. Lomax, Dan Morgenstern, the late Tony Parenti, Gordon Pheil, the late Bob Reisner, Jerome Richardson, Zutty Singleton, Jean and the late Marshall Stearns, Hsio Wen Shih and John A. Williams.

For this edition my thanks go to Andy Billek, Mike Doorley, Albert Goldman, Jan Kindler (once again), Bucky Pizzarelli, Dave Schnitter and Zoot Sims; and I owe an especial debt of gratitude for their super-expertise to Elliot Horne, to Dan Morgenstern (yet again) and to Peter Tamony (San Francisco's gift to lexicography).

Finally, my thanks to all those vital people who created the sounds—musical *and* verbal.

INTRODUCTION

Taking the stand one night at a West Coast jazz concert a quarter of a century ago, jazz's premier tenor saxophonist, Lester Young, turned to his drummer for the night, Louis Bellson, and said, "Lady Bellson, don't drop no bombs behind me, baby, just give me that *titty-boom, titty-boom* all night on the cymbal, and I'm cool." The uninitiated might have been mystified by the instruction, but the drummer wasn't: "bombs" are the sudden bass-drum explosions which had come into vogue a few years earlier and which Lester's Kansas City swing style was uncomfortable with; "cool," in context, means contented; "baby" is a popular term of address among jazzmen; the double "titty-boom" is simply Lester's onomatopoeic rendering of the desired rhythmic pattern; and "Lady" is what Lester aristocratically called everyone, an ironic-respectful term of address.

What's missing from the above transcription and exegesis is Lester's speaking style—the nuances achieved by phrasing and by tone and pitch variation, which are also aspects of Lester's musical style. (Proposition: Transcribed speech is to speech as transcribed music is to actual performance.)

A slang dictionary can provide definitions (and, sometimes, word origins), but no mere glossary will inflame the reader's auditory imagination; if jazz slang's spirit of rich musicality and existential wit is to be captured, there must also be examples of the terms as they are used in specific contexts.

Jazz Talk offers selective citations from an admittedly sketchy written record (it's unfortunate that those who most use slang are least likely to express themselves in writing). The thousands of quotations in this volume will serve to encapsulate jazz language within the larger perspective of the jazz life, spanning its 80-year-or-so history. As jazz has evolved from its funeral-march, brass-band and piano-rag beginnings to small-band New Orleans and Chicago style, big-band swing (or Kansas City) style, bop and post-bop, its special argot has undergone many changes, sometimes though not always parallel to changes in the music.

Slang—*any* slang—is the creation and property of people lacking formal education, and the blacks who created jazz in the first two decades of our century brought into the musical life a colorful rural and ghetto vocabulary that had resisted the standardization of language which typifies educated urban centers. As the new music became grist for the commercial mill, black folk idiom was infused with terms deriving from new conditions of musical performance and, most important, with underworld argot. Always close (though hardly by choice) to the most sordid aspects of big-city life, urban blacks had early assimilated the jargon of the rackets—dope peddling, prostitution, larceny and gambling; but now even the gin mills, brothels and nightclubs which housed jazz were owned by racketeers, most of them white.

As the jazz community coalesced, understandably an entire sub-vocabulary emerged—terms for musical styles, devices and effects; for instruments; for dances and dancers. Later, a critical vocabulary arose as writers struggled to describe freshly the quality of jazz art. These purely musical terms constitute a jargon such as exists in all occupations, and is perhaps the least interesting part of any specialized vocabulary.

It's the locutions that flow out from the center, registering feelings, behavior, and moral and esthetic judgments, that are most interesting, because they most crucially reflect the philosophy and "style" of the speakers. For example, *mean, dirty, low-down* and *nasty* (all current c. 1900), and *bad, tough, hard* and *terrible* all carry favorable connotations in jazz speech, while *sweet, pretty, square* and *straight* are usually unfavorable; it requires no cultural historian to detect the basic black distrust of white moral and esthetic standards lying behind such semantic reversals. If one is "bad" or "tough," he might just be bad enough or tough enough for the society not to ignore (an old habit of white officialdom when it comes to blacks). If one is "square," on the other hand, he might well enjoy *Mickey Mouse* or *ricky-tick* music or a *businessman's bounce* and not understand that many blacks still *feel a draft.*

The distrust of conventional white morality is also evident in the practice of assigning favorable connotations to terms of mental de-

x

rangement *(crazy, insane, nutty);* there is also an implied antipathy to the bleak realities of twentieth-century existence in such transcendant superlatives as *out of this world, far out, gas(sed), gone, out of sight* and *something else.*

The travails of survival can lead a musician (black *or* white) to feel *beat, brought down, bugged, drugged, hung up, strung out, hassled* or *up tight,* so that he must *scuffle* and *pay dues* in order to survive, and ease his way by being *hip, fly, down, booted* and *ready.*

Problems and solemnity aside, jazz slang most often reflects the basic affirmation of the music, its joy and ebullience: *jump, ride, rock, roll, romp, swing, stomp, jitterbug* and *boogie-woogie;* its fire and intensity: *hot, burning, cooking* and *smoking;* its colorful settings: *honkytonk, barrelhouse* and *gutbucket;* its people: *cats, chicks, studs, foxes* and *dudes;* its clothing: *togs, drapes, threads* and *vines;* and its good times: *jamming, balling, grooving,* and *getting one's kicks.*

In opting for color and incisiveness, slang necessarily sacrifices the standard vocabulary's finer distinctions and exactitude of expression. Jazz slang gets plenty of mileage from its narrow range of locutions, particularly from its verbs. *Pick up,* for example, covers a lot of waterfront: to get, take, learn, find, understand, appreciate, etc. Most jazz slang verbs are multiple-meaning action verbs *(blow, broom, cook, cop, dig, jump, knock, latch on, make,* and *put down),* a linguistic image of jazz's playfulness and vitality.

Obviously most slang is metaphoric, but less obvious is why metaphors tend to be elaborately decorative in one period and severely functional in another, though World War II is a divider between the easy-going, loose hyperbole of the Louis Armstrong-Cab Calloway generation *(collar the jive; like the bear, I ain't nowhere; plant you now and dig you later)* and the unsmiling incisiveness of the boppers *(dig it; ax; cool).* The always prevailing tendency, however, is the movement toward simplicity, of pruning away as much of a phrase as seems extraneous: *split the scene* becomes simply *split; dig you later* simply *later.*

The high casualty rate of emotionally charged slang terms (especially superlatives, which sometimes have only a three- or five-year vogue) has led some students of language to regard the entire slang vocabulary as ephemeral. Not so. Some staples of jazz slang have been around for a long time: *dig, jive, cop, gig, scarf, hip, jazz* itself and dozens more have survived the ravages of linguistic fickleness.

The slang casualty rate, however, does exceed that of the standard language. Sometimes the fatality is caused by the spontaneous discovery of a fresher or wittier metaphor or image (*stud* with its macho connotation, for example, yielding to the more humorous tenderfoot image of *dude*), and sometimes by the coterie value of a term's being destroyed by the general public's adoption of it (these days even DAR members may be heard intoning that someone "tells it like it is" or assuring a host that they've "had a ball"). Jazzmen are not especially flattered by imitation, particularly when their language is aped by people with no appreciation of the life that produces it. The media's tendency to caricature jazz slang is not very different from Hollywood's antique and dishonorable practice of using jazz on a sound-track to suggest tawdriness or sleaziness.

In the 1960s there were copious borrowings from jazz slang by the rock-youth culture, and many of these terms were further disseminated among the general public by TV dramas, ads and talk shows; the upshot of all the media attention was to blur the already fuzzy distinctions among the various specialized slangs (jazz, black, rock, narcotics, hot rod, underworld, etc.). For its part the jazz world seems to have resisted the rock-youth linguistic impact: jazzmen will only occasionally be heard using terms like "rap," "rip off," "where (someone) is coming from," "bummer," "trip," "let it all hang out," "good (or bad) vibes" and "right on!" (the jazz equivalent remains *straight ahead!*).

There is evidence lately, for better or worse, of a rapprochement between jazz and rock: many young musicians play both; some of the middle-generation of established jazzmen (Freddie Hubbard, Herbie Hancock and McCoy Tyner among them) have converted to the rock practice of using heavily amplified rhythm sections; jazz publication *Down Beat* now gives considerable coverage to rock. Add one more heavy fact—the inevitable dying out of the older generation of jazzmen—and it's plain to see that the future of jazz slang is in question.

Whether its identity as a separate vocabulary is preserved, or the behavioral segment of it continues to be absorbed into the thickening amalgam of general slang available to a Madison Avenue plugged-in public, historically jazz slang is a triumph (albeit a minor one set beside the music). To be sure, there are egregious lapses of taste in the usage: jazzmen can be as corny as American Legionnaires in matters of money, intoxication and—God help us!—women (those appalling blues lyrics!). But overall, jazz slang is like the music and the musical life it reflects, a vital, creative and socially significant form of human expression.

Jazz Talk

A & R, *adj.* [abbreviation; primarily a music trade term; current since c. 1950] Artists and repertory man.

1959 *N.Y. Times,* 15 Nov., Sec. II, p. 4M. In the recording business, A means artists; R, repertory. In a general way, an A & R man is the demiurge who selects A & R, herds the former into a studio, supervises their rendition of the latter, and edits the taped results with an engineer at his side.

1960 *Jazz: A Quarterly of American Music,* Winter, p. 48. We just happen to have an A & R man with a lot of soul.

ace, *n.* 1. [from gambling slang; cf. 1930 *American Tramp and Underworld Slang,* s.v. *ace:* "dollar bill"; widely current among jazzmen since c. 1935]

1945 *Hepcats Jive Talk Dictionary,* s.v. *ace:* dollar bill.

1952 *Who Walk in Darkness,* p. 13. Can you lend me an ace?

2. [by analogy with the highest of playing cards; current c. 1940–c. 1950, rare since]

1950 *The Book of Negro Folklore,* p. 481. *ace:* bosom friend.

1960 *Beat Jokes Bop Humor & Cool Cartoons,* p. 40. The Ham's tight ace, Horatio, had brought news of the ghost of The Big Ham.

adj. [current c. 1935–c. 1945, rare since] Primary; best.

1944 *Dan Burley's Original Handbook of Harlem Jive,* p. 133. *ace-lane:* husband.

1960 *Hiparama of the Classics,* p. 15. Hip to the cool sweet groove of Liberty and solid sent upon the Ace Lick that all Cats and Kitties, Red, White, or Blue! are created Level, in FRONT.

v.t. [cf. 1929 *American Speech,* June, "The Vocabulary of Bums,"

p. 337. *"ace in:* to place yourself or a friend in the good graces of someone"; current since c. 1935] To help [someone], usually by getting [oneself or one's friend] work as a musician or, less frequently, an introduction to a woman.

1962 *Down Beat,* Jan., p. 2. Sis, you've aced me again.

action [prob. from the gambling slang sense (i.e., bets); cf. 1960 *Dictionary of American Slang* s.v. *action:* "Activity, excitement"; cf. also its Early Modern English use (i.e., in the sense of sexual intercourse): c. 1607 *Pericles,* IV, ii. 8–9, "They with continual action are even as good as rotten"; current since c. 1930; see also HAPPENINGS, PLAY, *n.*] Any activity, but especially that relating to jazz and to women.

1944 *Dan Burley's Original Handbook of Harlem Jive,* p. 133. *action:* motivating force, issue, situation, proposition.

1960 *Hiparama of the Classics,* p. 21. Man that Chick is puttin' down some action!!

1971 *N.Y. Times Mag.,* 28 Nov. p. 92. Only action he get is with his hand.

ad lib [from standard musical terminology (see 1949 quot.); widely current c. 1920–c. 1935, obs. since except historical; replaced by the standard term *improvise* and the slang term *blow*]

1926 *Jazz* (Whiteman & McBride), p. 73. Perhaps I should mention that "ad lib" is a jazz musical term meaning to improvise, to invent as you go along.

1949 *Music Library Association Notes,* Dec., p. 35. Many . . . familiar terms come direct from "longhairs" [q.v.] —*ad lib.*

after hours, *prep. phr.* [refers to a practice common only c. 1925–c. 1945, when musicians could, unpaid, play uninhibitedly and to their own liking only at certain clubs and at special hours, and hardly ever at their regular, paying music jobs; rare since 1945] See note above and 1960 quot.

1942 *After Hours* (tune written by Avery Parrish, recorded by the Erskine Hawkins Orchestra).

1960 *The Story of the Original Dixieland Jazz Band,* p. 167. These enthusiastic youngsters, who were much in demand in jazz-hungry New York, often gathered with members of the Dixieland Band "after hours" for jam sessions and the inevitable sounds of nocturnal revelry in which girl friends played no little part.

adj. 1959 *The Permanent Playboy*, p. 243. We would play our regular jobs until 3:00 A.M., then go to an after-hours place until around 7:00.

air check [*check* in the sense of executive control; current in the trade since c. 1935] A (musical) radio broadcast recorded and preserved by the broadcasting company for its own purposes, sometimes released commercially many years later.

1962 *Billie Holiday: The Golden Years* (boxed-set booklet), p. 6. Three tracks, previously unreleased . . . are airchecks of Billie Holiday singing with the Count Basie orchestra.

1973 *Benny Goodman from the Congress Hotel* (Sunbeam SB 128 liner notes). For years collectors have been aware of the probable existence of air checks from the Congress engagement.

alley fiddle [see quot. for key to semantic development—i.e., the natural association of a "primitive" style with the attributive *alley;* primarily in the Midwest, esp. in Chicago, where jazz bands frequently used violins, the phrase had some currency c. 1910–c. 1925, obs. since except historical]

1939 *Jazzmen,* p. 18. Freddie Keppard . . . played violin in a primitive style known as "alley fiddle."

alligator, *n.* [term poss. an expanded form of *gate* q.v., although jazz critic Martin Williams suggests that Armstrong coined the term as a criticism of young white musicians who, like alligators, followed the black players on riverboats in order to sop up their ideas: see last quot.; widely current esp. among white jazzmen c. 1935–c. 1940, obs. since except historical]

1938 *N.Y. Post,* 3. Feb., p. 15. Now, then, the alligators, that's the swing fans, get the drift.

1955 *Hear Me Talkin to Ya,* p. 97. We'd call them alligators . . . because they were the guys who came up to swallow everything we had to learn.

all-in, *adj.* [refers to the practice in traditional jazz of *all* the instruments coming back *in* after the individual solo choruses have been played; current c. 1917–c. 1945, rare since except historical; see also EVERY TUB, (LET'S) GO HOME and RIDE-OUT] In traditional jazz, the final chorus; see 1946 quot.

3

1926 *Melody Maker,* Oct., pp. 62–63. If an "all-in" chorus has been used first, a repetition of the same movement is, of course, unnecessary.

1941 *Gems of Jazz; Vol. III,* p. 3. The ending has . . . four bars of all-in jamming.

1946 *The PL Yearbook of Jazz,* p. 32. Their improvisatory urge found its expression in the disjointed "Jam session," with its string of solos followed by a chaotic "all-in" chorus.

all over, see s.v. OVER.

all reat, all reet, alreet, all root [corruptions of *all right;* cf. *1960 Dictionary of American Slang,* s.v. *all reet:* "orig. jive use c. 1935; pop. student use c. 1940; archaic"; see also REET]

1943 *New Yorker,* 19 June, p. 15. "All reat" . . . is the rug-cutter's way of saying "all right."

1944 *Esquire,* June, p. 170. *all root:* universally okay.

1970 *The World of Duke Ellington,* p. 140. Back in the days of "all reet" and "all root," Ben Webster gave Ray Nance the nickname of "Root," appropriate to many of those qualities that distinguish him [i.e., taste, stylishness].

all that, *adj. phr.* [one of several quantitative terms given a qualitative meaning by jazzmen (see also LOT, GANG); current since c. 1935] Excellent; superb.

1972 *Jazz Masters of the Thirties,* p. 181. Not only did he play all that piano . . .

apple, (big) [by analogy with the shape of the world, then by synecdoche; also, see 1966 quot. for etym.; current since c. 1930] New York City; also see first two quots.

1938 *Cab Calloway: Hi De Ho,* p. 16. *apple:* the big town, the main stem, Harlem.

1944 *Dan Burley's Original Handbook of Harlem Jive,* p. 133. *apple:* the earth, the universe, this planet. Any place that's large. A big Northern city.

1946 *Really the Blues,* p. 165. As soon as we hit the Big Apple, we'll ditch the buggy.

1950 *Gutbucket and Gossamer,* p. 26. Why should she stay in the Apple over a July weekend?

1966 *Record Research,* June, p. 7. My suspicion [is] that *Big Apple* is a transliteration of the older Mexican idiom "Manzane principale" for the main square of the town or the downtown area.

ass, *n.* [synecdoche; prob. from black and/or armed forces slang; current since c. 1950] Person; self.

1958 *Somewhere There's Music,* p. 180. If I knew it'd kill my ass, I'd follow.

1960 *The Jazz Word,* p. 109. There's not really a living ass to talk to.

1967 *Black on Black,* p. 136. All someun wants to do is get my ass in jail.

1969 *The Life and Loves of Mr. Jiveass Nigger,* p. 118. He liked that crazy ass Ula.

-assed, *suffix* [general slang emphasis additive, esp. common among jazzmen since c. 1930] Vulgar intensifier.

1956 *Lady Sings the Blues,* p. 65. All alone in a room upstairs, snoring up a breeze and cuddling a big-assed bottle of champagne. —pp. 225–226. They slapped a high-assed old bail of seventy-five hundred dollars on us.

1963 *Nugget,* Feb., p. 46. I've hated chicks since the day I first laid eyes on my bad-assed mother.

1969 *The Life and Loves of Mr. Jiveass Nigger,* p. 149. That peroxide blonde from the States, with them green-ass eyes.

-aureenie (& variants) [from a diminutive-affectionate impulse; some currency c. 1945–c. 1960, rare since] Playful, meaningless suffix.

1943 *Linger Awhile* (Lester Young's recorded version). Take it, Prez-aureenie!

1966 *New Yorker,* 25 June, p. 38. We'll have a little taste, a little Scotcherini.

1970 *Blue Movie,* p. 56. The highest paid darling of the silver screen—nailing ten percent of the boxoroonie.

1971 *Beneath the Underdog,* p. 287. Maybe we all can—Lee-Marie, Donna, you know, a little daisy chainerooney.

ax, axe, *n.* [see 1958 quot. for semantic explanation; current since c. 1950]

1956 *Sideman,* p. 25. You wanta make it with me tonight? Bring your ax.

1957 *N.Y. Times Magazine,* 18 Aug., p. 26. *axe:* any musical instrument, even a piano.

1958 *Publication of the American Dialect Society,* Nov., p. 43. *ax:* any of the solo reed or (less commonly) brass instruments. Orig. a saxophone. From fancied resemblance in shape plus the abbr. *sax.*

1959 *Esquire,* Nov., p. 70H. *ax:* instrument, horn. Extended to mean any tool of work. Example: Hemingway's ax is his typewriter.

1960 *Jazz: A Quarterly of American Music,* Winter, p. 20. I am digging a recorded group from Canada though, with four axes.

B

baby, *n.* [some general slang use, but with esp. currency among jazzmen since c. 1945 to anyone, regardless of sex] See second 1959 quot.

1925 *English Words & Their Background,* p. 59. *Oh, baby! Jazz baby.*

1959 *Selected Poems,* Langston Hughes, p. 111. *I asked you, baby,/If you understood.*

1959 *Newport Jazz Festival: 1959,* p. 45. *baby:* a general appellation directed at either sex.

1965 *Down Beat,* 25 Mar., p. 21. *Hey, baby, glad to have you in the band.*

back, *v.t.* [extension of the standard meaning (i.e., to support); current since c. 1930; see also COMP] To provide accompaniment (for solo instruments); as noun: accompaniment.

1940 *Swing,* Jan., p. 24. *Everyone, however, seems happy in the rowdy backing, which gives plenty of punch to a good old barroom song.* —June, p. 17. *The backing is based on a riff that's been used for several other numbers lately.*

1961 *Jazz Journal,* July, p. 4. *I've heard a record or two of Lang backing a singer, and his harmonies and little fill-ins are really something.*

back, from (way) back, *adv. & prep. phr.* [logic of its use derives from a belief in the positive correlation of worth with experience; current c. 1925–c. 1945, rare since] An intensifier (usually implying only the sense given in 1928 quot.).

1928 *The Walls of Jericho,* p. 300. *from way back:* of extraordinary experience and skill.

1944 *Dan Burley's Original Handbook of Harlem Jive,* p. 16. That's a gasser from back.

1952 *Flee the Angry Strangers,* p. 249. She smoked enough for ten way-back vipers.

1959 *Diggeth Thou?,* p. 40. The spielers were shucking some hard jive from back.

back beat [so called because less prominent than the major accent; current since c. 1920] A secondary rhythmic accent.

1928 *Melody Maker,* Dec., p. 1295. Back Beats! (column title).

1948 *Metronome,* Nov., p. 28. I'd rather use the high-hat as a back beat and break up the bass drum rhythms.

1971 *Down Beat,* 23 Dec., p. 34. It seemed like a leader got a session together and put today's backbeat—it used to be called a shuffle.

back of the beat, see s.v. BEHIND THE BEAT.

bad, *adj. & adv.* [*Dictionary of American Slang* (1960) is mistaken in characterizing the term as an "understatement" (p. 13); the term is one of several which *emphatically* reverse the standard meaning: see also HARD, MEAN, TERRIBLE, TOUGH; cf. 1928 black slang listing in *The Walls of Jericho,* s.v. *too bad:* "marvelous"; widely current among jazzmen since c. 1945]

1958 *Publication of the American Dialect Society,* Nov., p. 43. *bad:* Good. However, at times, it may mean "bad," and the listener must determine meaning from context, tone of voice, facial expression, etc.

1959 *Esquire,* Nov., p. 70H "*bad:* good." Example: A bad man on flute. A superlative musician on flute.

1959 *Jazz: A Quarterly of American Music,* Fall, p. 294. He's bad—he can play his ass off.

1965 *A Drop of Patience,* p. 63. "You a bad man, Ludlow Washington." There was admiration in her voice.

the baddest [combination of *bad* with the tendency to form superlatives by adding the suffix *-est* (q.v.) to any word; some currency since c. 1955] The very best (usually, performer).

1969 *The Life and Loves of Mr. Jiveass Nigger,* pp. 61–62. I have great confidence in you. You're the baddest nigger in this section of the country.

bad face, see s.v. FACE.

bad scene, see s.v. SCENE.

bag [prob. by analogy with "bag of tricks"; current since c. 1958; see also GROOVE] Initially, the imaginary repository of a musician's ideas, conception, style, attack; by extension, the source of one's behavior.

1960 *The Jazz Word,* p. 188. Man, that's really in another bag.

1961 *Down Beat,* 2 Feb., p. 30. Soul is appropriately earthy, medium tempoed, and melodically a bit doubtful as to what jazz bag it belongs in.

1962 *Jazz Journal,* March, p. 30. "Bag" is a current piece of trade jargon for hip musicians, and means something between a personal style and a body of work.

1962 *N.Y. Times Magazine,* 20 May, p. 45. *bag:* a point of view or pattern of behavior.

1970 *Death of a Blue-Eyed Soul Brother,* p. 20. I dig everything about this lady, but what was her bag?

ball, *n.* [prob. by analogy with the pleasure derived from being at a ball (i.e., a formal dance); cf. *1960 Dictionary of American Slang,* s.v. *ball.* "Some early c. 1935 Negro jive use. Orig. popularized by bop and cool use, and associated with jazz and avant-garde groups. Now common student and teen-age use, with less emphasis on being unrestricted and exciting, and some general use"; see also *pitch a bitch* s.v. BITCH]

1938 *Cab Calloway: Hi De Ho,* p. 16. *have a ball:* to enjoy yourself, stage a celebration.

1948 *Trumpet on the Wing,* p. 68. One ball we pitched got to be just too much.

1954 *Esquire,* Nov., p. 135. "Life was like one long ball in those days," Norvo recalls. "We played and imbibed, played and imbibed."

1959 *The Holy Barbarians,* p. 52. They sent me to Saipan, which was even more of a ball.

v.i. 1. [formed from *n.;* current since c. 1940]

1942 *American Mercury,* July, p. 94. *balling:* having fun.

1954 *Esquire,* Nov., p. 131. In Norvo's youth, he balled with the best, . . . he drank a lot, he experimented with the dread weed, he stayed up for long stretches.

2. (also *v.t.*) [extension of sense 1; current since c. 1940] To engage in sexual intercourse (with).

1959 *Easy Living,* p. 30. I ain't balled her yet, if that's what you're asking.

1960 *The Jazz Review,* May, p. 30. Look, sweetheart, I don't care if they're gonna ball in the streets.

1963 *The Realist,* June, p. 29. Is it bizarre that married guys have to jerk off more than anyone else, because your old ladies won't ball you and you can't chippie [i.e., philander]?

ballin' the jack [cf. *1960 Dictionary of American Slang,* s.v. *ball the jack:* "To go, move, or work very rapidly or fast. Orig. logger use, from *highballing*"; current c. 1913–c. 1927, obs. since except historical] A dance in vogue c. 1913–c. 1927, consisting largely of bumps and grinds.

1913 *Ballin' the Jack* (title of song composed by Chris Smith & Jim Burris).

1943 *The Jazz Record,* 15 Apr., p. 3. In 1917 . . . there were several dances in vogue, namely: "walkin' the dog," "jazz dance," and "ballin' the jack."

band man [cf. sports slang "team man" (i.e., cooperative ballplayer); some currency since c. 1935] A jazzman who excels in ensemble playing, though is not necessarily a distinguished soloist.

1946 *The PL Yearbook of Jazz,* p. 148. King was always a "band man," playing lead and keeping fairly close to the melody, rather than a flashy soloist.

barbecue, *n.* [one of a number of food metaphors for a woman; also, according to jazzmen, the term often has a hidden reference to female genitalia; current esp. among black jazzmen c. 1925–c. 1945, rare since] See 1944 quot.

1928 *Struttin' with Some Barbecue* (tune written by Lil Armstrong and Don Ray).

1944 *Dan Burley's Original Handbook of Harlem Jive,* p. 133. *barbecue:* a very attractive girl.

bari, bary, *n.* [abbreviation; current since c. 1935] A baritone saxophone.

1955 *Down Beat,* Sep., p. 30. It might have been Gerry on bary.

1961 *Metronome,* Feb., p. 41. I told her I played bari in Duke's band!

barrelhouse, barrel-house, *n., v.,* & *adj.* [cf. 1938 DAE, s.v. *barrelhouse:* "a cheap saloon: 1883"; also cf. 1913 Vachel Lindsay, *The Congo:* "Barrel House kings, with feet unstable"; also see quots. for explanation of semantic development; obs. since c. 1940 except historical] See 1949, 1952, 1956 quots.

1913 *Memphis Blues* (song composed by Handy & Norton). I don't care what Mister Crump don't 'low,/I'se gonna bar'l-house anyhow.

1926 *So This Is Jazz*, p. 99. Trumpets and trombones . . . impart half-confidences in that semi-muffled voice aptly described by the term "barrel-house tone."

1935 *Vanity Fair*, Nov., p. 71. Additional synonyms for hot music are . . . barrel-house (slang for "cheap saloon").

1949 *Music Library Association Notes*, Dec., p. 39. *barrelhouse:* a style of piano playing, rhythmic, syncopated, seductive and "blue." Term seems to have originated in relation to the type of piano entertainment offered in cheap saloons and in New Orleans houses of prostitution about 1910.

1952 *A History of Jazz in America*, p. 349. *barrelhouse:* after the New Orleans cabarets in which liquor was dispensed from barrels; music that is rough and ready, chiefly applied to Dixieland, but not exclusively.

1956 *Guide to Jazz.* s.v. *barrel house:* Southern term once used to describe small beer joints. Since the early years of the 20th century, a pianist or a small group usually playing unpretentious but excellent jazz in the barrel houses, so good that the word becomes a synonym for rough, spontaneous, uninhibited jazz. On piano the style is harsh and strident . . . so it can be heard above the bedlam going on around.

battle, *n.* [special application of the standard sense; current c. 1915–c. 1945, very rare since except historical; see also CUTTING CONTEST] A musical competition, usually between orchestras, sometimes between instrumentalists.

1929 Savoy Ballroom advertisement, 8 May [1962 *Jazz: A History of the New York Scene*, p. 198]. For this "Battle of Jazz" the Savoy at a tremendous cost is bringing to this city three of the South's best orchestras.

1932 *The Inter-State Tattler*, 5 May, p. 10. What a battle of music will be waged between three of the leading orchestras in New York City.

1946 *Esquire's 1946 Jazz Book*, p. 29. This group participated in many "battles" with the best Negro organizations.

1958 *Jam Session*, p. 210. Or it may be "battle" wherein two similar instruments show each other their strength, friendly or unfriendly.

Bean, see s.v. HAWK.

bear, *n.* 1. [according to jazzmen, the term derives from the nickname of a legendary New Orleans pianist, fl. 1890; cf. *1960 Dictionary of American Slang,* p. 24: "c. 1915 pop song: 'Everybody's doin' it. Doin' what? Turkey trot. Ah, my honey, honey, I declare! It's a bear! It's a bear!' "; widely current c. 1900–c. 1925, rare since: see sense 2] See 1960 quot.

1916 *Walkin' the Dog* (song composed by Matzan & Atteridge). But there,/it's a bear now.

1924 (Columbia Records publicity release) If you ever heard a plea that came from the bottom of an apprehensive heart, you have a very slight idea of how the "gal" put her stuff over. It's a bear.

1959 *The Eddie Costa-Vinnie Burke Trio* (liner notes on LP album Jubilee 1025). My man, Eddie Costa—he's a bear!

1960 *Dictionary of American Slang,* s.v. *bear:* a remarkable, first-rate person or thing, a humdinger.

2. [from the rhyming slang vogue c. 1935–c. 1940: word was rhymed with *nowhere,* q.v., and c. 1937–c. 1943 the term was usually pejorative; obs. since c. 1943] An unsuccessful or unhappy state or condition; impoverishment.

1942 *American Mercury,* July, p. 96. *the bear:* confession of poverty.

1959 *The Jazz Scene,* p. 292. *Jack the Bear:* nowhere [jazz sense].

1970 *Dictionary of Afro-American Slang,* p. 24 *bear:* (1930s–1940s) unpleasant life style; an ugly woman.

beat, *n.* [from verb in phrase "beat time"; current since c. 1900; see also TIME]

1926 *Melody Maker,* Sep., p. 11. The Charleston is a fast fox-trot with an unusual beat.

1952 *A History of Jazz in America,* p. 349. *beat:* jazz time; more meaningful to jazz musicians as an honorific description of rhythmic skill ("he gets a fine beat") than as a description of an underlying 2/4 or 4/4 or 6/8 or any other time.

1956 *Guide to Jazz,* s.v. *beat:* not merely the number of beats to the bar, but the pulse created within and around those beats.

adj. [cf. *1960 Dictionary of American Slang,* s.v. *beat:* "Prob. from 'beat-out' or 'beat-up' gen'l slang since c. 1750"; widely current among jazzmen since c. 1935; cf. its non-jazz adaptations, e.g., *beat generation, beatnik*]

1935 *We Who Are About to Die,* p. 194. Boy, I'll bet that kid was very beat.

1939 *Jitterbug Jamboree Song Book,* p. 32. *beat:* tired, lacking anything, low in spirit.

1939 *Jazzmen,* p. 5. He came from the beat side of town.

1956 *Sideman,* p. 53. I believe I'll go to bed. I'm sure beat.

1957 *On the Road,* p. 61. He had fallen on the beat and evil days that come to young guys in their middle twenties.

beat to the (or **one's**) **socks** [cf. general slang intensifying phrase "from the top of my head to the tips of my toes"; widely current c. 1935–c. 1945, obs. since except historical] Intensified form of *beat.*

1935 *San Francisco Call-Bulletin,* 8 Feb. "Beat to the socks" (broke).

1939 *Fortune,* July, p. 78. Harlem is "beat to its socks."

beat (it) out [shortened form of "beat out the rhythm"; current c. 1900–c. 1945, obs. since except historical]

1938 *Cab Calloway: Hi De Ho,* p. 16. *beat it out:* play it hot, emphasize the rhythm.

1939 *Jazzmen,* p. 62. Jones, beat it out in B-Flat.

1955 *Saturday Review,* 25 June, p. 49. I'd stand there listening to King Oliver beat out one of those ole good-ones like "Panama."

bebop, be-bop, *n. & adj.* [see 1959 quots. for explanation of semantic development; widely current only c. 1944–c. 1948, when it was almost completely replaced in the speech of jazzmen by *bop;* hence, rare since 1948 except in print] See second 1959 quot.

1944 *Beebop Blues* (tune by Dizzy Gillespie; spelling is unique).

1947 *Metronome,* Nov., p. 38. Fats doesn't like the name *bebop.* "It's just modern music. What they call bebop is really a series of chord progressions."

1959 *Toledo* (Ohio) *Blade,* 15 Feb. However, the word itself, Tamony writes, appears in numerous forms back through the history of jazz as early as 1928 . . . it faded away until applied to Gillespie and his music at Minton's.

1959 *New Yorker,* 7 Nov., p. 158. Of all the queer, uncommunicative, secret-society terms that jazz has surrounded itself with, few are lumpier or more misleading than "bebop." Originally a casual onomatopoeic word used to describe the continually shifting accents of the early work of Charlie Parker, Dizzy Gillespie, Kenny Clarke, and Thelonious Monk, it soon became a free-floating, generic one as well,

13

whose tight, rude sound implied something harsh, jerky, and unattractive.

1961 *Ibid.,* 18 Feb., p. 127. Describing bebop in the past tense is not wholly accurate, for it survives, in diffused shapes, in the work of almost all modern-jazz musicians.

be-bop glasses [current c. 1945–c. 1950, very rare since: supplanted by *shades,* q.v.] Dark (tinted) glasses.

1956 *Sideman,* p. 121. May have to get me a beret and some be-bop glasses.

behind the beat [from a tendency common in jazz; current since c. 1920] Of a singer or instrumentalist, lagging deliberately and relaxedly behind the metronomic beat of the tune.

1972 *Down Beat,* 25 May, p. 27. I always sing behind the beat.

1974 *Down Beat,* 9 May, p. 29. He doesn't play that way, it's a little behind the beat.

bells, *interj.* [poss. with reference to the pleasant sound of bells, or to the name of a New York City bar frequented by jazzmen; according to jazzmen, term was first used in a jazz sense by Lester Young and has had some currency since c. 1940]

1948 *New Yorker,* 3 July, p. 28. The bebop people have a language of their own; their expressions of approval include "Cool!" "Gone!" and "Bells, man!"

1948 *Life,* 11 Oct., p. 139. Bebop greeting begins as Gillespie . . . hails Benny Carter with "Bells, man! Where you been?"

1959 *Down Beat,* 30 Apr., p. 11. This was revelatory for Pres, who usually limited his answers to "bells" or "ding dong."

bend, *n., v. & adj.* [see 1952 quot. for key to semantic development; according to jazzman Eubie Blake, term originates c. 1904 with Bendin' Boots Butler's manner of playing piano triplets; still current] See 1952 quot.; for adjective use, see 1965 quot.

1949 *Music Library Association Notes,* Dec., p. 39. *bend:* effect employed by the brass section of modern bands. It is achieved by manipulation of the lip and involves a slight upward or downward variation in pitch.

1952 *A History of Jazz in America,* p. 350. *bending:* the process of altering pitch between notes, up or down, sometimes called "scooping pitch."

1956 *Eddie Condon's Treasury of Jazz,* p. 214. You must be very, *very* careful not to use the bell. Use the valves. Then what you *hit* will bend.

1965 *Down Beat,* 9 Sep., p. 28. His *Cheree* solo work contains some judiciously placed bent tones.

benny, 1. [from 19th c. British slang: *Benjamin,* by oblique association with Joseph's many-colored coat; current among jazzmen since c. 1900] An overcoat.

1944 *Dan Burley's Original Handbook of Harlem Jive,* p. 109. Ole man, where's your benny?

2. [from narcotics slang; some jazz use since c. 1935] Benzedrine or a benzedrine inhaler.

1956 *Second Ending,* p. 230. You want to crack a benny?

1959 *The Holy Barbarians,* p. 22. He'd seen me go into my purse a couple of times after bennies.

1960 *The Jazz Titans,* p. 150. *bennies:* benzedrine pills.

bet you a fat man, I'll, see s.v. i'll . . .

big apple, 1. The big town: see s.v. APPLE.

2. [current c. 1937–c. 1939]

1937 *Life,* 9 Aug., p. 22. Copied from Negroes, "The Big Apple," a loose-hipped, free-hand combination of "truckin'" and the square dance.

1937 *N.Y. Amsterdam News,* 4 Sep., p. 12. All the "cats" on the avenue are "breakin' it up" with a new dance they call "The Big Apple," a swing square dance.

big band [current since c. 1925] See last quot.

1926 *Melody Maker,* Feb., p. 35. The Kit-Cat Band has again scored with "The Camel Walk," which gives the lie to those who say that a "big band" is unwieldy and not suitable for "dirt" arrangements.

1960 *Dictionary of American Slang,* s.v. *big band:* pertains to swing or jazz music played by a large band, usually composed of 14 to 20 men, as opposed to smaller or pick-up groups.

big ears, see s.v. EARS.

big eyes, see s.v. EYES.

15

bill, *n.* [cf. 1950 *Dictionary of American Underworld Lingo,* s.v. *bill:* "a one-hundred dollar note"; current among jazzmen since c. 1945]

1960 *Dictionary of American Slang.* s.v. *bill:* $100 bill; the sum of $100.

1961 *The Sound,* p. 189. You mean I only get a bill out of it?

Bird, *n.* [see semantic explanation s.v. YARD(BIRD) for which this is the shortened form; one of the five or six indispensable jazz nicknames (see also LADY, PREZ, SATCH); widely current since c. 1946] Nickname for Charlie Parker (1920–1955), alto saxophonist; most musicians and critics agree that he was at once the most influential innovator and the greatest instrumentalist in the history of jazz.

1947 *Chasing the Bird* (tune by Charlie Parker).

1949 Birdland (famous jazz night club in New York City named for Charlie Parker, closed in 1965).

1956 *Enjoyment of Jazz* (EJ402) p. 2. One can hardly name an important modern alto man, or any other modern instrumentalist who has not been influenced by "Bird."

birdie, *n.* [by analogy with a bird's sound, esp. its unexpectedness; some currency since c. 1917]

1935 *Vanity Fair,* Nov., p. 71. Impromptu grace notes are "birdies."

bit, *n.* [extension of its theater slang sense (i.e., minor part or performance); widely current since c. 1943] See 1958 and second 1960 quots.

1956 *Sideman,* p. 275. Gigs are hard to get, so I do this bit at Macy's.

1958 *American Speech,* Oct., p. 225. When, on the other hand, he *does the bit,* he is merely part of a short incident.

1959 *The Holy Barbarians,* p. 71. It's the old Oedipus bit, ain't it?

1960 *Down Beat,* 27 Oct., p. 26. Actually, the hugging bit is the thing that bugs me.

1960 *Dictionary of American Slang,* s.v. *bit:* Any expected or well-defined action, plan, series of events, or attitudes, usually, but not necessarily, of short duration; the role which one assumes in a specific situation or in life. Orig. bop and cool use.

bitch, *n.* 1. [cf. 1928 *American Speech,* Feb., "Kansas University Slang," p. 218: "*bitch:* something difficult or formidable"; current among jazzmen since c. 1935, though term, like several others (see BAD, TOUGH,

16

HARD, TERRIBLE, etc.), has acquired increasingly favorable connotations since c. 1945] Anything formidable; also, a formidable person.

1946 *Really the Blues*, p. 19. That boy was really a bitch.

1955 *Hear Me Talkin to Ya*, p. 196. The depression for musicians in New York—man, it was a bitch!

1956 *Eddie Condon's Treasury of Jazz*, p. 207. His followers, both white and Negro, often affectionately declare that Dizzy is "it," that he is "real crazy," "a bitch," and "a killer."

1970 *The World of Duke Ellington*, p. 138. Technically you may be a bitch, but to play his music you've also got to feel it.

2. [cf. Early Modern English pejorative connotation: c. 1605 *King Lear*, II, ii, 23. "The son and heir of a mongrel bitch"; also some general slang use, but with esp. currency among jazzmen since c. 1935 in a less pejorative than neutral sense] A woman (note: the term does not necessarily have a pejorative connotation).

1956 *Lady Sings the Blues*, p. 80. If they had caught Pop having a drink with a white bitch, the management would have flipped.

1972 *Bessie*, p. 56. You could hear Bessie yelling things about "these Northern bitches."

pitch a bitch, 1. [inspired by rhyming-slang vogue c. 1935–c. 1940; some currency c. 1938–c. 1945, rare since] To cause a disturbance.

1956 *Lady Sings the Blues*, p. 46. Bernie pitched such a bitch up there at the office, he finally made them pay me.

2. [same dates as sense 1; see also BALL, n.] To have an exciting party or an enjoyable evening in the company of others. Oral evidence only.

black bottom [from general slang for black buttocks: cf. 1928 *The Walls of Jericho*, p. 14. "Been wantin' to spank yo' little black bottom"; current c. 1919–c. 1929, obs. since except historical] A jazz dance popular in the 1920s.

1919 *The Original Black Bottom Dance* (dance-song written by Perry Bradford).

blackstick, black-stick, *n.* [some currency c. 1920–c. 1940, obs. since except historical; see also LICORICE STICK]

1937 *This Thing Called Swing*, p. 9. *black stick:* clarinet.

1937 *Metronome*, June, p. 26. The black-stick man gets off well on his own.

blast, *v.i.* 1. [extension of the standard meaning; some currency since c. 1930] To play loudly; refers esp. to brass instruments.

1946 *King Oliver*, p. 6. The band's sound could fill the largest hall with nobody blasting (they never did) and no microphones.

1956 *The Heart of Jazz*, p. 181. I try to keep my band from blasting.

2. [from narcotics slang; by analogy with the effect on the smoker: cf. 1958 *Southern Folklore Quarterly*, Sep., "The Anonymous Verses of a Narcotics Addict," p. 130. "*blast:* smoke, by cupping the hands and drawing deeply"; current since c. 1935] To smoke marijuana.

1952 *Go*, p. 125. Hell, you should come along though and blast with us!

1958 *The Subterraneans*, p. 73. We'd been drinking French Bordeaux and blasting.

1959 *The Naked Lunch*, p. 18. I blasted my last stick of Tangier tea.

blewy, blooey, *n.* [prob. from general slang *blew* (i.e., mismanaged) and comic strip onomatopoeia for something ruined or exploded; some currency c. 1930–c. 1945, rare since; see also the more common CLAM, CLINKER, FLUFF, GOOF] A misplayed note.

1970 *Dictionary of Afro-American Slang*, p. 27. *blewy, blooey:* (obscure) in jazz, an out-of-place note.

blip, *n.* 1 [etym. unknown; current c. 1930–c. 1945, obs. since except historical]

1944 *Dan Burley's Original Handbook of Harlem Jive*, p. 134. *blip:* a nickel.

[1944] *Black on Black*, p. 207. Ain't got one white quarter, not even a blip.

1946 *Really the Blues*, p. 114. Managers would murder their own mothers for a deuce of blips.

2. [poss. by analogy with sense 1.: i.e., the scarcity of money during the depression 1930s; 1960 *Dictionary of American Slang*, p. 43: "Jive use since c. 1935"; obs. since c. 1945]

1938 *Cab Calloway: Hi De Ho*, p. 16. *blip:* something very good.

1945 *Hepcats Jive Talk Dictionary*, s.v. *blip:* superlative.

block (or blocked) chord [from the fixed, blocklike relation of the hands to each other when playing these chords; widely current since c. 1945; see also LOCKED HANDS]

1948 *Down Beat*, 19 May, p. 14. The final chorus is git [i.e., guitar] and block chords.

1957 *The Book of Jazz*, p. 68. This was the "locked hands" or "block chord" style, in which the left hand moves parallel with the right, playing extra notes in the chord or duplicating the right hand's chord, instead of supplying a bass line.

blood, *n.* [some currency c. 1945– c. 1960, rare since]
1959 *Esquire*, Nov., p. 70H. *blood:* wine.

blow, *v.t.* 1. [metonymy: i.e., "blow smoke"; current since c. 1930] To smoke (marijuana); used with any of the many analogues for *marijuana.*
1953 *Night Light*, p. 136. We're all out of charge [i.e., marijuana], so I'll dash in and get some and we'll blow one more.
2. (also *v.i.*) [by analogy with the method of performing on any instrument (for which *blow* mostly replaced *play* c. 1945): see 1958 quot.; as applied to performing on any instrument in any art medium or simply to behaving, current since c. 1955] See 1957 and 1958 quots.
1950 *Neurotica*, Autumn, p. 46. We just cut out of a gone session and they're still blowin'.
1955 *Solo*, p. 107. You've been blowing piano a long time, right?
1957 *N.Y. Times Magazine*, 18 Aug., p. 26. *blow:* to play a musical instrument, any instrument. Also to perform any act: "He blows great conversation." "She blows scrambled eggs from endville."
1958 *Publication of the American Dialect Society*, Nov., p. 44. *blow:* orig. to play a wind instrument. Generalized to performing upon any instrument (thus, one can "blow guitar"). Probably from fact that all solo instruments in traditional jazz are wind instruments.
1959 *The Holy Barbarians*, p. 26. Are we gonna blow some poetry, maybe?
1968 *I Want It Now*, p. 59. Or perhaps you blow drums.
blow (one's) ass off [by analogy with general slang "work (one's) ass off"; *play* . . . current since c. 1935; *blow* . . . since c. 1945] To play music superlatively.
1959 *Jazz: A Quarterly of American Music*, Fall, p. 294. He's bad—he can play his ass off. —p. 295. Cannonball, you're blowing your ass off.
1965 *Down Beat*, 20 May, p. 31. He's playing his tail off.
1973 *Down Beat*, 11 Oct., p. 33. These pros really, really play their asses off.

blow (someone) down (or **into the ground, off the stand** [or **scene**], **out, out of the house**) [hyperbole; *blow down* and its less common variations have had some currency since c. 1935, gradually largely replacing *cut* by c. 1950; see also COOK ON 'EM, SMOKE ON 'EM]. To best (someone's) musical competition (can apply to either an instrumentalist or a group); also, less commonly, to impress (the audience) favorably with musical skill or volume (this is the sense in which the first quot. is to be taken).

1954 *See*, Sep., p. 34. They won't listen unless you're blowing them out of the house.

1956 *Lady Sings the Blues*, p. 55. He blew him out with his horn.

1958 *The Horn*, p. 85. When some goony sideman tenor can blow me off the stand.

1961 *Down Beat*, 13 Apr., p. 22. There were eight other saxophone players, and Zoot blew them all into the ground.

1967 *Down Beat*, 21 Sep., p. 14. He is still blowing everyone off the scene!

1972 *Down Beat*, 22 June, p. 15. A lot of people knock Dizzy, but ain't nobody going to blow him down.

blow (one's) soul [current since c. 1957] To play music with great sincerity and passion.

1961 *The Sound*, p. 268. Prez blew his soul on that one, man!

blow the gig [general slang *blow* (i.e., to fail [at something]) + jazz slang *gig*, q.v.; current since c. 1955] To fail to appear for a one-night musical engagement; also, less commonly: to appear, but to play badly.

1960 *Jazz: A Quarterly of American Music*, Winter, p. 32. They're always putting *me* down for blowing the gig. I never do that. *I'm* here—it's them musicians who ain't here! —p. 37. He's playing beautifully now—he must feel like playing—not like that Hollywood Bowl gig. I asked him, Monk, what happened at the Hollywood Bowl? What I hear, you really blew it [i.e., the gig]!

blow the roof off [hyperbole; current c. 1930–c. 1940, very rare since] To play music loudly and well.

1957 *Paris Blues*, p. 7. They let go on "Tiger Rag" . . . and they blew the roof off.

blow (one's) top, wig or **cool** [see 1952 quot. for semantic explanation; prob. from underworld slang; cf. 1934 *The Thin Man*, p. 70. "How did I know he was going to blow his top?"; cf. also 1940 *American Speech*, Oct., "Jargon of Marihuana Addicts," p. 336. "to blow one's *top*: to become sick from excessive use of marihuana"; . . . *top* current among jazzmen since c. 1935 . . . *wig* since c. 1940, both obs. since c. 1945; . . . *cool* current since c. 1955] Note progressive shift in connotation (c. 1945) from *pleasant* excitement to *unpleasant*.

1938 *Cab Calloway: Hi De Ho*, p. 16. *blow the top:* to be overcome with emotion (delight).

1944 *The World*, Oct., p. 33. Real jazzmen . . . work twice as hard . . . if allowed to "blow their top" in a small combination of . . . musicians who know solid jazz.

1944 *The New Cab Calloway's Hepsters Dictionary*, p. 4. *blew their wigs:* excited with enthusiasm, gone crazy.

1946 *The Jazz Record*, July, p. 9. They sent me down South, Georgia. That was enough to make me blow my top.

1952 *A History of Jazz in America*, p. 350. *blow one's top:* phrase expressing exasperation, enthusiasm, or insanity; synonymous with "flip one's lid," "snap one's cap" or "wig," each of which describes the process of losing the hair or skin of the head.

1966 *The Wig*, p. 72. "Don't blow your cool," I warned him.

1973 *Travel and Leisure*. I almost blew my cool the night of the first jam session at Radio City.

blow up a breeze (or **storm**) [current c. 1935–c. 1945, very rare since] To play music excitingly.

1940 *Blowing Up a Breeze* (tune recorded by Chu Berry on Commodore C-541).

1955 *Solo*, p. 25. Mahn, but he blows up a storm.

blower, *n.* [chiefly a writers' term; some currency since c. 1955] A soloist; the hearer or reader must judge from the context whether the term is being used in a pejorative sense (a desultory *blower*), or a neutral sense (a soloing *blower*).

1960 *Sal Salvador: The Beat for This Generation* (liner notes on LP album Decca DL 74026). Adequate space is allotted in each arrangement for one or two of the "blowers" to have their say.

1961 *Down Beat*, 5 Jan., p. 16. He stresses that he is not referring to those who work more or less regularly in studios but to those usually referred to as "the blowers." —p. 20. It has been the blowers—and Louis, Bird, and Pres were at heart blowers—who have shown the way.

blowing room [jazz slang *blowing* + general slang *room* (i.e., time); some currency since c. 1955; see also STRETCH OUT] Sufficient improvisational time allowed a jazzman in which to develop his musical ideas.

1963 *Down Beat*, 20 June, p. 21. Each soloist is permitted blowing room.

blowing session [chiefly a writers' term; some currency since c. 1955] A musical performance characterized by improvisation (rather than by arrangements), usually at a recording studio or a concert hall.

1961 *Jazz News*, 15 Mar., p. 5. Nor will the prospect of another uncharted "blowing" session with Gillespie and Co. fail to attract him.

1961 *Down Beat*, 12 Oct., p. 29. This is no helter-skelter "blowing session," although there is surely a lot of inspired blowing going on.

1962 *Jazz Monthly*, Oct., p. 25. A "blowing session" depends essentially on the strength of the soloists, for formal qualities are usually little in evidence.

blowtop, *n. & adj.* [formed from *blow (one's) top;* current c. 1935–c. 1950, very rare since] (One who is) excitable, violent, or unstable.

1940 *Blow Top* (tune recorded by Count Basie Orchestra).

1946 *Really the Blues*, p. 323. That's the musical mania of the blowtops.

1955 *Find a Victim*, p. 52. He was drunk when he told me. He was always full of blowtop tales about her.

blue note [prob. from its melancholy sound; according to jazzman Eubie Blake, current since c. 1895; see also OFF NOTE] See 1955, 1958 quots.

1926 *Melody Maker*, Apr., p. 42. They are according to the strict laws of music, "out of chord." . . . They are simply "blue" notes and sound most pleasing and effective when incorporated in a melody part.

1947 *Frontiers of Jazz*, p. 45. Handy's interpolated minor third has acquired a name of its own: "the blue note."

1955 *The First Book of Jazz*, p. 20. These blue notes are "off notes," just a little bit flat and in between the usual notes. They most often are a somewhat flatted third or seventh note of the scale. They are impossible to show in written music, although they are indicated as flatted notes.

1958 *Jam Session: An Anthology of Jazz*, p. 23. Louis Harap explains the "blue note" that they [the blacks] brought into jazz: "The third and seventh of all Negro music from spirituals to hot jazz are not pitched steadily. They are, as Abbe Niles has said, 'worried,' wavering between flat and natural."

blues, *n.* [cf. 1933 OED s.v. *the blues* "(for 'blue devils'): depression of spirits, despondency. *colloq.*"; first citation is 1807 W. Irving (1824) 96 "In a fit of the blues"; current among jazzmen since c. 1895] See 1949, 1956 quots.

1905 *Jelly Roll Blues* (tune composed by Jelly Roll Morton, copyright 1915).

1939 *The International Cyclopedia of Music and Musicians,* p. 897. Though the type of Negroid song known as the "blues" probably existed in improvised form before he devoted his talents to it, it was Handy who introduced it to popular favour. The "blues" attained this popularity about 1914, just as the "rag" craze was dying out.

1949 *Music Library Association Notes,* Dec., p. 40. *blues:* song form, style, and harmony originating with the American Negro. The "blues" form involves a 12 measure sequence instead of the 8 or 16 measure unit of popular song. The minor mode and the flatted seventh figure prominently.

1956 *Guide to Jazz,* s.v. *blues:* a short piece of 12 bars divided into 3 sections of 4 bars each—has become standardized into a classic form both musically and with regard to the lyrics. There are variations (16 bars, etc.), but blues is then given to the style of playing.

1959 *The Jazz Scene,* p. 95. The blues is not a style or phase of jazz, but a permanent substratum of all styles; not the whole of jazz, but its heart.

bombershay, *n.* [etym. unknown; current c. 1897–c. 1917]

1934 *Beale Street: Where the Blues Began,* p. 105. The Pasamala was a ragtime dance originated, according to Isaac Goldberg, in tin pan alley at about the same time as the bombershay, in 1898, in which the girls chanted as they danced: "Fust you do a rag, then you bombershay."

bombs, *n. pl.* [so called because of the volume and suddenness with which they erupt; current since c. 1944] Unexpected bass drum accents which were made an integral part of drumming by Kenny Clarke in the first years of bop (c. 1944), though occasional accidental or humorous use of them predates Clarke.

1961 *Metronome,* Apr., p. 34. Dodds underscores the work of the hornmen with "bombs" and off-beat rolls.

1961 *The Sound,* p. 108. That kid on drums dropped too many bombs.

1962 *Dinosaurs in the Morning*, p. 26. He depends on the relentless use of bass-drum explosions, or "bombs."

1973 *Jazz Style in Kansas City*, p. 153. Lady Bellson, don't drop no bombs behind me, baby, just give me that *titty-boom, titty-boom* all night on the cymbal, and I'm cool.

bone, 'bone, *n.* [shortened form; some currency since c. 1917, but with wide currency only since c. 1935; see also earlier TAILGATE, SLIPHORN]

1942 *The American Thesaurus of Slang*, p. 559. *bone:* trombone.

1956 *Sideman*, p. 14. Oh, Dick's a hell of a 'bone man.

1957 *The Book of Jazz*, p. 79. The trombone, contrary to popular belief as propagated by the movies, is never known among musicians by such terms as "slushpump" and "sliphorn," but is frequently known simply as a "bone."

boo, *n.* [shortened form of *jabooby,* etym. of which is unknown; some currency from c. 1935–c. 1955, rare since; see also GAGE, MARY JANE, POT, TEA]

1959 *Esquire*, Nov., p. 70H. *boo:* marijuana.

boogie, boogie-woogie, *n.* [see 1942, 1943, 1957 quots. for suggested etyms.; current c. 1920–c. 1945, rare since except historical] See 1944 quot.

1928 *Pine Top's Boogie Woogie* (tune composed by Pine Top Smith).

1942 *American Mercury*, July, p. 94. *boogie-woogie:* type of dancing and rhythm. For years in the South, it meant secondary syphilis.

1943 *The Jazz Record*, 15 Apr., p. 3. The word "boogie" was derived from our old grandmothers' use of the word meaning the devil. When the kids broke the rules in any way, we were told that the "Boogie man" was going to get us. The blues was considered bad music as it usually alluded to love affairs.

1944 *Esquire*, Feb., p. 129. Boogie-Woogie is any kind of jazz or swing, solo or orchestral, generated by certain eight-to-the-bar rhythms, mostly using the twelve-measure Blues pattern for a theme.

1957 *Just Jazz*, p. 13. I don't know the origin of the word "boogie woogie," but it seems obvious to me that it is onomatopoeic—it simply describes the noise that the music makes. A "boogie," of course, is a "bad girl." Brothels were called "boogie houses" in many parts of the old South. "Pitchin' boogie" was a raw term for "makin' a chick."

v. To dance to the music or to have a good time.

1955 *Big Bill Blues*, p. 30. Oh let's boogie, children.

1960 *Dictionary of American Slang*, s.v. *boogie:* to enjoy oneself thoroughly. Some Negro use. Also *boogie woogie.*

book, *n.* [metonymy: the repertory of arrangements are in loose book form; current since c. 1925]

1949 *Music Library Association Notes*, Dec., p. 40. *book:* the repertoire of a band.

1955 *A Pictorial History of Jazz*, p. 155. Goodman set the pace here as well, by the extremely astute move of hiring Fletcher Henderson to create the foundations of his "book."

1956 *Sideman*, p. 12. Get down to the club an hour or so before the job, look the book over.

boot, 1. *v.i. & v.t.* [by analogy with *kick,* q.v.; some currency since c. 1930] To play (an instrument) pulsatingly, energetically, and excitingly; also, for adjective form, see last two quots.

1937 *Metronome*, Nov., p. 11. After Louis boots, the cats truck on to their various domiciles.

1957 *Down Beat*, 25 July, p. 24. On "Get Happy" . . . he boots the group, and, in turn, is booted by Candido's driving congas.

1960 *Down Beat Record Reviews*, p. 11. For a happy, booting 40 minutes, you can't beat this one.

1967 *Down Beat*, 2 Nov., p. 23. Desmond artfully used pauses and booting phrases à la Zoot Sims.

2. *v.t.* [from *booted, adj.,* q.v.; some currency c. 1935–c. 1945, obs. since; see also HIP, *v.t.*] To inform or enlighten (someone).

1944 *Dan Burley's Original Handbook of Harlem Jive*, p. 15. Let me boot you to my play [i.e., plan].

1945 *Hepcats Jive Talk Dictionary*, s.v. *boot:* clarify or understand.

booted, *adj.* [see 1958 quot. for explanation of semantic development (validated by jazzmen); prob. from *got (one's) boots on*, q.v.; current esp. among black jazzmen c. 1920–c. 1945, very rare since; see also HIP, *adj.*] Sophisticated; socially and/or metaphysically aware.

1949 *Down Beat*, 28 Jan., p. 6. Another "booted" character on WJLB's assembly line of jockeys is Phil McClain, who spins an all-night record show.

1958 *Jive in Hi-Fi*, p. 13. It comes from a story of a fisherman warning young fishermen never to wade in deep water without hip boots on because they could run into trouble. So, when you hear the words, "I'm hip" or "I'm booted," it's said to let you know they have no fear of trouble or that they understand what's shaking [i.e., happening].

boots on (or **laced**), **got (one's)** [analogue for a state of readiness: i.e., to have one's boots on is to be ready for any kind of weather—hence, by extension, for any eventuality; according to jazzmen, some currency esp. among black jazzmen c. 1900–c. 1945, obs. since; see also HIP, *adj.*, DOWN, *adj.*]

1938 *Cab Calloway: Hi De Ho*, p. 16. *got your boots on:* you know what it is all about, you are a hep cat, you are wise.

bop, *n. & adj.* [See 1957, 1959 quots. for etym., first 1956 quot. for beginning date; still current with, though much rarer than, *modern jazz*; see also HARD BOP and BEBOP]

1947 *Bongo Bop* (tune recorded by the Charlie Parker Sextet).

1955 *Say*, 28 Apr., p. 53. They're calling him [bop] "Modern Music" now. But he's the same cat who was making crazy sounds back in the '40s—only the critics didn't start cheering until he changed his name.

1956 *Guide to Jazz*, s.v. *bop:* originally meaningless syllables in scat singing (as, for example, in the piece, *Hey ba ba re bop*). Since about 1945 the name be bop (re bop, or today more frequently just bop) has been applied to the new jazz: (1) the bop rhythm section breaks the continuity of the swing, the drums constantly introducing figures which spring from pseudo-Spanish figures introduced from Cuba and certain Latin American countries.

1956 *Chicago Review*, Autumn-Winter, p. 13. The ultimate in pushing the words away, of course, is "scat" or "bop" talk where the singer produces familiar sounds which don't make words at all.

1957 *Giants of Jazz*, p. 188. The word "bop" is a contraction of "bebop" or "rebop." The two-syllable word was merely a way of describing the staccato two-note phrase that became the trade-mark in its playing.

1959 *Jazz: A Quarterly of American Music*, Spring, p. 116. Apart from their employment in scat, it does not appear that rebop/bebop/bop had any widely known connotations. The printed *bop!*, an onomatopoeic term, crashed off the comic pages, and has been employed colloquially since to mean *to whop, to hit, to clobber.*

v.i. 1. [from *n.*; some currency c. 1945–c. 1950, rare since] To play in "bop" style.

1947 *He Beeped When He Shoulda Bopped* (tune recorded by Dizzy Gillespie Orchestra).

1962 *Down Beat*, 6 Dec., p. 23. We all started bopping.

1966 *Down Beat*, 28 July, p. 40. BG's band bops only on one out of 10 numbers.

2. [playful extension of 1.; some currency since c. 1950]

1974 *Ladies and Gentlemen—Lenny Bruce!!*, p. 385. I bopped out to the short [q.v.]. —p. 442. I bop around to the driveway and he follows.

bopper, bopster, *n.* [current c. 1945–c. 1950, rare since] A musician who plays bop.

1948 *New Yorker*, 3 July, p. 28. Boppers call themselves "the left wing" and their opponents "the right wing."

1957 *American Speech*, Dec., p. 281. But occasionally, backed to the wall by monetary considerations, bopsters would make a partial concession by playing at weddings and other social functions where musical authenticity is held in low esteem.

1963 *Down Beat*, 31 Jan., p. 24. In the 40s the boppers moved toward a less symmetrical method of construction in their improvising.

boppish, *adj.* [some currency since c. 1948] Like bop; i.e., in that musical vein.

1955 *The First Book of Jazz*, p. 55. Sometimes, for fun, singers sing "oo-ya-koo" syllables to boppish backgrounds.

1965 *Down Beat*, 6 May, p. 30. "Tempo's" is a nice, boppishly melodic line.

boss, *adj. & n.* [by analogy with the colloq. sense (i.e., someone of authority); 1904 *Dictionary of Slang & Its Analogues*, "boss: pleasant, first-rate, chief"; 1888 *Brooklyn Daily Eagle*, 18 Mar. "Take it all together, with scarcity of food and little sleep, we had a hard, but a boss time." Some currency, esp. among black jazzmen, since c. 1950; very widely current since c. 1958] Authoritative or excellent; initially, applied to jazzmen or jazz performance; by extension, applied to anyone or anything (see last quot.). As noun, one who performs authoritatively.

1953 *Ebony*, Aug., p. 68. Bop pianists still refer to him as "the Boss Man."

1959 *Gene Ammons: Boss Tenor* (LP album Prestige PRLP7180).

1961 *Metronome*, Apr., p. 32. He has always been a boss arranger.
1961 *N.Y. Times Magazine*, 25 June, p. 39. Man, she brews some boss stews!
1970 *Blue Movie*, p. 17. And her mouth was boss beauty.

bossa nova [see quots. for etym., though jazz critic Martin Williams says term derives from *nova* + *boss* (jazz sense); term orig. used in U.S. by jazzmen c. 1962, soon popularized] See last quot.
1962 *Shorty Rogers and His Giants: Bossa Nova* (liner notes on Reprise LP album). The word "nova" in Portuguese means "new." "Bossa" is a pagan word, not yet found in the dictionary. It is, however, a sincere term created to express the ability of playing well.
1962 *High Fidelity*, Dec., p. 108. Bossa nova, the Brazilian-based music that has suddenly flooded American recording studios, is like jazz, unsusceptible to precise definition. The term itself is translated as "the new beat" or "the new wrinkle," and the music is derived from the samba. But when one says "bossa nova," according to Charlie Byrd, the guitarist who was one of those principally responsible for launching it in this country, one refers not to a rhythm or to a melody but to "a mood, a feeling, a way of playing."

Boston, *n.* [poss. from the style originating in Boston, Mass., but according to jazzman Eubie Blake, the term derives from jazzmen's habit of referring humorously to the bass notes as being "way up North" and, subsequently, extending the verbal association to a specific Northern city; some currency c. 1917–c. 1935 when this piano style had its vogue, obs. since except historical] A piano style characterized by accented bass figures; also, the bass figures themselves.
[1923] 1966 *Down Beat*, 5 May, p. 23. You can bet a man that they can get off on them horns and blow a "Boston" that will swing you into bad health (a Boston was a real get-off).
1943 *Harlem Jazz, 1930*, p. 3. Willie "The Lion" Smith was biting cigars in half, taking his "Boston" (accented bass figures) in "piano battles" with Fats Waller.
1970 *The World of Duke Ellington*, p. 148. We were setting riffs and each taking a "Boston," as they called solos then [1929].

bounce, *n.* [by analogy of rhythmic accents with the bounce of a ball; current c. 1930–c. 1945, rare since; see also BUSINESSMAN'S BOUNCE]

1932 *Melody Maker*, June, p. 511. The "bounce" of the brass section has degenerated into a definitely "corny" and staccato style of playing.

1935 *Vanity Fair*, Nov., p. 71. Additional synonyms for hot music are *bounce* (indicating pronounced rhythm) . . .

1937 *American Speech*, Feb., p. 45. *bounce:* a light-medium-fast tempo, with a light accent on the first and third beats.

1939 *Metronome*, Dec., p. 46. Mary Lou Williams' piano helps Andy Kirk's band obtain a fine bounce.

1952 *A History of Jazz in America*, p. 350. *bounce:* used by some musicians, especially Duke Ellington, to describe a particularly buoyant beat.

box, *n.* 1. [see 1958 quot. for semantic explanation; current prob. since c. 1920]

[1927] 1966 *Down Beat*, 20 Oct., p. 17. Smack, let's see you sit down to that box.

1936 *Metronome*, Feb., p. 61. *box:* piano.

1958 *Publication of the American Dialect Society*, Nov., p. 44. *box:* a piano (undoubtedly from shape of upright piano and spinet, usually found in jazz night clubs).

1959 *The Art of Jazz*, p. 101. When Yancy wasn't hired to play at a party, he might have been found in almost any joint along 31st or State Street which had a "box" on which he could practice.

2. [from its general shape; current prob. since c. 1930; see also GITBOX] A guitar.

1933 *Metronome*, Aug., p. 16. Eddie was playing the kind of banjo I wanted, but I got him to learn that "gitter box."

1948 *Tremolo*, p. 115. A dark little guitar player had appeared from nowhere and he could make that old box talk, all right.

1972 *Down Beat*, 8 June, p. 13. Very few people, unless they have a classical box, know the true sound of guitar.

3. [from its general shape; current since c. 1935] A record player or a juke box.

1937 *N.Y. Amsterdam News*, 11 Dec., p. 20. The music box, plus Tommy Dorsey, ground out "Once in a While."

1959 *The Holy Barbarians*, p. 88. They put Mozart on the box.

1973 *Down Beat*, 13 Sep., p. 17. We were over at his girl friend's house and she had some records on the box.

boxed, *adj.* [by analogy with being boxed in; some currency since c. 1955; see also HIGH, JUICED, STONED, ZONKED] Intoxicated.

1958 *Somewhere There's Music*, p. 18. We were sitting in the front row, so boxed that the musicians were looking at us!

1959 *Jazz for Moderns*, p. 20. *boxed:* stoned, c. 1959.

boy, *n.* (generally preceded by a personal pronoun, usually **my**) [orig. black slang, but esp. common among jazzmen c. 1925–c. 1945, very rare since because of its servile connotation, offensive to the militant post-World War II black: largely supplanted by *man* (with personal pronoun)] See first quot.; also, a favorite musician (see 1955 quot.).

1928 *The Walls of Jericho*, p. 295. *boy:* friend and ally. Buddy.

1941 *Down Beat*, 1 Sep., "My boy, Bunny Berigan," says Louis Armstrong, "I've always admired."

1948 *PM*, 22 Feb., p. M6. This was inscribed, "To Monk, my first inspiration. Stay with it. Your boy, Dizzy Gillespie."

1955 *Down Beat*, 7 Sep., p. 29. O.P. is my boy; bass or cello, he's very clean, and he swings.

1960 *Hiparama of the Classics*, p. 27. If you do this little favor for me Lord, you've got yourself a Boy!!!

brass section [current since c. 1925]

1937 *American Speech*, Feb., p. 48. In the *brass section* are trumpets and trombones.

bread, *n.* [see 1958 quot. for explanation of semantic development; cf. *1811 Dictionary of the Vulgar Tongue*, "bread: employment"; some currency esp. among black jazzmen since c. 1935; widely current since c. 1945; see also LOOT, GOLD] See 1958 quot.

1939 *Jazzmen*, p. 63. Inside the low, smoky room, the musicians sweated for their bread.

1952 *Down Beat*, 18 June, p. 15. If I had bread (Dizzy's basic synonym for loot) I'd certainly start a big band again.

1958 *Publication of the American Dialect Society*, Nov., p. 44. *bread:* money. A double pun—(1) "dough," (2) bread, the necessity.

long bread [formed from *bread* and *long green*; current since c. 1945] Much money.

1963 *Nugget*, Feb., p. 71. Tania's parents, and Tania, all seem to find me singularly repulsive, and will offer me pretty long bread to get out of their lives and keep my mouth shut.

small bread [some currency since c. 1945; see also CRUMBS]

1957 *N.Y. Times Magazine*, 18 Aug., p. 26. *crumbs:* a small amount of money.

Also **light bread,** oral evidence only.

break, *n.* [an extension of the standard sense (i.e., a pause); current c. 1917–c. 1945, obs. since: replaced largely by *chorus*] See 1959 quot.

1922 *How to Play and Sing the Blues Like the Phonograph and Stage Artists* [1962 *Jazz: A History of the New York Scene*, p. 97] Harmony break.

1926 *Melody Maker*, Jan., p. 31. With the exception of . . . the additional special chorus containing the violin breaks, the score used . . . is . . . identical with that issued by the publishers.

1929 *The Music Quarterly*, Oct., p. 611. As to what possibilities such free-will tricks as the jazz "break" . . . hold . . . he would be bold who would predict.

1936 *Esquire*, June, p. 92. It was "breaks" originally. Then it became "licks." Today it is "riffs." In all truth hot is redundant with any of these words.

1944 *This Is Jazz*, p. 24. Still another musical device developed in jazz is the break. This is an unaccompanied interpolation of one or two measures for solo instrument or group of instruments. It is freely improvised.

1959 *The Jazz Scene*, p. 290. *breaks:* open passages in the performance when the rhythm is suspended, more generally, solo passages.

break it down [prob. from *breakdown;* current c. 1930–c. 1937, obs. since except historical]

1937 *This Thing Called Swing*, p. 3. *break it down!:* Get hot! Swing it!

1959 *Jazz: A Quarterly of American Music*, Fall, p. 284. "Break it down" was reported to be Harlem's pet expression of 1933, and was synonymous with "get hot."

break it up [hyperbole: by analogy with dispersing a gathering—i.e., leaving nothing more to be said or done; current since c. 1935] See 1938 quot.

1937 *N.Y. Amsterdam News*, 4 Sep., p. 12. All the "cats" on the avenue are "breaking it up" with a new dance they call "The Big Apple," a swing square dance.

1938 *Cab Calloway: Hi De Ho*, p. 16. *break it up:* to win applause, to stop the show.

31

1944 *The Jazz Record*, Jan., p. 7. When the band really started sounding right, Wingie broke it up and away we went to the studio.

break up [hyperbole: by analogy with fragmenting or dissolving (here from either a comic or thrilling stimulus); current since c. 1940] To convulse with laughter; also: to excite musically.

1956 *Lady Sings the Blues*, p. 48. Then the house broke up.

1959 *The Cool World*, p. 16. George Cadmus was breaken evrybody up.

breakdown, break-down, *n.* [see first 1959 quot. for semantic development; cf. 1904 *Dictionary of Slang & Its Analogues*, "*break-down:* a noisy dance, a convivial gathering, spec. a Negro dance"; current among jazzmen c. 1920–c. 1940, obs. since except historical] An energetic jazz dance originated by American blacks and popular among them c. 1920–c. 1935; also, the energetic music to which it was danced; for its adj. use, see last quot.

1927 *Birmingham Breakdown* (tune recorded by Duke Ellington).

1941 *Central Avenue Breakdown* (tune recorded by the Lionel Hampton Orchestra on Victor 26652).

1959 *Jazz: A Quarterly of American Music*, Fall, p. 284. A noisy, rollicking reel with the descriptive name [*breakdown*] is reported in Virginia prior to 1820, and by the middle of the century the word had reached currency in America and England to denote a convivial gathering. Duke Ellington recorded "Birmingham Breakdown" in 1927; the Chocolate Dandies cut their version in 1928.

1959 *The Jazz Review*, July, p. 12. Breakdown music was the best for such sets, the more solid and groovy the better.

breeze, up a [variant of general slang phrase "up a storm"; current from c. 1935–c. 1945, rare since] Exceedingly; to the utmost.

1939 *Blowing Up a Breeze* (recorded by Chu Berry on Columbia C-541).

1946 *Really the Blues*, p. 122. Bix cussed up a breeze.

1956 *Lady Sings the Blues*, p. 65. All alone in a room upstairs, snoring up a breeze.

1960 *Hiparama of the Classics*, p. 30. He stated that everyone should ball up a breeze.

bringdown, bring-down, bring down, *n.* [from *bring (one) down;* current c. 1940–c. 1950, rare since; see also DRAG, n.]

1944 *The New Cab Calloway's Hepsters Dictionary*, s.v. *bring down:* something depressing.

1952 *A History of Jazz in America*, p. 350. *bringdown:* one who depresses.

1959 *The Naked Lunch*, p. 19. And our habits build up with the drag, like cocaine will build you up staying ahead of the C [q.v.] bringdown.

bring (one) down [extension of the standard sense: here, to reduce *in spirit* from an exalted state to a depressed one (though very briefly, c. 1935, effect could be good or bad: see 1935, 1958 quots.); also cf. 1940 *American Speech*, Oct., "Jargon of Marihuana Addicts," p. 337. "*to bring someone down:* to calm someone when he is violent"; widely current c. 1935–c. 1950, rare since; replaced largely by *drag;* see also BROUGHT DOWN]

1935 *His Hi De Highness of Ho De Ho*, p. 35. "That brings me down" . . . can be applied to anything that affects you strongly, whether favorably or even adversely.

1940 *You Bring Me Down* (tune recorded by the Erskine Hawkins Orchestra on Bluebird 10756).

1952 *A History of Jazz in America*, p. 350. *bring down:* to depress.

1958 *Publication of the American Dialect Society*, Nov., p. 44. *bring down:* to make one feel low. (Obs.—to make one feel good—out of use since the '30s.)

broad, *n.* [see 1959 quot. for explanation of semantic development; prob. from underworld slang: cf. 1930 *American Tramp and Underworld Slang*, s.v. *broad:* "a woman, more especially one of loose morals" (note: in jazz slang, the term has no pejorative sense); also cf. 1928 *American Speech*, Feb., "Kansas University Slang," p. 218. "*broad:* a plump, shapely girl"; some general slang use, but with esp. currency among jazzmen since c. 1930, supplanted considerably by *chick* c. 1938–c. 1952, but again widely current since c. 1952] A woman, esp. a young woman.

1926 *Walk That Broad* (tune recorded by Ed Allen on Okeh 8629).

1942 *American Mercury*, July, p. 88. The right broad would, or might, come along.

1958 *Somewhere There's Music*, p. 35. Jess is the craziest broad I've ever known, even finer than that chick in New Orleans.

1959 *Jazz: A Quarterly of American Music*, fall, p. 283. Usually assumed to refer to the physical dimensions of a woman, *broad* is more accurately a clipped form of *broad-gauge,* and in the complex embracing *broad-minded.* After 1850-USA the interests of people were centered in railroads spanning the continent. From such activity a whole vocabulary developed. One source of concern was financing, and narrow-gauge/broad-gauge tracking was a battle of costs versus stability and speed. *Broad-gauge* developed extensions and association, and from the easy grade and level of a moral judgment it was sidetracked to an inferred physical attribute.

broom, *v.i.* [prob. from witches' mode of transportation; cf. 1795 *A New Dictionary of the Cant and Flash Languages,* s.v. *broom:* "to run away"; also cf. 1936 *San Francisco News,* 30 April, p. 25. "*Broom:* disappear hastily"; some currency among jazzmen since c. 1935] Travel, esp. fly.

c. 1940 *Lips' Blues* (tune recorded by Hot Lips Page). I guess I'll dust my broom.

1970 *Dictionary of Afro-American Slang,* p. 32. *broom:* walk or run.

1973 *Bird Lives,* p. 16. What's happened to Bird? He cut out or broom back to the Apple [q.v.]?

1974 *Ladies and Gentlemen—Lenny Bruce!!* p. 212. Lenny would take off for a couple of days and broom down to L.A.

brought, brought down [from *bring (one) down;* current c. 1940–c. 1950, rare since; see also the more recent DRAGGED]

1942 *The American Thesaurus of Slang,* p. 581. *brought:* downcast, depressed.

1958 *Somewhere There's Music,* p. 162. I figured you'd be brought down about that.

1960 *Beat Jokes Bop Humor & Cool Cartoons,* p. 22. Don't be brought down 'cause you didn't wig up this plan.

brushes, *n. pl.* [short for *wire brushes,* which, in turn, derives from their brushlike appearance; current since c. 1925 when they came into use in dance bands] See 1960 quot.

1933 *Metronome,* Nov., p. 54. Brushes (paragraph heading in drum instruction column).

1948 *Tremolo,* p. 33. The drummer maybe starts it soft with the brushes.

1960 *Dictionary of American Slang,* s.v. *brushes:* a pair of thin drum sticks used to give the drums a soft, smooth, muted sound. Orig. jazz use; now the most common word for these items in all forms of jazz and popular music.

bruz, *n.* [short for *brother;* from common slang practice of retaining only the first syllable of a word, then substituting "z" sound for all succeeding syllables: cf. *Muzz* for *Murray,* etc.; according to jazzmen, Lester Young introduced the term into jazz use c. 1935; some currency until c. 1950, very rare since] A casual term of address to a man.

1958 *Somewhere There's Music,* p. 35. Romance? No, bruz, that's not my groove.

buck, *v.i.* [spec. application of the standard meaning; current c. 1910–c. 1930, obs. since except historical; see also CUT]

1971 *Louis Armstrong,* p. 6. Louis and Kid Rena used to buck every time they met. "To buck" means to try to outplay the other fellow.

bucking contest [spec. application of *bucking;* current c. 1910–c. 1930, obs. since except historical; see also CUTTING CONTEST, BATTLE]

1960 *Treat It Gentle,* p. 63. Sometimes we'd have what they called in those days "bucking contests"; that was long before they talked about "cutting contests."

bug, *v.t.* [from underworld slang; cf. 1930 *American Tramp and Underworld Slang,* s.v. *bug:* "an insane or simple-minded individual"; current since c. 1940]

1949 *Music Library Association Notes,* Dec., p. 40. *bug:* to be annoying.

1958 *Publication of the American Dialect Society,* Nov., p. 44. *bug:* to bother, especially to get one in such a state that he cannot play well. Extended to mean getting annoyed at anything.

1960 *Hiparama of the Classics,* p. 7. The Lion was buggin' India.

bugged, *adj.* [from *bug,* v.t.; current since c. 1942; see also DRAGGED, HACKED, HUNG] Bewildered or annoyed.

1958 *American Speech,* Oct., p. 225. *bugged:* annoyed.

1959 *San Francisco Chronicle,* 4 June, p. 35. Them people down there must be plenty bugged if a book like this can get them so tore up.

bugged on [variant of *bugged;* current c. 1943–c. 1953, rare since; see

35

also the more recent STRUNG OUT.] Obsessed with; dedicated to; exceedingly enthusiastic about.

1956 *Sideman*, p. 414. Madame Luke, gonna get her a screen test, for these art films she's bugged on.

bump, bumpty-bump, bump-the-bump, *n.* [according to jazzman Eubie Blake, the dance originated in 1907 in Washington, D.C.; obs. since c. 1930 except historical]

1928 *The Walls of Jericho*, p. 296. *bump; bumpty-bump; bump-the-bump:* a *shout* characterized by a forward and backward swaying of the hips.

bunny hug [dance designations frequently refer to animal movements: cf. CAMEL WALK, FOX TROT, TURKEY TROT; current during the dance's vogue, 1907–c. 1927, obs. since except historical] A jazz dance.

1914 *Modern Dancing* [1962 *Jazz: A History of the New York Scene*, p. 37]. Drop the Turkey Trot, the Grizzly Bear, the Bunny Hug, etc.

1926 *Nigger Heaven*, p. 84. She was good at the new ones, too, the turkey trot and the bunny hug.

1933 *Metronome*, July, p. 19. The Bunny-hug . . . came into popularity on the Barbary Coast.

burn, *v.i.* [by analogy with jazz slang *cook;* current since c. 1958; see also SMOKE] To play music intensely and expertly; also, by extension: see 1962 quot.

1959 *Newport Jazz Festival: 1959*, p. 45. *burn:* cook [q.v.]

1962 *N.Y. Times Magazine*, 20 May, p. 45. *burn:* to do something well, quickly or efficiently.

1968 *Down Beat*, 16 May, p. 17. Jazz to Farrell means "burning," another expression for hyper-swinging.

1971 *Down Beat*, 10 June, p. 16. In order to assert himself Coleman has to bear down and *burn*.

v.t. [from underworld slang; cf. 1904 *Dictionary of Slang & Its Analogues.* s.v. *burn:* "to cheat, to swindle"; 1605 Shakespeare *Lear* III, ii, "No heretics burn'd, but wenches' suitors"; current among jazzmen since c. 1940] To cheat.

1958 *Somewhere There's Music*, p. 31. The cat never burned me before.

1959 *Esquire*, Nov., p. 70I. *to burn:* to rob.

burn (someone for bread) [extension of *burn, v.t.;* esp. current among narcotics addicts but also with some currency among jazzmen since c. 1955]

1957 *N.Y. Times*, 25 Aug., Sec. 2, p. 8. *burn (someone) for bread:* borrow money.

business straight, get (one's) [from jazz slang *straight, adj.* 2, q.v.; some currency since c. 1935] To attend to something.

1947 *Jive and Slang*, s.v. *I have to get my business straight:* I have something to do.

businessman's bounce [see 1950, 1952 quots. for semantic explanation; current c. 1935–c. 1945, obs. since except historical]

1940 *Business Man's Bounce* (tune composed and recorded by Raymond Scott).

1950 *Lingo of Tin-Pan Alley*, s.v. *business man's bounce:* term of derision. . . . Originated during the thirties, when swing music, loud and fast, was the vogue. Referred to the type of soft, smooth style in which songs were played by bands like Guy Lombardo's; it was designed to appeal to the middle-agers rather than the teen-agers.

1952 *A History of Jazz in America*, p. 350. *businessman's bounce:* a monotonous two-beat played fast, usually by society bands, for the delectation of tired businessmen and their dance partners.

1970 *The World of Duke Ellington*, p. 12. What we played in that first hour to impress the chaperons was a little "businessman's bounce."

buss, buzz, *v.t.* [from Middle English: cf. 1959 *Webster's New World Dictionary*, s.v. *"buss:* (? akin to G. [dial.] *bus,* kiss, or W. & Gael, *bus,* kiss, lip) (Archaic or Dial.), kiss, especially in a rough and playful manner"; also cf. 1904 *Dictionary of Slang & Its Analogues*, s.v. *"buss:* (or *bus*) (once literary, now colloquial) to kiss (c. 1500)"; some currency esp. among black jazzmen c. 1935–c. 1945, obs. since except historical]

1945 *Hepcats Jive Talk Dictionary.* s.v. *buzz:* kiss.

1972 *Jazz Masters of the Thirties*, p. 100. He flashes his devilish smile, and lately has taken to bussing everyone, men included, in the French manner, on each cheek.

bust (one's) conk (or **top**) [hyperbole; some currency c. 1935–c. 1945, obs. since except historical] To feel exhilarated (see 1939 quot.); for a further, rare meaning, see 1938 quot.

37

1938 *Cab Calloway: Hi De Ho*, p. 16. *bust your conk:* apply yourself diligently, break your neck.

1939 *Jitterbug Jamboree Song Book*, p. 32. *bust your conk:* something [sic] that will make you enthuse.

1946 *Really the Blues*, p. 10. Negroes and whites side by side busting their conks.

1955 *Hear Me Talkin to Ya*, p. 232. We called it a "ninety-nine percent," one more either way would bust your top.

busted, *adj.* [hyperbole; from underworld and drug addicts' slang; cf. 1958 *Southern Folklore Quarterly*, Sep., "The Anonymous Verses of a Narcotics Addict," p. 131: "*busted:* arrested by the police or federal agents"; current in jazz slang since c. 1940]

1948 *Metronome*, Apr., p. 33. You hear that such-and-such a musician has been "busted" (arrested).

1958 *Somewhere There's Music*, p. 143. He got busted last week by the local fuzz.

1965 *Down Beat*, 11 Mar., p. 16. We had never heard such terms as "busted" for arrested, "fuzz" for police, and all the other jargon that came into common use in bop circles after a vast clique of junkies had fanned out from Bird.

busy, *adj.* [special application of standard term; current since c. 1950] Extremely energetic or supportive (sometimes, too much so: see last quot.): said of an accompanist, esp. a drummer.

1962 *Jazz Journal*, July, p. 11. Milt's a busy bass player, you must give him credit for that.

1962 *Down Beat*, 6 Dec., p. 30. He is busy, but not loud.

1964 *Down Beat*, 13 Aug., p. 29. The drummer seemed to be a little busy in places.

buzz, *v.t.* See s.v. BUSS.

buzz, *n.* [prob. synesthesia—i.e., feeling represented as sound; see quots. for dates]

1960 *Dictionary of American Slang*, s.v. *buzz:* a thrill, a kick, a charge, a feeling of excitement, pleasure, satisfaction or the like. Since c. 1935.

1970 *Dictionary of Afro-American Slang*, p. 33. *buzz:* (1930s) the first effects of smoking marijuana or using some other kind of "dope."

buzz mute [from its buzzing sound; current since c. 1930]

1957 *The Book of Jazz*, p. 76. He made effective use of a strange contraption known as the "buzz mute," which sounded like the product of an illicit meeting between a trumpet and a kazoo.

C

C [abbreviation; from underworld slang; cf. 1930 *American Tramp and Underworld Slang,* s.v. *C:* "cocaine"; some currency among jazzmen since c. 1930]

1953 *Junkie,* p. 11. *C:* Cocaine.

1959 *The Naked Lunch,* p. 65. Eukodol is like a combination of junk and C.

cack, *v.e.* [etym. unknown; current since c. 1948]

1959 *Newport Jazz Festival: 1959,* p. 45. *cack:* fall asleep, fall out, go under. [Note: usually from too much stimulant]

cake-walk, cakewalk, *n.* [cf. 1957 *Funk & Wagnalls New "Standard" Dictionary,* s.v. *cakewalk:* "an entertainment originating among Negroes of the Southern United States, in which a cake is the prize for the most graceful walking"; current c. 1890–c. 1920, obs. since except historical, despite the fact that parts of the dance survive in other dances]

1910 *Cake Walk* (tune composed by Hayden & Eldridge).

1947 *Jazzbook 1947,* p. 37. Right along with the two-step, came a dance of American Negro origin that had a tremendous vogue—the cake-walk. The name "cake-walk" was applied to the dance and likewise to the music for it.

1958 *The Decca Book of Jazz,* p. 31. Both the coon song and the cake-walk made use of syncopation, and they were also alike in being invariably the work of white composers, although they included material taken from Negro sources.

camel walk [dance designations frequently refer to animal movements: cf. BUNNY HUG, FOX TROT, TURKEY TROT; current from c. 1913–c. 1945, obs. since except historical] A jazz dance in which shoulder and back movements simulate somewhat those of a camel.

1925 *The Camel Walk* (tune recorded in England by the Kit-Cat Band).

1926 *Nigger Heaven*, p. 242. Camel Walk!

canary, *n.* [from a shared activity—i.e., singing; despite skepticism of last quot., term had some currency, esp. among white big band musicians and jazz writers c. 1935–c. 1945, very rare since; see also CHIRP]

1937 *American Speech*, Feb., p. 45. *canary:* a woman vocalist.

1953 *The Hot and the Cool*, p. 48. Where the hell do you get off blowing in here, copping a job some poor canary could use?

1956 *Enjoyment of Jazz* (EJ410), p. 2. The band "canary" was a pretty girl named Ginnie Simms.

1956 *The Real Jazz Old and New*, p. 150. Canary or mouse for woman is just used in smart fiction about jazz.

cap, *v.t.* [prob. from black slang *backcap* (retort): in answering definitively, to put the lid or cap on the situation; current since c. 1940]

1944 *The New Cab Calloway's Hepsters Dictionary*, s.v. *capped:* outdone, surpassed.

1952 *Who Walk in Darkness*, p. 173. "You capped me, man," he said.

1958 *The Subterraneans*, p. 97. To cap everything . . . Adams opens the door.

cap on [extension of jazz slang *cap;* some currency since c. 1960] To censure.

1960 *Lenny Bruce: I Am Not a Nut, Elect Me* (LP album Fantasy 7007). It would be different if the sharks were flagrant offenders, but, I mean, they made *one* mistake and everybody capped on them immediately.

capper, *n.* [from *cap,* v.t.; current since c. 1942] The ultimate.

1960 *The Jazz Review*, May, p. 30. But dig, here's the capper.

1974 *Ladies and Gentlemen—Lenny Bruce!!* p. 443. The last flick we take is the capper.

carve, *v.t.* [hyperbole; some currency c. 1920–c. 1940, obs. since except historical; see also the more common cut] To defeat (someone) in musical competition, or simply to play better than one's contemporaries.

1950 *Mister Jelly Roll*, p. 145. George Smith is frank to admit that Morton carved everybody.

carving contest, see s.v. CUTTING CONTEST.

cat, *n.* [semantic etym. obscure; 1946 quot. logical but of doubtful validity; also see 1972 quot.; most prob. shortened form of general and black slang *tomcat* (i.e., a female-chasing male); also poss. related to the itinerant nature of early jazzmen: cf. 1930 *American Tramp and Underworld Slang*, s.v. *cat:* "Itinerant worker. . . . Possibly so called because he slinks about like a homeless cat"; see 1958 quot. for semantic development; according to jazzmen, Louis Armstrong introduced the term into jazz slang c. 1922, very widely current since; see also STUD and DUDE]

1936 *Swing That Music*, p. 42. All jazz musicians from New Orleans called each other "cats" and still do.

1946 *Really the Blues*, p. 218. They even called each other *cats* approvingly because they wanted to be as alert and keen-sighted as an alley cat.

1958 *Publication of the American Dialect Society*, Nov., p. 44. *cat:* orig. one who was "hep." Obsolete in this sense; now, any person. (Thus, a musician can now speak of a "square cat"—a contradiction in terms in the '30s.)

1972 *Black English* (inside front jacket). *Cat*, for example, is a West African word for person.

catting, *part.* [prob. from general and black slang "tom-catting" (i.e., pursuing women), reinforced by jazz slang *cat;* some currency esp. among black jazzmen since c. 1925] Questing after women; also, occasionally: moving about a great deal (see note s.v. *cat*).

1946 *Hollywood Note*, Apr. A hustler, he lives in Greenwich Village . . . catting around Manhattan in the wake of the Ellington and Herman bands.

1961 *The Jazz Review*, Jan., p. 7. Davis, the featured tenor soloist at the time, was "catting" with a young lady at ringside.

1967 *Down Beat*, 7 Sep., p. 26. Albert Ayler out "catting" with a powerfully bright, varied wardrobe.

catch, *v.t.* [by analogy with the general meaning—i.e., the ears performing a function that is normally the hands'; some currency esp. among white jazzmen from c. 1930–c. 1940, rare since; see also DIG] To hear; to listen (to).

1939 *Metronome*, Mar., p. 40. Catch those lyrics in *Don Redman's Auld Lang Syne!*

1948 *Metronome*, Sep., p. 26. I caught them down at the Royal Roost.

1955 *Solo*, p. 172. Catch this, Jones.

1959 *The Horn*, p. 221. This Kelcy Crane. Have you caught him yet?

catch-up bass [according to jazzman Eubie Blake, current from c. 1900–c. 1910, obs. since except historical]

1940 *New Orleans Jazz*, p. 12. Thus we had, in various places from Pensacola to Dallas and from St. Louis to Chicago, such interesting names for what the left hand does (and the right hand knows it!) as *catch-up bass* (a walk [q.v.] and a chord).

cents, *n. pl.* [understatement: see 1961 quot.; current since c. 1935]

1938 *Better English*, Nov., p. 51. *two cents:* $2.

1961 *The Sound*, p. 157. Twenty cents meant twenty dollars; Red always spoke of dollars in amounts under one hundred as cents; perhaps it expressed his contempt for money.

1962 *N.Y. Times Magazine*, 20 May, p. 45. *cents:* dollars.

changes, *n. pl.* [shortened form of *chord changes;* some currency since c. 1920, but with wide currency only since c. 1945] See 1955, 1956, 1958 quots.

1926 *Melody Maker*, Mar., p. 33. No consideration seems to be given to arranging the notes of the chords so that the fingers of a player may execute a minimum series of changes.

1955 *The Encyclopedia of Jazz*, p. 346. *changes:* harmonic progression of a tune.

1956 *Guide to Jazz*, s.v. *variations:* improvisational transformations of melody by a soloist (obs.), now "changes" since Bop revolutionized improvisation by innovating frequent key changes and many more rhythm changes than were possible in the pre-Bop era.

1958 *Publication of the American Dialect Society*, Nov., p. 44. *changes:* the chords for whatever melody is being used as a basis for improvisation.

43

changes, go (or put) through [extension of jazz slang *changes* to the realm of personal experience; current since c. 1952] See last two quots.

1962 *Down Beat*, 29 Mar., p. 23. Anyone who's got white skin must be aware he's white when he looks at himself in a mirror and because he does not get refused at a restaurant. He does not have to go through the changes that I go through.

1964 *Down Beat*, 27 Feb., p. 21. Anyone who had been through those changes before and was used to the schedule knew that Monk never got there until around 11 P.M.

1969 *Hip Manual*. *To put through changes:* to disorient, to startle and amaze.

1970 *Dictionary of Afro-American Slang*, p. 35. *changes, go through (put through):* (since c. 1952) to endure a series of intense emotional or psychological reactions.

changes, make the [formed from jazz slang *make* and jazz slang *changes;* some currency since c. 1955] To successfully perform harmonic progressions.

1960 *Jackie McLean: Making the Changes* (LP album New Jazz 8231).

1973 *Down Beat*, 15 Mar., p. 28. He had a uniquely ingenious way of making the changes with breathtaking ease and subtlety.

changes, run (the) [formed from jazz slang *run* and jazz slang *changes:* some currency since c. 1947, though increasingly pejorative since c. 1955] Uninspired and mechanical reliance on the progressions as a substitute for genuine musical invention.

1959 *Evergreen Review*, Nov.-Dec., p. 138. Silver indirectly exposed many of the adept fakers who merely "ran the changes" in familiar keys, jumping from one chord to the next with stock phrases.

1961 *The Jazz Life*, p. 37. Harmonically, the modernists became so intrigued by the challenging, expanded chordal possibilities of improvisation advanced by Charlie Parker and his colleagues that, until recently, most players "ran changes" (improvised on the chords of a tune) instead of developing melodic variations on the theme.

channel, *n.* [extension of standard meaning (i.e., a body of water joining two larger bodies of water); current since c. 1945; see also the earlier RELEASE] A connecting passage between two statements of the theme: the equivalent of *bridge* in standard musical terminology.

1951 *Down Beat*, 20 Apr., p. 18. You know, the channel of our theme song when I was playing with Columbus' band in the Rendezvous 10 years ago was the channel of *Nothing But D. Best.*

1955 *The Encyclopedia of Jazz*, p. 346. *channel:* bridge.

1955 *Down Beat*, 19 Oct., p. 33. In the first chorus, he changed the channel completely for the strings.

charge, *n.* 1. [cf. 1934 *A Dictionary of American Slang*, p. 6. *charge:* "a shot of dope"; also cf. *Dictionary of American Slang*, s.v. *charge:* "General jazz use since c. 1935; from underworld and addict use c. 1925"; rare since c. 1950: see GAGE, POT, TEA, etc.]

1944 *Dan Burley's Original Handbook of Harlem Jive*, p. 52. Charge is marijuana.

1952 *Flee the Angry Strangers*, p. 248. She's the queen of small and large,/Ridin the sky on a ton of charge.

1953 *Night Light*, p. 135. It's a funny thing about smoking charge.

2. [see note, sense 1; current since c. 1935]

1959 *The Holy Barbarians*, p. 172. "Charge" and "explode" are also terms used by the head and the hype to describe the kick of the drug at the moment of "turning on."

Charleston [from *Charleston*, S.C., its place of origin; see 1956 and 1968 quots. for dates]

1926 *Melody Maker*, Sep., p. 11. The Charleston . . . is a fast fox-trot with an unusual beat.

1956 *Guide to Jazz*, p. 59. *Charleston:* dance step done in the 1920s (recently revived) to the syncopated rhythm of two notes, one falling on the first beat of the bar and the other between the weak second beat and the strong third beat.

1968 *Jazz Dance*, p. 112. The Charleston didn't last very long in the thirties—it was soon superseded by the Black Bottom . . . it has been revived many times.

Charleston cymbal(s) [by association with the dance, for which they supplied part of the accompaniment; current c. 1922–c. 1932, obs. since except historical; replaced by *high hat*, q.v.] Two cymbals facing each other and made to meet through pedal control.

1927 *Melody Maker*, July, p. 697. A pair of cup cymbals or "Charleston" cymbals, as they are commonly called, hung together on a thong.

1956 *Guide to Jazz*, p. 59. *Charleston cymbals:* generally called "high hat cymbals."

chart, *n.* [by analogy with standard meaning; current since c. 1955]

1957 *N.Y. Times Magazine*, 18 Aug., p. 26. *charts:* musical arrangements.

1960 *Down Beat*, 9 June, p. 13. And don't leave out Gil Fuller and John Lewis and their charts for Dizzy Gillespie's big band years ago.

1961 *Down Beat*, 30 Mar., p. 29. Have you dug that album they did on all those Saxie Dowell charts?

chase (chorus) [extension of standard meaning; current since c. 1935] See first 1959 quot.; also, for a rare verb use, see last 1959 quot.

1942 *Gems of Jazz:* Vol. 4, p. 7. It's one of the most exciting "chase" choruses on wax.

1949 *Down Beat*, 11 Mar., p. 14. *Duel* is, of course, a chase in which each tries to outdo the other by alternating first choruses, then half choruses, then four-bar phrases and so on until finally they are squalling at each other simultaneously like a couple of terrified sows.

1959 *The Jazz Scene*, p. 289. *chase:* a series of choruses by two or more players each playing several bars in turn.

1959 *The Horn*, p. 34. The drummer for the house band good-naturedly chased Wing's warm-up runs with precise rim shots.

1960 *The Jazz Review*, Nov., p. 22. And the chase fours [i.e., four-bar choruses] between Bird and Fats are thrilling indeed.

cheat, *v.i.* (usually in the present participle), [according to jazzmen, current since c. 1910, largely supplanted c. 1925 by *fake*]

1970 *Dictionary of Afro-American Slang*, p. 36. *cheat:* (1910–1925) in jazz, stretching harmonic or rhythmic variations to cover limited musical skill.

cheat on the rhythm [see quot. for semantic explanation; current c. 1910–c. 1925, obs. since except historical]

1947 *The Musical Digest*, July, p. 24. The changes which make up the music are felt equally in the melody and the harmony, but the most important ones are those which, in the words of the drummer Baby Dodds, "cheat on the rhythm." This quality of altering accents, with regard for and in relation to each other, is the essence of the work of New Orleans musicians.

cheaters, *n. pl.* [from gambling slang: cf. 1934 *A Dictionary of American Slang,* p. 318. *"cheaters:* eyeglasses"; current among jazzmen since c. 1930, largely supplanted c. 1945 by *shades,* q.v.] Dark (tinted) glasses.

1938 *Jeepers Creepers* (tune composed by Harry Warren). Golly gee, when you turn those peepers on,/Woe is me, got to put my cheaters on.

1946 *Really the Blues,* p. 173. Tesch mumbled . . . cocking his sorrowful eyes over those horn-rimmed cheaters.

check it (or someone or something) out [black and general slang, but with esp. currency among black jazzmen since c. 1970] Look into; pay close attention to.

1972 *Gorilla, My Love,* p. 139. You need to check out what she saying.

1973 *Bird Lives,* p. 18. If this is the first mixed club on the Coast, he wants to check it out.

1973 *Down Beat,* 29 Mar., p. 18. Hey, man, there's a new drummer in town; check him out.

Chicago style [see 1958 quot.; current since c. 1927, but its use since c. 1940 is chiefly historical] See last three quots.

1936 *Transatlantic Jazz,* p. 45. Bud Freeman . . . plays in the "Chicago style" (using "choppy" phrasing).

1956 *Guide to Jazz,* s.v. *Chicago style:* a slight departure from New Orleans style, predominating jazz during the 1920s, marked by the substitution of a tenor saxophone for a trombone in the melody ensembles and by the distinctive individual styles of its performers.

1958 *Hi Fi & Music Review,* Aug., p. 35. There was a "Chicago style" loosely ascribed to young white musicians of the Midwest whose playing had been shaped by listening to New Orleans musicians.

1963 *Blues People,* p. 152. Unlike New Orleans style, "Chicago" sacrificed ease and relaxation for tension and drive.

chick, *n.* [cf. general slang term *chicken:* 1925 *English Words & Their Background,* p. 58. *"chicken:* girl"; also cf. 1961 *N.Y. Herald Tribune,* 12 Oct., p. 36. "Girls were known in those days [1917] as chicks"; current among jazzmen since c. 1930; see also BROAD]

1937 *N. Y. Amsterdam News,* 11 Dec., p. 20. Chicks run out without a final accounting.

1959 *The Holy Barbarians,* p. 20. A chick with free-wheeling hips and no cover charge.

1959 *Swinging Syllables,* s.v. *chick:* girl, woman, female.

47

chinchy, *adj.* [poss. a portmanteau word (slightly varied): *cheap* + *stingy;* cf. 1934 *A Dictionary of American Slang,* p. 319. "*Chinchy:* stingy"; some general slang use but with esp. currency among jazzmen c. 1930–c. 1945, very rare since] Stingy.

1952 *Music Out of Dixie,* p. 71. I aims for the piano player to stay on the stool an' earn his pay. Same time, I don't aim to be chinchy.

1961 *The Sound,* p. 216. What in the *world* would these important big-time musicians want to hang around a chinchy old uptown joint like this for?

chirp, *n.* [by analogy (with a bird) and metonymy (with its sound): see also CANARY; some currency since c. 1935]

1944 *The New Cab Calloway's Hepsters Dictionary,* s.v. *chirp:* female singer.

choice, *adj.* [some teen-age and general slang use, but with esp. currency among jazzmen c. 1947–c. 1952, obs. since except historical] Excellent.

1958 *American Speech,* Oct., p. 225. Among nonhipsters, the most widespread of all hip expressions are those expressing warm approval: choice.

chops, *n. pl.* [dialectal English term given special application by jazzmen: cf. 1811 *Dictionary of the Vulgar Tongue:* "*chops:* the mouth"; also cf. 1959 *Webster's New World Dictionary,* s.v. *chap:* "ME. *chaft;* ON. *kjaptr,* 1. a jaw. 2. a cheek: also *chop*"; current among jazzmen since c. 1900; see also IRON CHOPS] Initially, see 1959 quot.; see also 1969 quot.; also, by extension, the use a musician makes of his embouchure or of his natural equipment—i.e., his technique (see 1962 quot.).

1939 *Jazzmen,* p. 141. Louis . . . daubs away with his handkerchief and silently fingers the valves, while "getting his chops set."

1947 *Metronome,* Jan., p. 32. He might not have the chops he used to have, but his ideas are always fine.

1959 *Swinging Syllables.* s.v. *chops:* a musician's lips.

1962 *Down Beat,* 27 Sep., p. 41. He's got a lotta chops, but he played way too long.

1969 *Hip Manual.* A pianist's chops are his hands, a tap dancer's chops are his feet.

iron chops [formed from noun above; according to jazzmen, phrase was coined by Louis Armstrong c. 1925, but it did not gain wide currency until c. 1935; still current; see also FREAK LIP] An extraordinary capacity on the part of a trumpeter or a trombonist to play in the upper register and/or for any horn player to play very long choruses.

1961 *The Village Voice*, 16 Feb., p. 13. He acknowledged playing a good deal with "Little Jazz" and credited him with having "iron chops."

1965 *Down Beat*, 11 Mar., p. 8. Henry, may your iron chops blow out candles for years to come.

chorus, *n.* [standard music term used by jazzmen in an altered sense; widely current since c. 1935] One or more thirty-two-bar (in a blues, q.v., twelve-bar) choruses played by an instrumentalist, usually with rhythmic support.

1936 *Hot Jazz: The Guide to Swing Music*, p. 17. Tunes used in jazz generally comprise a "chorus" and a "verse," like many folk songs. Most often hot musicians use only the chorus. Hence the expression, "to take a chorus," meaning that a musician is to do a solo on the tune.

1963 *Down Beat*, 3 Jan., p. 13. Cooper got off an electrifying chorus.

city, *suffix* [humorous superlative; according to jazzmen, first used by either Lester Young or Emmett Berry c. 1938, but has been widely current only since c. 1947] An intensifying suffix or word signifying the quintessential state of whatever precedes it.

1960 *Hiparama of the Classics*, p. 16. With that wild incense flyin' all over the place and that Buddha-headed moon pale Jazzmin colored flippin' the scene. It was Romance City.

1969 *Hip Manual*, "You went to the Elk's meeting—what was it like?" "What can I tell you? It was Clyde city."

clam, *n.* [poss. partly from being alliterative with its older synonym CLINKER, q.v.; more prob. shortened form of the derogatory sense of CLAMBAKE, q.v.; current since c. 1950; see also GOOF] A misplayed note; also, for a rare verb use, see 1961 quot.

1955 *Down Beat*, 30 Nov., p. 47. I'd say that was a band that doesn't work together regularly . . . because there were a few clams in the ensemble.

1961 *Down Beat*, 2 Feb., p. 30. Hubbard sounds positively uncomfortable and clams in royal style at the beginning.

1964 *New Yorker*, 25 Apr., p. 195. Stridency creeps into his tone, clams proliferate, and one senses that he has difficulty translating into sound what he hears in his head.

clambake, *n.* [by analogy with the standard sense; current c. 1930–c. 1938 in an approbative or a neutral sense, but increasingly since c. 1938 in a pejorative sense]

1937 *American Speech*, Feb., p. 46. *clambake:* same as *jam session.*

1938 *Cab Calloway: Hi De Ho*, p. 16. *clambake:* ad lib session, every man for himself, a jam session not in the groove.

1949 *Music Library Association Notes*, Dec., p. 41. *clambake:* gathering of hot musicians. Also used in a derogatory sense to mean an affair that does not come off well.

1955 *Hear Me Talkin to Ya*, p. 265. Everybody got kind of half-high and it ended up in a clambake.

clary, clarry, *n.* [shortened form; some currency among white jazzmen and esp. jazz writers since c. 1935]

1942 *American Thesaurus of Slang*, p. 558. *clarry:* clarinet.

1952 *Music Out of Dixie*, p. 187. My clary was in that mess.

clean, *adj.* 1. [from underworld slang: cf. 1930 *American Tramp and Underworld Slang*, s.v. *clean:* "out of funds; penniless"; current among jazzmen since c. 1925]

1960 *The Jazz Titans*, p. 152. *clean:* free from money.

2. [by analogy with sense 1; from narcotics slang; current among jazzmen since c. 1930]

1952 *Flee the Angry Strangers*, p. 262. She knew where she had to go to get clean.

1958 *Somewhere There's Music*, p. 194. He was *clean*, in the dictionary sense and the hipster sense.

1960 *The Jazz Titans*, p. 152. *clean:* not to have any narcotics on one's person or free from the habit.

3. [current since c. 1930] Technically precise.

1934 *Metronome*, June, p. 22. An outstandingly clean outfit with pretty tones.

1955 *Down Beat*, 21 Sep., p. 33. I never heard anybody play in a higher register like that. So clean.

1961 *Down Beat*, 13 Apr., p. 23. Some of Horace Silver's things sound professional to me—clean.

the scene is clean, see s.v. SCENE.

clinker, *n.* [onomatopoeic; current c. 1930–c. 1950, then largely replaced by *clam* and *goof*] See 1958 quot.; also, for a rare verb use, see 1948 quot.; also, by extension: any mistake.

1937 *Metronome,* Jan., p. 25. Hey, you dope, watch them there clinkers.

1940 *Esquire,* May, p. 202. In the Crosby band, "clinkers" fall on deaf ears.

1948 *Down Beat,* 14 July, p. 14. Though he clinkers several times on the first slow chorus, he gets off a good one.

1958 *Publication of the American Dialect Society,* Nov., p. 44. *clinker:* a missed note, or other error in playing. Largely replaced by *goof.*

1961 *Metronome,* Feb., p. 20. This ingenuous belief that Louis Armstrong can smile away the egregious clinkers in our foreign policy is akin to having Frank Sinatra do a policy paper on Algeria.

cloud (followed by a number), *n.* [poss. by analogy with transcendent superlatives: e.g., *out of this world, far out, way out;* some currency since c. 1950] See last quot.

1956 *Sideman,* p. 120. Oh, she's off on Cloud Seven—doesn't even know we exist.

1959 *Down Beat,* 14 May, p. 20. I don't like strange music, I'm not on Cloud Nine.

1959 *Swinging Syllables,* p. 6. *Cloud Nine:* Heaven, to fly, complete contentment.

clown, *n.* [cf. its general colloquial meaning (i.e., foolish person); poss. its extension to all people reflects the jazzman's skepticism regarding humanity; current in the earlier sense since c. 1940, in the latter sense since c. 1950] As in general slang: a foolish or an ineffectual person; but also, any person (hearer must judge connotation from the context).

1953 *Night Light,* p. 135. Most clowns you meet are real square.

1959 *Blow Up a Storm,* p. 71. "This clown's higher than a kite," he said.

1959 *Diggeth Thou?,* p. 10. Let's jive this clown into runnin' 'em around.

coast, *v.i.* [extension of standard sense; some currency since c. 1930] To play music uninspiredly; by extension, performing in any art in an uninspired way (see last quot.).

1936 *Stage,* Mar., p. 58. *coasting:* just playing notes, not socking it.

1961 *The Jazz Life,* p. 23. The man who coasts too long may retain the admiration of the critics long after he's lost the respect of other musicians.

1967 *Down Beat,* 10 Aug., p. 27. With Louis at the helm, there is little opportunity for coasting.

1971 *Down Beat,* 27 May, p. 12. I think the author was coasting on a lot of it.

collar the jive [underworld slang *collar* (i.e., to grab) and jazz slang *jive* or *swing*; current c. 1935–c. 1945, obs. since except historical] See 1960 quot.

1938 *Cab Calloway: Hi De Ho,* p. 16. Do you collar this jive?

1960 *Dictionary of American Slang,* s.v. *collar the jive:* to understand and feel rapport with what is being said; to be in the know; to be hip. c. 1935 jive term.

collecting hot [shortened phrase; some currency since c. 1935] Collecting "hot" jazz records.

1973 *Jazz Style in Kansas City,* p. 91. When the collectors of jazz and blues became active, 1923 vintage recordings would command high prices, sometimes as much as $50 to $150 apiece in good condition. "Collecting hot" became a fascinating hobby.

combo, *n.* [cf. 1931 *American Speech,* Dec., "Underworld Argot," p. 107. "*combo:* combination of a safe": from the common linguistic practice of reducing a polysyllabic word to its first syllable and adding *o;* widely current in its jazz sense since c. 1935] See 1949 and 1957 quots.

1935 *Metronome,* May, p. 28. As a soft fiddle-sax combo, it clicks.

1949 *Music Library Association Notes,* Dec., p. 41. *Combo:* abbrev. of "combination." Refers generally to an instrumental group usually smaller than a band.

1956 *It's Always Four O'Clock,* pp. 106–107. I was playing with an ordinary little combo.

1957 *The Book of Jazz,* p. 159. The term "combo," in common use for the past twenty years among jazz musicians, is usually employed to distinguish between the small group, ranging generally from trio to octet size, and the full orchestra.

come down, 1. [from narcotics slang; to reduce in spirit from a "high";

current among jazzmen since c. 1935; see also COME OFF] To sober up from the effects of narcotics or liquor.

1959 *The Holy Barbarians,* p. 21. But between fixes, coming down, he was one of the best sex partners I ever had.

2. [by analogy with sense 1; current among jazzmen c. 1940–c. 1950, then largely replaced by *cool it*] To stop behaving irresponsibly—i.e., as if one were "high."

1953 *Night Light,* p. 144. Why don't you come down, man?

1959 *Music '59,* p. 80. "Come down, man," Billy said.

come off [prob. from narcotics slang; current among jazzmen since c. 1935] To rid (oneself) of the effects of (a stimulant).

1952 *Flee the Angry Strangers,* p. 314. But an easy charge [i.e., marijuana] to come off of.

come on, 1. [extension of standard sense (i.e., to come on stage in order to begin performing); widely current since c. 1930] To perform music, but invariably either given emphasis (indicating approval) or modified approvingly or disapprovingly (see last two quots.).

1939 *Metronome,* Apr., p. 51. Bauduc . . . really comes on with some very fly and superb drumming.

1958 *American Speech,* Oct., p. 225. The cat who blows well . . . is said to *come on.*

1958 *Publication of the American Dialect Society,* Nov., p. 44. *come on:* strictly, to begin a chorus, but almost always used with an approving or disparaging phrase.

2. [extension of sense 1; current since c. 1935)

1953 *Junkie,* p. 12. *come on:* the way someone acts, his general manner and way of approaching others.

1956 *Sideman,* p. 39. He's a good guy, . . . just comes on weird sometimes.

1959 *The Horn,* p. 49. I'll come on square, I'll hustle strangers, I'll hit everybody I can think of.

come on like gang busters [variant of *come on,* sense 2; currency roughly contemporaneous with vogue of radio program *Gang Busters,* c. 1937–c. 1945, obs. since except historical]

1942 *American Mercury,* July, p. 89. Man, I come on like the Gang Busters.

1944 *The New Cab Calloway's Hepsters Dictionary,* s.v. *comes on like gang busters:* playing, singing or dancing in a terrific manner.

1952 *Flee the Angry Strangers,* p. 296. Nothing can hold me down. 'Cause I'm like Gangbusters. Watch me come on.

come on strong [variant of *come on,* sense 2; widely current since c. 1950] To behave impressively, for good or ill.

1956 *Intro Bulletin,* May, p. 5. "These cats come on so strong," a musician . . . says.

1961 *The Sound,* p. 270. Now let's us go see how strong this Frenchmans is gonna come on.

1969 *Hip Manual.* To say that someone "comes on strong" means that he has an overdeveloped personality. Also, to make sexual overtures.

come on weak (or lame) [variant of *come on,* sense 2; widely current since c. 1950] To behave reprehensibly. Oral evidence only.

come on with the come on [nonsense phrase; current from c. 1940–c. 1944, obs. since] An intensified approving form of *come on,* q.v.

1942 *Jazz,* Sep., p. 26. Comin' On With the Come On (headline).

commercial, *adj.* [from jazzman's feeling that financial success and art are usually antithetical; current since c. 1925]

1926 *Melody Maker,* Aug., p. 35. *commercial orchestration:* one arranged for sale by the music publisher and in such a manner that it can be played by all and sundry combinations.

1936 *Metronome,* Feb., p. 21. *commercial:* appreciated corn [jazz sense].

1952 *A History of Jazz in America,* p. 350. *commercial:* music or musicianship designed solely to garner money and/or fame; usually inflected with great scorn.

1954 *Américas,* Aug., p. 31. Waller is criticized by some ultra-ultras as leaning toward the "slick" and "commercial"—two of the dirtiest words in the vocabulary of jazz.

comp, *v.i. & v.t.* [shortened form of *accompany,* poss. reinforced by *complement;* current since c. 1930]

1955 *Hear Me Talkin to Ya,* p. 305. Count is also just about the best piano player . . . for comping soloists.

1956 *Enjoyment of Jazz* (EJ402), p. 3. Basie "comps" chords on the piano here and there.

1957 *The Book of Jazz,* p. 119. The pianist and guitarist may "comp" (fill in with rhythmic punctuations and syncopation).

con, *v.t.* [from underworld slang: orig. abbreviation of *confidence man;* also poss. reinforced by *convince;* general slang but with esp. currency among jazzmen since c. 1925] To persuade effectively; convince. For a rare *v.i.* use, see 1961 quot.

1950 *Lingo of Tin-Pan Alley,* s.v. *con:* used . . . with reference to the technique of persuasion and promotion.

1956 *Sideman,* p. 48. Jimmy conned him into keeping him on.

1959 *The Horn,* p. 113. For all their hipness they did not notice he was conning them.

1961 *The Sound,* p. 206. She's seen the seamiest side of life, taken her lumps, starved, lied, stolen, conned.

connection, *n.* [from narcotics slang; some currency among jazzmen since c. 1925]. See 1959 quot.

1946 *Really the Blues,* p. 238. My friends began pestering me again about a hop connection.

1959 *The Holy Barbarians,* p. 315. *connection:* contact man for drugs.

cook, *v.i.* [by analogy with *heat;* also cf. general slang *What's cooking?* (i.e., What's happening?), *cooking with gas* (i.e., doing something well); term had some currency, esp. among black jazzmen, c. 1930–c. 1940, disappeared largely from oral vocabulary c. 1940–c. 1950, reappeared c. 1950, widely current since; see also WAIL, SMOKE]

1955 *The Encyclopedia of Jazz,* p. 346. *cook:* to play with rhythmic inspiration.

1956 *Down Beat,* 31 Oct., p. 17. Big Nick Nicholas had the band there . . . and it always came up cooking.

1959 *Jazz: A Quarterly of American Music,* Spring, p. 166. We had to be playing at our absolute best, really "cooking," to reach the audience.

cook him out [current since c. 1955; see also CARVE, CUT] To best him musically (frequently hortatory). Oral evidence only.

cook on 'em [current since c. 1955] To play music exceedingly well (frequently hortatory). Oral evidence only.

cooker, *n.* [from *cook, v.i.;* some currency since c. 1950; see also the more common SWINGER] A musician who plays excitingly; also an exciting piece of music.

1962 *Down Beat,* 13 Sep., p. 28. A hard cooker in the bop or post-bop groove he is not—he has his own slick style and stays with it.

1963 *Down Beat,* 3 Jan., p. 25. Despite Ira Gitler's earnest notes assuring us that Garland is really a cooker, this set seems to confirm that the pianist is at his best a very able ballad player.

1970 *All What Jazz*, p. 151. "Teo" is a dark, close-knit cooker, with Larry Gales' bass to the fore.

cool, *adj. & interj.* [cf. earlier general colloquial *keep a cool head*, black slang *keep cool, fool;* term is linguistic parallel of the new post-World War II musical temper (more relaxed, cerebral, sophisticated): see 1950 and second 1958 quots.; widely current since c. 1947; see also COOL JAZZ, UNCOOL] In addition to the several meanings in the 1948, 1952, 1955, the second 1958, and the five 1959 *Esquire* quots., this most protean of jazz slang terms also means, among other things: convenient, off dope (see 1956 and 1971 quots.), on dope, comfortable, respectable, perceptive, shrewd—virtually anything favorably regarded by the speaker.

1948 *New Yorker*, 3 July, p. 28. The bebop people have a language of their own; . . . their expressions of approval include "cool!"

1948 *Down Beat*, 28 July, p. 4. *cool:* some entity which, in colloquial terms, "gasses" [q.v.] the witness; an adjective describing something which impresses visibly the speaker.

1950 *Harper's*, Apr., p. 93. Another reversal of the usual jazz procedure, parallelled by the Bop musician's use of "cool" instead of "hot" as a word of the highest praise, is the tendency while taking a solo to lag tantalizingly a fraction of a second behind the beat.

1952 *A History of Jazz in America*, p. 350. *cool:* superlative, usually reserved for sizable achievement within a frame of restraint.

1955 *The Encyclopedia of Jazz*, p. 346. *cool:* restrained, relaxed. "Cool" is also used as an interjection meaning "fine" or "okay."

1956 *Second Ending*, p. 215. You don't show signs of a man who's been cool a week.

1958 *After Hours Poetry*, p. 67. This joint is run by two ex-convicts/ And a dope head/they're "cool people."

1958 *Publication of the American Dialect Society*, Nov., p. 44. *cool:* agreeing with the generally received aesthetic standards of the modern jazzman.

1959 *Esquire*, Nov., p. 70H. "Do you want to go to the movies?" "It's cool with me (acquiescence)." —*Ibid.* "Do you have enough money?" "I'm cool (in good financial condition)." —*Ibid.* "Then you must be feeling lean and strong?" "I'm cool (in good shape)." —*Ibid.* "All right, let's go." "Cool." —*Ibid.* "I am moved to censure X strongly for stealing my fiancée." "Be cool, man."

1959 *Jazz: A Quarterly of American Music*, Fall, p. 289. I'd like to make enough money to be cool.

n. [substantive formed from adj. above; current since c. 1965] Poise; composure.

1967 *Down Beat*, 13 July, p. 22. He never loses hold of his cool.

cool it [widely current since c. 1950] See both 1959 quots.

1953 *The Hot and the Cool*, p. 13. Cool it, girl. Nobody's interested.

1959 *Newport Jazz Festival: 1959*, p. 45. *cool it:* to stop something, to relax, to take it easy.

1959 *Esquire*, Nov., p. 70H. In stopping a fight or cautioning a person against losing his temper or the approach of a policeman, one can also say: "Cool it."

1961 *Down Beat*, 5 Jan., p. 20. Some guys say, "Why don't you cool it the first set—take it easy?"

cool on (current since c. 1958; see also COOL (ONE) OUT]

1959 *Esquire*, Nov., p. 70H. "Shall I call on X and take him with us?" "I'm cooling on him (ignoring a person or subtly snubbing him)."

1960 *The Jazz Titans*, p. 153. *cool on:* to ignore or snub (someone).

cool (one) out [current since c. 1958] To restrain or calm (usually musically) a tendency toward overenthusiasm; by extension, to ignore, rebuke, or break off relations with (someone).

1961 *Metronome*, Dec., p. 32. In fact, I'm of the opinion that when he is cooled out just slightly, as he is on this date, he is even a fine musician.

1963 *Down Beat*, 20 June, p. 21. When I had that problem with my hands in 1960, well, it was pretty frightening, even to me. Fortunately I found a doctor who could cool me out.

1966 *Down Beat*, 10 Feb., p. 15. Even you freaks with the paper ears should get this album; it might cool you out from hurting somebody!

cooling, *adj.* [cf. underworld and general slang *cooling (one's) heels* (i.e., relaxing); note also that term is appropriately antonymous to standard term *sweating;* current since c. 1935]

1938 *Cab Calloway: Hi De Ho*, p. 16. *cooling:* laying off between engagements, not working.

1959 *Esquire*, Nov., p. 70H. "But aren't you supposed to play with that orchestra you have been rehearsing with?" "I'm cooling tonight (I'm refraining from playing)."

1971 *The Street That Never Slept*, p. 298. As years went by, Bird started cooling.

cool jazz (or sound) [adapted as a generic term for a style of playing because it suggests the unemotional and unexcitable qualities which characterize that musical style; widely current since c. 1948, though the popularity of the style has waned since c. 1957; see also *West Coast jazz*] The most popular jazz style c. 1950–c. 1957, characterized by restraint, intellectuality, and a studied relaxation; its popularity with the *cognoscenti* waned markedly in the 1960's (see 1961 quot.), though its practitioners remained legion, esp. on the West Coast.

1949 *Inside Be-Bop*, p. 5. Lester was a radical in that he symbolized the gradual evolution from hot jazz to "cool" jazz.

1956 *Enjoyment of Jazz* (EJ410), p. 3. That was the first time [i.e., 1947] an entire section had affected the "cool" sound that was to become *the* sound of the '50s.

1961 *Metronome*, Apr., p. 13. The lid was put on "cool" by hard bop. There was a search for a sound, for a *soul* sound that brought back the "group" feeling, perhaps inspired by gospel music and some aspects of rock and roll.

cootie crawl [cf. 1959 *Webster's New World Dictionary*, s.v. *cootie:* "Polynesian *kutu*, parasitic insect . . . (Slang), a louse"; often, dance designations refer to animal movements: cf. BUNNY HUG, CAMEL WALK, FOX TROT; current c. 1916–c. 1920, obs. since except historical] A jazz dance popular c. 1916–c. 1926.

1934 *Beale Street: Where the Blues Began*, p. 105. In the golden days of 1912 . . . brown beauties . . . danced the Pasamala, long before the "cootie crawl," "black bottom" and "snake hips" were thought of.

cop, *v.i.* [special application of *cop*, v.t.; some currency since c. 1945]

1958 *Jive in Hi-Fi*, p. 25. cop: to get something.

1961 *Metronome*, Dec., p. 31. All in all, this is a good record and you really ought to cop.

v.t. [cf. 1933 OED, s.v. *cop*: "north, *dialect* and *slang* (Perhaps a broad pronunciation of *cap*) . . . To capture, lay hold of": first citation is dated 1704; special applications by jazzmen widely current since c. 1935]

1938 *Cab Calloway: Hi De Ho*, p. 16. cop: to get, to obtain.

1938 *Metronome*, Feb., p. 24. Much swing, too, in "Harlem," with Hodges and Williams' plunger copping most glory.

1953 *The Hot and the Cool*, p. 48. Where the hell do you get off blowing in here, copping a job some poor canary could use?

1956 *The Book of Negro Folklore*, p. 482. *cop:* to take, receive, understand, do.

1959 *Newport Jazz Festival: 1959*, p. 45. *cop:* to buy, to take, borrow, indulge in, or steal.

n. [from the *v.* above; some currency since c. 1965] Theft; borrowing.

1973 *Down Beat*, 1 Mar., p. 9. One piece on the album was a "cop" from Miles Davis' "In a Silent Way."

cop a nod [jazz slang *cop* + jazz slang *nod;* some currency since c. 1940; see also the more recent COP z's]

1958 *Jive in Hi-Fi*, p. 15. *to cop a nod:* to sleep.

1961 *N.Y. Times Magazine*, 25 June, p. 39. *copping a nod:* taking a nap.

cop a plea [from underworld slang: cf. 1950 *Dictionary of American Underworld Lingo*, s.v. *cop a plea:* "to apologize; to ask mercy"; current c. 1935–c. 1950, then largely replaced by *cop out*, q.v.] To excuse oneself, usually evasively.

1958 *Jive in Hi-Fi*, p. 25. *to cop a plea:* to ask someone to listen to your story [i.e., excuse or plea].

1959 *The Holy Barbarians*, p. 315. *cop out:* to settle down, go conventional, in the sense of "sell out" or "cop a plea."

cop out [from *cop a plea*, which it supplanted c. 1950] See 1955, 1959 quots. (Note that the meanings are allied, in that going to sleep is the supreme form of excusing oneself from company.)

1955 *The Encyclopedia of Jazz*, p. 346. *cop out:* go to sleep.

1958 *The Subterraneans*, p. 90. So I cop out, from the lot, from life, all of it, go to sleep.

1959 *Esquire*, Nov., p. 70I. *cop out:* go to sleep. Evasiveness.

1960 *Down Beat*, 13 Oct., p. 6. Ralph Gleason's review of the new Ornette Coleman album (*Down Beat*, Aug. 18) was one of the grossest examples of ambiguity, copping out, padded writing and incompetency that I have ever read.

cop z's [jazz slang *cop* + comic-strip representation of sleep; some currency since c. 1955; see also earlier COP A NOD]

1961 *N.Y. Times Magazine*, 25 June, p. 39. *coppin' zzzz:* taking a nap. Variant: "copping a nod."

1963 *Hiptionary*, p. 18. Nobody cops *zzzz's* here.

cop-out, *n.* [from phrase *cop out;* current since c. 1955, but now chiefly youth culture slang] An evasion; an alibi.

1963 *Down Beat*, 4 July, p. 30. The liner notes state, "There is much controversy as to who the sidemen were." . . . This seems like a cop-out.

1964 *Down Beat*, 9 Apr., p. 26. But today my critical ear whispers into my receptive ear that see-saw convention is a cop-out.

corn, *n.* [see note s.v. *corny;* some currency among white jazzmen and jazz writers c. 1930–c. 1945, very rare since] Anything, but esp. jazz, that is either dated or badly conceived.

1936 *Metronome*, Feb., p. 21. *corn:* rooting-tootin' 1921 vintage.

1936 *Stage*, Mar., p. 58. *corn:* fake hot jazz.

1946 *Really the Blues*, p. 32. I thought George was going to knock out some of the usual corn.

corny, *adj.* [see 1944, 1958 quots. for semantic development; also cf. 1960 *Dictionary of American Slang*, s.v. *corny:* "orig. pejorative use by musicians and theatrical folk"; some earlier general slang use, but widely current esp. among white jazzmen and jazz writers c. 1930–c. 1945, very rare since; see also TICKY] See 1952 quot.

1932 *Melody Maker*, June, p. 511. The "bounce" of the brass section . . . has degenerated into a definitely "corny" and staccato style of playing.

1933 *Fortune*, Aug., p. 47. *Corny* is the jazz musician's term for what is old-fashioned.

1944 *Esquire's 1944 Jazz Book*, p. 53. To define it succinctly, corny (derived from "cornfed") means out-of-date, rustic, old fashioned.

1952 *A History of Jazz in America*, p. 350. *corny:* stale, insipid, trite, usually the worse for age.

1958 *Publication of the American Dialect Society*, Nov., p. 44. *corny:* non-jazz, extremely commercial music. Origin doubtful, but since it often is expanded to "corn-fed" and "corn-ball" (or may actually have been a clipped form of one of these words), I think it once meant "country" music: polkas, square dance music, etc.

corona, *n.* [etym. obscure; according to jazzman Eubie Blake, term current c. 1900–c. 1910, obs. since; see also BIRDIE] An impromptu grace note. Oral evidence only.

covered, see S.V. HAVE IT COVERED.

crack up [by analogy with jazz slang *break up*, q.v.; some currency since c. 1950] To convulse (someone) with laughter.

1960 *Beat Jokes Bop Humor & Cool Cartoons*, p. 56. Where's all your hip talk, man; those way-out things you did that cracked up the house?

crazy, *adj. & interj.* [explanation of semantic development in 1958 quot. is essentially correct, though it is doubtful that the term's creation was a reaction to criticism; more prob., since jazzmen, like most creators, greatly admire the imaginative, they are here anticipating the hostile characterization (see, for example, 1939 quot., which is pre-bop); despite 1939 quot., an accidental use, widely current only c. 1945–c. 1955, rare since; see also INSANE, NUTTY] Splendid.

1939 *Jazzmen*, p. 59. Bunk Johnson was "puffing on his cornet" in a way that made everyone "real crazy."

1948 *Down Beat*, 28 July, p. 4. *real crazy:* a visible impression, usually meant to imply that the musician so described is playing fairly well, often even excellently.

1952 *A History of Jazz in America*, pp. 350–351. *crazy:* superlative of the late forties, synonymous with "gone," "the end."

1958 *Publication of the American Dialect Society*, Nov., pp. 41–42. Likewise, the adverse criticisms of bop were taken over almost wholesale and made into favorable ones. Such terms as "crazy," "weird," "wild," and "nervous," all used to express favorable responses to music, are adaptations of terms levelled against the bop musicians. Since they knew the music which people called "crazy" was actually good, they took over the word in a good sense.

1959 *The Holy Barbarians*, p. 22. If a little mayonnaise dripped onto the paper you just rubbed it into the drawing with a deft thumb—crazy, man, crazy.

crib, *n.* [cf. 1933 OED, s.v. *crib:* "(Thieves' slang) a dwelling-house, shop, public-house, etc.": first citation is dated 1812; still in general Br. slang use; some currency among jazzmen since c. 1940; see also the more common PAD]

1955 *Babs Gonzales: Dem Jive N.Y. People* (song lyrics on LP album Crazy C-0001-B). But every morning he's at my crib to wash up.

1958 *Jive in Hi-Fi*, p. 15. *crib:* house, home, or room.

1971 *N. Y. Times*, 7 July, p. 41. Mrs. Armstrong went to live in the Perdido-Liberty Street Area, which was lined with prostitutes' cribs.

Crow Jim [reversal of the more common term by analogy with reversal of the more common, discriminatory practice; some currency esp. among white jazzmen since c. 1955] Racial discrimination by blacks against whites, esp. in the jazz world.

1956 *San Francisco Examiner*, 7 Jan., p. 3. A form of racial bias known in the trade as "Crow Jim."

1961 *Commonweal*, 24 Mar., p. 658. It was during those years of the late 1950s that I heard several white jazzmen in New York wish dolefully that they had been born Negro. In part of jazz at least, Crow Jim reigned.

1965 *Down Beat*, 8 Apr., p. 8. Taylor implies strongly by his negative viewpoint that Crow Jim is sounding its bleak dissonances within his private unconscious.

crumbcrusher, *n.* [some currency among black jazzmen since c. 1935; see also CRUMBSNATCHER]

1959 *Esquire*, Nov., p. 70I. *crumbcrusher:* baby.

1971 *Beneath the Underdog*, p. 191. But Mingus, how about them crumb-crushers of yours when their little stomachs get to poppin' . . . ?

crumbs, *n. pl.* [by analogy with jazz slang *bread,* q.v.; current since c. 1955, though some humorous and accidental use prob. since c. 1935; see also phrase *small bread,* s.v. BREAD]

1957 *N.Y. Times Magazine*, 18 Aug., p. 26. *crumbs:* a small sum of money; also called small bread.

1961 *Metronome,* Apr., p. 1. And the rich foundations and civic organizations are still sustaining symphony orchestras and classical music and throwing crumbs to jazz.

light crumbs [according to jazzmen, some currency since c. 1955; see also *small bread* s.v. BREAD] Very little money. Oral evidence only.

crumbsnatcher, *n.* [some currency among black jazzmen since c. 1935; see also CRUMBCRUSHER]

1958 *Jive in Hi-Fi*, p. 27. *a crumb snatcher:* a baby.

1959 *Esquire*, Nov., p. 70I. *crumbsnatcher:* child.

1960 *Beat Jokes Bop Humor & Cool Cartoons*, p. 59. The broad's old man tried to sound him that his crumb snatcher was yet too young to indulge in the marriage action.

cut, *v.i.* See s.v. CUT OUT.

v.t. 1. [hyperbole: see first 1959 quot.; current since c. 1920; see also CARVE, CAP]

1937 *American Speech*, Oct., p. 182. *cut:* musicians vie with one another to see who can blow the hotter lick. The winner is said to have "cut" the loser.

1952 *A History of Jazz In America*, p. 351. *cut:* to best a soloist or band in competition.

1959 *The Horn*, p. 17. He would do him the honor of "cutting" him to pieces, bar by bar, horn to horn. —p. 18. For "cutting" was, after all, only the Indian wrestling of lost boyhood summers, and the trick was getting your man off balance.

2. [from recording process of cutting grooves into a record; current since c. 1930] Note noun use (see TAKE, TRACK) in 1949 and 1967 quots.

1939 *Jazzmen*, p. 19. "High Society" became a test piece which forever afterwards all aspiring clarinetists had to "cut" before they could get a job.

1949 *Music Library Association Notes*, Dec., p. 42. *cut:* recording term used as noun and verb. A recording artist *cuts* a master and the recording executive may reject the *cut*.

1959 *Melody Maker*, 4 Aug., p. 3. In any case, I have always been willing to cut sides with any good musician.

1967 *Down Beat*, 13 July, p. 32. For the longest cut in the album, Holmes chooses "Old Folks."

cut (it) [extension of jazz slang *cut*, sense 1 (in the sense of something *superlative*) and jazz slang *cut*, sense 2 (in the sense of a *successful* recording); some currency since c. 1960] Usually used of a piece of music, but also of any performance or experience: to succeed, or be handled acceptably.

1970 *The World of Duke Ellington*, p. 149. "This band can't cut the shows," they said.

cut (out) [see 1958 quot. for poss. explanation of semantic development; widely current since c. 1940 (the shorter form *cut*, since c. 1945) and still some currency though largely replaced by *split*, q.v., c. 1950]

1944 *The New Cab Calloway's Hepsters Dictionary*, s.v. *cut out:* to leave, to depart.

1958 *Publication of the American Dialect Society*, Nov., p. 45. *cut:* to leave. Usually to "cut out" (cut = leave out, leave).

1959 *The Horn*, p. 85. I'm gonna cut this time, Baby. . . . Like all I need is bus fare.

63

1959 *The Naked Lunch*, p. 117. No, we do not want to buy any used condoms! Cut!

cutoff, *n.* [some currency since c. 1935] Literally, a cutting off of sound by the brass section (i.e., a stop) to create a desired effect.

1961 *Down Beat*, 19 Jan., p. 41. This is especially noticeable in the dynamics, shakes, falloffs, and cutoffs of the brass section.

cutting (or **carving**) **contest** [hyperbole: see 1959 quot. for beginning date; obs. since c. 1945 except historical; see also BATTLE] See 1956 quot.

1955 *Hear Me Talkin to Ya*, p. 24. They used to have "cutting contests" every time you'd get on the streets.

1956 *Guide to Jazz*, p. 73. *cutting contest:* a form of musical competition joined in by bands or individual musicians, in which audience applause determines the winner. A popular competition in the 1930s, early '40s.

1959 *A Compendium for the Teaching of Jazz History*, p. 66. In the 1910s . . . a battle of bands known as a "carving" contest was on.

1961 *The Jazz Life*, p. 34. We used to call them cuttin' contests. . . . Like you'd hear about a very good tenor in some night spot, and I'd have to go down there and cut him.

D

dad, *n.* [antedated in jazz slang by *daddy*, q.v.; also some general and student use: cf. 1955 *American Speech*, Dec., "Wayne University Slang," p. 303: "*dad:* good friend"; more common among jazzmen from c. 1945–c. 1960 than *pops, papa, daddy, daddy-o,* q.v., since c. 1960 largely supplanted by *baby*, q.v.] Term of address to a male.

1959 *The Horn*, p. 128. Here, dad, have a brew while I get these boys set up.

1963 *Nugget*, Feb., p. 44. The public, that means you, dad, does not respond favorably.

dada mama [onomatopoeic; some currency since c. 1920] A drum roll.

1934 *Metronome*, Sep., p. 64. We must distinguish between three kinds of rolls of sustentation (1) the double stroke ("dada mama"). . . .

daddy, *n.* [from black slang; also some general slang use, but with esp. currency among jazzmen c. 1920–c. 1940, rare since] A male lover; also, term of address to a male lover.

1927 *Cheatin' Daddy* (song title listed in *Columbia 1927 Race Catalogue: The Latest Blues by Columbia Race Stars*, p. 9).

1928 *The Walls of Jericho*, p. 298. *daddy:* provider of affection and other more tangible delights.

1959 *Selected Poems*, Langston Hughes, p. 148. Keep on a-lovin' me, daddy/Cause I don't want to be blue.

daddy-o, daddy, *n.* 1. [some currency since c. 1940; cf. widespread general colloquial practice of affixing "o" to a term of address; see also the more common DAD, POPS, PAPA, BABY]

1948 *New Yorker*, 3 July, p. 28. The bebop people have a language of their own. They call each other Pops, Daddy, and Dick.

1949 *Music Library Association Notes*, Dec., p. 42. *daddy-o:* friend, buddy. Originated with Negro musicians.

1959 *Selected Poems*, Langston Hughes, p. 179. He wouldn't write so/Bad that way,/Daddy-o.

2. [also some general slang use, but with esp. currency among jazzmen since c. 1940] A profound musical influence or a musical progenitor; by extension, one who is a seminal influence in any art form or in any activity.

1955 *Hear Me Talkin to Ya*, p. 290. Like that Ellis Burton was the daddy of us.

1957 *Down Beat*, 17 Oct., p. 33. That was the daddy of them all—Charlie Christian!

1962 *Jazz Monthly*, Oct., p. 9. Jazz has always had a "daddy-o"—the only man "who could really blow"—and Parker's occupancy of this role made his publicized drug-taking very important to many young musicians.

1962 *Dinosaurs in the Morning*, p. 17. Black introduced Rexroth as a horse wrangler and the Daddy-O of the jazz-poetry movement.

dap, *adj.* [from black slang; shortened form of *dapper;* current since c. 1950; for other terms which evolve from words descriptive of clothing see BOOTED, HIP, SHARP] Nattily attired (i.e., dapper); also, by extension: alert, aware, perceptive, knowledgeable, sophisticated.

1956 *Eddie Condon's Treasury of Jazz*, pp. 303–304. "You don't say hep any more," Hampton said. "It means aware, or sharp, but you don't say it, man. The word now is *dap.* You want somebody to know a man is sharp, is au reet, you say he's dap."

1959 *Esquire*, Nov., p. 70I. *dap:* dapper. Sharp is obsolete.

1960 *Beat Jokes Bop Humor & Cool Cartoons*, p. 12. Looking confused, a stranger asks a dap one, "How do I get to Carnegie Hall?"

date, *n.* 1. [shortened form of *recording date* (i.e., an appointment for the purpose of recording music); current since c. 1920] See 1937 quot.

1924 *Variety*, 24 Sep. Out west they recorded for the Gennett disks, but although less than a week on Broadway, they have had "dates" with a number of minor companies.

1937 *American Speech*, Oct., p. 183. *date:* this is the appointment with the recording company to appear at a certain time to record.

1965 *Down Beat*, 6 May, p. 28. Usually all-star dates don't make it because they tend to be too loosely organized.

2. [extension of sense 1; current since c. 1950; see also the older GIG] A night club or concert engagement for musicians (though night club engagements are sometimes distinguished from recording sessions by being called "club dates": see first quot.).

1956 *Sideman*, p. 275. He's giving me tips on club dates.

1961 *Down Beat*, 19 Jan., p. 40. One afternoon a group of us did a date at a New York City college.

3. *(preceded by a possessive)*, [shortened form (i.e., signifies the one who, in a recording session, is designated as leader and, therefore, under whose name the record appears); current since c. 1935]

1959 *Jazz: A Quarterly of American Music*, Fall, p. 291. I did a thing with "Bags" before that was a "soul" session, only it was his date.

day gig, see s.v. GIG.

deuce, *n.* 1. [prob. from gambling slang; cf. 1930 *American Tramp and Underworld Slang*, s.v. *deuce:* "a two dollar bill"; current esp. among black jazzmen since c. 1925]

1945 *Hepcats Jive Talk Dictionary*, s.v. *deuce:* two dollars.

1948 *Trumpet on the Wing*, p. 90. We did what we could to help along the merriment by selling gin under the piano, at a deuce a throw.

2. [extension of sense 1; current since c. 1935] See 1944 quot.

1937 *I Repent* (tune recorded by Fats Waller). I'm talkin' to you on bended deuces [i.e., my knees].

[1938] *Black on Black*, p. 145. Fill those glasses for that deuce [those two people] over there.

1944 *Dan Burley's Original Handbook of Harlem Jive*, p. 137. *deuce:* two, a pair.

1946 *Really the Blues*, p. 114. Well, she went on for years, being robbed by stinchy managers who would murder their own mothers for a deuce of blips [i.e., two nickels].

1960 *Beat Jokes Bop Humor & Cool Cartoons*, p. 56. And here hung his deuce of slobbers [i.e., lips] that drove the broads out of their hair.

Dick, *n.* [one of several given names made generic; some currency since c. 1945; see also JACK, JIM]

1948 *New Yorker*, 3 July, p. 28. The bebop people have a language of their own. They call each other Pops, Daddy, and Dick.

1953 *American Thesaurus of Slang,* p. 545. *Dick:* term of address among "bebop" players.

dicty, dickty, *adj.* [etym. unknown; from black slang; current esp. among black jazzmen since c. 1920; see also HINCTY] High-class, high-toned (frequently derisive: see first 1928 quot.); also, for a very rare noun use, see first 1928 quot.

1923 *Dicty Blues* (tune recorded by Coleman Hawkins).

1926 *Nigger Heaven,* p. 285. *dicty:* swell, in the slang sense of the word.

1928 *The Walls of Jericho,* p. 3. Despite the objections of the dickties, who prefer to ignore the existence of so-called rats, it is of interest to consider Henry Patmore's Pool Parlor on Fifth Avenue in New York. —p. 4. Fifth Avenue's shame lies in having missed these so-called dickty sections.

1946 *Duke Ellington,* p. 94. *The Dicty Glide,* like its adjective, a "dicty" piece, very flashy, very sophisticatedly aware of all tricks of the times.

1971 *Down Beat,* 9 Dec., p. 28. Jazz has returned to New York's dicty East Side.

dig, *v.i. & v.t.* [see 1958 quot. for poss. explanation of semantic development; also poss. African, from the Wolof *degan:* to understand (Dorothy Z. Seymour, "Black English," *Commonweal*); also cf. 1960 *Dictionary of American Slang,* s.v. *dig:* "to study a subject diligently. *Some student use since c. 1850";* also cf. 1925 *English Words & Their Background,* p. 67: "*dig up:* get"; introduced into jazz speech by Louis Armstrong c. 1925, but widely current only since c. 1935; see also PICK UP, PUT DOWN, MAKE] See first and last quots.; also: to recognize; listen to; hear (which of its many meanings is intended must be inferred from the context).

1938 *Cab Calloway: Hi De Ho,* p. 16. *dig:* meet.

1947 *Frontiers of Jazz,* p. x. I dig good jazz when I hear it.

1952 *A History of Jazz in America,* p. 351. *dig:* to understand; often to penetrate a hidden meaning, hence used of the process of intellection of the jazz initiate ("he digs!").

1956 *Chicago Review,* Autumn-Winter, p. 15. "Dig that jive," to which Louis Armstrong could probably still lend meaning, is a similar expression used *ad nauseam* even by the hotel orchestras of the period.

1958 *Publication of the American Dialect Society*, Nov., p. 45. *dig:*
. . . (Perhaps from a sense of "getting to the bottom" of things).

1959 *The Holy Barbarians*, p. 24. I'm not modest either, dig?

1959 *Swinging Syllables*, s.v. *dig:* understand; also: look, see, enjoy,
like.

dig it (!) [from *dig* above and/or *dig the jive* below; current esp.
among black jazzmen since c. 1965] Punctuative phrase akin to
"Amen!" or "Pay attention!"

1969 *Hip Manual.* We were walking down Tenth Avenue, you dig it.

1974 *Location Shots*, p. 89. $120,000 for 20 pounds of pure coke! Dig
it?

dig the jive, see COLLAR THE JIVE; also see last 1956 quot. S.V. DIG.

dig the play [jazz slang *dig* + jazz slang *the play:* current c. 1935–c.
1945, rare since]

1940 *Current History*, 7 Nov., p. 22. *Do you dig the play?* Do you
understand me?

I don't dig the scene [from jazz slang *dig* + jazz slang *scene;* some
currency from c. 1955–c. 1965, rare since] I don't comprehend the
situation, the environment, the music—whatever it is that is occupying
my attention. Oral evidence only.

dime note [understatement (cf. CENTS); cf. 1934 *A Dictionary of
American Slang*, p. 295: "*dime:* money in general"; current since c.
1935] $10; by extension: ten of anything (see last quot.).

1938 *Better English*, Nov., p. 51. *dime note:* $10.

1971 *Bird Lives*, p. 264. Here's a dime note for your trouble.

1974 *Harper's*, June, p. 47. Three years later I was back in Fort Worth
. . . ten years for sticking a needle in my arm . . . I had just written a
letter to the Attorney General telling him a dime was a long time for
what I did.

Dip, the (Beale Street) [according to jazzmen, the dance was almost
always referred to as simply *the Dip* (which suggests the dance's
movement); current c. 1912–c. 1916, obs. since except historical] Jazz
dance.

1942 *Beale Street Sundown*, p. 32. They wanted to make pictures of
couples doing the Beale Street Dip.

dirt (music) [by analogy with its earthiness; current c. 1910–c. 1935, obs.

since except historical] "Hot," earthy, driving (jazz), characteristic of the small jazz bands.

1926 *Melody Maker*, Jan., p. 31. The former is conspicuous for an excellent hat-muted trumpet solo and some real "dirt" on the fiddle by that super-jazz artist, Hugo Rignold. —March, p. 39. They are full of "dirt" and everything else that's good.

1955 *Hear Me Talkin to Ya*, p. 37. He was a great man for what we call "dirt music."

dirty, *adj.* [one of several standard terms the connotation of which jazzmen have reversed (i.e., from bad to good): see also BAD, MEAN, TERRIBLE, TOUGH; current c. 1900–c. 1945, very rare since]

1926 *Melody Maker*, May, p. 48. Fine "hot" record, with a special "dirty" piano solo.

1929 *Jacobs' Orchestra Monthly*, June, p. 6. It [i.e., jazz] is "hot," "dirty," maybe, at times, a little blasphemous.

1936 *Hot Jazz: The Guide to Swing Music*, p. 89. His tone almost always has a pronounced rasp, the effect of which is magnificently "dirty."

1939 *American Jazz Music*, p. 45. And the term "dirty" is often applied to the general tone of certain players who favor robust, somewhat rough tone production.

1959 *The Jazz Scene*, p. 116. "dirty"—instrumentally unorthodox because emotionally expressive (the word was used as a synonym for "hot" in the 1920s).

dirty dozens, the, see S.V. DOZENS.

district, the [see 1955 quot. for semantic explanation; widely current c. 1910–c. 1917, when it was the geographic center of jazz, obs. since except historical] The Storyville (q.v.) sector of New Orleans, an important locale in the early history of jazz.

1948 *Trumpet on the Wing*, p. 11. But I never played in "the district."

1955 *Hear Me Talkin to Ya*, p. 4. I never heard it called Storyville . . . It was always The District—the red light district.

Dixieland, Dixie, *n.* [see 1939 quot. for explanation of semantic development; current since c. 1916; see also NEW ORLEANS.] See 1937, 1939, 1959 quots.

1916 *Original Dixieland Jazz Band* (name of famous jazz group, which made its first restaurant appearance on January 19, 1917).

1917 advertising poster [1962 *Jazz: A History of the New York Scene*, p. 58] Due to the expense of bringing The Original Dixie Land Jazz Band. We are forced to Charge a small sum of 25¢ per Person during their Stay Only.

1937 *American Speech*, Feb., p. 47. When the melody of a chorus is played by a combination of trumpet, tenor saxophone, and clarinet, it is said to be played *Dixie*. It is voiced peculiarly in that the lead melody is carried lower than the clarinet, which carries a third harmony usually an octave above its normal position in a chord and always above the lead. So called after the style of playing of the *Original Dixieland Jazz Band*, the first great dance orchestra.

1939 *Jazzmen*, p. 39. Many years before, a bank in New Orleans had issued a ten-dollar bill with the word *dix* printed in large letters on one side. From this, the words "Dixie" or "Dixieland" meant New Orleans, long before the word was used as a general name for the South. This designation, in its original sense, gave a name to hot jazz played by New Orleans musicians. Today, it is applied more specifically to improvised hot music as played by small five- or six-piece orchestras.

1955 *Hear Me Talkin to Ya*, p. 402. One great thing about Dixie . . . is its use of counterpoint.

1956 *Guide to Jazz*, s.v. *Dixieland:* synonymous with New Orleans or Chicago, i.e., the jazz which flourished in the 1900–1935 (pre-Swing) period.

1959 *Jazz: A Quarterly of American Music*, Fall, p. 273. *Dixieland:* music involving the technical idiom established by certain players and composers, especially in New Orleans, in the second decade of this century.

dog, *n.* [prob. from black slang; some currency esp. among black jazzmen since c. 1925; for other terms in which the connotation can be either good or bad, see LOOSE, SOMETHING ELSE, WIG, WEIRD (note, however, that *dog* has increasingly been used in a pejorative sense)]

1928 *The Walls of Jericho*, p. 299. *dog:* any extraordinary person, thing, or event. "Ain't this a dog?" is a comment on anything unusual.

1961 *Swank*, July, p. 72. The *ABC* [album] is a dog, the *Impulse!* a mild winner.

1961 *Down Beat's Jazz Record Reviews: Vol. V*, p. 210. The only real dog in the set is *Friday the Thirteenth*, a doleful, badly balanced performance.

doghouse, dog-house, *n.* [cf. 1950 *Slang Today and Yesterday*, p. 433: "dog-house: a bass violin (musicians—1922)"; very rare since c. 1945]

   1925 *English Words & Their Background*, p. 45. *dog-house:* bass violin.

   1936 *Esquire*, June, p. 131. What type of people get a thrill . . . out of listening to Wellman Braud "slap the doghouse"?

   1960 *The Jazz Titans*, p. 20. "Doghouse" is the old slang term for the cumbersome instrument.

dog tune [cf. teenage slang *dog* (i.e., an unattractive girl); some currency since c. 1945]

   1952 *A History of Jazz in America*, p. 351. *dog tune:* a song of questionable musical quality.

   1964 *Down Beat*, 30 Jan., p. 32. "Bésame Mucho," something of a dog tune, became more fascinating with every chorus the way he played it.

   1974 *N.Y. Times*, 9 June, II, p. 24. Everything moves, even the dog tunes.

do it! (or **that thing!, your stuff!**) [current esp. among black jazz dancers c. 1920–c. 1935, rare since] Cries of encouragement to either jazz musicians or dancers.

   1926 *Nigger Heaven*, p. 10. Do that thing.

   1928 *The Walls of Jericho*, p. 299. *Do it! Do that thing! Do your stuff!:* shouts of encouragement.

domie, domi, dommy, *n.* [shortened form of *domicile;* some currency esp. among black jazzmen c. 1930–c. 1940, rare since; see also CRIB, PAD] A room or apartment.

   1944 *The New Cab Calloway's Hepsters Dictionary*, p. 6. I live in a righteous domi.

   1958 *Jive in Hi-Fi*, p. 15. *domie:* house, home, or room.

   1959 *Diggeth Thou?*, p. 34. She cut into his dommy and helped kill the fifth.

don't take down [according to jazzman Eubie Blake, current c. 1900–c. 1917, obs. since except historical]

   1955 *Hear Me Talkin to Ya*, p. 59. The order, "Don't take down," was a signal to everyone in the band to play all the time—no laying down the horn for a minute.

doodle, *v.i.* [prob. of sexual or scatological origin; according to jazzman Eubie Blake, some currency c. 1900–c. 1935, obs. since except historical] To play music very informally and relaxedly.

1955 *Hear Me Talkin to Ya*, p. 164. Get out your horn, let's doodle a little.

1964 *Down Beat,* 19 Nov., p. 21. Lee Morgan adds a lot with all those quick doodling phrases.

dots, *n. pl.* [from the appearance of sheet music; some currency since c. 1920] Originally, the notes on sheet music, now also extended to the sheet music itself.

1927 *Melody Maker*, June, p. 586. I will give you the "dots" for them.

1958 *Teach Yourself Jazz*, p. 39. Firstly, most St. Louis musicians could read music, and were seen "carrying their 'dots' about with them."

double, *v.i. & v.t.* 1. [cf. circus slang *double in brass;* current since c. 1920 (i.e., with the advent of the *big band,* q.v.)] See 1946 quot.; also, for noun use—an instrument so used—see 1934 quot.

1926 *Melody Maker*, Feb., p. 13. It is able to do so successfully since, owing to its musicians doubling, the combination of three fiddles, 'cello, bass, with, of course, piano, is obtained.

1934 *All About Jazz*, p. 68. All the foregoing applies equally to clarinets and the instruments used as "doubles" by the saxophonists in the band.

1946 *Jazzways*, p. 52. Or, if a musician is able to "double," that is, play another instrument in addition to his regularly assigned one (for example, most saxophonists double clarinet, flute, etc.), he receives added compensation for that.

1955 *A Pictorial History of Jazz*, p. 40. The excess of instruments on these bandstands indicates how much "doubling" a musician was expected to do.

1957 *The Book of Jazz*, p. 27. "He doubled on bass and piano."

2. (occasionally with *up*) [current since c. 1925; see also DOUBLE TIME] To double the tempo; for its adjective use, see first quot.

1948 *Down Beat*, 14 July, p. 13. Ventura's doubled up tenoring on "Body" is some of the best that he has set down on wax.

1950 *Mister Jelly Roll*, p. 75. As Picou saw it, jazz consisted of "additions to the bars—doubling up on notes—playing eight or sixteen for one."

1958 *American Thesaurus of Slang*, p. 554. *double it up:* to double the tempo.

1959 *The Horn*, p. 231. Even the doubling of the bass was distinctly audible.

double time [variant of *double*, sense 2; current since c. 1925]

1957 *The Book of Jazz*, p. 224. "Double time," a gambit normally associated with bop; frequent use is made of 16th notes . . . in . . . uninterrupted fashion . . . among bop soloists.

do up [cf. Early Modern English use of *do* (i.e., of a man, to copulate): c. 1592 *Titus Andronicus*, IV, ii, 76, "I have done thy mother"; current among jazzmen since c. 1948] To effect (something), take action with regard to (something or someone—food, music, sex, etc.); also (with ref. to narcotics), see first quot.

1959 *The Holy Barbarians*, p. 24. About the second day I was with him he offered me a fix—did I want to do up—and I said no.

1959 *Easy Living*, p. 89. I figure, give her a couple days rest and then do her up right, you dig?

1959 *Esquire*, Nov., p. 70I. *do up, to:* term of action. Example: let's go out and do up this club. Enjoy it to the utmost.

down, *adj.* 1. [from *down with it,* q.v. poss. reinforced by general slang *down to earth;* cf. *1811 Dictionary of the Vulgar Tongue:* "*down:* aware of a thing. Knowing it"; widely current only since c. 1950]

1959 *Esquire*, Nov., p. 70I. *down:* dirty, earthy. Example: a down stud. A fellow devoid of pretense, fundamentally honest.

1960 *Beat Jokes Bop Humor & Cool Cartoons*, p. 50. The old man, respected throughout the kingdom for being a down kitty, lay but a few weeks in his grave.

1961 *Down Beat*, 2 Feb., p. 30. Collette's playing is faultless and at times he manages to work up a "down" jazz feeling.

1964 *N.Y. Times Magazine*, 23 Aug., p. 64. *down:* hip, just right and true, as in "That was a down movie."

1972 *Down Beat*, 8 June, p. 26. Dupree is as down a guitar player as there is out there.

2. [special application of standard sense; some currency since c. 1920] Out of practice; uninspired.

1973 *Bourbon Street Black,* p. 40. When he gets out, his lip is "down" and he never makes the good gigs again.

adv. [poss. from general colloquial *down to his toes* (or *socks*); current esp. among black jazzmen c. 1925–c. 1945, very rare since; see also BACK, *adv.*] Extremely; well.

1928 *The Walls of Jericho,* p. 299. *drunk down:* the nadir of inebriation.

1942 *American Mercury,* July, p. 94. *draped down:* dressed in the height of Harlem fashion; also *togged down.*

down for [prob. from gamblers' slang; current since c. 1935] Agreeable to.

c. 1941 *Down for Double* (tune recorded by Count Basie orchestra).

down with [prob. from gambling slang to *be down* (i.e., to have one's bet placed) and poss. from general colloquial *down to his toes* (or *socks*); current esp. among black jazzmen since c. 1935] See 1957 and 1959 quots.

1944 *Dan Burley's Original Handbook of Harlem Jive,* p. 47. Iago is down with the action.

1946 *Really the Blues,* p. 369. *down with it:* top-notch, superlative.

1955 *Down Beat,* 5 Oct., p. 51. I don't know who the singer is 'cause I'm not down with all the singers now.

1957 *The Book of Negro Folklore,* p. 483. *down with it:* to get acquainted with, to understand.

1959 *Esquire,* Nov., p. 70I. *down with something, to be:* to know something thoroughly.

down with (one's) ax [jazz slang *down with* + jazz slang *ax;* current since c. 1955; cf. *all over (one's) horn, get around on (one's) horn*] To be thoroughly proficient technically on one's instrument. Oral evidence only.

downhome, down-home, down home, *adj.* [from black jazzman's identification of his emotional roots with the earthiness of the Southern black (and esp. with rural life); despite some earlier use, widely current only since c. 1950; see also FUNKY, SOUL] Earthy, honest, and unpretentious.

1938 *N.Y. Amsterdam News,* 12 Mar., p. 17. The allusion to "peppermint candy" stirs almost primal emotions, hangover from the old "down home house rent strut" days.

1960 *The Jazz Word*, p. 213. All the current terms of approbation among jazzmen—"soul," "funk," "down home"—all mean basically that if a man can play the blues from inside himself without straining to play a part, he's a legitimate jazzman.

1960 *Down Beat*, 24 Nov., p. 18. The ever-changing jazz argot is consistent in one thing: Through the years the most cogent and expressive words and terms relating to good jazz have without exception been down to earth and colorful. Jazz is not sissy music. What could be more natural than that words like "funk," "dirty," and terms like "gut-bucket" and "down home" be indigenous to it?

1973 *Bourbon Street Black*, p. 16. It didn't matter if they were "note" lessons, or just straight "blowin' down home style."

dozens, the (dirty) [according to lexicographer Peter Tamony, term derives poss. from 18th c. *dozen* (*v.*): to stun, stupefy, daze; some currency esp. among black jazzmen since c. 1925 (see 1960 quot.)]

1928 *The Walls of Jericho*, p. 9. For it is the gravest of insults, this so-called "slipping in the dozens." To disparage a man is one thing; to disparage his family is another.

1960 *N.Y. Citizen-Call*, 30 July, p. 19. An etymologist might be led to define "The Dozens" as the "Science of Disparaging One's Ancestors." . . . Research reveals that the Dozens were of American slave origin and took the place of physical assault by the "field slaves" on the more favored "house slaves" on Southern plantations. . . . It was during the 1920s . . . that some unknown blues pianist and singer composed an uncopyrighted tune called "The Dirty Dozens" complete with words, which because of their very nature never got on paper. But at barrelhouse and buffet flat house rent parties "The Dirty Dozens" became the rage.

1970 *Death of a Blue-Eyed Soul Brother*, p. 70. "Don't play the dozens with me, bitch," I warned her.

draft, feel a, see s.v. FEEL A DRAFT.

drag, *n.* 1. [from the delayed, pulling movement of the dance and the music to which it was danced: cf. 1959 quot.; current c. 1915–c. 1930, obs. since except historical, though the dance step survives in other dances; for synonymous names, see also MOOCH, SCRAUNCH] An early blues style and/or tempo; also, the concomitant jazz dance, c. 1917–c. 1935.

1916 *Walkin' the Dog* (tune). Do that slow drag 'round the hall.

1923 *Shoe Shiners Drag* (tune).

1924 *The Chicago Gouge* (tune). Down at a Chitlin rag,/They played a fiddlin' drag.

1938 *The Hot Jazz of Jelly Roll Morton*, p. 7. Jelly takes . . . passages . . . returning to the essence of *slow drag*, the blues style that Jelly knew so well.

1950 *They All Played Ragtime*, p. 247. The Slow Drag must begin on the first beat of each measure.

1955 *Hear Me Talkin to Ya*, p. 123. We had only two tempos, slow drag and the two-four one-step.

1959 *The Jazz Scene*, pp. 290–291. Terms for emotion were formed by metaphor, e.g. by the widespread practice of equating . . . grief with depth . . . thus the quality most desired in the old blues is that it should be *low-down* or *dragging*.

1960 *Jazz: A Quarterly of American Music*, Winter, p. 25. By that name or by other names ("ditties," "slow drags"), blues were as basic to early jazz as brass bands.

2. [cf. jazz slang *drag the beat;* also cf. 1925 *English Words & Their Background*, pp. 61–62. "If she [i.e., a girl] is unpopular, she is . . . *a drag"*; widely current from c. 1940–c. 1960, less common since] See 1960 quot.

1946 *The Jazz Record*, July, p. 9. They sent me down South, Georgia. That was enough to make me blow my top. It was a drag, Jack.

1952 *Go*, p. 240. It's all such a drag, . . . all these relationships, hangups, conflicts.

1960 *Dictionary of American Slang*, s.v. *drag:* a person, thing, event, or place that is intellectually, emotionally, or aesthetically boring, tedious, tiring, or colorless.

v.t. (also, occasionally, *drug:* see 1961 quot.) [see note in *n.*, 2; current from c. 1940–c. 1960, rare since] See 1958 quot.

1955 *Down Beat*, 21 Sep., p. 33. If there's anything that drags me, it's when they put the piano up too loud in the control room.

1958 *The Book of Negro Folklore*, p. 483. *drag:* humiliate, upset, disillusion.

1961 *Down Beat*, 19 Jan., p. 22. Something's really drugging you that evening.

v.i. (current since c. 1900] In music, to fall behind the beat.

1953 *Night Light*, p. 223. "You're draggin'."

Also **drag the beat.**

dragged, drug(g), drugged, *adj.* [from *drag, v.t.;* current since c. 1940; see also BROUGHT DOWN, BUGGED, HUNG]

1946 *Really the Blues*, p. 298. I was one drugg cat. —p. 369. *drugg:* brought down [jazz sense], depressed.

1958 *American Speech*, Oct., p. 225. Somewhat less frequently paired are the synonyms for *annoyed: bugged, dragged.*

1959 *The Holy Barbarians*, p. 27. Before I light up I'm drug with ten thousand things.

1959 *Esquire*, Nov., p. 70I. *dragged:* depressed. Example: I'm dragged with this scene. I'm annoyed by these surroundings. —*drugged:* annoyed, disgusted, extremely depressed.

1960 *Hiparama of the Classics*, p. 12. Drag not, and Thou Shalt not be Drug!

drape(s), *n.* (also *v.i.:* oral evidence only) [from standard sense: 1959 *Webster's New World Dictionary*, s.v. *drape:* "1. *usually in pl.* cloth hanging in loose folds"; current from c. 1935–c. 1960, rare since; see also VINES, THREADS]

1938 *Cab Calloway: Hi De Ho*, p. 16. *drape:* suit of clothes, dress, costume.

1946 *Really the Blues*, p. 41. Jack, the drapes they handed me a jungle bum wouldn't wear on weekdays.

1952 *Park East*, Dec., p. 31. His drapes were all crummy, his toupee was beat.

draped, *adj.* [current since c. 1935] Attired.

1942 *American Mercury*, July, p. 94. *draped down:* dressed in the height of Harlem fashion.

drive, *n.* [special application of standard sense (i.e., energy); current since c. 1930] Musical power, energy, or pulse.

1938 *Metronome*, June, p. 21. Mr. Gray's band at times achieves a drive.

1947 *Metronome*, June, p. 16. The former [i.e., swing] bumped and chugged along like a beat locomotive; this was known in some quarters as drive.

1951 *Down Beat*, 5 Oct., p. 12. There's a lot of drive to the rhythm section.

1960 *The Story of the Original Dixieland Jazz Band*, p. 193. With great patience he proceeded to teach Henry . . . the idea of "drive"—

when to hit hard on the downbeat, when to drop out to let the clarinet and trombone come through, how to lead into a chorus.

v.i. & v.t. [special application of a standard sense; current prob. since c. 1930]

1952 *A History of Jazz in America*, p. 351. *drive:* to play with concentrated momentum.

1957 *Down Beat*, 11 July, p. 19. Listening to Hamp Hawes, he'll comment, "Yeah. He plays a driving piano."

1960 *The Story of the Original Dixieland Jazz Band*, p. 33. No one ever "drove" a band like La Rocca, and to this day his secrets of "drive"—the tricks of "blowing in" a phrase, of hitting slightly ahead of the beat, of dropping out at a critical moment—have never been equalled.

drive-notes, *n. pl.* [current c. 1930–c. 1945, obs. since]

1935 *Vanity Fair*, Nov., p. 71. Ensemble chords that mark a transition to a new key are *drive-notes.*

drop off, see s.v. FALLOFF.

dropping bombs, see s.v. BOMBS.

drug(g), drugged, *adj.* See s.v. DRAGGED.

dude, *n.* [humorous application of term formerly applied to a "tenderfoot"; cf. *Dictionary of Slang & Its Analogues.* "*dude:* a man of spirit"; youth and black slang, but also current among jazzmen since c. 1965] Fellow.

1969 *The Life and Loves of Mr. Jiveass Nigger*, p. 109. Bob was a tough dude with them Swedish broads.

1973 *Down Beat*, 25 Oct., p. 26. Well, whoever the dude is, he sure can play.

1973 *Down Beat*, 6 Dec., p. 17. If there was anything that dude loved, it was the drums.

dues, *n. pl.* [extension of standard meaning; some currency since c. 1945, but wide currency only since c. 1955] See 1969 quot.

1946 *Good Dues Blues* (tune recorded by Dizzy Gillespie).

1960 *Hiparama of the Classics*, p. 15. It is for us the swingin' to pick up the dues of these departed Studs.

1969 *Hip Manual. dues:* the disadvantages you will put up with in order to get what you want. The punishment for unwise behavior.

pay (one's) dues [extension of *dues*, n. pl.—i.e., in jazz slang, one "pays" with personal suffering instead of with money; some currency since c. 1945, but wide currency only since c. 1955] To serve an apprenticeship in life by absorbing a share of the hardships that experience brings.

1942 *Call House Madam*, p. 292. She was mixed up later in one of the rottenest shooting messes ever staged in Hollywood, but she got away with her end of it and never paid her dues.

1956 *Esquire*, Feb., p. 63. Some of the commercial jazz guys think they're playing real jazz, but they aren't making it because they haven't paid their dues. (Suffering enough of the trials and tribulations of life to realize that jazz comes from the heart.)

1961 *The Sound*, p. 61. I paid my dues in them big bands. —p. 206. She's seen the seamiest side of life, taken her lumps, starved, lied, stolen, conned—paid her dues.

1961 *The Jazz Life*, p. 29. "Paying dues" is the jazz musician's term for the years of learning and searching for an individual sound and style while the pay is small and irregular.

1970 *The Jazz People*, p. 1. "To pay one's dues" originates from the actual monthly dues paid to the Union, but it is a universally accepted comment on the hazards of the day-to-day jazz existence.

duster, *n.* [from its incidental function of dusting off chairs and benches; some currency esp. among black jazzmen c. 1925–c. 1945, very rare since; see also RUSTY DUSTY] The buttocks.

1946 *Really the Blues*, p. 196. Keep on wriggling your saucy duster.

dusty butt [some currency esp. among black jazzmen c. 1900–c. 1945, very rare since]

1942 *American Mercury*, July, p. 94. *dusty butt:* cheap prostitute.

E

ear man [general colloquial phrase but with esp. currency among jazzmen c. 1917–c. 1940, very rare since] A musical improviser: one who doesn't read music.

1939 *Jazzmen*, p. 190. Ammons, although strictly an "ear" man, has always been an excellent orchestra pianist.

ear music [general colloquial phrase but with esp. currency among jazzmen c. 1917–c. 1940, very rare since; see also the more common HEAD, *adj. & n.*] Improvised music; also, for a rare adjective use, see first quot.

1936 *Stage*, Mar., p. 58. *ear-music boys:* improvisers; literally those who play by ear.

1939 *Jazzmen*, pp. 40–41. They played by note for marches and played by note at some of the more sedate balls, but had plenty of opportunity to play "ear music" at house parties, at the race track, and in "the district."

ears, *n. pl.* [according to jazzmen, Lester Young was the first to apply this term in a special jazz slang sense c. 1940; reinforced by idiomatic *a good ear (for music);* still current] A desire to listen or hear; also, a keenly discriminating responsiveness to music.

1958 *Nugget*, Dec., p. 42. In 1957, George Avakian, one of the notable A & R men with "ears" in the record business, decided that Miles and Gil Evans had to be reunited.

1963 *Down Beat*, 3 Jan., p. 34. Only people with minimum preconception and maximum ears took him seriously.

big ears [extension of *ears* above; current since c. 1945] The knack of hearing very accurately.

1971 *Down Beat*, 15 Apr., p. 19. He has big ears, he only needs to hear it once to play it as if he wrote it!

East Coast (jazz) [chiefly a writers' term; some currency since c. 1955] Generic since c. 1955 for the countermovement to West Coast (i.e., *cool*, q.v.) jazz; earthy modern jazz (see also FUNK).

1957 *New York Jazz Festival: 1957*, p. 19. *The school:* East Coast, "bluesy" or "funky" jazz, highlighted by such musicians as trumpeters Donald Byrd, Kenny Dorham, Art Farmer.

1957 *Charles Mingus: East Coasting* (LP album Bethlehem BCP-6019).

eel-ya-dah, *n.* [see quot. for etym.; current c. 1945–c. 1950, rare since; see also OO-BLA-DEE]

1949 *Music Library Association Notes*, Dec., p. 43, *eel-ya-dah:* nonsense syllables for the triplet figure common in bebop.

eight-to-the-bar, *adj.* [see 1955 quot. for etym.; some currency c. 1930–c. 1945, very rare since] Boogie-woogie (q.v.).

1931 *Melody Maker*, May, p. 399. A fine trumpet gets going against a most modern eight-in-a-bar rhythm.

1955 *The First Book of Jazz*, p. 27. Some people started calling all boogie-woogie music the "fives." Others call it "eight-to-the-bar," because the rolling bass consists of eight eighth-notes in each bar.

eighty-eight, *n.* [from number of keys on a piano; some currency esp. among white jazzmen c. 1925–c. 1945, rare since; see also BOX]

1942 *The American Thesaurus of Slang*, p. 559. *eighty-eight:* piano.

1944 *Down Beat*, 15 Feb., p. 8. Nowhere can one find a more solid 88 solo.

1949 *Down Beat*, 11 Mar., p. 15. Eighty-eight tinkler Allen plays most of his capitol dance dates with only himself and three rhythm.

eighty-eighter, *n.* [some currency esp. among white jazzmen c. 1925–c. 1945, rare since]

1949 *Music Library Association Notes*, Dec., p. 43. *eighty-eighter:* popular musician's term for pianist.

1971 *The Street That Never Slept*, p. 287. Bud Powell, regarded as the foremost of bop eighty-eighters, sat in with Bird for one set.

end, the [hyperbole: that point beyond which one can't go; widely current from c. 1952–c. 1965, less common since; see also THE MOST, OUT OF SIGHT] The very best.

1950 *Neurotica*, Autumn, p. 45. Senor, this shit [i.e., narcotic] is the end!

1958 *Somewhere There's Music*, p. 200. I wanted to tell you I thought your singing was the end. Really nice.

1960 *The Jazz World*, p. 81. Diz played with Bird's group and sounded the end. —p. 123. One of my paintings is named "Requiem for Bird," a tribute for the end alto.

1963 *Nugget*, Feb., p. 44. I dyed it . . . to complement my end hair. —p. 46. I was blowing some jazz in the student lounge on this end Steinway.

-est, *suffix* [wide use and, consequently, rapid turnover of superlatives in jazz slang has led since c. 1950 to the affixing of *-est* to unlikely words more frequently than happens in general slang or colloquial speech.] To the nth degree.

1955 *Solo*, p. 191. These mixed-up cats get the *gon*est chicks, I swear.

1955 *Bop Fables*, p. 47. She is the swingin'est, but let's take it from the top again. —p. 57. "Man," said the stranger, "they're the jumpin'est!"

1957 *On the Road*, p. 282. Victor is the . . . franticest . . . cat I've ever . . . met.

1957 *New York Jazz Festival: 1957*, p. 43. Al "Jazzbo" Collins WRCA is one of the outest.

every man for himself [general colloquialism given special application by jazzmen; current c. 1917–c. 1940, obs. since except historical; see also EVERY TUB] In traditional jazz, complete improvisation: no written music.

1955 *Hear Me Talkin to Ya*, p. 59. It was "every man for himself," with trumpeter taking the lead and everyone else filling in the best he could.

every tub [taken from *every tub on its own black bottom* q.v.; some currency esp. among black jazzmen since c. 1935] Each individual.

[1927] 1966 *Down Beat*, 20 Oct., p. 18. Tell them New York cats to look out. Here comes Tatum! And I mean every living 'tub' with the exception of Fats Waller and Willie the Lion.

1938 *Every Tub* (tune recorded by Count Basie).

1968 *Down Beat*, 7 Mar., p. 19. In those days, the late Buster Bailey could cut every living tub on the clarinet.

1972 *Jazz Masters of the Thirties*, p. 150. When Hawk finished off the blues, every tub began cheering.

every tub on its (own black) bottom [cf. 1952 *Invisible Man*, p. 472. "After that it's every tub on its own black bottom!"; nautical expression adopted by rural Southern blacks, then given a special application by black jazzmen; current c. 1917–c. 1940, obs. since except historical; see also EVERY MAN FOR HIMSELF] In traditional jazz, complete improvisation; in life, every man for himself.

1966 *New Yorker*, 25 June, p. 35. You had to go out and find a room—which was called every tub on its bottom, or being on your own.

1972 *Down Beat*, 20 July, p. 15. The "every-tub-on-its-own-bottom" approach to group playing by Davis' combos permitted Trane and Shorter to work out their improvisational styles in an empathetic setting.

evil, *adj.* [special applications of standard term; from black slang; cf. 1926 *Nigger Heaven*, p. 248. "Cause Ah's evil an' bad."; current esp. among black jazzmen since c. 1935] As applied to people, see 1939 and first 1946 quots.; as applied to nature, malign (see second 1946 and 1957 quots.).

1939 *Jitterbug Jamboree Song Book*, p. 32. evil: in bad humor.

1946 *Big Book of Swing*, p. 124. evil: nasty.

1946 *Really the Blues*, p. 160. This evil dim [i.e., night], as we sat around our table at the Nest, I was still as a hoot-owl, sad and sick at heart.

1956 *Eddie Condon's Treasury of Jazz*, p. 239. They forgave him his trespasses when Bird felt evil.

1957 *On the Road*, p. 61. He had fallen on the beat and evil days that come to young guys in their middle twenties.

1957 *The Horn*, p. 52. She's one of them rich, *evil* junkies.

explosion, *n.* [from its sound; some currency since c. 1945; see also FLARE] A loud musical chord or phrase.

1955 *Hear Me Talkin to Ya*, p. 134. We would build up to an explosion, then go down soft.

eyes, *n. pl.* [prob. suggested by *I Only Have Eyes for You*, 1934 song which became a jazz standard; according to jazzmen, Lester Young was the first to use the term in a special jazz slang sense c. 1940] A desire or inclination (for something); see 1955 quot. for special, rare uses.

1948 *New Yorker*, 3 July, p. 28. Have you eyes for a sandwich?

1955 *Say*, 28 Apr., p. 53. *historical eyes:* outdated, passé. *Hollywood eyes:* a fine girl.

1958 *Somewhere There's Music*, p. 19. Oh, a girl here's got eyes to meet you.

1961 *The Sound*, p. 174. You always had downtown eyes.

1971 *Beneath the Underdog*, p. 287. I think I can make a little bed eyes if I cool it with her and her friend.

big eyes, 1. [current since c. 1950] A great desire (for something).

1956 *Sideman*, p. 276. I'm all happy about it—*big-eyes.*

1959 *Esquire*, Nov., p. 70I. I have big eyes to make it with this chick.

1961 *The Sound*, p. 108. Big eyes to hear you blow, man!

2. [comic-strip externalization of an inner capacity; some currency since c. 1955] The ability to read music expertly.

1971 *Down Beat*, 15 Apr., p. 19. He only needs to hear it once to play it as if he wrote it! He hides behind the cats with big eyes.

no eyes [current since c. 1950] An aversion; a disinclination.

1959 *The Horn*, p. 56. I got no eyes for that now.

1970 *Death of a Blue-Eyed Soul Brother*, p. 83. She had no eyes for Stokes' bag.

F

face, *n.* [synecdoche; cf. 1960 *Dictionary of American Slang*, s.v. *face:* "Negro use"; some currency esp. among black jazzmen since c. 1940] Initially, a stranger, any anonymous individual (hence, frequently for blacks, a white man); increasingly, any person.

1946 *Hepcats Jive Talk Dictionary.* s.v. *face:* white man.

1946 *Really the Blues*, p. 369. *face:* a form of greeting.

1952 *Flee the Angry Strangers*, p. 316. You go down and cook up some soup for the Face.

1955 *Solo*, p. 39. "Real cool tonight!" said one face.

1960 *The Jazz Titans*, p. 155. *face:* person, man.

1969 *Hip Manual.* He's a West Coast face.

bad face [some currency esp. among black jazzmen since c. 1940]

1961 *N.Y. Times Magazine*, 25 June, p. 39. *bad face;* hipster's version of Rasputin (either sex); i.e., a surly, mean, no-good cat [jazz sense].

1969 *Hip Manual.* He's a bad face, man, and I don't want him around.

fake, *v.i. & v.t.* [see 1958 quot. for explanation of semantic development; current c. 1915–c. 1945, less common since, primarily because modern jazz is so technically demanding that most modern jazzmen must be able to read music well: consequently, the practice now derives from choice, not from necessity] See 1937, 1958 quots.; also, by extension, to improvise or be resourceful in any situation: see 1962 quot.

1926 *Melody Maker*, Jan., p. 20. In those days, it must be remembered, the dance band was not studied by the orchestrator as it is now, and one had to "fake" saxophone and banjo parts from those of such other instruments as were catered for in the score.

1929 *The Musical Quarterly*, Oct., p. 623. "Faking" . . . is increasingly giving way to the printed part.

1936 *Harper's*, Apr., p. 574. Thus in a typical "jam session" one instrument will lead off with a slightly modified form of the general melody, the other instruments "faking" the harmony.

1937 *American Speech*, Oct., p. 183. *fake:* at a formal engagement, to play a piece of music without orchestration as though there were one.

1944 *Spotlight*, Jan., p. 18. And according to what I hear played today there was enough good music "faked" in those days to last this generation of "readers" the rest of their days.

1958 *Publication of the American Dialect Society*, Nov., p. 41. The term "fake" has been applied to improvising for a good many years. It originally implied that the player was not doing his job correctly, and possibly that he could not read music at all and thus was forced to make it up as he went along. Jazzmen, perhaps in self-defense, made the word a synonym for "improvising" and use of it implies nothing bad about a man's performance.

1962 *Jazz Monthly*, Oct., p. 10. In a typical "bop joke" a musician passenger tells a taxicab driver who says he doesn't know how to get to a particular address: "That's all right, man, fake it."

fake book [from *fake;* current c. 1925–c. 1945, very rare since] Any of the various books containing the basic chord progressions for many popular songs, an indispensable book for many of the dance (hotel) musicians of the 1920s and 1930s.

1958 *American Speech*, Oct., p. 225. The . . . "fake book" . . . guides most small combos through this weary world.

1965 *New Yorker*, 2 Jan., p. 46. Bring that fake book, please, in case they ask me to play something I recorded forty years ago.

fake fingering, see s.v. FALSE FINGERING.

faker, *n.* [from *fake;* some currency c. 1915–c. 1945, rare since except historical]

1934 *All About Jazz*, p. 50. The early jazz drummers were nearly all "fakers," in that they could not read music.

fall by (or **in, out, over, up**) [understatement; current since c. 1940]

1946 *Really the Blues*, p. 369. *fall in:* arrive.

1953 *Night Light*, p. 141. You'll have to fall over to the apartment sometime.

1958 *Somewhere There's Music*, p. 34. Why don't you fall out with your axe some night?

1959 *The Horn*, p. 220. I fell by here looking for a chick.

1960 *Metronome*, Sep., p. 15. *fall by, fall in, fall up:* arrive, enter.

1961 *The Sound*, p. 107. Gee, I can't get over you cats falling in like this.

1969 *Hip Manual. fall by:* visit; *fall in:* enter.

falloff, drop off [current since c. 1925]

1949 *Music Library Association Notes*, Dec., p. 50. *drop off:* instrumentalist begins on written note, and usually by relaxed lip pressure, slides down four or five tones, reducing volume at same time.

1961 *Down Beat*, 19 Jan., p. 41. This is especially noticeable in the dynamics, shakes, falloffs, and cutoffs of the brass section.

fall out [prob. hyperbole; see 1960 quot. for partial semantic explanation, though dating is inaccurate; current since c. 1935] Initially, see 1938 quot.; more recently, see first 1959 quot.

1938 *Cab Calloway: Hi De Ho*, p. 16. *fall out:* to be overcome with emotion. Ex.—"The cats fell out when he took that solo."

1944 *Dan Burley's Original Handbook of Harlem Jive*, p. 138. *fall out:* to be aroused emotionally, to be taken by complete surprise.

1959 *Esquire*, Nov., p. 70I. *fall out:* to leave, to sleep. Pass out from too much drugs.

1959 *The Holy Barbarians*, p. 186. We were down there about an hour and I kept falling out.

1960 *Dictionary of American Slang*, p. 177. *fall out:* to be emotionally aroused; to be surprised; to "fall apart." Orig. c. 1946 bop use; now some teenage use. Prob. reenforced by the Army command "fall out"—dismissed.

1965 *Down Beat*, 11 Mar., p. 14. Everybody fell out laughing.

false (or fake) fingering [from improper or unconventional technique; some currency since c. 1920] A special technique for fingering a stop on a valve instrument, esp. on a trumpet, that produces certain effects (choking, etc.) which cannot be achieved conventionally.

1926 *Melody Maker*, May, p. 29. Higher notes must be obtained by "fake" fingering and special lip pressure.

1955 *Hear Me Talkin to Ya*, p. 275. He was very interested in the false-fingering ideas I was working out.

1961 *The Jazz Review*, Jan., p. 22. "Housewarming" is a good track, with Lips showing some of the "false-fingering" that was his own and some of the strength that was his, too.

1964 *(letter from jazz critic Martin Williams)* False fingering does not mean half-valve à la Rex Stewart; it means literally pressing down the wrong valve, using the wrong finger, but getting the right note, as many self-taught brassmen did.

fangs, *n. pl.* [current since c. 1957; see also earlier CHOPS, LIP] For literal sense, see 1959 quots.; more generally, a musician's embouchure—the skill and power of his blowing apparatus.

1958 *Down Beat*, 6 Feb., p. 31. The trumpet section probably includes Bernie Glow, Ernie Royal, Jimmy Nottingham, and all the guys with—to use the hip vernacular—they're saying "fangs" now instead of chops . . . a beautiful trumpet section.

1959 *Esquire*, Nov., p. 70I. *fangs:* lips.

1959 *Swinging Syllables*, s.v. *fangs:* teeth.

far out [see last quot. for accurate but partial explanation of semantic development: it overlooks the fact that the other-worldliness of the term derives at least in part from the new, extreme value placed by modern jazzmen on imaginativeness (see 1958 and first 1959 quots.); current from c. 1950–c. 1960, rare since: term has moved over to youth and Madison Ave.] Imaginative, experimental; hence, excellent.

1956 *Esquire*, Sep., p. 79. "Far out" is the new *hip,* not *hep,* term of critical approval, superseding the swing era's *hot* and the bop era's *cool.*

1958 *Somewhere There's Music*, pp. 15–16. Mike wondered what he would play. Nothing too far out, but a real old tune wouldn't get it either.

1959 *The Horn*, p. 131. Curn, it's wild, the greatest band you've ever had, but it'll bomb because it's too far out for the average gin-mill owner.

1959 *Jazz: A Quarterly of American Music*, Fall, p. 284. The power of musicians of skill to transport is verbalized in *send me.* It is little wonder that swing devotees . . . on the general observations of music as "heavenly" and "melody of the spheres," proclaimed they were sent—propelled by that centrifugal force *out of the world.* In the 1940s *far out* and *away out* became integral to bop and cool.

fast Texas, see S.V. TEXAS.

fat, *adj.* [some currency prob. since c. 1935] Full-toned.

1958 *Somewhere There's Music,* p. 164. The clarinet was as woody and fat as a clarinet can be.

1961 *The Sound,* p. 108. And Bernie, man, I need them big fat chords.

1962 *Down Beat,* 8 Nov., p. 32. Goldie has a big, fat sound, a dark, lustrous tone.

faust, *n. & adj.* [from Faust's association in legend with the devil: see 1946 quot.; from black slang; current esp. among black jazzmen c. 1930–c. 1945, very rare since]

1938 *Cab Calloway: Hi De Ho,* p. 16. *Faust:* an ugly girl.

1945 *Hepcats Jive Talk Dictionary,* s.v. *faust:* blind date.

1946 *Really the Blues,* p. 369. *Faust:* ugly (as the devil).

fay, ofay, *n. & adj.* [from black slang; the most prob. etym. (see both 1959 quots.) is that since the white man was considered a foe, *ofay* comes from *foe:* in pig Latin an initial consonant or cluster is dropped and added at the end with an [ay] following it; the *fay* form, then, would be a shortened form; however, jazz critic Martin Williams suggests that the term may derive from Louisiana Creole parents' admonition to children, "au fait"—i.e., show good manners à la genteel whites; for a third etym. see 1928 quot.; current esp. among black musicians since c. 1917, and fairly widespread among white musicians as well since c. 1945; both forms of the word are still widely current; see also GRAY] See last quot.

1925 *The Inter-State Tattler,* 6 Mar., p. 8. We hear that "Booker Red" has three ofays on his staff.

1928 *The Walls of Jericho,* p. 299. *fay, ofay:* a person who, as far as is known, is white. *Fay* is said to be the original term and *ofay* a contraction of "old" and "fay."

1946 *Really the Blues,* p. 178. The whole area was overrun with fay gangsters.

1959 *The Horn,* p. 89. She learned . . . even to order coffee from an ofay waitress in a voice that could be heard.

1959 *Harper's,* June, p. 75. "Ofay," the term for a white, is said by some theorists to be pig Latin for "foe," but whatever its etymology, the usual connotation of the word is at best neutral and usually hostile.

1959 *Esquire*, Nov., p. 70J. *ofay:* a white person. Sometimes shortened to fay. Derivation: Pig Latin for foe.

feature, *v.t.* [relation, if any, to its general slang sense (i.e., to imagine, believe, conceive of) unknown; current esp. among black jazzmen c. 1935–c. 1945, obs. since] To like or approve of (something). Oral evidence only.

feed, *v.i. & v.t.* [some currency since c. 1940; see also the more common BACK, COMP] To provide a chord background (for an instrumentalist); for adjective use, see second quot.; for noun use, see 1965 quot.

1961 *The Sound*, p. 108. I mean he really feeds me good. —p. 141. He was passing beyond the feed pianist stage.

1965 *Down Beat*, 17 June, p. 36. Kenny Burrell is one of the great feeders on guitar.

1971 *Down Beat*, 27 May, p. 20. Flanagan is a masterful accompanist —enhancing, underlining, feeding, supporting.

feel a draft [by analogy with the discomfort; introduced into jazz use by Lester Young c. 1945, but widely current only since c. 1955] To feel hostility directed against oneself: see 1960 quot.; also, to feel that something is amiss (esp. musically): see 1961 quot.

1957 *The Charles Mingus Jazz Workshop: The Clown* (liner notes on LP album Atlantic 1260). Mingus feels the slightest draft, sometimes even when no draft is there.

1960 *Playboy*, Aug., p. 106. "If somebody like J. J. or Gil Evans or John Lewis is obviously not impressed by what he's doing," says a friend, "Miles feels a draft."

1960 *Esquire*, Sep., p. 91. The term, "I feel a draft," is used by Negro musicians when there's evidence in a restaurant—or elsewhere—of Jim Crow. Ironically, white musicians who have played with Negro groups have sometimes used the same phrase in order to tell each other that they're being frozen out of the conversation or an afterhours party.

1961 *Metronome*, Sep., p. 14. I'm playing and all of a sudden I feel a draft. Either you should keep the trumpet going all the way or cut him sooner.

1968 *Down Beat*, 16 May, p. 17. The black audience would send a strong draft toward a Negro leader who hired a white man instead of a black man of comparable talent and stylistic inclination.

feeling, *n.* [special application of standard meaning (i.e., emotion); current c. 1935–c. 1945, rare since; see also the more recent SOUL] Emotional depth.

1939 *Down Beat's Yearbook of Swing*, p. 25. That musician who believes only in "feeling" is sadly deluding himself.

1940 *Swing*, Nov., p. 27. There's still a world of feeling in his improvisations on this swell old tune.

feel (one's) stuff, feel it [cf. general slang *to have the feel of (something);* some currency c. 1930–c. 1945, rare since] To be in touch with one's own creative springs; hence, to play music well.

1938 *N.Y. Post*, 3 Feb., p. 15. If he's in the mood, we say he's in the groove, or feeling his stuff.

1955 *Hear Me Talkin to Ya*, p. 356. He couldn't feel it.

fig, *n.* See S.V. MOLDY FIG.

fine, *adj.* [some general colloquial use but with esp. currency among jazzmen c. 1935–c. 1945, rare since]

1938 *N.Y. Amsterdam News*, 19 Feb., p. 17. He doesn't have to be good looking or dress so fine.

1940 *Swing*, Jan., p. 13. There was only one band that ever cut us down—and that was Woody's. They're fine!

1960 *Dictionary of American Slang*, s.v. *fine:* pleasing; wonderful; exciting . . . *associated with bop and cool use.*

fine and mellow [jazz slang *fine* + jazz slang *mellow;* innovated by jazz song with that title (see 1939 quot.); some currency since] Thoroughly pleasing.

1939 *Fine and Mellow* (song recorded by Billie Holiday on Columbia C-526).

1959 *Blow Up a Storm*, p. 19. Sounds fine and mellow.

fine as wine [from rhyming slang vogue, c. 1935–c. 1940, rare since] Excellent.

1957 *American Speech*, Dec., p. 276. Jazz Lingo abounds in . . . similes, e.g. . . . *fine as wine.*

finger popper, popping [see 1960 quot. for explanation of semantic development; some currency esp. among white jazzmen since c. 1950; see also the older ALLIGATOR, GATE] Initially, see 1959, 1960 quots.; also by extension, see last quot.; also, for its adjective use, see 1955 quot.

1955 *Metronome,* July, p. 22. Lord Buckley . . . addresses this album of *classics* in *bop talk* to Hipsters, Flipsters and Finger Poppin' Daddies.

1959 *Jazz for Moderns,* p. 20. *finger-popper:* a tune that lends itself to popping one's fingers.

1960 *Dictionary of American Slang,* s.v. *finger popper:* literally, one who snaps his fingers; figuratively, a musician or listener who is carried away by jazz music.

1963 *Hiptionary,* p. 72. *finger-popper:* a swinging [jazz sense] anything; play, book, meal, ball-game, musician, hipster.

finger style [some currency since c. 1920] See 1957 quot.

1927 *Melody Maker,* Jan., p. 22. There are also solos that are guaranteed to start the feet tapping and are issued for the finger style of playing in addition to plectrum style.

1957 *The Book of Jazz,* p. 117. An innovation introduced in the Kenton band in 1947 was the incorporation, in a jazz setting, of an unamplified Spanish concert guitar, played "finger style" (without a plectrum or pick).

five, lay (or **give me**) [from the number of fingers on the hand; current from c. 1940–c. 1955, rare since; see also SKIN] As a greeting (or parting), to slap someone's palm.

1972 *Village Voice,* 31 Aug., p. 62. We who still give skin or lay five on friends are, by Bill's standards, square.

five, take, see s.v. TAKE.

fives, the [semantic development unknown; some currency c. 1920–c. 1935, obs. since except historical] An earthy, sorrowful blues style on the piano. (Jazzmen say that this is its only meaning; hence, 1955 quot. is somewhat misleading.)

1955 *The First Book of Jazz,* p. 27. Some people started calling all boogie-woogie music the "fives."

1959 *The Jazz Scene,* p. 130. Even the research of the jazz lovers has failed to turn many of its casually recorded pioneers into more than names, vaguely attached to a location, a blues or two, or a particular pianistic trick ("the chimes," "the rocks," "the fives," "the chains").

flagwaver [by analogy with common vaudeville practice of winning applause by performing a familiar, often patriotic, tune; some currency since c. 1930] A spectacular piece of music or part of a musical performance intended to excite the listeners and win their applause.

1937 *The New York Woman,* 24 Feb., p. 29. "A flag waver" is the last chorus in which everybody goes to town ending up like a full ensemble of Valkyrie and Norse Gods.

1957 *Al Cohn-Zoot Sims Quintet: Al and Zoot* (liner notes of LP album Coral CRL 57171). *Just You, Just Me,* taken at a "flagwaver" tempo, closes the album.

1960 *Leisure,* Dec., pp. 40–41. If you remember, the things people liked most about Benny in the old days were the Gene Krupa solos, the screaming-type solos of Harry James, the flagwaving.

Also **flag waver.**

flam, *n.* [like most drum figures, onomatopoeic; current since c. 1930]
1967 *New Yorker,* 26 Aug., p. 74. *flams:* flat, clumping beats traded rapidly back and forth between the hands.

flare, *n.* [by analogy with standard meaning; current since c. 1935; see also EXPLOSION]
1942 *The American Thesaurus of Slang,* p. 562. *flare:* to play a note with a sharp attack and hold it for extra beats gradually letting it fade away.

1956 *Guide to Jazz,* p. 95. *flare:* a note held by a player at the end of a chorus to lead the band into a final collective improvisation.

flick(s), flicker(s), *n.* [earlier general slang term (flickers) adopted by jazzmen (usually without the *s*) c. 1935, shortened form dates from c. 1945]
1944 *Dan Burley's Original Handbook of Harlem Jive,* p. 138. *flickers:* moving pictures.

1946 *Really the Blues,* p. 231. To me the flickers were just a mild Minsky's on Celluloid.

1959 *Swinging Syllables,* s.v. *flick:* movie.

1960 *Down Beat,* 7 Jan., p. 26. I will stand by this one from here to eternity (a pretty groovy flick).

flip, *adj. & n.* [from *v.i.;* current from c. 1950–c. 1965, rare since] As adj., exciting or excitable: hence, eccentric or unstable; as n., see 1959 quot.
1952 *Flee the Angry Strangers,* p. 388. You crazy broad. Jeez, you flip broad.

1955 *Hear Me Talkin to Ya*, p. 347. He's not a flip as far as business is concerned.

1959 *Esquire*, Nov., p. 70I. *flip:* eccentric person.

v.i. [shortened form of *flip (one's) lid* or *flip (one's) wig;* current since c. 1948]

1950 *Neurotica*, Autumn, p. 44. If I'm not right back don't flip.

1952 *Life*, 29 Sep., p. 67. *flip:* to react enthusiastically.

1955 *Hear Me Talkin to Ya*, p. 119. Everybody flipped. It was wonderful.

1959 *Esquire*, Nov., p. 70I. To flip means to go wild. Example: He flipped over the record. He waxed enthusiastic over the record. . . . Flipped can also mean going insane.

flip (one's) lid (or **top** or **wig**) [see first quot. for semantic explanation; current c. 1943–c. 1948 when it was largely replaced by *flip:* see 1959 quot.]

1952 *A History of Jazz in America*, p. 351. Expressing exasperation, enthusiasm, or insanity . . . "flip one's lid" . . . describes the process of losing the hair or skin of the head.

1952 *Who Walk in Darkness*, p. 47. He flipped his wig when it was finished and they took him to a sanitarium.

1959 *Esquire*, Nov., p. 70I. Obsolete: flipped his lid or flipped his wig. This has been shortened to just flipped.

flip side [from the practice, c. 1920–1948, when phonograph records were played at 78 rpm, of recording just one piece of jazz music per side; some currency esp. among jazz writers since c. 1940, though increasingly rare since c. 1950] The reverse and, usually, less important side of a phonograph record.

1949 *Down Beat*, 11 Mar., p. 14. The flip side ("South") will be a shade slower but with the same general routine.

fluff, *n. & v.t.* [from entertainment (i.e., radio, theater) slang; some currency since c. 1935; see also GOOF] A note or phrase played incorrectly; as verb, to play a wrong note (in this sense, oral evidence only); also, by extension: see 1959 quot.

1942 *The American Thesaurus of Slang*, p. 560. *fluff:* discord.

1959 *Newport Jazz Festival: 1959*, p. 45. *fluffed:* to be brushed off, ignored, cast aside.

flutter, *n. & v.t.* [special application of standard meaning; current since c. 1920] To triple- or quadruple-tongue (the reed of any reed instrument) in order to produce a flutter sound; also, the effect so produced.

1926 *Melody Maker*, Mar., p. 30. Take one of the more simple figurations of the Chinese effect and play it . . . using less of the flutter tongue.

1927 *Melody Maker*, June, p. 541. I should be greatly obliged if you could explain how the flutter is done on the trumpet.

1942 *The American Thesaurus of Slang*, p. 561. *flutter-tongue:* the effect produced by fluttering the tongue against the mouthpiece.

fly, *adj.* [cf. 1959 *Webster's New World Dictionary*, s.v. *fly:* "orig. thieves' slang"; also cf. *1811 Dictionary of the Vulgar Tongue.* "*fly:* Knowing. Acquainted with another's meaning or proceeding"; still current esp. among black jazzmen from c. 1900–c. 1960, rare since]

1928 *The Walls of Jericho*, p. 156. I got a picture o' myself lettin' any guy alone that gets fly with my girl.

1939 *Metronome*, Apr., p. 51. Bauduc . . . really comes on with some very fly and superb drumming.

1952 *A History of Jazz in America*, p. 351. *fly:* smooth; to describe looks or manner or performance, usually the first two ("he's a fly cat").

1955 *Hear Me Talkin to Ya*, p. 226. Elmer Snowden played banjo in our band, and was considered to be very fly.

1958 *The Book of Negro Folklore*, p. 483. *fly:* fresh, impudent, sassy, flirtatious.

1972 *Town Hall program*, 30 Nov., p. 6. "Fly" was once used to describe someone who was very sharp, very hip.

forget it [cf. general slang meaning (i.e., never mind); some currency since c. 1950] See last quot.; also, expression of contempt or dismissal (see first quot.) or of unparallelled admiration (in this sense, oral evidence only).

1961 *Down Beat*, 25 May, p. 24. If five stars for all three volumes implies to you that this is a flawless set of records, forget it.

1969 *Hip Manual. forget it:* expression of contempt.

fours (trade), *n. pl.* [shortened form of *four bar passages;* some currency since c. 1935, but wide currency only since c. 1950; see also CHASE]

1955 *The Encyclopedia of Jazz*, p. 346. *fours:* a "chase" [q.v.] in which the soloists play four bars apiece.

1960 *The Jazz Review*, Nov., p. 22. And the chase fours between Bird and Fats are thrilling indeed.

1960 *Esquire*, July, p. 112. At this time the drummer was "trading fours" with the pianist or exchanging four-bar phrases.

1961 *Down Beat*, 16 Feb., p. 36. The "fours" between guitar and piano on . . . "I Remember You" build beautifully as they unfold.

fox, *n.* [by analogy with both the beauty and the cunning; some currency esp. among black jazzmen since c. 1958 (it is, oddly, considerably predated by *foxy*)]

1962 *N.Y. Times Magazine*, 20 May, p. 45. *fox:* a beautiful girl.

1970 *Shaft*, p. 97. His life was on the line and he was thinking about some fox.

1971 *The Female Eunuch*, p. 262. The splendidly ambiguous expression "fox" emanates from the Chicago ghetto.

fox trot [from common practice of designating jazz dances by reference to animal movement (see also BUNNY HUG, CAMEL WALK, TURKEY TROT); current since c. 1917] Generic term for popular jazz dance (and its tempo) since c. 1917.

1926 *So This Is Jazz*, p. 25. A tune played doubly slow for a "toddle" is no less jazz than when performed at its original fox-trot tempo.

1929 *Jacobs' Orchestral Monthly*, June, p. 6. Jazz grew up around the fox trot and is still mainly supported by it.

1968 *Jazz Dance*, p. 109. Another Negro composer and arranger, W. Benton Overstreet, assembled a number entitled "The Jazz Dance" (subtitled "Song and Foxtrot") which named the Texas Tommy, The Eagle Rock, the Buzz, and the Shimmy. All of these steps had been used before, and Overstreet was apparently improving his chances by calling it a fox-trot.

foxy, *adj.* [cf. 1942 *American Thesaurus of Slang*, p. 251: "*foxy:* stylish; 'chic'"; current esp. among black jazzmen since c. 1925] Beautiful (applied only to a woman).

1959 *Esquire*, Nov., p. 70I. *foxy:* beautiful. Example: Man, but she's foxy.

1961 *The Sound*, p. 218. I mean all the studs in fancy duds and foxy chicks togged to the bricks is gonna be there.

1963 *Down Beat,* 24 Oct., p. 25. Hire six foxy young chicks to massage my aching head.

framming, *participle* [etym. obscure: poss. onomatopoeic (i.e., with the sound of guitar chords); according to jazzmen, term had some currency c. 1900–c. 1925, obs. since except historical]

1959 *Jazz* (Hentoff & McCarthy) p. 107. The first guitar player was "picking" and the second was "framming," that is, playing chords while the lead carried the melody.

frantic, *adj.* [extension of standard meaning; current from c. 1940–c. 1960, rare since] Exciting, thrilling.

1946 *Jazzways,* p. 51. The meaning of "jump tune" should be clear enough from the term itself; literally, it jumps, it's exciting or frantic, as the fan would describe it.

1958 *The Dharma Bums,* p. 194. You never saw a more frantic dancer.

1959 *Esquire,* Nov., p. 70I. *frantic:* something of wild beauty. Anything of a frenzied nature.

1960 *Dictionary of American Slang,* s.v. *frantic:* exciting; satisfying; wonderful.

freak, *adj.* [special application of standard meaning; current since c. 1925] Technically unusual or unorthodox.

1955 *Hear Me Talkin to Ya,* p. 42. We were both freak trumpet men.

1959 *Jazz* (Hentoff & McCarthy), p. 241. Jonas Walker . . . was probably the first . . . to apply the New Orleans "freak" sounds to the trombone.

n. [from *freakish,* q.v., one of several standard terms from which the pejorative connotation has been removed because of an antipathy for the mundane, the ordinary, the conventional; current since c. 1945] One who is inordinately (not perversely) passionate (about someone or something). (Usually preceded by an adjective; where there is none, the term is short for *musician freak:* see second 1959 quot.).

1946 *Duke Ellington,* p. 270. "I'm a train freak," Duke says.

1956 *Lady Sings the Blues,* p. 65. She's a hat freak, that girl.

1959 *The Holy Barbarians,* p. 39. He looked more like one of those beachcomber Nature Boy health freaks than a real hipster.

1959 *The Horn,* p. 112. White babies, jazz babies, freaks (as musicians called them) who attached themselves to hornmen, like camp followers, to be hurt.

1960 *The Jazz Word*, p. 150. Called camp followers,/they're verbally abused/but not before they're physically used/One girl follows ball-players/her sister, sailors seeks/but these chicks/are something else—they're musician freaks.

freak lip [current since c. 1925; see also IRON CHOPS S.V. CHOPS]

1936 *Metronome*, Feb., p. 21. *freak lip:* a brass man who can play three octaves for three hours at least.

1942 *The American Thesaurus of Slang*, p. 546. *freak lip:* the ability to play high notes accurately; also strong, untiring lips.

freak out [from the noun above; some currency since c. 1955] To lose control; to become over-excited.

1970 *Down Beat*, 20 Aug., p. 28. The others enthusiastically freak out.

freakish, *adj.* [current since c. 1940] Initially, and sometimes today, perverted (esp. sexually); now, usually, out-of-the-ordinary, adventure-some, stimulating.

1956 *Lady Sings the Blues*, p. 36. But any kind of freakish feelings are better than no feelings at all.

1958 *Somewhere There's Music*, p. 190. Everything was good, fine, swell, freakish.

freebee, freebie, freeby, *adj. & n.* [from common practice of forming a slang term by adding a rhyming syllable to a word; current among jazzmen since c. 1900]

1928 *The Walls of Jericho*, p. 300. *freeby:* something for nothing, as complimentary tickets to a theatre.

1938 *Cab Calloway: Hi De Ho*, p. 16. The meal was a freeby.

1946 *Really the Blues*, p. 252. It's the brakeman who throws freebie passengers off.

1959 *Esquire*, Nov., p. 70I. *freebee:* something for nothing, a person who always looks for free things.

from in front, see S.V. FRONT.

from the top (down), see S.V. TOP.

front, *n.* [cf. 1930 *American Tramp and Underworld Slang*, s.v. *front:* "a good appearance; anything designed to make a good impression"; current since c. 1940; see also DRAPE(S), THREADS, TOG]

1944 *The New Cab Calloway's Hepsters Dictionary*, s.v. *front:* suit of clothing.

1958 *American Speech*, Oct., p. 224. The cat . . . dons his front.

v.t. [See note in *n.* above; current since c. 1930] To act as nominal head (of a band), as bandleader.

1937 *American Speech*, Feb., p. 46. *to front:* to serve as leader.

1946 *Jazzways*, p. 48. Hampton was with the Les Hite Orchestra, occasionally "fronted" by Louis Armstrong.

1955 *Hear Me Talkin to Ya*, p. 260. Fats tried fronting a big band on a southern tour.

from in front, in front, from front, out front, up front [prob. by analogy with sheet music, the front being the beginning; current since c. 1948] See 1959 quot.

1956 *Lady Sings the Blues*, p. 187. Every musician is a friend of mine from front, we don't need any introductions.

1959 *The Holy Barbarians*, p. 316. *from in front:* first, from the beginning.

1960 *Hiparama of the Classics*, p. 11. My frame is bent, Naz. It's been bent from in front!!! —p. 15. Hip to the cool sweet groove of Liberty and solid sent upon the Ace Lick that alls Cats and Kitties, Red, White, or Blue! are created Level, in FRONT.

1960 *Lenny Bruce: I Am Not a Nut, Elect Me* (skit dialogue on LP album Fantasy 7007). I need a little bread [i.e., money] out front.

front line [poss. by analogy with parade positions in early New Orleans street marches (see SECOND LINE), or poss. simply from approximate positions on the bandstand (see first 1959 quot.); current since c. 1950] The featured group of instrumentalists (usually the winds) with a small jazz band (i.e., up to eight pieces); for its adjective use, see second 1959 quot.

1959 *A Compendium for the Teaching of Jazz History*, p. 36. Trumpets (or cornets), trombones, clarinets, saxophones and occasionally other instruments make up the front line, a name which doubtless grew out of the fact that they sat in a line, in front of the rhythm section.

1959 *The Collector's Jazz: Modern*, p. 49. Brown makes some adept front-line uses of his bass on *Bass Hit*, Verve 8022.

1961 *Down Beat*, 30 Mar., p. 17. I've started a group with *four* vibes players in the front line.

1961 *The Sound*, pp. 11–12. The Sultans were six. Three rhythms and three horns. In the front line were a trumpet . . . an alto saxophone and a tenor saxophone.

fruit, *v.i.* [from black slang; poss. related to general slang term for homosexual; some currency esp. among black jazzmen c. 1935–c. 1945, very rare since]

1938 *Cab Calloway: Hi De Ho,* p. 16. *fruiting:* fickle, fooling around with no particular object.

1946 *Really the Blues,* p. 369. *fruit:* romance playfully.

fucked up [prob. from armed services slang meaning (i.e., badly performed or in trouble); cf. 1960 *Dictionary of American Slang,* s.v. *fucked up:* "in trouble; obsessed with a personal problem; confused; neurotic"; current among jazzmen in several senses since c. 1945; see also WASTED] In addition to the meanings in the note above: extremely drunk or high from effects of liquor, marijuana, or drugs; addicted to drugs; crippled; emotionally distraught.

1970 *Dictionary of Afro-American Slang,* p. 56. *fucked up:* (1940s–1970s) confused or experiencing great misfortune, or both.

funk, *n.* [see note s.v. FUNKY; also cf. 1960 *Webster's New International Dictionary,* s.v. *funk:* "cf. OF *funkier* to emit smoke. . . . Offensive smell or smoke. *Now rare*"; widely current in the jazz sense since c. 1957; see also SOUL] Earthiness.

[1925] *Bessie,* p. 85. "The funk is flyin'," said Bessie approvingly as she opened the front door and smelled the heavy odor of food, liquor, smoke, and perspiration.

1959 *Jazz Poems,* p. 14. Miles Davis blowing his sophisticated funk.

1960 *The Jazz Word,* p. 213. All the current terms of approbation among jazzmen—"soul," "funk," "down home"—all mean basically that if a man can play the blues from inside himself without straining to play a part, he's a legitimate jazzman.

1960 *Down Beat,* 24 Nov., p. 18. "Funk," then, may best be described as a broad use of blue tonality.

funky, *adj. & n.* [cf. 1956 *American Speech,* Dec., p. 309. "Tobacco is said to be funked if it has become spoiled or moldy after it has been taken down, piled closely on the floor in bulk, and stripped. . . . *The American Dialect Dictionary* notes that it is used only as a participle and as an adjective with the meaning of 'rotten,' 'molded.' Its earliest recorded use is from Kentucky in 1892"; also cf. 1959 *The Holy Barbarians*, p. 316: "*funky:* Old French *funicle,* terrible"; see 1959 quot. for further etym.; also cf. what was prob. first jazz use in the old sense: Buddy Bolden's c. 1900 jazz tune *Funky Butt;* widely current since c. 1955; see also HARD BOP] As adj., see first 1960 quot.; as n., a jazz movement: see 1959 quot.

1956 *Down Beat*, 31 Oct., p. 17. What is funky? Oh, a sort of low-down blues feeling.

1959 *Evergreen Review*, Nov.-Dec., p. 138. The "gospel music" of Negro churches and a kind of blues playing that had matured as long ago as the late twenties rediscovering an *emotional* basis on which jazz could continue in the same kinds of sources from which it had originally sprung. . . . And the style acquired a name, "funky"—a term borrowed from Negro argot for a certain kind of body odor.

1960 *The Village Voice*, 3 Feb., p. 13. This term *funky* is taken, half a century later, to describe a return to earthy and blue tonalities.

fuzz, n. [from underworld slang: cf. 1930 *American Tramp and Underworld Slang*, s.v. "*fuzz:* a detective; a prison guard or turnkey. Here it is likely that 'fuzz' was originally 'fuss,' one hard to please or over-particular"; also see last quot.; some currency esp. among black jazzmen since c. 1935, but wide currency only since c. 1950; see also LAW] The police or a policeman.

1952 *Flee the Angry Strangers*, p. 137. No Law in there, baby, I can smell Fuzz from fifty yards.

1956 *Lady Sings the Blues*, p. 33. The place was full of what they called "wayward women" in those days, and of course the vice squad fuzz.

1965 *Down Beat*, 11 Mar., p. 16. We had never heard such terms as "busted" for arrested, "fuzz" for police, and all the other jargon that came into common use in bop circles after a vast clique of junkies had fanned out from Bird [q.v.].

1969 *Hip Manual. fuzz:* Originally a pickpockets' term, stemming from the fact that police had nothing in their pockets but fuzz.

G

gage, gauge, *n.* [cf. *1811 Dictionary of the Vulgar Tongue.* "*gage:* a pipe of tobacco"; current since c. 1930; see also MARY JANE, SHIT, TEA] See last quot. (Note: the definition in the first quot. is mistaken.)

1945 *Hepcats Jive Talk Dictionary*, s.v. *gage:* intoxicating liquor.

1955 *Solo*, p. 40. You can carry about five sticks of gauge in the beard.

1959 *The Naked Lunch*, p. 81. They smoke gage in cigarettes made of wrapping paper.

1959 *Esquire*, Nov., p. 70H. *gage:* marijuana.

galloping piano (or rhythm) [from resemblance of the sound; some currency c. 1917–c. 1930, obs. since except historical].

1937 *American Speech*, Feb., p. 46. *gallop:* a type of rhythm used in drumming, resembling the sound of a horse's gallop.

1958 *The Jazz Review*, Nov., p. 14. The regular pianist, Turk Thomas, had been with the Satisfied Five in Texas, and played what we called "galloping piano"—no equilibrium.

gang, *n.* [see 1959 quot. for semantic explanation and approx. beginning date; term largely obs. since c. 1950; see also LOT, MESS] A great quantity (see 1959 quot.) or something of great quality—that is, excellent.

1933 *Fortune*, Aug., p. 47. "Yeah," said the other, "he plays a gang o' horn."

1936 *Swing That Music*, p. 1. It made a whole gang of sound, for sure.

1959 *Jazz: A Quarterly of American Music*, Fall, p. 285. In requesting a *gang of gin*, Bessie voices a use of gang in the sense of "much, several, a number" which had been developing a special sense in the gangster era of the twenties. Perhaps, as in the thirties, *gang* may have had the connotation of a medley, a number of songs or musical compositions strung together.

gang busters, come on like, see s.v. COME ON.

gappings, *n. pl.* [etym. obscure; according to jazzmen, term had some currency c. 1910–c. 1925, obs. since except historical] Salary.

1955 *Hear Me Talkin to Ya,* p. 8. Their tips were so great until they did not even have to touch their nightly gappings.

gas, *v.t.* [see note in *gas, n.;* current from c. 1945–c. 1965, rare since] To excite or please enormously.

1953 *The Hot and the Cool,* p. 76. And man, that was something would gas the folks back home in Lynton Bridge, Mass.!

1960 *Jazz: A Quarterly of American Music,* Winter, p. 47. I was THUNDERSTRUCK. I couldn't say a word. He gasses me.

gas, gasser, *n.* [by analogy with immobilizing effects of being, literally, gassed; *gasser* current since c. 1942; the shortened form, *gas,* was poss. formed directly from *gas, v.t.,* and largely replaced *gasser* c. 1957; rare since c. 1965]

1944 *The New Cab Calloway's Hepsters Dictionary,* p. 7. When it comes to dancing, she's a gasser.

1948 *Down Beat,* 28 July, p. 4. *gasser:* that instrumentalist, vocalist, arrangement, performance or 1949 convertible which is "cool," "real crazy," "half-gone" . . . which visibly impresses the speaker.

1959 *The Holy Barbarians,* p. 40. Any sound behind poetry was a novelty, exciting, a *gas.*

1959 *Swinging Syllables,* s.v. *gas:* anything enjoyable, satisfying.

gate, gatemouth, gate-mouth, *n.* [see 1959 quot. for etym.; also cf. 1942 *American Mercury,* July, p. 94: "*gator-faced:* long, black face with big mouth"; current c. 1935–c. 1945, obs. since except historical; see also ALLIGATOR]

1938 *Cab Calloway: Hi De Ho,* p. 16. *gate:* a male person (a salutation), abbr. for "gate-mouth."

1945 *Band Leaders,* Mar., p. 20. Within a horn blast of Hollywood and Vine, the crossroads of Glamour-town, can be found many lairs of the hepcats—haunts of gates and ride men [q.v.].

1947 *The Harder They Fall*, p. 189. Where you been, gate?

1959 *Jazz: A Quarterly of American Music*, Fall, p. 284. Louis Armstrong writes that he originated the term *gate* which through the swing era was applied to musicians (*Swing That Music*, p. 77). Early in New Orleans Louis was given the nickname "Gatemouth," an allusion to his formidable lips, teeth and general kisser. . . . As gates swing, two words in the field patterned an associated, which helped the currency of *gate*.

gauge, *n.* See s.v. GAGE.

gee, ghee, *n.* [from underworld slang: cf. 1934 *A Dictionary of American Slang*, s.v. *gee:* "from first letter of 'guy,' reenforced by an imitated French pronunciation"; some currency among jazzmen c. 1935–c. 1945, obs. since].

1939 *Jitterbug Jamboree Song Book*, p. 32. *ghee:* a fellow, man, guy.

1960 *Dictionary of American Slang*, s.v. *gee:* a fellow; a guy.

geets, geetz, *n. pl.* [see last 1960 quot. for poss. etym.; cf. 1953 *American Speech*, May, "Carnie Talk" p. 116: "*geetus:* money"; some currency since c. 1945; see the more common BREAD]

1957 *N.Y. Times Magazine*, 18 Aug., p. 26. *geets:* money.

1960 *The Jazz Word*, p. 81. I'm spendin' my hard-earned geets.

1960 *Dictionary of American Slang*, p. 211. *geets:* dollars. That which "gets" or buys things.

1971 *Beneath the Underdog*, p. 189. You can bet it ain't jazz no more when the underworld moves in and runs it strictly for geets.

get around (on [one's] horn) [special application of general slang "get around" (i.e., to be experienced, to fare well); current since c. 1935; see also ALL OVER, DOWN WITH (ONE'S) AX]

1937 *American Speech*, Feb., p. 46. *get around on a horn:* to be able to play fast and difficult passages well.

1950 *Metronome*, Aug., p. 16. He sure gets around on the horn, doesn't he? . . . He does so many little tricky things that are really not easy, and he does them with finesse.

1964 *Down Beat*, 27 Feb., p. 22. Monk can get around to any place on the piano he thinks he needs to be.

get down (with) [prob. by analogy with "getting to the bottom of things"; current since c. 1955] To become deeply familiar with; also, by extension, see 1971 quot.

1961 *Lenny Bruce in Concert* (LP record). But you didn't *really* know them—get down with them.

1971 *N.Y. Times Magazine*, 6 June, p. 93. *get down:* start taking care of business or acting efficiently. A popular musician's phrase.

1973 *Down Beat*, 1 Feb., p. 28. It's not easy to get down with a group in which every instrument except the drums has some sort of electronic augmentation.

get hot! [for etym. see HOT; current c. 1925–c. 1940, obs. since except historical or, very rare, derisive] An exhortation to a musician or musicians to play excitingly (though note in 1956 quot. the pejorative connotation that the phrase has taken on in its rare post-World War II use).

1946 *Really the Blues*, p. 141. The unhip public took over the expression "hot" and made it corny by getting up in front of a band and snapping their fingers in a childish way, yelling "Get hot! Yeah man, get hot!"

1956 *Jazz: Its Evolution and Essence*, p. 232. "Getting hot" is relatively easy; a student band can do it as well as anybody. Exasperated, distorted sonorities played fortissimo are generally sufficient.

get in there [for etym. see IN THERE; some currency c. 1935–c. 1945, obs. since] An exhortation to a musician or musicians to play excitingly.

1938 *Cab Calloway: Hi De Ho*, p. 16. *get in there:* (an exclamation) go to work, get busy, make it hot, give it all you've got.

get into [from the sense of penetrating the surface; current since c. 1960] See 1971 quot.

1964 *Down Beat*, 18 June, p. 15. I think this is one of the things that John and Elvin got into without a bass player.

1971 *N.Y. Times Magazine*, 6 June, p. 93. *get into:* become interested in and/or knowledgable about.

get it [current since c. 1925] Exhortation or simple instruction to a musician to play a solo chorus; also, to satisfy musically; also, by extension: to be eminently satisfactory.

1942 *Well, Get It!* (tune recorded by the Tommy Dorsey Orchestra).

106

1952 *The Record Changer*, Aug.-Sep., p. 22. Buster says, "Now let's get it."

1958 *Somewhere There's Music*, p. 69. Fine, but that doesn't get it.

1961 *The Sound*, p. 159. Even that one night a week gets it for me.

1973 *Down Beat*, 15 Mar., p. 15. Now there are some guys who, once you say, "Okay, you got it," just start to play with no relationship to the song form or the construction of the tune.

get off [cf. general slang *get off the ground;* current c. 1920–c. 1945, obs. since except historical] To improvise skillfully; also, for its rare noun form, see 1935 quot.

[1923] 1966 *Down Beat*, 5 May, p. 23. You can bet a man that they can get off on them horns.

1932 *Melody Maker*, July, p. 593. There is an abundance of trumpet-playing of the first order from the local "get-off" man.

1933 *Fortune*, Aug., p. 47. Returning to Trombonist Brown, he can *get-off* (. . . syncopate to beat the band).

1935 *Vanity Fair*, Nov., p. 71. Breaks are sometimes known as *get-offs* or *take-offs*.

1936 *Metronome*, Feb., p. 21. *getting off:* really swinging.

1972 *Down Beat*, 20 July, p. 38. These two had the ability, all important in a big band, to "get off" at a moment's notice.

get on, see s.v. ON.

get (one's) business straight, see s.v. BUSINESS.

get oneself together, see s.v. TOGETHER.

get to [general slang, but esp. current among jazzmen since c. 1960] Impress (favorably).

1965 *Down Beat*, 28 Jan., p. 30. This didn't get to me.

1967 *Down Beat*, 4 May, p. 34. It got to me—I'd give it about 2½ stars.

1970 *Down Beat*, 10 Dec., p. 30. The tenor player didn't get to me as much as the other players.

ghee, *n.* See s.v. GEE.

ghost note [by analogy with its faintness; some currency since c. 1920] On a wind instrument, a note deemphasized in a series—that is, fingered, but barely blown; also, as a verb, to blow such a note (oral evidence only in this form).

1927 *Melody Maker*, July, p. 695. Ghost note . . . is *barely audible.*

gig, *n.* [poss. from *gigue,* a lively dance form of Italian origin commonly used as the last movement of a suite (cf. English counterpart *jig*): from Old French *giguer;* also, see 1964 quot.; according to jazzman Eubie Blake, bandleader James Reese Europe used the term in its jazz sense as early as c. 1905; widely current since c. 1920] Initially, see 1955 quot.; since c. 1955, see last 1959 quot. (though, it should be noted, for the non-jazz job, the term is applied only to a non-jazzman; for the jazzman, the non-jazz job is a *hame* or a *day gig,* q.v.).

1926 *Melody Maker,* Sep., p. 7. One popular "gig" band makes use of a nicely printed booklet.

1955 *The Encyclopedia of Jazz,* p. 346. *gig:* job (esp. one-night stand).

1959 *The Holy Barbarians,* p. 89. He returned to the bass fiddle and started making night club gigs again.

1959 *Newport Jazz Festival: 1959,* p. 45. *gig:* a job of any kind, musical or non-.

1964 *Deep Down in the Jungle,* p. 266. *gig:* may have sexual origin, as *gig* or *gigi* means vagina or rectum.

v.i. (sometimes with *around*) [widely current since c. 1940] See 1947 quot.; also, since c. 1955: to work at any job (see also HAME).

1947 *N.Y. Herald Tribune,* 10 Mar. At present he is "gigging around," a musician's term for those who take casual dates whenever they can find them.

1952 *Music Out of Dixie,* p. 158. I only played with him a few times, jes' giggin' aroun'.

1955 *The Encyclopedia of Jazz,* p. 346. *gig:* to work one-night jobs.

day gig [jazz is generally performed at night: hence, the logic of the distinguishing term; current since c. 1945; see also HAME, SLAVE] A non-jazz job reluctantly taken by a jazzman for purely monetary reasons.

1962 *The Village Voice,* 14 June, p. 13. Shepp, Dixon, and even a leader of the advance guard like Cecil Taylor must rely on the day gig in order to survive.

gitbox, git, gitter, gitterbox, *n.* [dialectal; some currency c. 1920–c. 1945, rare since; see also BOX, 2] See 1937 quot.

1933 *Metronome*, Aug., p. 16. Eddie was playing the kind of banjo I wanted, but I got him to learn that "gitter box."

1936 *Metronome*, Feb., p. 61. *gitter:* guitar.

1937 *American Speech*, Oct., p. 181. *gitbox:* guitar.

1948 *Down Beat*, 19 May, p. 14. The final chorus is git and block chords and knocked-out at that.

give (one) some skin, see s.v. SKIN.

give (out) [current c. 1930–c. 1945, obs. since except historical] To play excitingly: frequently hortatory.

1936 *Esquire*, June, p. 92. And the singer with the outfit can do with his or her voice just what the soloist can do with his instrument, he can *give.*

1937 *This Thing Called Swing*, p. 8. *give:* a command or plea meaning "give it all you've got, put the heat on it, go to town."

1952 *A History of Jazz in America*, p. 351. *give* or *give out:* swing [i.e., c. 1935–c. 1945] parlance for "let yourself go."

1955 *Hear Me Talkin to Ya*, p. 151. We would give out with such tunes as "Tiger Rag."

gliss, *n. & v.* [shortened form of technical musical term *glissando:* current since c. 1920] See 1936 quot.: in jazz, applied chiefly to trumpet and esp. trombone.

1926 *Melody Maker*, Mar., p. 31. The aforementioned mute modifier . . . is used to get the necessary "gliss" which I have marked by means of slurs.

1936 *Metronome*, Feb., p. 21. *gliss:* glissando.

1946 *Jazzways*, p. 31. The engineer handed them the instruction sheet and listened to Dutrey warm up with a few glisses on the long slide trombone.

1967 *Down Beat*, 7 Sep., p. 30. Davis proves once again that he is *the* bassist: fretting, glissing the strings, etc.

go, *v.i.* [by analogy with action or movement; some currency since c. 1920 but wide currency only since c. 1947; see 1958 quot. for the term's status among musicians and fans; see also MOVE, WORK] See 1937, 1958 quots.

1926 *Melody Maker*, Jan., p. 19. Atta-boy, let's go!

1935 *Vanity Fair*, Nov., p. 71. Hot artists or bands that can put across their licks successfully . . . can "go."

1937 *American Speech*, Feb., p. 46. *go:* to improvise rhythmically and expertly on a given melody.

1953 *Night Light*, p. 131. One of them was saying urgently, "Go, go."

1958 *Publication of the American Dialect Society*, Nov., p. 45. *go:* really a fan's word, to express excitement at a particularly "swingin'" solo. Often used derisively, sometimes approvingly, by musicians. (The fan's phrase is "Go, man, go!").

1959 *The Horn*, p. 144. You can't take it away from him, that man goes.

1961 *Jazz Journal*, Feb., p. 8. Lester goes first, and how he goes.

go down [etym. unknown; cf. 1937 *A Dictionary of Slang and Unconventional English*, s.v. *go down:* "to be accepted (by); be approved or allowed" (first citation given is from Smollett); current since c. 1940; see also SHAKING] To happen.

1947 *Time*, 10 Feb., p. 12. But until the groovy cats dig each other or a Webster happens by to help us pick up on what's going down, *Time* will igg [i.e., ignore] the issue.

1956 *Lady Sings the Blues*, p. 190. In view of what went down later, who can say?

1958 *Jazz in Hi-Fi*, p. 13. To say . . . "I dig what's going down" . . . means you are aware of the situation.

go to town [by analogy with the excitement (i.e., of rural folk going to town); current c. 1933–c. 1943, obs. since] To play music or do anything excitingly.

1935 *Stage*, Sep., p. 45. *go to town:* play hot.

1935 *His Hi De Highness of Ho De Ho*, p. 35. "Goin' to town," meaning to get fast and hot.

1936 *Swing That Music*, p. 30. That phrase, "goin' to town," means cuttin' loose and takin' the music with you.

1938 *Pic*, 5 Apr., p. 31. Goin' to town with a vengeance! This looks like mass murder but is only the Savoy version of hot dancing.

go home, go out [according to jazzmen, current c. 1925–c. 1945, obs. since except historical; see also ALL-IN, RIDE-OUT] In traditional jazz, a signal to play the final chorus.

1952 *Jazz: A Quarterly of American Music*, Summer, p. 191. It seems such a perfect "goin' home" riff.

1964 *Down Beat*, 30 July, p. 35. The last solo was just a typical Basie going-out thing.

gold, *n.* [from underworld and general slang, but with esp. currency among jazzmen c. 1900–c. 1945, when it and *loot* were largely replaced by *bread*] Money.

1952 *Who Walk in Darkness,* p. 12. Can you lend me some gold?

golden-leaf, *n.* [some currency c. 1920–c. 1945, very rare since; see also PANATELLA] See 1946 quot.

1925 *Golden Leaf Strut* (tune recorded by the Original New Orleans Rhythm Kings).

1946 *Really the Blues,* p. 370. *golden-leaf:* the best marijuana.

gone, *adj. & interj.* [one of several terms favorably connoting transcendence: see also OUT OF THIS WORLD, SENT, SOMETHING ELSE; current c. 1945–c. 1955, rare since]

1946 *Really the Blues,* p. 370. *gone:* out of this world, superlative.

1948 *New Yorker,* 3 July, p. 28. Their expressions of approval include "Cool!," "Gone!" and "Bells, man!"

1955 *Down Beat,* 30 Nov., p. 47. The drummer was gone!

and gone [peculiar conjunctional intensifier; current since c. 1945] Intensifying phrase for whatever precedes it.

1971 *Beneath the Underdog,* p. 159. You know them Jew boys got the soul and gone.

real gone [current c. 1945–c. 1955, rare since]

1949 *Music Library Association Notes,* Dec., p. 44. *real gone:* intensified form of *gone.*

1953 *Night Light,* p. 130. You're so real gone, Pops.

the gonest [see first quot.; current c. 1945–c. 1955, rare since]

1954 *Esquire,* Nov., p. 131. Jazz musicians and enthusiasts thrive on hyperbole, of course; if anything is good, it's far and away ahead of everything else, it's "the gonest."

1957 *On the Road,* p. 60. I have found the gonest little girl in the world.

good looking out [prob. from the idiom "looking out for" (i.e., taking care of); some currency since c. 1950] (Expression of) thanks: "You did me a favor."

c. 1965 *Good Lookin' Out* (tune recorded by Stan Turrentine).

goof, *n. & v.i.* [cf. 1959 *Webster's New World Dictionary* s.v. *goof:* "prob. < or akin to ME. *gofisshe, goofish,* foolish"; prob. reinforced by armed services use of *goof off* (shun duty); also see first 1956 quot., for poss. explanation of semantic development; current among jazzmen since c. 1943; see also CLINKER, FLUFF] See both 1952 quots.; also, to carouse (no pejorative connotation): see 1957 and first 1959 quots.

1948 *Just Goofin'* (tune composed by Hubie Wheeler).

1952 *Life*, 29 Sep., p. 67. *goof:* to blow a wrong note or to make a mistake.

1952 *A History of Jazz in America*, p. 351. *goof:* to wander in attention, to fail to discharge one's responsibility (as for example, not to show up for an appointment and not to be provided with a clear excuse); in musical performance, to play without much attention, to miss coming in on time, etc.

1956 *Tennessee Folklore Society Bulletin*, Mar., p. 26. The verb *to goof* (to do something stupid) obviously stems from *goof balls* [i.e. barbiturates], since one might do anything under their influence.

1956 *Sideman*, p. 20. If the band didn't all take the same route, there'd be mistakes—some goofs.

1957 *On the Road*, p. 177. Dean and I goofed around San Francisco.

1959 *The Horn*, p. 85. I get me some real rest, just goof a while. — p. 87. She had heard him goof, play sour, pretend.

goola, *n.* [etym. unknown; according to jazzmen, term had some currency c. 1917–c. 1940, obs. since except historical; see also BOX 1., EIGHTY-EIGHT]

1944 *Dan Burley's Original Handbook of Harlem Jive*, p. 139. *goola:* piano.

grass, *n.* [metonymy: marijuana derives from a weed; some currency since c. 1930; see also BOO, GAGE, POT, TEA]

1943 *Time*, 19 July, p. 54. Marijuana may be called . . . grass.

1972 *Village Voice*, 31 Aug., p. 50. "Grass" is referred to by Cab Calloway in his "Reefer Man" number in the 1933 *International House*.

gray, *n. & adj.* [from black slang; some currency esp. among black jazzmen since c. 1930; see also PINK, FAY]

1960 *Dictionary of American Slang*, s.v. *gray:* a white person.

1961 *The Sound*, p. 43. One of those pale, taut, overeager grays that seemed drawn in increasing numbers to the new jazz, like moths to the flame. —p. 101. I dunno, old man, to the average colored person the average gray acts like he's in a sweat most of the time.

1968 *Black Music*, p. 132. Some slick-haired gray poet gave me his booklet.

grease, *n. & v.i.* [cf. 1928 *American Speech,* Feb., "Carnival Slang," p. 253: "*grease joint:* hamburger stand"; also poss. shortened from *grease one's chops,* q.v.; some currency as *v.i.* since c. 1940, as *n.* since c. 1955; see also SCOFF] See 1959 quot.

1944 *The New Cab Calloway's Hepsters Dictionary,* s.v. *grease:* to eat.

1959 *Jazz for Moderns,* p. 20. *grease:* food, or "to eat."

1961 *Night Song,* p. 86. Look, man, can we take off our things and get some grease?

1969 *The Life and Loves of Mr. Jiveass Nigger,* p. 32. No, man, I wanna grease.

2. [analogous to rock musician's *grease* (i.e., the engineer's board), source of the power; some currency since c. 1965] Of music or a musician: earthiness, directness, power.

1974 *Harper's,* June, p. 47. Those of us who were affected the strongest felt we'd be willing to do anything to warm ourselves by that fire, get some of that grease pumping through our veins.

1974 *Raise Up Off Me,* p. 6. In the forties Bud Powell had grease in his veins and burned the motherfucker up.

grease (one's) chops [see note in *grease* 1.; some currency c. 1935–c. 1945, very rare since]

1946 *Really the Blues,* p. 370. *grease your chops:* eat.

1950 *Gutbucket and Gossamer,* p. 19. Then the suggestion that we grease our chops was advanced.

greatest, the [see 1954 quot.; widely current c. 1940–c. 1955, rare since; see also THE END, THE MOST] See 1954 quot.

1946 *Jazzways,* p. 56. "Duke's the greatest" is certainly the easiest cliché tossed around swing circles.

1954 *Esquire,* Nov., p. 131. Jazz musicians and enthusiasts thrive on hyperbole, of course; if anything is good . . . it is "the greatest."

1956 *Sideman,* p. 25. Lips is the greatest. Farther out than J. J.

green, long green [cf. 1960 *Dictionary of American Slang,* s.v. *green:* "orig. sporting and underworld use. From 'long green' "; according to jazzman Eubie Blake, term has had some currency esp. among black jazzmen since c. 1900, though it has had wide currency only since c. 1950; see also BREAD, GEETS, GOLD, LOOT]

1955 *Say*, 28 Apr., p. 53. *long green:* over $1,000.

1957 *N.Y. Times Magazine*, 18 Aug., p. 26. *green:* money.

1958 *This Week Magazine*, 28 Sep., p. 33. Money is "green," and "long green" is much money.

grey, *n.* see S.V. GRAY.

grind [from the hip-grinding movements of the dance; current c. 1900–c. 1920, obs. since except historical] A jazz dance or movement of Congolese origin popular c. 1900–c. 1920.

1963 *Blues People*, p. 116. Hundreds of dancers would crowd into the "blue light" parties to "grind" or "slow-drag."

1968 *Jazz Dance*, p. 117. In those days critics were hard-pressed in commenting upon American vernacular dances—especially the hip movements of the grind.

grit, *n.* [from *grits*; synecdoche: i.e., one kind of food to denote any food; according to jazz dancer Leon James, the term was introduced into jazz speech by Southern black musicians c. 1940; see also SCOFF]

1962 *N.Y. Times Magazine*, 20 May, p. 45. *grit:* food.

grizzly bear [dance designations frequently refer to animals and their movements; current during the dance's vogue, c. 1910–c. 1920, and its brief revival in 1930s, obs. since except historical] A jazz dance.

1914 *Modern Dancing* [1962 *Jazz: A History of the New York Scene*, p. 37]. Drop the Turkey Trot, the Grizzly Bear, the Bunny Hug, etc.

groove, *n.* [from jazz slang *in the groove, groovy,* q.v.; current since c. 1940] Routine, preference, style, source of pleasure.

1940 *Swing*, Nov., p. 27. "Travelin'" has a sax-unison melody somewhat in the Tuxedo groove.

1958 *Somewhere There's Music*, p. 35. Romance? No, bruz, that's not my groove.

1959 *Esquire*, Nov., p. 70l. *groove:* category. A person's predilection. Example: Chess is his groove.

v.i. & v.t. [widely current since c. 1945]

1945 *Groovin' High* (tune written and recorded by Dizzy Gillespie).

1959 *Esquire*, Nov., p. 70I. To groove someone means to provide them with enjoyment. Example: Her singing grooved me.

1973 *Down Beat*, 13 Sep., p. 16. The average person can't tap his foot to them and groove on them.

in the groove [from the manner of making and/or playing phonograph records (i.e., with the needle in the groove of the record); widely current c. 1936–c. 1945, obs. since except historical] Excellent, esp. applied to music: see first quot.; also, by extension, excellent or sophisticated (in this sense, oral evidence only; see also IN THERE).

1936 *Delineator*, Nov., p. 49. *in the groove:* carried away or inspired playing. Swing that fairly carries away the player. A fine compliment from other members of the band—"He's in the groove tonight."

1947 *Frontiers of Jazz*, p. 141. They simply got a great *burn* from playing *in the groove*. Also *in a groove*.

groovy, *adj.* [from *in the groove*, q.v.; current from 1938–c. 1960, rare since: the term has moved over into youth slang]

1944 *The New Cab Calloway's Hepsters Dictionary*, s.v. *groovy:* fine. "I feel groovy."

1952 *A History of Jazz in America*, p. 351. *groovy:* applied to a good swinging beat (earlier, "in the groove").

1953 *Night Light*, p. 154. That dance you were doing . . . was real groovy.

growl, *v.i. & v.t., n. & adj.* [current c. 1925–c. 1945, very rare since except historical] See 1956 quot.

1934 *Metronome*, Nov., p. 25. A trumpet . . . growls really effectively for a change.

1935 *His Hi De Highness of Ho De Ho*, p. 35. Even white musicians will say "growl it" to a trumpet player when they are asking him to play it "lowdown" or "dirty."

1946 *Jazzology*, Sep., p. 32. Nanton's fame as the foremost exponent of the "growl" trombone is known far and wide.

1956 *Guide to Jazz*, s.v. *growl:* a deep, rough tone produced with the lips on wind instruments in imitation of tones used by some blues singers.

gully-low, *adj.* [see 1939 quot. for semantic development; some currency c. 1910–c. 1940, obs. since except historical]

115

1939 *Jazzmen*, p. 12. From barrel-houses and honky-tonks came many of the descriptive words which were applied to the music played in them; such as . . . "gully-low," meaning, as its name implies, low as a ditch or a "gully," hence "low-down."

1946 *Really the Blues*, p. 102. They wanted to blast every high-minded citizen clear out of his easy chair with their yarddog growls and gully-low howls.

gutbucket, gut-bucket, *adj. & n.* [see 1939 and 1961 quots. for semantic development (the explanation in 1944 quot. is of extremely doubtful validity); current c. 1910–c. 1940, obs. since except historical] See 1939 and last quots.

1929 *New York Age*, 23 Feb., [1962 *Jazz: A History of the New York Scene*, pp. 191–192]. Using a mute, occasionally a small megaphone inserted at the bell of his trumpet, he eschews the tin pail, hat, plunger and other devices of the "gut bucket" player.

1939 *Jazzmen*, p. 12. From barrel-houses and honky-tonks came many of the descriptive words which were applied to the music played in them; such as . . . "gut-bucket," referring originally to the bucket which caught drippings or "gutterings" from the barrels, later to the unrestrained brand of music that was played by small bands in the dives.

1944 *Metronome*, Nov., p. 17. The word gutbucket must have stemmed directly from Irvis's style and his use of a real bucket for a mute.

1961 *Esquire*, May, p. 153. "Gutbucket," meaning a lowdown type of blues (the term originated from the name of the bucket that caught the drippings of the big, reclining barrels from which gin was sold), perforce left its stain on the singer as well as the music.

guts, *n. pl.* [special application of general slang meaning, prob. reinforced by *gutbucket,* q.v.; according to jazzmen, some currency c. 1930–c. 1945, obs. since; see also FUNK, SOUL] Earthiness (of an instrumentalist).

1964 *Down Beat*, 22 Oct., p. 28. This is pop jazz with a bit more guts than this type of music usually contains.

gutter music [from early (c. 1900) parade and funeral march practice (i.e., of marching in the gutter), reinforced by jazzmen's awareness of the disesteem of the general public; according to jazzmen, some currency c. 1900–c. 1917, obs. since except historical] New Orleans jazz.

1936 *Transatlantic Jazz*, pp. 16-17. Actually, the Negro bands in New Orleans were the originators, but unfortunately no company was interested in making records of their so-called "gutter music."

gutty, *adj.* [from *guts:* some currency c. 1930–c. 1945, rare since] Musically earthy.

1939 *Blues* (Decca Records pamphlet), p. 2. Buster Bailey's reaction can be felt in the "gutty" clarinet tone he uses.

1965 *Down Beat,* 25 Mar., p. 26. Carter makes excellent use of a rich and gutty trombone section.

H [abbreviation; from underworld and narcotics slang: cf. 1934 *A Dictionary of American Slang*, p. 18: "*H:* heroin"; some currency among jazzmen since c. 1935; see also HEAVY SOUL, HORSE]

1942 *American Thesaurus of Slang*, p. 474. *H:* heroin.

1961 *Esquire*, May, p. 155. "Fat Girl," as he [i.e., trumpeter Fats Navarro] was known, was dead in his twenties of tuberculosis aggravated by his bouts with the big H.

habit, *n.* [from underworld and narcotics slang: cf. 1930 *American Tramp and Underworld Slang*, s.v. *habit:* "the drug habit"; some currency among jazzmen since c. 1935]

1952 *Flee the Angry Strangers*, p. 302. I don't get close to a guy with a habit everybody can tell.

hacked, *adj.* [prob. by analogy with a standard meaning (i.e., chopped up); current c. 1945–c. 1955, rare since; see also BUGGED, DRAGGED]

1958 *American Speech*, Oct., p. 225. Somewhat less frequently aired are the synonyms for *annoyed: bugged, dragged, spooked, hacked,* and *hung.*

1959 *Esquire*, Nov., p. 70I. *hacked:* tired, irritated.

hall, *n.* [from New Orleans practice of shortening *dance hall* to *hall:* e.g. Mahogany Hall (immortalized by Louis Armstrong's *Mahogany Hall Stomp*); some currency in a jazz sense c. 1900–c. 1940; see also JOINT, ROOM] Any place where musicians play—be it a café, a ballroom, or a concert hall.

1960 *Down Beat*, 24 Nov., p. 6. He never left it (thereby solving the hall, gig, and transportation problems).

hame, hime, *n.* [poss. by analogy with restraining connotation of standard meaning; current since c. 1945; see also DAY GIG, SLAVE]

1955 *The Encyclopedia of Jazz*, p. 346. *hame:* job outside the music business.

1961 *N.Y. Times Magazine*, 25 June, p. 39. *hame:* any unpleasant job, from mowing the lawn to playing a trumpet in a Mickey Mouse [q.v.] band.

1971 *Beneath the Underdog*, p. 191. That's what jazz originally was, getting away from the usual tiddy, the hime, the gig.

hamfat, *n. & adj.* [cf. *1960 Dictionary of American Slang*, s.v. *hamfatter:* "an inferior, obvious entertainer . . . an actor whose subtlety is no greater than that of a Negro minstrel show. Since c. 1880"; according to jazzmen, some currency c. 1900–c. 1930, obs. since except historical] Mediocre (musician).

1938 *N.Y. Amsterdam News*, 12 Mar., p. 17. The Harlem Hamfats grind out the tune on myriad Harlem piccolos (i.e., juke boxes].

1946 *Really the Blues*, p. 58. A lot of beat-up old hamfats . . . sang and played.

1959 *The Country Blues*, p. 86. The singing of these little "hamfat" bands never reached the artistic intensity of men like Blind Lemon.

ham kick [see quot. for etym.; according to jazzmen, some currency c. 1900–c. 1917, obs. since except historical]

1939 *Jazzmen*, p. 35. One night a week, as a special added attraction, the 28 Club put on a "ham kick." A ham was hung up high, and the contest was won by the girl who could kick the highest.

hang, *v.t.* [by analogy with standard meaning's connotation of immobilization; current since c. 1940; see also HUNG (UP)] To inconvenience (someone).

1959 *The Beat Generation Dictionary*, s.v. *hang:* delay.

hangup, *n.* [from the *v.t.* above: current since c. 1950]

1969 *Hip Manual*, *hangup:* a fascinating object or concept. Also, a psychological block or personality quirk.

119

1970 *Death of a Blue-Eyed Soul Brother*, p. 55. The fragrance of the stockyard isn't the only hangup.

happen, *v.i.* [term reflects selective or preferential attitude of the jazzman in his acknowledgement of events: cf. music trade use (1949 *Music Library Association Notes*, Dec., p. 44. "A song *happens* . . . when the preparatory work results in a successful bid for popularity"); current since c. 1945; see also SHAKING] To occur, but only if the consequence is beautiful and/or significant.

1955 *Down Beat*, 13 July, p. 33. I don't think much of anything happens here.

1961 *The Jazz Life*, p. 158. A lot of musicians think the public is stupid, but the audiences know what's happening.

1962 *Down Beat*, 8 Nov., p. 38. It sounded like they were all striving to create and get away from the standard things, but it didn't really happen.

1974 *Down Beat*, 14 Mar., p. 29. Yeah. That was happening, that was happening.

happenings, haps, *n. pl.* [from *happen;* some currency since c. 1948; see also ACTION] Occurrences, but only those of some immediacy or significance.

1953 *Later* (tune recorded by Ella Fitzgerald on Decca DL8149). Later for the happenings, baby.

1958 *Jive in Hi-Fi*, p. 41. Our two friends, standing in a corner, were diggin' [i.e., observing] the happenings.

1961 *N.Y. Times Magazine*, 25 June, p. 39. *haps:* an event, an occurrence.

1966 *The Wig*, p. 30. What's the haps?

hard, *adj.* [one of several jazz slang terms which reverse the standard connotation (i.e., from unfavorable to favorable): see also BAD, MEAN, TERRIBLE, TOUGH; current since c. 1935]

1938 *Cab Calloway: Hi De Ho*, p. 16. *hard:* fine, good. Ex.—"That's a hard tie you're wearing."

1959 *Diggeth Thou?*, p. 40. The spielers were shucking some hard jive from back.

1962 *Down Beat*, 13 Sep., p. 28. A hard cooker in the bop or post-bop groove he is not—he has his own slick style and stays with it.

1965 *Down Beat*, 6 May, p. 35. I give this one three stars, because it's a hard tune.

hard bop [*hard* is used here in the general slang sense of tough, virile, masculine (in opposition to what its advocates and practitioners regard as sissified music—i.e., *cool* or *West Coast jazz*, q.v.); current esp. among jazz writers since c. 1955; see also FUNKY, SOUL, and the earlier BOP] That modern jazz or jazz style innovated c. 1954 on the East Coast, predominantly by black jazzmen, which retains all of the characteristics of bop (q.v.) but rejects the overly relaxed quality into which it had been led esp. by West Coast jazzmen, most of whom are white; aggressive, intense modern jazz with the tension of hot jazz reinstated.

1957 *The Book of Jazz*, p. 102. Symbolizing a partial reaction against the ultra-cool sounds of the late 1940s is the work of another school of tenor men, whose style has been labeled, perhaps a little arbitrarily, "hard bop," but might better be described as "extrovert modern."

1958 *N.Y. Journal-American*, 22 Mar. According to Sid, New York's younger jazz fans like "the hard bop," the fast, driving jazz of men like Art Blakey and Sonny Rollins.

1959 *Evergreen Review*, Nov.-Dec., p. 136. Jazz was not to lose its way in the temporary dead end of an increasingly tepid cool style, but would find a crucial rebirth in a modified version of the bop style of the forties' . . . "hard bop."

1961 *Down Beat*, 16 Feb., p. 16. I'm an extrovert . . . and hard bop is played by bands of extrovert people.

1961 *Metronome*, Apr., p. 13. The lid was put on "cool" by hard bop. There was a search for a *soul* sound that brought back the "group" feeling, perhaps inspired by gospel music and some aspects of rock and roll.

hard bop-funky [some currency esp. among jazz writers since c. 1957] That modern jazz style made up of two important allied styles (see HARD BOP, FUNKY).

1959 *Evergreen Review*, Nov.-Dec., p. 140. Blakey's is only one of several rediscoveries that the by now fashionable swing to the hard bop-funky style has brought about.

hard bopper [some currency esp. among jazz writers since c. 1957] A musician who plays hard bop.

121

1960 *Jazz Monthly,* Nov., p. 29. He seems to be particularly severe on the hard boppers.

1960 *Esquire,* Dec., p. 74. Some of the current "soul fever" being incorporated into the music of musicians who used to be called "hard boppers" is legitimately come by and is yet another way of forcefully reminding white audiences—and themselves—of a basic part of their heritage.

hard swing, hard swinging, hard-driving, hard-blowing [from *hard bop,* combined with *swing, drive,* or *blow,* q.v.; some currency since c. 1955] Noun phrase: hard bop; adj.: aggressive, intense (musical attack); also, v. and adv. (see first 1960 quot.).

1958 *Down Beat,* 29 May, p. 13. If they have the right people there, perhaps they'd do some good. You know, some. of the hard swinging cats from both bands.

1959 *Esquire,* Jan., p. 115. In the second half of the Fifties, the hard-blowing school seems to have a much bigger influence on the younger players than the soft-blowing school.

1960 *The Jazz Review,* Nov., p. 10. My lip went bad after a year in the Earl Hines band. They swung so hard and played so much.

1960 *Down Beat,* 24 Nov., p. 26. Bacalao maintains the same ingredients—"hard" swing, extensive solo work, by tenor and organ, and the ever-present congas and bongos.

1961 *Metronome,* Feb., p. 30. This review is directed at the more hard-driving jazz tastes like my own.

Harlem, *n. & adj.* [named for the black section of New York City where the style originated; some currency c. 1930–c. 1945, obs. since except historical; see also the more common JUMP] A popular but obvious swing music style, incorporating a very pronounced rhythm and very earthy tonal qualities.

1934 *Metronome,* Oct., p. 49. The band, its style and the vocalist is strictly Harlem.

1959 *The Jazz Scene,* p. 112. Often vulgar and showy, this "Harlem music" (often played by non-New Yorkers) tended to commercialism.

hash, *n.* [abbreviation; from narcotics slang; some currency among jazzmen since c. 1935]

1960 *The Jazz Titans,* p. 157. *hash:* hashish.

1961 *The Sound,* p. 22. "Hash" all through them Moslem countries, man.

hassel, hassle, *n.* [cf. 1959 *Webster's New World Dictionary,* s.v. *hassle:* "? < dial. *hassle,* to breathe noisily"; from general slang, but esp. common among jazzmen since c. 1945] A difficulty, a problem, an argument; also, rare, *v.t.:* to cause a difficulty or an argument (in this sense, oral evidence only); as *v.i.:* to be in trouble or difficulty.

1946 *Hollywood Note,* July, p. 7. Jay C. Higgenbotham, Onyx Club's noted jazz trombonist, quipped, "That'll be a hassel."

1958 *The Village Voice,* 1 Oct., p. 5. Jazz musicians . . . have been temporarily brought down by life's hassels.

1959 *The Horn,* p. 215. Anyone makes a hassle this next set, I'll show 'em put-downs if that's all they're after.

1959 *The Holy Barbarians,* p. 75. You *are* hassled if you haven't got loot.

hat, *n.* [obscene semantic development: i.e., an analogy is drawn between putting on a hat and mounting a woman in coitus and/or the man's head performing cunilingus; some currency esp. among black jazzmen since c. 1940]

1963 *Hiptionary,* p. 8. *hat:* girl, chick [jazz sense], wife.

have a ball, see S.V. BALL.

have it covered [special application of general colloquial phrase (i.e., to have something under control); current since c. 1955; see also ALL OVER, GET AROUND ON (ONE'S) HORN] To play (an instrument) with great virtuosity; to do something admirable.

1961 *Down Beat,* 17 Aug., p. 13. This was one of the most talented youngsters I've seen come up in a long time. For his age, he really had it covered.

1963 *Down Beat,* 9 May, p. 15. Oscar Brown Jr. really had those lyrics covered.

Hawk, *n.* [shortened form of his surname; one of the five or six indispensable nicknames in the jazz world (see also BIRD, PREZ, SATCH); although close associates frequently call him "Bean," jazz writers and fans have, since c. 1930, most often referred to him as "Hawk"]

Coleman Hawkins, 1904–1969, tenor saxophonist, acclaimed by musicians and critics as one of the all-time great performers on his instrument.

1935 *Metronome*, May, p. 37. For phrasing, tone, and original ideas . . . you can't beat old Hawk!

1973 *Jazz Style in Kansas City*, p. 147. Hawkins, called "Hawk" or "Bean," was held in awe by contemporaries and dominated the instrument in the same way that Louis Armstrong dominated the trumpet.

hawk, hawkins, *n.* [see 1973 quot. for poss. etym.; or, poss., the name of a fearsome person (poss. a New Orleans or Chicago policeman c. 1900); according to jazzmen, *hawkins* has been current esp. among black jazzmen since c. 1900, *hawk* since c. 1935] See 1958 quot.

1944 *Dan Burley's Original Handbook of Harlem Jive*, p. 44. Listen ole man; all yon jive I have spread only has been put down to knock thee a Benny when/Mister Hawkins rides his December chariot. — p. 140. *hawkins:* cold winter wind.

1958 *The Book of Negro Folklore*, p. 484. *hawkins:* the wind, wintertime, cold weather, ice, snow.

1969 *Village Voice*, 23 Jan., p. 31. The hawk (the old-fashioned black word for cold weather winds) passed out gingersnaps coated with dry ice.

1973 *N.Y. Post*, 4 Dec., p. 3. The Hawk is coming. Those icy breezes—which ghetto dwellers often compare to the predatory bird—carry a special wind-chill factor when you're on the skids.

head, *adj. & n.* [from where it is "kept" (as contrasted to "sheet" music); current since c. 1925] See 1958 quot.

1955 *Solo*, p. 26. There isn't anything wrong with blowing the way it's written, or if it's just a head arrangement, with the *mood* of the thing.

1955 *Atlantic Monthly*, July, p. 55. Most of the music grew out of fertile memories and atavistic impulses rather than out of conscious study. "Head music" they still call it.

1958 *Publication of the American Dialect Society*, Nov., p. 46. *head arrangement:* a musical arrangement which is not written down and never has been, but is known by all the members of the ensemble.

1959 *The Horn*, p. 193. But maybe if we do a whole set of heads, old ones.

head, *n.* 1 [synecdoche; current since c. 1935; before c. 1950, preceded by an *adj.* or *prefix,* used largely alone since] A person who uses marijuana or narcotics.

1938 *N.Y. Amsterdam News,* 2 Apr., p. 17. The thousands of lushheads and "tea" worms that are being hatched daily . . . are a peril.

1959 *The Holy Barbarians,* pp. 171–172. When the marijuana head (vipers, we called them in the thirties) or the hype turns on, he has the feeling of setting something in motion inside himself.

1960 *Hiparama of the Classics,* p. 7. So Mr. Rabadee . . . sent out Notices to . . . the Reed Heads, the Lute Heads, and the Flute Heads.

1961 *The Sound,* p. 22. Like, man, if Hitler and Mussolino had of been heads, there never would have been no Big Scuffle on the other side.

2. [metonymy and/or synecdoche; current since c. 1935] Fellatio.

1956 *Sideman,* p. 103. She's wild, man! Gives the craziest head!

1974 *Ladies and Gentlemen—Lenny Bruce!!* p. 443. The other fox [q.v.] is giving Lenny head.

hear, *v.t.* [some general colloquial use, but given special application by jazzmen; some currency since c. 1925] To understand (usually, music) esthetically and/or emotionally.

1946 *Really the Blues,* p. 318. Yeah, I hear you.

1961 *The Sound,* p. 55. It took me almost a month of listening . . . before I actually heard this music. —p. 206. It all comes out in what Red plays. It's not just a certain arrangement of notes. It's the way he hears it.

heavy, *adj.* [special applications of standard meaning (i.e., serious, profound); current esp. among black jazzmen from c. 1935–c. 1965, rare since: the term has moved over into youth slang] As in the standard sense, important or profound, but here the application is to people, ideas, money, and music rather than to responsibilities, etc.

1944 *Dan Burley's Original Handbook of Harlem Jive,* p. 3. Recently, in a rather heavy article in a heavy magazine, the *Journal of Negro Education* (Spring, 1944), I had occasion to speak of Dan Burley's work.

1959 *Afro Magazine Section,* 3 Oct., p. E4. Ya see, I'm not one of those cats who is always trying to break in on all the heavy loot.

1961 *The Sound,* p. 190. Baby, this is Bernie, Bernie is a real heavy cooker on piano.

1963 *Down Beat,* 15 Aug., p. 31. The average human being who understands jazz, I don't believe, could interpret this, because it's quite heavy.

heavy drums (or **drumming, beat**) [some currency since c. 1935] See 1953 quot.

1937 *This Thing Called Swing*, p. 9. *mugging heavy:* soft swing with a heavy beat.

1940 *Swing*, July, p. 17. Very fast semi-boogie blues in Gabriel with nasty, heavy off-beat drumming.

1953 *The American Thesaurus of Slang*, p. 552. *heavy drums:* forceful drumming.

heavy soul [jazz slang *heavy* + jazz slang *soul* (i.e., marijuana) = a powerful narcotic; some currency since c. 1958; see also H, HORSE] Heroin.

1963 *Heavy Soul* (tune recorded by Bill English on LP album Vanguard 9127).

heavyweight [from *heavy* above and prizefighting terminology; some currency since c. 1965] An important or profound musician; an important or profound person.

1973 *Down Beat*, 29 Mar., p. 14. We weren't trying to surpass Parker or the heavyweights.

hemp, *n.* [cf. 1959 *Webster's New World Dictionary*, s.v. *hemp:* "a drug, especially hashish, made from the flowers and leaves of this plant"; some currency among jazzmen since c. 1935]

1944 *Dan Burley's Original Handbook of Harlem Jive*, p. 140. *hemp:* marijuana cigarette.

1952 *Flee the Angry Strangers*, p. 131. Now, smoking hemp, she let out the laughter she'd choked back with food.

hep, *adj.* [though frequently represented as jazz slang (even jazzmen have made concessions to this popular misapprehension: cf. *The New Cab Calloway's Hepsters Dictionary*), jazzmen have never used this term in speech except derisively. Lexicographer Peter Tamony (*Americanisms*, March 1967) makes a good case for *hep* having had a long general slang life of its own, but *not* in jazz circles.] See s.v. HIP.

hepcat, hepster, *n.* [see note in *hep*] See s.v. HIPSTER.

hey now! [current c. 1938–c. 1946, obs. since] Hello.
1946 *Hey Now, Hey Now* (song recorded on Columbia 37081).

hide beater [from *hides:* some currency since c. 1935, very rare since c. 1945; see also SKIN-BEATER]
1938 *Cab Calloway: Hi De Ho*, p. 16. *hide beater:* a drummer.
1971 *The Street That Never Slept*, p. 159. He was the hide beater on that great record of "Body and Soul" by Coleman Hawkins.

hides, *n. pl.* [synecdoche; some currency since c. 1925; see also SKINS, TUB]
1942 *The American Thesaurus of Slang*, p. 559. *hides:* drums.
1961 *The Sound*, p. 287. "Still beating his hides and winning all the polls," Vann said.

high, *adj.* [cf. 1930 *American Tramp and Underworld Slang*, s.v. *high:* "elevated through drink; in high spirits"; widely current among jazzmen since c. 1917; see also BOXED, JUICED, STONED, ZONKED]
1928 *The Walls of Jericho*, p. 306. Not "drunk" in the usual sense, for which the Harlemese is "high."
1935 *His Hi De Highness of Ho De Ho*, p. 36. A person who is experiencing the exhilaration produced by a reefer is described as "high."
1939 *Jitterbug Jamboree Song Book*, p. 32. *high:* intoxicated by liquor or marijuana.

high hat, high-hat (cymbal) [from its similar collapsibility; current since c. 1932]
1948 *Metronome*, Nov., p. 28. I'd rather use the high-hat as a back beat and break up the bass drum rhythms.
1957 *The Book of Jazz*, p. 126. The foot-cymbal gave way, soon after 1930, to the "high hat cymbal," two cymbals facing each other and made to meet through pedal control.

hincty, hinkty, *adj.* [etym. unknown; cf. 1934 *A Dictionary of American Slang*, p. 19: "*hinkty:* suspicious"; current esp. among black jazzmen c. 1930–c. 1945, rare since]
1941 *Goin' to Chicago Blues* (tune recorded by vocalist Jimmy Rushing with Count Basie Orchestra). Well, I am hinkty and I'm lowdown too.

127

1944 *The New Cab Calloway's Hepsters Dictionary,* s.v. *hincty:* conceited, snooty.

1946 *Really the Blues,* p. 62. I had to cut loose some way, to turn my back once and for all on that hincty, kill-joy world of my sister's.

1974 *Location Shots,* p. 20. Lots of Negroes go there, but they're not my type. Too hincty.

hip, *adj.* [cf. 1930 *American Tramp and Underworld Slang,* s.v. *hip:* "wise, knowing"; last two quots. are completely mistaken about the etymology, but are much circulated (see 1944 quot.); according to jazzmen, the term has always been *hip,* never hep (q.v.), and it derives by analogy with having one's hip boots on (see 1938, 1958 quots.)—i.e., the way in which they protect the wearer from bad weather or dangerous currents is analogous to the way in which awareness or sophistication arms one against social perils; according to jazzmen, current since c. 1900; see also BOOTED, DOWN]

1938 *Cab Calloway: Hi De Ho,* p. 16. hip: wise, sophisticated, anyone with boots on.

1944 *Esquire,* Feb., p. 129. Don't believe all you read in the daily papers and the fan magazines. Very few of the terms attributed to musicians are now in use. The word "hep" is "hip" in Harlem, which is where most of this jargon originated.

1958 *Jive in Hi-Fi,* p. 13. The correct word is "hip." It comes from a story of a fisherman warning young fishermen never to wade in deep water without hip boots on because they could run into trouble. So, when you hear the words "I'm hip" or "I'm booted" it's said to let you know they have no fear of trouble or that they understand what's shaking [i.e., happening].

1959 *Toronto Telegram,* 31 Mar., p. 3. hip: equipped with enough wisdom, philosophy and courage to be self-sufficient, independent of society; able to swing on any scene [jazz slang sense].

1960 *Dictionary of American Slang,* s.v. *hip:* orig. a variant of "hep."

1961 *Encounter,* June, p. 56. Hip and hipster themselves derive from opium smoking for which the addict reclines on one hip.

v.t. [widely current since c. 1935] To advise, to tell, or to make (someone) understand.

1938 *American Speech,* pp. 316–317. Hip me to the Jive and Lace my boots! means "put me wise!"

1958 *The Subterraneans,* p. 90. Sand must have hipped him quietly in a whisper somewhere what was happening with the lovers.

128

hipness, *n.* [some currency esp. among jazz writers since c. 1950] Modishness (with a pejorative connotation); fashionability; feigned sophistication.

1958 *Saturday Review*, 8 Feb., p. 44. Parker's line on "The Song Is You" is an anthology of "licks" still played by jazzmen striving for "hipness."

1959 *The Horn*, p. 35. The very name conjured up a specter of a hipness he had renounced.

1960 *The Jazz Review*, Feb., p. 9. If this is natural for you, doesn't current hipness force you into unnatural strictures?

hipped to the jive, hipped on [variants of *hip*; cf. earlier general slang use of *hipped (on)*: enthusiastic about; *hipped*: some currency since c. 1900, *hipped to the jive* c. 1935–c. 1945, obs. since] Aware, knowledgeable—esp., see 1938 quot.: sometimes shortened to *hipped*; also rhyming slang *hip(ped) to the tip,* c. 1935–c. 1945: oral evidence only.

1938 *American Speech*, Dec., p. 314. *hipped to the jive:* well informed on the latest slang expressions.

1947 *Esquire*, Apr., p. 76. "Are there any squares in this outfit?" "No, man, we're all hipped."

1967 *Americanisms*, Mar., p. 5. Those *hipped on* any subject or field are generally in possession of knowledge about it.

hippy, hippie, *n.* [though formed from *hip,* the term, like *hipness,* has a pejorative meaning; current since c. 1945] A would-be hipster; one who affects awareness, sophistication, wisdom, but is deficient in these qualities.

1953 *Night Light*, p. 157. Man, I really get a bellyfull of these would-be hippies.

1959 *The Village Voice*, 18 Nov., p. 13. Imagine coming on so jaded, so epicurean, so hippie, so barbwire and fed up?

1959 *Jazz for Moderns*, p. 20. *hippy:* generic for a character who is supercool, overblasé, so far out that he appears to be asleep when he's digging something the most.

1960 *The Jazz Word*, p. 149. The hippy is overdone/over-hip and he ain't no fun.

1960 *N.Y. Post*, 16 Nov., p. 50. A "hippy," in the lexicon of jazz, is a pretender to the truth of Hip. Or, in the words of Maynard Ferguson, "He's not a junkie, but he tries to act like one. He sits there in his uniform, with a blank stare and a lot of pseudo-jazz expressions in his

129

head, and he probably doesn't understand the music, but he says, like: 'Ha, ha, John Coltrane's really saying something.' "

hipster, *n.* [from *hip;* despite definition in 1952 quot. *hepcat* was never current among jazzmen except perhaps derisively or satirically; some currency since c. 1940] One who is hip (q.v.)—a person who is knowledgeable and resourceful.

1945 *Down Beat,* 1 Sep. Harry "the Hipster" Gibson is in Hollywood.

1952 *Life,* 29 Sep., p. 67. *hipster:* modern version of hepcat.

1959 *Esquire,* Nov., p. 70I. *hipster:* one who is aware, as opposed to one who is a square.

1959 *The Holy Barbarians,* p. 39. He looked more like one of those beachcomber Nature Boy health freaks than a real hipster.

hit, *n.* [from numbers racket slang (i.e., to win); some currency since c. 1940] See 1970 quot.

1960 *Hiparama of the Classics,* p. 15. Four big hits and seven licks ago, our Before daddies Swung Forth upon this sweet groovey land.

1970 *Dictionary of Afro-American Slang,* p. 66. *hit:* to take a puff on a reefer; a quantity of anything.

v.t. [prob. from the standard musical phrase *hit a note;* current c. 1925–c. 1945, obs. since except historical] To begin to play music: frequently hortatory.

1939 *Jazzmen,* p. 97. Hit it, gal.

1948 *Trumpet on the Wing,* p. 38. So he gave us the down beat and we hit it.

hit on [poss. from the jazz slang *hit,* n.; current since c. 1948; see also SOUND] See last two quots.; also, by extension, to address oneself to (someone)—with the intent of making *any* request or asking a question.

1959 *Diggeth Thou?,* p. 58. And right now I'm hitting on the cool young teens.

1959 *Esquire,* Nov., p. 70I. *to hit on:* to request money or the act of love. Example: To hit on a chick means to try to get intimate with her.

1963 *Hiptionary,* p. 18. *hit on:* pester, annoy; also, flirt.

holding [extension of standard meaning; from narcotics slang; some currency among jazzmen since c. 1945]

1959 *The Holy Barbarians,* p. 316. *holding:* to have marijuana or any drug in your possession.

1961 *The Sound*, p. 15. Don't jump the light, baby, mother's holding, you know.

1969 *Hip Manual. holding:* to have on one's person whatever is needed, usually drugs or money.

holes, *n. pl.* [special application of standard meaning; some currency since c. 1950] In music, the silent intervals between notes or between clusters of notes.

1960 *Jazz: A Quarterly of American Music*, Winter, p. 20. "What are you listening to now? . . . Jamal?" "Too many holes, man."

1962 *N.Y. Times*, 11 Feb., Sec. 2, p. 12X. The compositions leave none of the customary holes where the jazz soloist can take over.

1962 *Jazz Journal*, July, p. 11. Duke needs an exceptionally strong bass player. All those holes to fill, with no guitar, and even sometimes no piano.

honk, *v.i.* [onomatopoeic; some currency since c. 1930] (Note its pejorative connotation in the last quot., which derives from an overuse and consequent monotony of the effect).

1937 *American Speech*, Feb., p. 46. *honk:* to play a note on a reed instrument in the low register with force and in a definite rhythmic pattern. Used of reed instruments only.

1961 *Palaver*, Feb., p. 14. Shavers screams, the Hawk honks, and only Bryant and Duvivier show any real sense of proportion.

honker, *n.* [some currency since c. 1948] Generally applied to tenor saxophonists who engage in claptrap "honking," most frequently at jazz concerts. Oral evidence only.

honkytonk, honky-tonk, *n.* [cf. 1959 *Webster's New World Dictionary*, s.v. *honky-tonk:* "prob. echoic"; also cf. 1931 *American Speech*, p. 29. "*honky-tonk:* a disorderly house"; current among jazzmen since c. 1900; see also BARRELHOUSE, GUTBUCKET]

1939 *Honky Tonk Train Blues* (tune composed by Meade Lux Lewis).

1942 *The American Thesaurus of Slang*, p. 565. *honky-tonk:* primal "swing" of the style played in the bordels of New Orleans, Memphis, and St. Louis in which a free rein is given to improvising.

1952 *Music Out of Dixie*, p. 133. New Orleans music . . . deserved something a little better than being kicked around in the tonks and saloons.

1961 *Esquire*, May, p. 153. Nor could the performer in a honky-tonk (Negro slang for gin mill) or a barrelhouse, both of which became characterizations of ragtime piano style, easily escape the tie-up.
Also **honky tonk, tonk.**

hooked, *adj.* [from underworld and narcotics slang; by analogy with being caught on a hook; some currency among jazzmen prob. since c. 1935] Addicted (usually, to drugs, but not necessarily: see last two quots.).
1946 *Really the Blues*, p. 371. *hooked:* addicted.
1959 *The Holy Barbarians*, p. 102. It isn't genius that's got me hooked.
1960 *Hiparama of the Classics*, p. 17. The swinging Brutus hath laid a story on you,/That Caesar was hooked for power.

hop, *n.* See s.v. LINDY HOP.

horn, *n.* [special application of standard meaning; in its more restricted sense, current since c. 1900; in its less restricted sense, widely current since c. 1945; see also AX]
1937 *Metronome*, Jan., p. 25. Satchmo, I was only kiddin'. I'll give you your horn back!
1937 *American Speech*, Feb., p. 46. *horn:* any wind instrument, whether reed or brass.
1958 *Publication of the American Dialect Society*, Nov., p. 46. *horn:* any musical instrument, but especially (and originally *only*) the wind instruments.

horn, hornman, horn player, *n.* [see note above; current since c. 1945] A wind instrumentalist.
1955 *Solo*, p. 52. Take Buddy Bolden, if you will. A great horn.
1959 *Philadelphia Afro-American*, 7 Feb. There must be tongue, finger and thought control working simultaneously on a split-second basis for the modern hornman blowing his solo.
1960 *Jazz: A Quarterly of American Music*, Winter, p. 33. Tenorman Charlie Rouse is one of the handful of "horn players" capable of working with Monk.

horse, *n.* [alliterative, but semantic development unknown: see 1958 quot. for metaphoric possibility; from narcotics slang; some currency among jazzmen since c. 1935; see also H, HEAVY SOUL]

1953 *Junkie*, p. 13. *horse:* heroin.

1955 *Hear Me Talkin to Ya*, p. 374. Fats was a real sweet guy B.H.—before horse is what I mean.

1958 *Oakland Tribune*, 19 Jan., p. B-15. His inner turmoil led him to heroin, the horse no one can ride.

1960 *Beat Jokes Bop Humor & Cool Cartoons*, p. 57. No more arm with which to take horse?

hot (jazz) [prob. from black slang; cf. 1928 *The Walls of Jericho*, p. 301. "*hot:* kindling admiration"; term orig. prob. had a sexual connotation (see 1950 quot.); widely current c. 1920–c. 1945, obs. since except historical] Initially, jazz as distinguished from popular or commercial music; since c. 1948, in writing, traditional jazz as distinguished from modern jazz.

1924 *Variety*, 24 Sep. This "hot" septet hails from around Chicago.

1929 *The Inter-State Tatler*, 9 Aug., p. 11. Such "hot" music is one reason why all roads on a Sunday afternoon lead to the Paradise.

1936 *Esquire*, June, p. 92. *Hot* refers to a musical idiom and attitude, not to a tempo.

1944 *Metronome*, Apr., p. 23. As Nappy Lamare points out, even *hot jazz* is a confusing term, because it implies that there is more than one kind of jazz music.

1944 *Esquire's 1944 Jazz Book*, p. 26. That the popularity of hot jazz is not even more widespread may be attributed to the lack of any literature treating of hot as a special field, and also to the deadening effect of the shallow emotionalisms of sweet (popular) jazz upon the public ear.

1946 *Really the Blues*, p. 141. This word [i.e., *swing*] was cooked up after the unhip public took over the expression "hot" and made it corny by getting up in front of a band and snapping their fingers in a childish way, yelling "Get hot! Yeah man, get hot!"

1950 *They All Played Ragtime*, p. 92. The sub-title, "The Hottest Thing You Ever Saw," started a tempest among . . . teapots, and certain women's clubs in New York complained to the Post Office Department, which ruled it obscene and unmailable. A hasty reprinting substituted the word "sweetest" for the objectionable adjective.

1956 *Guide to Jazz*, s.v. *hot:* an expression current for many years to denote the warm vibrant intonations of jazz musicians and their extemporized variations on a theme. "Hot jazz" connoted real jazz as opposed to commercial music. In recent years the word has been less and less used.

hotel (style) [metonymy: style was most popular at hotel ballrooms and supper clubs; some currency c. 1925–c. 1945, rare since; see also SWEET] A soothing, musically unadventurous style of playing, popular in hotel ballrooms c. 1925–c. 1945, but scorned by jazzmen.

1935 *Metronome*, May, p. 28. Playing in the Chez Paree doesn't give him a chance to click via his sophisticated hotel style.

1936 *Metronome*, Feb., p. 21. *hotel:* sweet and soft.

1959 *Jazz Review*, Dec. You couldn't play our kind of music in the big places. They wanted hotel music.

house band [chiefly a trade term; according to jazzman Eubie Blake, current since c. 1900] A band playing more or less permanently at a particular place—theater pit, hotel ballroom, nightclub, etc.

1959 *The Horn*, p. 34. The drummer for the house-band good-naturedly chased Wing's warm-up runs with precise rim-shots.

1961 *Record Research*, Mar., p. 9. Reams have been written about the dance bands of the acoustical era, both straight and jazz, from Prince's, Earl Fuller's, ODJB through Whiteman and beyond, but I've seen nary a word about that which, to me, is one of the most fascinating products of these times: the house band.

1962 *Down Beat*, 4 Jan., p. 36. By now, Sims and Cohn are practically the house band at the Half Note because of their four regular engagements there each year.

house-rent party (or **stomp, strut**), see S.V. RENT PARTY.

how about that mess?! [from jazz slang *mess;* current esp. among black jazzmen since c. 1935] Isn't that impressive?!

1941 *How 'Bout That Mess* (tune written by Cat Anderson, recorded by Doc Wheeler and the Sunset Royals).

hummer, *n.* [from underworld slang: cf. 1934 *A Dictionary of American Slang*, p. 20: "*hummer:* a false arrest"; some currency among jazzmen since c. 1950] An accidental occurrence, with either good or bad consequences.

1959 *Esquire*, Nov., p. 70I. *hummer:* a minor mistake, something that shouldn't have happened. Example: I got busted [i.e., arrested] on a hummer.

hung, hung-up, hungup, *adj. & p.p.* [by analogy with the standard term's connotation of immobilization; *hung-up* current since c. 1943, shortened form *hung* since c. 1950]

1945 *Hepcats Jive Talk Dictionary,* s.v. *hung up:* mixed up.

1959 *Toronto Telegram,* 31 Mar., p. 3. *hung-up:* foolishly entangled, stalled, involved.

1959 *Newport Jazz Festival: 1959,* p. 45. *hung-up:* stood up, confused, misled, addicted.

1961 *Down Beat,* 19 Jan., p. 33. The two saxophonists have a tendency to get hung for ideas, but both of them have moments of brilliance.

be (or get) hung up on (or with) [some currency since c. 1950; see also STRUNG OUT] To be or become obsessed with (something or someone).

1962 *N.Y. Times Magazine,* 20 May, p. 45. *hung up:* to be obsessed. ("He's hung up on Matt Dillon always shooting last.")

hustle, *v.i.* [see note in *hustler;* general slang (see last quot.) but with esp. currency among jazzmen since c. 1900] See first quot.; also, by extension, since c. 1945: see last two quots.; for its adjective use, see first 1959 quot.

1944 *Dan Burley's Original Handbook of Harlem Jive,* p. 140. *hustle:* beg, not work, to borrow, to live by one's wits or ingenuity.

1959 *The Horn,* p. 27. I learned *my* horn . . . in nine-piece hustling bands.

1959 *Esquire,* Nov., p. 70J. *hustle:* to work at a job.

1959 *The Holy Barbarians,* p. 75. Hustle is a word Itchy always uses for work, any kind of paid-for work. Notice that it is a word borrowed from whores and pimps—who, in turn, borrowed it from peddlers and door-to-door canvassers. (During the boom twenties it lost its derogatory connotations and was being used quite honorably for all selling.)

hustler, *n.* [cf. 1930 *American Tramp and Underworld Slang,* s.v. *hustler:* "a . . . street woman; . . . one who 'hustles' or hurries, works quickly and in fear of detection"; also cf. 1931 *American Speech,* Dec., "Underworld Argot," p. 109. "*hustler:* illegal entrepreneur"; current esp. among black jazzmen since c. 1900]

1944 *Dan Burley's Original Handbook of Harlem Jive,* p. 140. *hustler:*

a beggar, one who refuses to work, a playboy, prostitute, lady of leisure, tramp, an illegitimate performer.

1946 *Really the Blues*, p. 371. *hustler:* prostitute; also: anybody who makes a living by hook or crook.

1946 *Hollywood Note*, Apr. A hustler, he lives in Greenwich Village . . . catting around Manhattan in the wake of the Ellington and Herman bands.

hype, *n. & v.* [from narcotics and underworld slang (orig. prob. from *hypodermic, hype* meant a supplier of narcotics attempting to induce a potential customer to use them); cf. 1930 *American Tramp and Underworld Slang*, s.v. *hipe:* "to cheat or shortchange"; also, for poss. etym. see 1967 quot.; some currency among jazzmen since c. 1925; see also SHUCK]

1938 *The New Cab Calloway's Catalogue. hype* (n., v.): build up for a loan, wooing a girl, persuasive talk.

1959 *Esquire*, Nov., p. 70J. *hype:* deception. Example: He pulled a hype on the crowd. (He fooled or cheated the crowd.)

1967 *Americanisms*, Mar., p. 6. *Hype*, a type of throw, is a second hoary term in the vocabulary of wrestling. Used now principally in the vocabulary of Negroes, it denominates a put-on, a con game, an operation involving subterfuge.

1970 *Down Beat*, 20 Aug., p. 4. It's rock festival time. Hype, hype, hooray.

I

icky, *adj. & n.* [see 1935 quot. for poss. etym., also poss. reinforced by *sticky* and by the general colloquial term *hick;* some currency esp. among white jazzmen c. 1933–c. 1943, very rare since; see also SQUARE] An unsophisticated person; hence, as adjective, lacking sophistication, overly-sentimental.

1935 *Vanity Fair,* Nov., p. 71. If the straight music is also oversweet, the term icky (a pseudo-baby-patter word, meaning "little") is frequently employed to denote this.

1937 *Metronome,* Mar., p. 30. Once again I'd like to rise up in arms against the "unseen horde" of ickies who under the guise of posing as musicians and "heppers" persist in burdening us readers.

1937 *New Yorker,* 17 Apr., p. 31. Dance musicians are known as *cats* and those not up on the current idioms are *corny* . . . and, if their playing is oversweet, *icky.*

ideas, *n. pl.* [special application of standard meaning; current since c. 1930] In solo improvisation (sometimes, in composition or arrangement), musical ideas or conceptions: interesting phrases or the development of those phrases.

1933 *Metronome,* July, p. 26. He's got the ideas, but his lip's weak yet.

1947 *Metronome,* Jan., p. 32. He might not have the chops he used to have, but his ideas are always fine.

1961 *Metronome,* Apr., p. 20. Some nights I play it and ideas come, but sometimes they won't.

I'll bet a fat man [Elliot Horne's etymological guess is that "a fat man" is $5 (from "5 by 5," a fat man); some general black slang use, but with esp. currency among black jazzmen c. 1932–c. 1942, very rare since] I'm quite sure (of something); despite 1970 quot., phrase is almost always in 1st person sing.

1963 *Frontier*, June, p. 6. I'll bet you, as they say in Harlem, a fat man, that not many American children being taught American history have any real sense of what that collision was like.

1970 *Death of a Blue-Eyed Soul Brother*, p. 122. You can bet a fat-ass cook that none of us pulled that trigger.

I'm with you (or **him,** or a name) [some general and black slang use, but with esp. currency among black jazzmen c. 1917–c. 1945, rare since; see also CRAZY, SOLID] I approve of what you (or he) just said or did.

1926 *Nigger Heaven*, p. 242. "Buddy, I'm with you!" cried Lasca.

1962 *Down Beat*, 12 Apr., p. 22. I'm with John; I'd like to know how they explain "anti-jazz."

-ingest, *suffix* [common method of forming a jazz superlative since c. 1950; see also -EST] The nth degree (of whatever activity is indicated in the root verb).

1955 *Bop Fables*, p. 47. She *is* the swingin'est, but let's take it from the top again. —p. 57. "Man," said the stranger, "they're the jumpin'est!"

1955 *Hear Me Talkin to Ya*, p. 217. Incidentally, that was probably one of the partyingest bands that ever was.

insane, *adj.* [one of several terms in which the standard connotation is reversed (i.e., from bad to good) through the jazzman's association of mental instability (at least, by conventional judgment) with imaginativeness; current since c. 1945; see also CRAZY, NUTTY]

1948 *Down Beat*, 28 July, p. 4. insane: only the musical literati are addicted to (and permitted to use) this word. Pertaining to an extraordinarily dissonant conception or chorus. Applied only when the subject is "too gone" for "crazy" description.

1952 *Park East*, Dec., p. 30. His eight tiny coursers were really insane.

1960 *Hiparama of the Classics*, p. 22. Five thousand Christians started to wail up the biggest breeze and most insane orchestration you ever dug.

inside, (stay) [current since c. 1955] Of an instrumentalist, to play within the established chord structure of a tune (connotation of unadventuresomeness).

1975 *Down Beat,* 16 Jan., p. 35. Most of his playing was, as the labels go, "straight" or "inside."

instrumental, *n.* [special application of standard musical term; current as a distinguishing term during the big band era (when most bands had vocalists) c. 1930–c. 1945, rare since]
1940 *Swing,* July, p. 17. Bob Mersey's "Blue Ink" is another slightly Wham-like instrumental.
1949 *Music Library Association Notes,* Dec., p. 45. *instrumental:* composition written for instrumental performance, solo or group. Also, any performance without benefit of vocal.

in there [from *in the groove,* q.v.; widely current c. 1938–c. 1945, obs. since except historical] Of a musician, playing superbly; of anyone, possessing sophistication or wisdom; of any thing or place, exciting or interesting.
1944 *Dan Burley's Original Handbook of Harlem Jive,* p. 104. Now, this skull [i.e. person] was in there, Jack.
1948 *Partisan Review,* June, p. 721. *In there* was, of course, some-whereness.
1955 *Hear Me Talkin to Ya,* p. 106. The Lincoln Gardens, of course, was still in there.

into something, (get) [current since c. 1958] See 1969 quot.
1961 *Down Beat,* 13 Apr., p. 43. I said to myself, "Now, at last, we're going to get into something, and then, wow, it fell apart completely."
1963 *Down Beat,* 5 Dec., p. 35. The trumpet player could have gotten into something more.
1969 *Hip Manual.* Someone who is putting good creative ideas into his work may be said to be "into something." A high compliment.
   what are they into?, what is he into? [current since c. 1958] What musical ideas or conceptions are those musicians exploring? Oral evidence only.

intro, *n.* [from standard musical slang; shortened form of *introduction;* current since c. 1925]
1928 *Melody Maker,* Dec., p. 1353. The intro is artistic as it is appropriate.
1937 *American Speech,* Oct., p. 181. *intro:* introduction.
1955 *Sideman,* p. 32. After the intro there was a unison brass-riff.

139

iron chops, see s.v. CHOPS.

ivories, *n. pl.* [from their component; according to jazzman Eubie Blake, some currency c. 1900–c. 1945, very rare since] See 1926 quot.; also, the piano itself.

1926 *American Speech*, Dec., p. 146. "Ivories" may mean . . . piano keys.

1937 *Metronome*, Mar., p. 30. Teddy Wilson is on ivories.

(ivory) tickler, tickle (the) ivories [cf. 1948 *Shakespeare's Bawdy*, s.v. *tickle:* "overtly or covertly, an allusion to amorous or sexual tickling or caressing"; according to jazzman Eubie Blake, phrases based on conjoining of *tickle(r)* and *ivories* current, though not widely, c. 1900–c. 1945, obs. since except historical] *(Ivory) tickler:* a pianist; *tickle (the) ivories:* to play piano.

1932 *The Inter-State Tattler*, 7 Jan., p. 8. That's where Earl Hines tickled ivories.

1962 *Down Beat*, 16 Aug., p. 26. He had a magnificent attack . . . combined with the gaiety and sly humor that one looks for in a true "tickler."

J

Jack, Jackson, n. [cf. 1930 *American Tramp and Underworld Slang*, s.v. *Jack:* "a generic term for any tramp or other man"; *Jackson* current only c. 1938–c. 1942 (obs. since except historical), *Jack* from c. 1935– c. 1955, rare since; see also DICK, JIM]

1938 *Cab Calloway: Hi De Ho*, p. 16. *Jack:* name for all male friends.

1961 *The Sound*, p. 210. "Hey there, Jackson!" Vann was trying to strike the right note but it didn't come off. "Jackson" was a year or two out of date.

1969 *The Life and Loves of Mr. Jiveass Nigger*, p. 50. And then she tells me she's in love with me, jack.

Jack the bear, see S.V. NOWHERE.

jam, n., v.i. & v.t. [one of several food terms given a sexual meaning by blacks (see also BARBECUE, JELLY) and then associated with jazz by black jazzmen; current c. 1930–c. 1945, rare since]

1935 *Stage*, Sep., p. 45. *jam:* to improvise hot music, usually in groups.

1937 *This Thing Called Swing*, p. 3. *jamming:* impromptu swing, improvisation by one player against rhythm background of other instruments.

1952 *Who Walk In Darkness*, p. 98. Decker finished his solo and then all the musicians jammed, coming in together.

jam band [from *jam* above; some currency c. 1930–c. 1945, obs. since except historical]

141

1965 *Down Beat*, 8 Apr. p. 26. A Dixieland band was in those days a "jam band" or "small swing band."

jam session, session [current since c. 1933, mostly shortened to *session* c. 1945: see 1958 quot.] See 1955 and 1956 quots.

1936 *Harper's*, Apr., p. 574. Thus in a typical "jam session" one instrument will lead off with a slightly modified form of the general melody, the other instruments "faking" the harmony.

1955 *A Pictorial History of Jazz*, p. 202. "Jam session" was a highly elastic term. It could mean a group hired to play on the night it [i.e., the night club] would otherwise be closed, it could mean added men sitting in on a formal or informal basis, it could even mean an impromptu, odd-hours gathering at home, bar, or rented studio—which was the original idea.

1956 *Guide to Jazz*, s.v. *jam session:* a gathering in a nightclub or studio in which a group of musicians play on their own time and improvise at length on a few numbers, usually held after work hours [i.e., after about 3:00 A.M.]. The audience consists of a few musicians and devotees.

1958 *American Speech*, Oct., p. 223. To use any form of *jam* at what is now called simply a *session* is to brand yourself an auslander.

jamf, see s.v. JIVE, sense 4.

JATP [abbreviation; a writers' term only; current since c. 1950]
1956 *Guide to Jazz*, s.v. *JATP:* Jazz at the Philharmonic. Title of a series of concerts organized by Norman Granz, a form of jam session [q.v.] on stage with only a loose format.

1972 *Down Beat*, 20 July, p. 38. Flip gets into his later-to-be-famous JATP groove.

jazz, jass, jas, jaz, *n. & adj.* [cf. early sports slang use: 1913 *San Francisco Bulletin*, 6 Mar., p. 16. "What is the 'jazz'? Why it's a little of that 'old life,' the 'gin-i-ker,' the 'pep,' otherwise known as the enthusiasalum"; etym. is uncertain, but the sexual association (see 1927, 1931, 1959 quots.) is the most prob., poss. reinforced by associations of speed and excitation (see 1950, 1954 quots.), esp. in dancing (see 1968 quot.); for dates see 1917, 1939, 1946, 1960 quots.] Note: the term has been mostly generic for the music since c. 1917, except during the *swing* (q.v.) era (c. 1935–c. 1945) and the *bop* (q.v.) era (c. 1945–c. 1950) when those were

142

the generic terms; *jazz,* with the attributives *cool, modern,* and *progressive,* was reinstated in its honorific sense c. 1950 (for a pejorative use, see 1944 quot.).

1917 *Victor Records* (catalog advertising the world's first jazz phonograph record, Mar. 17, 1917). Spell it Jass, Jas, Jaz or Jazz—nothing can spoil a Jass band.

1927 *The Journal of Abnormal and Social Psychology,* Apr.-June, pp. 14–15. Used both as a verb and a noun to denote the sex act, jazz has long been common vulgarity among Negroes in the South, and it is very likely from this usage that the term "jazz music" was derived.

1931 *Scribner's Magazine,* Nov., p. 461. The word jazz in its progress toward respectability has meant first sex, then dancing, then music. It is associated with a state of nervous stimulation.

1939 *Down Beat,* 1 Nov., p. 6. Back in the year 1910, Schiller Cafe . . . advertising . . . sign. . . . At the very bottom . . . appeared the inspiring words: "Music will be furnished by Jas.' Band."

1944 *Metronome,* Apr., p. 22. Some of them [i.e., swing musicians] use the noun "jazz" to denote corn, especially those who are opposed to the Dixieland type of music and sum it up derogatorily with the word "jazz."

1946 *Jazzology,* Feb., p. 6. The word "jazz" as a musical term, was born in New Orleans. The Original Dixieland Jazz Band, playing at the Casino in the tenderloin district of New Orleans in 1914, first employed the term. . . . I first heard the word "jazz" used musically in reference to the Original Dixieland Jass Band. That was in 1913.

1950 *N.Y. Times,* 30 June, p. 21. Dr. Bender, who joined the Princeton faculty in 1909 . . . was stumped by the word "jazz." In the three years in which he traced the word he had to write more than 500 letters before reporting that he had traced it to the West Coast of Africa, the contact point for the slave trade with colonial America. He said that the word meant "hurry up" in the native tongue, and was first applied in the Creole dialect to mean "speed up" in the syncopated music in New Orleans.

1954 *St. Louis Post-Dispatch,* 27 Aug. Whether spelled jass, as at first, or jas, jasz, or jaszz, as at various times, or jazz as now, "the Creoles of New Orleans used the word, taken from the Negro patois and signifying *excite,* to designate a music of syncopated and rudimentary type," Lafacadio Hearn wrote.

1958 *The Story of Jazz,* p. 282. We may define jazz tentatively as a semi-improvisational American music distinguished by an immediacy

of communication, an expressiveness characteristic of the free use of
the human voice, and a complex flowing rhythm; it is the result of a
three-hundred-years' blending in the United States of the European and
West African rhythm.

1959 *The Jazz Scene*, p. 290. From about the same time [i.e., 1916] the
term "jazz" (or jass, jaz) came to be used as a generic label for the new
dance music, since few knew that it had hitherto been an African slang
word for sexual intercourse.

1960 *The Anatomy of Jazz*, p. 10. Although the word "jazz" was
undoubtedly in use for a good many years before 1914, it was not until
then, according to Nick LaRocca, founder of the Original Dixieland Jazz
Band, that "jazz" appeared in an advertisement.

1968 *Americanisms*, Dec., pp. 8–9. This juxtaposition of the word *jazz*
and social dancing suggests the basic element in the word *jazz* prior to
its extension to lock in the sense of music may be associated with
chassé, a dance step (to which the American language is already
indebted for *sashay*).

n. [general slang use, but with esp. currency among jazzmen since c.
1945; see also JIVE, sense 3, SHIT] Thing(s); nonsense.

1953 *Night Lady*, p. 153. What do you call that jazz, alpaca or
something?

1960 *Hiparama of the Classics*, p. 11. They want him to do this gig
here, they want him to do that gig there, play the radio, do the video
and all the JAZZ.

jazzbo [lexicographer Peter Tamony says term may derive from French
chassé-beau (a dance step?); some currency c. 1910–c. 1925, obs. since
except historical] Jazz.

c. 1909 *Jazzbo Glide* (jazz dance, acc. to *Jazz Dance*, citing Perry
Bradford's memory).

1921 *Jazzbo Ball* (tune recorded by Mamie Smith).

1921 *Old Time Blues* (tune recorded by Perry Bradford). Listen, listen
to that jazzbo band.

1968 *Americanisms*, Dec., p. 20. Obviously, *jazzbo* was a standard
usage when Negro/Black entertainers finally got to record in large
numbers in the early nineteen-twenties.

jazz (it) up [some currency since c. 1917, though with a connotation
shift c. 1940] Initially: to play jazz (see 1955 quot.); since c. 1940: to
simulate a jazz feeling with the use of artificial or clichéd jazz devices
(see 1958 quot.).

1955 *Hear Me Talkin to Ya,* p. 78. I came home and started jazzing it up in Memphis.

1958 *The Jazz Review,* Dec., p. 10. Oscar is jazzy; he jazzes up the tune.

jazzy, *adj.* [from the sense of caricature (-y); despite the earlier 1928 quot., the term gained wide currency from the swing era (c. 1935–c. 1945) musician's association of the word *jazz* with the older traditional style of jazz, of which he disapproved (see 1944 quot.); still some currency] See 1937, 1944 quots.

1928 *Melody Maker,* Dec., p. 1323. The trumpet was far too "jazzy." A more legato style would be a distinct improvement.

1937 *American Speech,* Feb., p. 46. *jazzy:* outmoded, showy, ostentatious style of playing.

1944 *Metronome,* Apr., p. 22. Yet most musicians use the adjective "jazzy" to denote "corny." Some of them even use the noun "jazz" to denote corn, especially those who are opposed to the Dixieland type of music and sum it up derogatorily with the word "jazz."

1966 *Down Beat,* 24 Feb., p. 26. His improvising is conservative and dull; it's filled with stale "jazzy" devices.

Jeff, *n.* [from *Jeff*erson Davis, whom blacks disesteem; some currency among jazzmen prob. since c. 1935; see also the more neutral and more common FAY, GRAY] A white person, but esp. one who is hostile to blacks.

1938 *Cab Calloway: Hi De Ho,* p. 16. *Jeff:* a pest, a bore, an icky.

1961 *The Sound,* p. 144. Them Jeffs is workin' together!

jelly (roll), *n.* [from black slang (see 1927 quot.); current esp. among black jazzmen c. 1900–c. 1945, very rare since]

1919 *I Ain't Gonna Give Nobody None o' This Jelly Roll* (tune composed by Spencer Williams and Clarence Williams).

1927 *The Journal of Abnormal and Social Psychology,* Apr.–June, p. 13. Relatively few symbols for the sex organs are found in the blues, but these are worked to the utmost. By far the most common of these terms is *jelly roll.* As used by the lower class Negro it stands for the vagina, or for the female genitalia in general, and sometimes for sexual intercourse. . . . Yet because of its decent meaning, it passes fairly well in popular song society.

1940 *Jelly, Jelly* (tune recorded by Billy Eckstine).

1959 *The Country Blues,* p. 83. In 1930 and 1931, Lonnie began recording more and more blues like "I Got the Best Jelly Roll in Town."

Jim, *n.* [some currency since c. 1940; see also DICK, JACK]

1952 *A History of Jazz in America,* p. 352. *Jack:* means of address to the male. Also "Jim."

1963 *The Realist,* June, p. 29. So when I see brothers and sisters that don't look alike, that's it, Jim.

jitterbug, *n.* [see 1956 quot. for poss. etym; also cf. 1935 *His Hi De Highness of Ho De Ho,* p. 35: " 'jitter sauce,' meaning liquor, and also 'jitter bug,' meaning one who drinks"; current c. 1936–c. 1945, now rare; see also ALLIGATOR]

1938 *From Spirituals to Swing* (Carnegie Hall program, dated Dec. 23, 1938). But the jitterbug millions . . . have scared a lot of people away from hot jazz.

1939 *The Kingdom of Swing,* p. 181. Mere exhibitionism, which has won the epithet of "jitterbug" as descriptive of the purely physical response that accompanies the worst phases of sensationalism by certain players.

1950 *Metronome,* Dec., p. 20. It's too bad the jitterbugs are gone. In those days jazz was the thing.

1952 *A History of Jazz in America,* p. 352. *jitterbug:* a swing dancer, frantic.

1956 *The Real Jazz Old and New,* p. 151. *Boogie woogie* used to mean the secondary stages of syphilis, and *jitterbug* a sexual reaction to music.

1968 *Jazz Dance,* p. 316. "The Lindy." Later they called it the Jitterbug.

v.i. [general slang term, formed from n., but with esp. currency among jazzmen. c. 1940–c. 1955, obs. since except historical]

1952 *A History of Jazz in America,* p. 352. *jitterbug:* to do the Lindy Hop.

1952 *Who Walks in Darkness,* p. 101. I turned away to watch the people jitterbugging.

jive, 1. *v.t. & n.* [see first 1944 and first 1946 quots. for prob. etym; current esp. among black jazzmen since c. 1920; see also THE DOZENS, PUT ON]

1928 *The Walls of Jericho,* p. 301. *jive:* pursuit in love or any device

146

thereof. Usually flattery with intent to win . . . this word implies . . . deceit.

1938 *Cab Calloway: Hi De Ho,* p. 16. *jive:* (1) Harlemese speech or lingo. (2) To kid along, to blarney, to give a girl a line.

1944 *Dan Burley's Original Handbook of Harlem Jive,* p. 71. Jive is a distortion of that staid, old, respectable English word "jibe." . . . In the sense in which it came into use among Negroes in Chicago about the year 1921, it meant to taunt, to scoff, to sneer—an expression of sarcastic comment. Like the tribal groups of Mohammedans and people of the Orient, Negroes of that period had developed a highly effective manner of talking about each other's ancestors and hereditary traits, a colorful and picturesque linguistic procedure which came to be known as "putting you in the dozens." Later, this was simply called "jiving" someone. Subsequently ragtime musicians picked up the term and it soon came to mean "all things to all men."

1944 *Jazz Miscellany,* p. 8. If I had some money I'd stroll down the street/And jive some old broad I might meet.

1946 *Really the Blues,* p. 215. The word jive probably comes from the old English word *jibe,* out of which came the words *jibberish* and *gibberish,* describing sounds without meaning, speech that isn't intelligible. —p. 371. *jive:* (*v.*) to kid, to talk insincerely or without meaning, to use an elaborate and misleading line: *(n.)* confusing doubletalk, pretentious conversation, anything false or phony.

1952 *A History of Jazz in America,* p. 352. *jive:* comic speech, usually larded with ambiguous jazz terms; sometimes synonymous with "kid" ("don't jive me").

1955 *Solo,* p. 40. You just play that game there without none of your jive.

1955 *Hear Me Talkin to Ya,* p. 15. Bunk would be in the nearest barroom . . . jiving some sporting women.

2. *n. & v.i.* [prob. reinforced by alliteration of *jive* with *jazz;* some currency c. 1930–c. 1945, obs. since except historical]

1935 *His Hi De Highness of Ho De Ho,* p. 35. "Jiving," meaning to improvise.

1944 *Dan Burley's Original Handbook of Harlem Jive,* p. 71. Since 1930 Jive has been accepted as the trade name for swing music.

1944 *N.Y. Times,* 23 Jan., p. 39. Attack on "Jive" Brings a Dissent (headline).

1955 *Hear Me Talkin to Ya,* p. 104. King Oliver and I got . . . popular blending that jive together.

1960 *Down Beat*, 9 June, p. 15. Regarding the word jive, Wilson said, "It is nothing more than an obsolete slang term for jazz."

3. *n.* [broadening of sense 1; some currency since c. 1935; see also JAZZ, sense 2, SHIT]

1938 *Cab Calloway: Hi De Ho*, p. 16. *jive:* stuff and things.

1960 *Jazz: A Quarterly of American Music*, Winter, p. 36. George Shearing copies so much jive from me.

4. **jive, jiver, jive mother-fucker, jive-ass mother-fucker, jamf** (oral evidence only for the last three) [from sense 1, in the sense of flattering, practicing deceit, "kidding"; *-ass* is an emphasis suffix here (cf. jazz slang -ASSED); *mother-fucker* (see MOTHER) a common jazz slang appellation; *jamf* is an abbreviation of *jive-ass mother-fucker* and is said to have originated with Charlie Parker; some currency since c. 1940].

1959 *Newport Jazz Festival: 1959*, p. 45. *jive:* a zany fun-loving person; also used to describe an unscrupulous person.

1962 *Down Beat*, 11 Oct., p. 24. "So many of the jazz cats," he said, "have become jivers. You know, the way they do it is much more important than what they do."

1964 *Down Beat*, 16 July, p. 15. If a jive guitar player came out on a stand—as jive as some of the avant garde horn players—the rest of the guitar players would laugh him out of the country.

1966 *Down Beat*, 16 June, p. 24. Hippies were passed over for what they were—in an apt phrase, jive punks.

joint, *n.* 1 [cf. 1930 *American Tramp and Underworld Slang*, s.v. *joint:* "any hangout, . . . not always a 'low resort' "; general slang but with esp. currency among jazzmen since c. 1925] See 1946 quot.

1938 *Cab Calloway: Hi De Ho*, p. 16. *The joint is jumping:* the place is lively, the club is leaping with fun.

1946 *Big Book of Swing*, p. 124. *joint:* entertainment place or living quarters.

1963 *Down Beat*, 20 June, p. 21. You know, I like soulful joints.

2. [semantic development and relation, if any, to sense 3 unknown; some currency among jazzmen since c. 1935; see also STICK] A marijuana cigarette.

1952 *Flee the Angry Strangers*, p. 171. You got a couple of joints to take along?

1960 *Saturday Review*, 6 Feb., p. 12. The marijuana is "tea." The rolled cigarette, looking very much like a paper-wrapped toothpick, is a joint.

3. [semantic development and relation, if any, to sense 2 unknown; current since c. 1935]

1959 *The Holy Barbarians*, p. 156. "Joint" . . . can also mean the penis.

jook, *n. & v.i.* see s.v. JUKE.

jug, *n.* [special application of standard meaning; also some general and college student use, but with esp. currency among jazzmen since c. 1900]

1929 *Knockin' a Jug* (tune recorded by Louis Armstrong).

1945 *Hepcats Jive Talk Dictionary*, s.v. *jug:* bottle of liquor.

jug band [see last quot. for semantic development; some currency c. 1917–c. 1930, obs. since except historical] Any small band which used a jug or a bottle as one of its instruments.

1931 *Melody Maker*, Dec., p. 1051. The only similarity I can see between this new outfit and the jug and bottle mongers, is that each contributes something in the way of "style."

1959 *The Country Blues*, p. 108. The men of the Memphis jug bands came from the crowded neighborhoods around Beale Street.

1970 *Down Beat*, 15 Oct., p. 33. Long ago we had jug bands. Pick-up records with kazoo, comb, washboard, homemade fiddle.

juice, *n. & v.i.* [current since c. 1935; see also LUSH]

1942 *American Mercury*, July, p. 95. *juice:* liquor.

1946 *Really the Blues*, p. 371. *juice:* (n.) liquor; (v.) to drink a lot.

1960 *Hiparama of the Classics*, p. 23. Come on over daddy-O, we drink up a little juice and everything be cool!

juiced, *adj.* [from *juice, v.i.;* current since c. 1937; see also BOXED, HIGH, STONED, ZONKED]

1946 *Really the Blues*, p. 371. *juiced:* drunk.

1961 *The Jazz Review*, Jan., p. 7. If a guy comes in juiced, . . . Basie is likely to call a number on which that guy is featured.

juicehead, *n.* [jazz slang *juice* + jazz slang *head, n.;* current since c. 1935] A drunkard.

1955 *Solo*, p. 247. The juiceheads . . . got so fractured [i.e., drunk] that they wouldn't show up for a date.

juice joint [jazz slang *juice* + jazz slang *joint,* sense 1; some currency since c. 1935] A cabaret, a night club.

1958 *Somewhere There's Music,* p. 35. She tells me I should kick my habits and figure out what I really want out of life besides six lonely nights a week in a juice joint.

juke, jook, *adj., n. & v.i.* [cf. 1959 *Webster's New World Dictionary,* s.v. *juke box:* "Negro Gullah jook-house, roadhouse; orig., house of prostitution akin to W. Afr. *dzug, dzog, dzugu*"; also cf. general slang *juke box,* which derives from it; current among jazzmen c. 1917–c. 1930, obs. since except historical] A stringed-instrument band that played at a combination roadside inn-brothel; also, the music played in that manner; also, the dancing done to the music.

1942 *American Mercury,* July, p. 95. *jooking:* playing the piano, guitar, or any musical instrument in the manner of the Jooks.

1948 *The Record Changer,* June, p. 6. On the folk level in New Orleans and elsewhere in the South . . . the jazz group and the "jook" or string band still furnish music for dancing.

1956 *The Real Jazz Old and New,* p. 151. *Juke* . . . came from juke house—which was once a whorehouse.

1959 *Jazz* (Hentoff & McCarthy), p. 107. Such places were known as "jukes," the playing was called "juking."

1968 *Jazz Dance,* p. 5. For years it [dancing at discotheques] was known in the South as "jukin'."

jump, *v.i.* [hyperbole (see 1938 quot.); current since c. 1935; see also SHAKE] To be lively or animated; also: to dance animatedly (see first 1957 quot.).

1938 *Cab Calloway: Hi De Ho,* p. 16. *The joint is jumping:* The place is lively, the club is leaping with fun.

1946 *Really the Blues,* p. 26. The First World War was jumping then.

1960 *Hiparama of the Classics,* p. 12. Now the fame of The Naz is jumpin'!

adj. & n. [see note above; see 1956 quot. for beginning date; very rare since c. 1948; see also UP-TEMPO] See first 1956 quot.; also, *jump band:* a band specializing in *jump numbers.*

1938 *Carnegie Jump* (tune recorded on Columbia C-1500).

1943 *This Is Jazz,* p. 30. You have left only the intolerable monotony of "jump" phrases played over and over.

1945 *Band Leaders and Record Review,* Mar., p. 20. Jump music, swing, jazz, or whatever you want to call it, jumps in the movie-capital, too.

1946 *Jazzways*, p. 51. The meaning of a "jump tune" should be clear enough from the term itself; literally, it jumps. . . . A "jump" treatment can be applied to almost any kind of song with success.

1956 *Guide to Jazz*, s.v. *jump:* introduced about 1938 as a synonym for "swing." . . . A *jump number:* a tune played in a particularly bouncing rhythm affected by many bands in the late thirties.

jump in [hyperbole; current from c. 1940–c. 1960, rare since] see 1970 quot.

1960 *Beat Jokes Bop Humor & Cool Cartoons*, p. 50. The cat did jump in soon.

1970 *Dictionary of Afro-American Slang*, p. 72. *jump in:* (1930s–40s) to become involved.

jump salty, see s.v. SALTY.

jungle (music) [see 1935 quot. for etym.; some currency c. 1928–c. 1936, obs. since except historical] An earthy musical style, featuring tomtoms and growl (q.v.) trumpet, associated with a Harlem sound and esp. with Duke Ellington's Orchestra c. 1928–c. 1936.

1935 *Vanity Fair*, Nov., p. 71. Negro bands play "race music" (a curious euphemism spread by phonograph companies), and the savagery of their rhythm calls forth the terms "shake music" and "jungle music."

1966 *Down Beat*, 30 June, p. 22. There's no way you can get the "jungle" sound except with the growl.

junk, n. [from narcotics and underworld slang: 1931 *American Speech*, Aug., "Convicts' Jargon," p. 439: "*junk:* drugs"; prob. by analogy with its colloquial sense (i.e., trash); general slang but with some currency among jazzmen since c. 1935]

1934 *Black Mask*, Oct. Canales has a noseful of junk a lot of the time.

1958 *American Speech*, Oct., p. 225. *junk:* narcotics.

junkie, n. [cf. 1931 *American Speech*, Aug., "Convicts' Jargon," p. 439: "*junkie:* a drug addict"; also general slang but with some currency among jazzmen since c. 1935]

1942 *American Thesaurus of Slang*, p. 476. *junkie:* drug addict.

1948 *Metronome*, Apr., p. 33. Hanging around with 52nd Streeters you would get to know a whole new vocabulary used by the "junkies."

151

JUNKIE

1965 *Down Beat,* 11 Mar., p. 16. We had never heard such terms as "busted" for arrested, "fuzz" for police, and all the other jargon that came into common use in bop circles after a vast clique of junkies had fanned out from Bird. (Even the word junkie was unfamiliar.)

K

K.C., Kansas City (style) [after *Kansas City*, Missouri; current since c. 1935] A swing era (c. 1935–c. 1945) style of playing, some elements of which survive in modern jazz.

1938 *Count Basie's Kansas City Seven* (name of a jazz septet).

1946 *Harvard Dictionary of Music*, p. 376. Passing over the somewhat lighter and less percussive "Kansas City style" of the early 1930s with its riff technique (short ostinato melodic figures by the band against which one of the instruments improvises), mention must be made of a special type of blues piano.

1955 *A Pictorial History of Jazz*, p. 149. They had their own way of playing in Kansas City, their own beat, and the trumpets searing through the band sound, and the spirited repetitive riffs. Some argue that there is actually no specific Kansas City "style"; but no one can claim that this town wasn't a major jazz landmark.

1956 *Enjoyment of Jazz* (EJ401), p. 2. The K.C. version of Swing was freewheeling and flexible.

kick, *n.* 1. [semantic development unknown; from pickpockets' slang, but some currency among jazzmen since c. 1935]

1944 *The New Cab Calloway's Hepsters Dictionary*, s.v. *kick:* a pocket. Example: "I've got five bucks in my kick."

1947 *The Harder They Fall*, p. 131. I like to have enough in my kick to pay my tabs.

2. [poss. from *kicks*, q.v.: i.e., one's *kick* provides, is the source of, one's pleasure *(kicks)*; 1811 *Dictionary of the Vulgar Tongue*. "*kick:* a strange whim or peculiarity"; widely current since c. 1940; see also

153

GROOVE] A passion, philosophy, preference, attachment, interest, fad, vogue, style, practice, vein.

1946 *The Jazz Record*, July, p. 8. The whole jazz world was on a Hawkins kick.

1947 *Band Leaders and Record Review*, Feb., p. 17. "I'm still on the group kick," says Buddy.

1953 *The Hot and the Cool*, p. 38. This domestic kick with diapers is great.

1956 *It's Always Four O'Clock*, p. 44. Sometimes the Sauter-Finegan outfit sounds like it's trying to get off on a new kick.

1961 *Down Beat*, 5 Jan., p. 16. Everybody now is on that Les McCann kick.

v.i. & v.t. 1. [prob. from standard phrase *kick it out;* from narcotics slang: cf. 1934 *A Dictionary of American Slang*, s.v. *kick the habit:* "to try to break the drug habit"; some currency among jazzmen since c. 1935] To rid oneself of (usually, a narcotics habit).

1948 *Metronome*, Apr., p. 33. You hear that such-and-such a musician . . . is trying to "kick" (break the habit).

1958 *Somewhere There's Music*, p. 35. She tells me I should kick my habits.

2. (sometimes with *out*) [by analogy with the energy and impact; current c. 1935–c. 1945, rare since; see also BOOT, ROCK, STOMP]

1936 *Metronome*, Feb., p. 21. *kick out:* swing.

1937 *American Speech*, Feb., p. 47. *kick out:* to bring out heavily the rhythm of a tune with every member of the band assisting.

1938 *Metronome*, Aug., p. 17. The band is kicking like mad in this one.

1939 *Metronome*, May, p. 19. Artie really kicks the last two choruses of "Prosschai."

kick (it) around [old colloquial phrase used in special sense by jazzmen c. 1935–c. 1945, rare since] To improvise music freely and relaxedly.

1939 *Esquire*, May, p. 75. Speaking again of Swing: few tunes deserve its name till they've been "kicked around" by good performers.

1944 *Esquire's 1944 Jazz Book*, p. 49. Benny Goodman once answered it by saying that after a musician has played a tune over and over again, what can he do but "kick it around"?

1956 *It's Always Four O'Clock*, p. 13. Lonny was tired and just kicking it around.

kick (it) off [poss. from football slang and general slang (i.e., to begin something) but a very natural application to a jazz sense; current since c. 1917] To signal for the musicians to play by the leader's stamping his foot several times in the desired tempo; also, by extension, to begin playing.

1945 *The Jazz Record*, Nov., p. 10. Bunk "kicks off" with his heel, piano and drums pick it up and the band is off.

1948 *Trumpet on the Wing*, p. 44. In those days I didn't know how to give a down beat with my hand, like leaders do today. We'd just kick it off on the bandstand, "One, two."

1957 *Concerning Jazz*, p. 16. I started to kick off the tempo.

kicks, *n. pl.* 1. [from hobo slang: cf. 1930 *American Tramp and Underworld Slang*, s.v. *kicks:* "shoes, those things with which a kick is delivered"; current among jazzmen since c. 1925]

1958 *Somewhere There's Music*, p. 101. "She bought me these kicks," he said and held up a foot.

1959 *Swinging Syllables*, s.v. *kicks:* shoes.

2. [poss. from narcotics slang (i.e., by analogy with the jolting effect), poss. reinforced by general slang "getting a kick out of (something)"; according to jazzmen, current since c. 1928] See 1952, 1960 quots.

1937 *Metronome*, Mar., p. 31. Swing fans will get the biggest kicks from Swing.

1952 *A History of Jazz in America*, p. 351. *kicks:* pleasure.

1959 *The Holy Barbarians*, p. 22. I just like to take them for kicks now and then.

1960 *Dictionary of American Slang*. s.v. *kicks:* a surge of pleasurable emotion; a thrill of enjoyment or excitement.

kill, *v.t.* [hyperbole; also some general slang use, but with esp. currency among jazzmen since c. 1935] To affect (one) powerfully and favorably.

1938 *Cab Calloway: Hi De Ho*, p. 16. *kill me:* show me a good time, send me [jazz sense].

1955 *Hear Me Talkin to Ya*, p. 329. It killed me to be accepted as a regular member of the band.

1957 *Down Beat*, 9 Jan., p. 33. Dickie Wells on trombone—he kills me.

1960 *The New Edition of the Encyclopedia of Jazz*, p. 478. It's very well executed, doesn't kill me too much, but gets going nicely when he goes into the block-chords stuff.

155

1961 *Jazz Journal*, Mar., p. 11. Clark Terry killed everybody—biting, darting trumpet genius.

killer, killer-diller, *n.* [prob. from *kill; killer-diller* was part of the rhyming slang vogue c. 1935–c. 1940 and had slight currency; *killer* was current c. 1935–c. 1945, very rare since] Someone or something exceedingly formidable; also, by extension: a piece of music that's difficult to play (see first 1940 quot.).

1937 *Metronome*, Apr., p. 55. That Zutie drummer-man is really a killer!

1938 *Better English*, Nov., p. 51. *killer-diller:* a great thing, thrill.

1940 *Swing*, Jan., p. 26. "Farewell Blues" is another of those very fast killers.

1940 *Mademoiselle*, Feb., pp. 89, 141. The Krupa band . . . is not all the killer-diller affair that a lot of people anticipated.

1947 *Frontiers of Jazz*, p. 150. The long crashing finale—the "Killer-Diller," as Goodman calls any cumulative superlative—of the antiphonal "Sing, Sing, Sing!"

1955 *Hear Me Talkin to Ya*, p. 227. I'm a killer with my new shepherd plaid suit.

king, *n.* [general slang term for a topnotcher in any occupation, but used in special sense by jazzmen c. 1900–c. 1920, obs. since except historical; not to be confused with commercial uses in the 1920s (Paul Whiteman, King of Jazz) and the 1930s (Benny Goodman, King of Swing) etc.] A very great early (c. 1900–c. 1920) musician. (Since the trumpet was generally then the most important solo instrument, it is not surprising that this honorific title was bestowed primarily on trumpeters Buddy Bolden, Freddie Keppard, and Joe Oliver.)

1915 advertising poster, 22 Apr. [1962 *Jazz: A History of the New York Scene*, photostat p. 35]. Contest Between the Percussion Kings.

1946 *Jazzways*, p. 16. By 1907, Bolden had disappeared from the scene, confined to an insane asylum. But the succession of "kings" of the hot cornet showed no sign of giving out. —p. 20. Freddie Keppard was the jealous King of Jazz in 1910.

1958 *Teach Yourself Jazz*, p. 114. The great "kings" of New Orleans took jazz groups there.

1965 *Down Beat*, 15 July, p. 25. The horn wasn't born that could follow the King [i.e., Louis Armstrong].

kitty, kitten, *n.* [prob. orig. by analogy with *cat,* q.v., poss. reinforced by the colloquial *kiddy* (i.e., a child); some currency since c. 1935; see also BABY] A young man or woman; also, by extension, any person.

1946 *Really the Blues,* p. 194. Walking down the street, glimming [i.e., looking at] the cute kittens. —p. 372. *kitten:* very young girl.

1956 *Lady Sings the Blues,* p. 27. I was only thirteen, but I was a hip kitty.

1960 *Beat Jokes Bop Humor & Cool Cartoons,* p. 50. The old man, respected throughout the kingdom for being a down kitty, lay but a few weeks in his grave.

1960 *Hiparama of the Classics,* p. 10. Look at all you Cats and Kitties out there!

knock, *v.t.* [semantic development unknown; cf. 1930 *American Tramp and Underworld Slang,* s.v. *knock:* "inform"; current c. 1925–c. 1960, rare since] (Note: a verb extremely protean [see first 1944 quot.] in its meanings.)

1929 *Knockin'* [i.e., consuming] *a Jug* (tune recorded by Louis Armstrong).

1944 *Dan Burley's Original Handbook of Harlem Jive,* p. 142. *knock:* to put down, speak, walk, loan, borrow, give, ask, exhibit.

1944 *Esquire,* June, p. 170. *knock a slave:* get a job.

1944 *The New Cab Calloway's Hepsters Dictionary,* p. 9. Knock me a kiss.

1959 *Diggeth Thou?,* p. 40. He fell for a chick who knocked him for a deuce [i.e., borrowed two dollars from him].

1960 *Hiparama of the Classics,* p. 9. Knock [i.e., sew] a patch on the little Cat's pants. —p. 26. The Gasser sat down to knock [i.e., write] a note on [i.e., to] Ferdinand the First.

knock (one) out [hyperbole; current since c. 1935; see also GAS, KILL, SEND] See first quot.; also, to please (one) greatly, to thrill (one).

1942 *American Mercury,* July, p. 95. *knock yourself out:* have a good time.

[1944] *Black on Black,* p. 196. We was at the Creole Breakfast Club knockin' ourselves out when this icky, George Brown, butts in.

1947 *Band Leaders and Record Review,* Feb., p. 20. "When I heard it," Ella Mae says, "it knocked me out."

1950 *Metronome,* Mar., p. 29. Shearing always did knock me out.

1960 *Jazz: A Quarterly of American Music,* Winter, p. 36. Maybe it makes you laugh because it knocks you out.

knocked-out, *adj.* [from verb phrase; current c. 1938–c. 1946, rare since] Excellent, thrilling, superb.

1941 *Strictly Ding-Dong,* p. 73. It had had all the dignity of a jam session, what with the staring alligators outside the church, and knocked-out at that.

1952 *Who Walk in Darkness,* p. 170. You should dig that surf. It is really something. Knocked out.

1956 *Sideman,* p. 275. Sold knocked-out ties real cheap.

L

label, *n.* [metonymy: i.e., the phonograph record label bearing the recording company's name stands for the recording company; current since c. 1930] A recording company.

1955 *Hear Me Talkin to Ya*, p. 177. I know we recorded for every label possible.

Lady, Lady Day [one of the five or six indispensable jazz nicknames: see also BIRD, PREZ, SATCH; see 1956 quot. for etym.; current since c. 1940] Billie Holiday, 1915–1959; most jazz musicians and critics acclaim her as the greatest vocalist in the history of jazz.

1942 *Travelin' Light* (Paul Whiteman Orchestra recording; vocalist listed as "Lady Day").

1956 *Lady Sings the Blues*, p. 59. Back at the Log Cabin the other girls used to try and mock me by calling me "Lady," because they thought I thought I was just too damn good to take the damn customers' money off the tables. . . . Lester Young took it and coupled it with the Day out of Holiday and called me "Lady Day."

1958 *Melody Maker*, 18 Oct., p. 3. Lady Day is unquestionably the most important influence on American popular singing in the last twenty years. . . . The depth of Lady's singing has always rocked me.

laid-back, *adj.* [by association with the relaxed state of the body position; according to jazzmen, current since c. 1973] Of music or a musician (or any person), relaxed.

1974 *Different Drummer* Sep., p. 5. It's a simple, tasteful, laid-back session.

159

lame, *adj. & n.* [extension of standard meaning, poss. reinforced by the similarity of sound with the earlier *lane,* q.v.; some currency since c. 1950; see also SQUARE] As adjective: unaware, unsophisticated, inexperienced; as noun: an unsophisticated, unaware person.

1955 *American Speech,* Dec., p. 303. *Lame* is the opposite of *solid* [q.v.].

1959 *Esquire,* Nov., p. 70J. *a lame:* one who doesn't know what's happening. A square.

1961 *N.Y. Times Magazine,* 25 June, p. 39. *lame:* square, but not beyond redemption. If you're lame, man, you can learn.

1963 *Nugget,* Feb., p. 46. It takes a real lame stud to follow a sick-looking cat like me, with a green beard and shades, into a dark alley.

lane, lain, laine, *n.* [according to jazz dancer Leon James, the term was formed by metonymy: country lanes are where many rural (i.e., unsophisticated) people live; some currency c. 1930–c. 1945, very rare since; see also LAME, SQUARE] One who is inexperienced or unsophisticated.

1937 *Metronome,* Aug., p. 7. Nothing ever fed me up so much as that lain George Simon's review on Bunny Berigan in the July MET.

1944 *Dan Burley's Original Handbook of Harlem Jive,* p. 52. A lame is a lane, and a lane is a square.

1946 *Really the Blues,* p. 372. *laine:* hick, innocent, sucker.

1958 *Jive in Hi-Fi,* p. 30. A lane is a man not hip to jive.

latch on [Old English term which became obs. in standard English but survived in dialect: cf. 1954 *Webster's New International Dictionary,* s.v. *latch:* "ME. lacchen, fr. AS. læccan. . . . Obs. exc. Dial.* 1. To seize; lay hold of; take; also, figuratively, to comprehend"; current among jazzmen c. 1930–c. 1945, rare since; see also PICK UP (ON)]

1938 *Cab Calloway: Hi De Ho,* p. 16. *latch on:* grab, take hold, get wise to.

1948 *Trumpet on the Wing,* p. 52. One night I latched on to the screwiest job I ever had in my life.

1958 *The Book of Negro Folklore,* p. 485. *latch on:* become aware, understand, learn.

later, *adv. & interj.* 1. [see 1957 quot.; current since c. 1950] See 1956, 1957 quots.

1956 *Tennessee Folklore Society Bulletin*, Mar., p. 23. *later:* catchall word for "I'll be seeing you."

1957 *American Speech*, Dec., p. 281. The bopster's successor, the modern jazz enthusiast, is not only moderate, but pithy. He tends to condense meanings into single words, e.g., bop and pre-bop "I'll dig you later, man" becomes simply, "Later!"

1959 *The Horn*, p. 34. Well, I'll cut out then . . . later, pops.

1959 *The Holy Barbarians*, p. 115. Angel . . . says "Later" and leaves.

1960 *Jazz: A Quarterly of American Music*, Winter, p. 21. Reporter: "Good night." Hippie: "Yeah, man, later."

2. extension of sense 1: [figuratively, to bid goodbye to or want to be rid of someone or something; current since c. 1952]

1953 *Later* (tune recorded by Ella Fitzgerald on Decca DL8149). Later for the happenings, baby.

1957 *N.Y. Times*, 25 Aug. *Later with that, man!:* disinclination to participate in an activity or project.

1960 *Beat Jokes Bop Humor & Cool Cartoons*, p. 61. Cut out from thy old man, later for your name.

1962 *Down Beat*, 22 Nov., p. 26. Later for the music business.

1966 *Down Beat*, 16 June, p. 38. During the second half, though, I almost got seasick. A string quartet. Later!

1969 *Hip Manual*. Later is a derogatory term similar to "Forget it."

law, *n.* [from underworld slang: cf. 1930 *American Tramp and Underworld Slang*, s.v. *law:* "any police authority"; also some general slang use, but with esp. currency among jazzmen since c. 1900; see also FUZZ] See 1958 quot.

1942 *American Mercury*, July, p. 92. Oh, let's don't talk about the law.

1952 *Flee the Angry Strangers*, p. 137. No Law in there, baby, I can smell fuzz from fifty yards.

1958 *The Book of Negro Folklore*, p. 488. *the law:* the police.

lay back [prob. from general colloquial *lay back* (i.e., to stay behind); current since c. 1930; see also DRAG, *v.i.*] To fall behind the rhythm (frequently deliberately in order to achieve a particular effect).

1955 *Hear Me Talkin to Ya*, p. 200. Most singers . . . they're either layin' back or else runnin' away from you.

1972 *Down Beat*, 30 March, p. 27. If I sing an up tempo song and the rhythmic thing is moving underneath it, I like to kind of lay back.

lay dead, lay up (in) [cf. 1930 *American Tramp and Underworld Slang*, s.v. *lying dead:* "in hiding"; some currency among jazzmen since c. 1935; see also COOLING] To relax, to do nothing.

1958 *The Dharma Bums*, p. 99. Come and lay up in and learn to drink tea.

1959 *Esquire*, Nov., p. 70J. *lay dead:* to wait. To stay in one place, don't move. —*lay up:* to be off the scene.

lay down, *v.t.* [extension of standard meaning (i.e., to place or set down); current since c. 1935; see also PUT DOWN, sense 1] To present, perform, or contribute.

1950 *They All Played Ragtime*, p. 194. He laid down a terrific stomp.

1958 *Somewhere There's Music*, p. 47. Gene must have really laid down some shuck to Barton about your playing.

1960 *Down Beat*, 13 Oct., p. 23. Those fingers have more direction and lay down better time than 90 percent working today.

lay (some) iron [from the metal taps worn by dancers; poss. also by analogy with an earlier railroad slang term; current esp. among tap dancers, but also current to some extent since c. 1917 among jazzmen, since they frequently provided the musical accompaniment]

1938 *Cab Calloway: Hi De Ho*, p. 16. *lay some iron:* to tap dance. Example: "Jack, you really laid some iron that last show."

1946 *Really the Blues*, p. 212. He . . . can lay some iron, too.

lay (something) on (someone) [by analogy with standard meaning (i.e., to place on); widely current since c. 1935; see also PUT (SOMETHING) ON (SOMEONE)] To give or present or tell (something to someone).

1942 *American Mercury*, July, p. 86. Lay de skin on me [i.e., shake hands], pal!

1952 *Music Out of Dixie*, p. 243. If Danny or any o' the customers got any kicks they can lay 'em on me.

1953 *Night Light*, p. 200. Laying a story on me.

1954 *Metronome*, Aug., p. 20. Watch what happens when we forget to pay up, or even those terrible moments when we don't lay enough on the waiter.

lay out [prob. from general colloquial *lay* (i.e., stay), and adapted from card players' use (i.e., not to play a particular hand); current since c. 1920] To temporarily stay out of the playing (of music).

162

1935 *Vanity Fair*, Nov., p. 71. Extended rests are "lay-outs."

1955 *Bop Fables*, p. 21. The commercial little pig laid out for a few bars and then moved into a prefab.

1959 *Jazz: A Quarterly of American Music*, Summer, p. 204. Do you like the piano player to "lay out" while you're jamming?

1959 *The Jazz Review*, Sep., p. 10. Always leave some spaces—lay out.

1961 *The Sound*, p. 45. I gonna lay out just one more set.

1963 *Hiptionary*, p. 12. *lays out:* says nothing; does not join in the action.

lay up (in), see s.v. LAY DEAD.

lazy, *n. & adj.* [standard term given a special application by jazzmen; according to jazzman Eubie Blake, some currency since c. 1900]

1956 *Guide to Jazz*, s.v. *lazy:* relaxed playing devoid of any apparent effort.

1961 *New Yorker*, 18 Feb., p. 128. Gillespie's work was an exemplary balance of extraordinary arabesque passages and lazy legato turnings.

lead, *n. & adj.* [see 1958 quot. for semantic explanation; current since c. 1925] See last quot.

1934 *All About Jazz*, p. 99. He evolved what he called a "harmony chorus," the instruments all playing harmony, with a solo lead.

1937 *American Speech*, Feb., p. 47. It is voiced peculiarly in that the lead melody is carried lower than the clarinet.

1940 *Swing*, Jan., p. 21. He often uses the Glenn Miller saxophone voicing with a clarinet lead.

1956 *Sideman*, p. 9. He was playing lead sax for Matt MacNeal.

1956 *Guide to Jazz*, p. 165. The "lead man" is the musician who leads the band or section of it.

1958 *Publication of the American Dialect Society*, Nov., p. 46. *lead:* the top, or melody, part in an arrangement: therefore, the melodic line. *lead man:* one who plays the "lead" in his section of the ensemble.

leader, *n.* [from *band leader;* current since c. 1935] The leader (cf. *sideman*) of a jazz band of any size.

1926 *Melody Maker*, Mar., p. 4. The drummer . . . disdains the leader.

1960 *Jazz Street*, p. 14. There are sidemen as well as leaders in this book.

163

lead sheet [from *lead, adj.;* current since c. 1925]

1949 *Music Library Association Notes,* Dec., p. 46. *lead sheet:* a song as written down in its simplest form—melody line and lyric.

1959 *The Horn,* p. 144. He picked up the lead sheet again.

least, the, *adj. & n.* [formed as antonym to *the most,* q.v.; some currency since c. 1952; see also NOWHERE] As adjective: mediocre; as noun: something mediocre.

1955 *Bop Fables,* p. 36. Honey, your grandma is feeling the least.

1958 *Publication of the American Dialect Society,* Nov., p. 46. *the least:* opposite of the most.

left hand [special application of standard phrase; current prob. since c. 1900] A pianist's left hand; also, his skill or inventiveness with the left hand.

1926 *Melody Maker,* Jan., p. 24. The bass, or left-hand part, is customarily the most neglected.

1944 *Metronome,* Nov., p. 17. Everyone wanted to treat the piano player. Drinks were lined up ten deep all night long . . . and to keep the ball rolling, the box-beater [i.e., pianist] had to reach for a drink with his right hand and keep the melody going with his left. That's how left-hands were born!

1961 *The Jazz Review,* Jan., p. 26. Granted he has a great left hand, but the way he uses it detracts from his right.

1961 *Monsieur,* Apr., p. 36. That's Teddy Wilson. Listen to his left hand.

left town [by analogy with standard meaning; some currency since c. 1900; see also QUIT THE SCENE, SPLIT THE SCENE] Died.

1960 *Lester Left Town* (tune written by Wayne Shorter as an elegy for Lester Young, who died in 1959).

legit, legitimate, *adj. & n.* [both the standard term and the shortened form derive from a parallel usage among theater people; some currency since c. 1925; see also LONG-HAIR] See 1937 quot.

1933 *Metronome,* Jan., p. 36. Naturally, the man who can play both legitimately and "hot" is the more valuable.

1937 *American Speech,* Feb., p. 47. *legitimate, legit:* applied to other than popular music. Also applied to a musician who does not play dance music well, although he may play other music perfectly.

1955 *Hear Me Talkin to Ya*, p. 59. He tried . . . to avoid a "legit" tone.

1956 *Sideman*, p. 10. Writes symphonies, you know? Legit stuff.

less, *adv.* [one of several quantitative terms given a qualitative meaning by jazzmen (see also GANG, LEAST, THE MOST); some currency since c. 1950] Not as well.

1959 *Jazz: A Quarterly of American Music*, Fall, p. 290. Man, I'm playing *less*.

let's do a set!, let's go back home! [according to jazzmen, some currency c. 1910–c. 1930 esp. among those blacks who danced to jazz, obs. since except historical; see also PUT US IN THE ALLEY!] Shouts of encouragement to jazz musicians c. 1910–c. 1930 to play fast, energetically and intensely.

1959 *The Jazz Review*, July, p. 12. When they got tired of two-steps and schottisches (which they danced with a lot of spieling), they'd yell: "Let's go back home!" . . . "Let's do a set!"

let's go home, see s.v. GO HOME.

let the good times roll [according to jazzman Eubie Blake, some currency esp. among black jazzmen since c. 1900] Let's enjoy ourselves —drink and talk and listen to or play music.

1948 *Let the Good Times Roll* (tune composed by Fleecie Moore and Sam Theard).

1959 *Jazz: A Quarterly of American Music*, Summer, p. 188. This invests the whole solo with a raucous, "let-the-good-times-roll" quality.

1960 *Hiparama of the Classics*, p. 29. He loved to hear the horns of joy blowin' that fine Jazz, plenty of juice flowin', and let the Good Times roll.

lick, *n.* 1. [prob. from its colloquial meaning (i.e., a blow): cf. 1939 *Jazzmen*, p. 60: "It was said Joe had a bad forehead wound caused by 'a lick on the haid' delivered by a wicked broomstick"; also cf. 1947 *Horn of Plenty*, p. 141. "Give it a solid lick!"; poss. reinforced by another meaning of the standard term: cf. 1938 *Cab Calloway: Hi De Ho*, p. 16: "*licking the chops*: what the cats do when they are warming up for a swing session"; widely current from c. 1930–c. 1945, obs. since except historical; see also BREAK] See 1933 quot.

1932 *Melody Maker*, June, p. 509. They manage to steal a "lick" from an American record.

1933 *Fortune*, Aug., p. 47. His *licks* (musical phrases) are original to the point of being *screwy* (fantastically exciting).

1936 *Esquire*, June, p. 92. The mutations of musicians' slang are interesting. It was "breaks" originally. Then it became "licks."

2. [extension of sense 1 (i.e., from a musical idea to any idea); current since c. 1940; see also RIFF] The idea, the gimmick, the plan, the situation.

1955 *Bop Fables*, p. 54. So here's the lick. Take this beat-up bovine to market.

1960 *Hiparama of the Classics*, p. 10. They're Pushin' The Nazz! Cause they wanted to dig his Lick, you see, Dig his Miracle Lick! —p. 11. He's a carpenter kitty and he's got his own lick.

1974 *Down Beat*, 14 Mar., p. 36. The whole band singing together or something like that, we had a good solid lick that really went across.

licorice stick [from its resemblance; some currency c. 1930–c. 1940, obs. since except historical; see also BLACKSTICK]

1935 *Vanity Fair*, Nov., p. 71. *licorice stick:* clarinet.

lid, *n.* [cf. 1937 *A Dictionary of Slang and Unconventional English*, s.v. *lid:* "a hat, a cap . . . from c. 1905"; current among jazzmen since c. 1935; see also SKY, WIG] Initially, see 1959 quot.; by extension, since c. 1943, the mind: see FLIP (ONE'S) LID.

1956 *Lady Sings the Blues*, p. 20. All the big-time whores wore big red velvet hats then with bird-of-paradise feathers on them. These lids were the thing.

1959 *Swinging Syllables*, s.v. *lid:* cap, hat.

lift, *adj. & v.t.* [by extension of standard meaning; some currency c. 1920–c. 1935, rare since]

1937 *Melody Maker*, June, p. 585. This was done chiefly by . . . placing before the original melody notes lift notes (usually a semi-quaver in value).

1934 *Metronome*, Dec., p. 52. *Lift* . . . implies extra accents in certain mensural time places. The "lifting" of a beat means extra accents.

light, *adj.* [special application of standard meaning (cf. *heavy beat*); some currency since c. 1935] As applied to a rhythm instrument or instrumentalist: weakly accented, having little power; as applied to the tone of a wind instrument or instrumentalist: thin.

1962 *Jazz Journal*, July, p. 11. Duke needs an exceptionally strong bass player. . . . I do think the man he has now . . . is a bit light for the band.

1966 *New Yorker*, 25 June, p. 38. He had a light tone; and it just didn't fit with the arrangements.

light crumbs, see s.v. CRUMBS.

lightly and politely [from rhyming slang vogue c. 1935–c. 1940, very rare since] Neatly, "niftily," effortlessly, smoothly, satisfactorily (done).

1939 *American Jazz Music*, p. 54. Louis Armstrong somewhere says, "Lightly and politely."

1961 *The Sound*, p. 118. "Lightly and po-lightly!" Red exclaimed.

light up [cf. its general colloquial use (i.e., to light a cigarette); some currency among jazzmen since c. 1930; see also TURN ON]

1938 *Cab Calloway: Hi De Ho*, p. 16. *light up:* to smoke a reefer or weed.

1953 *Night Light*, p. 136. You light up and you get yourself a hen and maybe shack up with her.

1959 *The Holy Barbarians*, p. 27. Before I light up I'm drug with [i.e., troubled by] the ten thousand things.

like, *adv.* [see last quot. for humorously expressed but accurate insight into the rationale of the word; also cf. OED "1500-20 Dunbar *Poems* xix, 19 yon man is lyke out of his mind. 1596 Spenser *F.Q.* iv. x. 56 all looking on and like astonisht staring"; also cf. 1960 *Dictionary of American Slang*, s.v. *like:* "reenforced by Yiddish speech patterns"; widely current since c. 1943] See 1956 and 1959 quots.

1950 *Neurotica*, Autumn, p. 45. Like how much can you lay on [i.e., give] me?

1954 *Esquire*, Nov., p. 82. He is a man who laughs often, and explosively, and in this case, he flipped, or as he put it later, he like flipped (Norvo, in common with many musicians, has a great fondness for the adverb "like").

1956 *Tennessee Folklore Society Bulletin*, Mar., p. 23. *like:* filler word for pauses of uncertainty.

1958 *Nugget*, Oct., p. 51. They also tell about the hipster at the beach

167

who got out beyond his depth and hollered to the life guard: "Like help!"

1959 *Newport Jazz Festival: 1959*, p. 45. *like:* replaces the comma in jazz parlance.

1959 *The Holy Barbarians*, p. 316. *like:* the theory of relativity applied to reality.

like it is, tell it [current from c. 1960–c. 1968 when its use by Richard M. Nixon and others signaled its demise among jazzmen] See 1970 quot.

1964 *Down Beat*, 19 Nov., p. 8. Mann tells it like it is.

1970 *Dictionary of Afro-American Slang*, p. 77. *like it is (telling it):* the real condition as one sees it.

Lindy (hop) [see 1958 quot. for etym., 1937 quot. for initial date] See 1937 quot.; also, for its v.i. use, see 1932 quot.

1931 *Zit's Theatrical Newspaper*, 2 May, p. 11. The winners of the all-Harlem Lindy Hop contest drew rounds of applause nightly.

1932 *The Inter-State Tattler*, 23 June, p. 8. They Lindy hopped.

1937 *American Speech*, Oct., p. 183. The Lindy Hop is a Negro dance which reached its present popularity during the summer of 1927. It contains elements of the previously popular Charleston and Black Bottom, and the subsequently introduced Truckin'.

1958 *Melody Maker*, 11 Oct., p. 4. In 1927, shortly after Lindbergh's flight to Paris, he [i.e., "Shorty George" Snowden] observed a group of unusually lively dancers. "Who do you think you are, hopping around like that?" he asked—"Lindbergh?" The Lindy Hop was christened.

line, *n.* [prob. from the fact that the music, if and when written, is set down on the long parallel lines that make up the staff (also in the sense of a continuum); current since c. 1935] A melody (and harmony); melodic (and harmonic) continuity in the building of an improvised chorus.

1940 *Swing*, Nov., p. 27. There's . . . a lovely, smooth melodic line in his improvisations on this swell old tune.

1958 *Saturday Review*, 8 Feb., p. 44. Parker's line on "The Song Is You" is an anthology of "licks" still played by jazzmen striving for "hipness."

1960 *The Jazz Review*, Nov., p. 18. The session started slowly, confining itself, strangely yet somehow logically, to early bop lines.

1961 *The Jazz Review*, Jan., p. 25. Red Allen is a soloist, not an ensemble improvisor; his lines are too active to be leads for this kind of polyphony.

liner, *n. & adj.* [chiefly jazz trade term; current since c. 1950] The back of a long-playing record cover, on which appears notes about the music and musicians.

1955 *Saturday Review*, 15 Jan., p. 41. For the covers of these new jazz albums . . . are being covered . . . with thousands and thousands of words known as "liner notes."

1960 *The Jazz Word*, p. 154. They couldn't come up with any less information than on some liners today.

lip, *n.* [metonymy; current since c. 1930; see also CHOPS, FANGS]

1933 *Metronome*, July, p. 26. He's got the ideas, but his lip's weak yet.

1937 *American Speech*, Feb., p. 47. *lip:* technically, embouchure. Used in relation to the state of muscular strength of brass instrument players' lips and their resultant ability to play high notes accurately.

1948 *Trumpet on the Wing*, p. 54. I noticed that he didn't have much of a lip.

1959 *Easy Living*, p. 57. I can't even do that until I get my lip back.

1960 *The Jazz Review*, Sep.-Oct., p. 14. He didn't have it with the lip, but he had it here, in his head.

lip (it) up, [current esp. among reedmen since c. 1935] To bring an instrument into tune.

1970 *The World of Duke Ellington*, p. 96. There's so much lipping to be done. You have to lip up to get it [the soprano saxophone] in tune.

Lipton's, *n.* [because jazz slang *tea* means marijuana, a brand name of the standard sense of *tea* has become synonymous with all marijuana of poor quality—i.e. having no more effect on the smoker than . . . ; current since c. 1940]

1970 *Dictionary of Afro-American Slang*, p. 77. *Lipton's:* (1940s) fake or poor marijuana.

listen, *v.i.* [spec. application of standard sense; current since c. 1935] To be musically sensitive and responsive, esp. as an accompanist.

1962 *Down Beat*, 6 Dec., p. 25. One gets the impression that everyone is listening to Bellson all the time.

169

1970 *The World of Duke Ellington*, p. 195. When you've got someone like Freddie Greene in the section, there's no sweat, because he listens and he's never stiff.

Little Jazz [prob. from his short stature; one of the five or six indispensable ones of the many jazz nicknames (see also BIRD, LADY, PREZ); current since c. 1938] Roy Eldridge, 1911–   , generally acclaimed by jazz musicians and critics as one of the great trumpeters in jazz history.

1941 *Little Jazz* (song recorded by Gene Krupa Orchestra, featuring Roy Eldridge on trumpet).

1961 *The Village Voice*, 16 Feb., p. 13. He acknowledged playing a good deal with "Little Jazz."

locked hands [from the fixed position of the hands in relation to one another when playing in this manner; current since c. 1945; see also BLOCK CHORD.]

1957 *The Book of Jazz*, p. 68. This was the "locked hands" or "block chord" style, in which the left hand moves parallel with the right, playing extra notes in the chord or duplicating the right hand's chord, instead of supplying a bass line.

1959 *The Collector's Jazz: Modern*, p. 268. Shearing has run practically the entire jazz gamut . . . through the locked hands block chords.

1961 *Metronome*, Aug., p. 7. He often generates enough thunder to blast off an army, and thus forces pianist Kuhn to rely heavily on a locked-hands style.

long bread, see s.v. BREAD.

long green, see s.v. GREEN.

longhair, long-hair, *n. & adj.* [from stereotyped image of the classical musician; chiefly 1930s teenage slang but with some currency among jazzmen c. 1930–c. 1945, obs. since except historical; see also LEGIT, STRAIGHT]

1935 *Vanity Fair*, Nov., p. 71. Straight or commercial musicians are often derisively called *salon-men* or *long-haired boys*.

1939 *Metronome*, Nov., p. 24. The jury was completely longhair, however.

1943 *Tangleweed*, p. 174. It ain't a song. It's a composition. Longhaired.

1949 *Music Library Association Notes*, Dec., p. 46. *long-hair:* one who plays, appreciates, composes, or writes about concert music.

long underwear, long-underwear (gang) [by analogy with the cautious, conservative nature of the apparel; chiefly teenage slang but with some currency esp. among white jazzmen c. 1930–c. 1940, obs. since except historical; see also HOTEL, SWEET, TICKY]

1933 *Fortune*, Aug., p. 47. And *corny* music is what generally happens when a *sweet* band, or *long-underwear gang*, tries to play *hot*.

1936 *Stage*, Mar., p. 58. *long underwear gang:* musicians who can play only "as written."

look out! [cf. its general colloquial meaning (i.e., "attention!"): widely current c. 1940–c. 1947, rare since] That's formidable! (Esp. though not exclusively applied to music.)

1946 *Big Book of Swing*, p. 124. *look out:* expression of one's interest in ad-lib musical break.

1960 *Stanley Turrentine: Look Out!* (LP album Blue Note BLP 4039).

loose wig, see s.v. WIG.

loot, *n.* [from underworld slang: cf. 1937 *A Dictionary of Slang and Unconventional English*, s.v. *loot:* "(n) pillage, plunder"; current among jazzmen c. 1930–c. 1945 when it was largely replaced by *bread;* see also GOLD] Money.

1951 *Esquire*, Dec., p. 210. He must have made a nice little "taste," (meaning) the tune made quite a bit of "loot."

1953 *Night Light*, p. 147. He's been stealin' all his old lady's loot.

lot, *adj.* [one of several quantitative words given a qualitative meaning by jazzmen (see also GANG, LEAST, THE MOST); current since c. 1935] Excellent; of great quality.

1946 *Duke Ellington*, p. 59. "Damn," said Harry, "that's a lot of horn, that really is."

1956 *Down Beat*, 14 Nov., p. 13. He plays an awful lot of trumpet.

1961 *Down Beat*, 5 Jan., p. 43. Well, I would rate it two stars for the orchestral technique, for being able to handle an orchestra that size, even though it's not a lot of music.

low-down, *adj.* [see 1939, 1959 quots. for semantic development; prob. reinforced by the old colloquial term: cf. 1959 *Webster's New World Dictionary*, s.v. *low-down:* "colloq. mean; contemptible; despicable"; note absence of pejorative connotation in jazzmen's use of the term (one of many such: see also BAD, DIRTY, MEAN, TERRIBLE, TOUGH); according to jazzman Eubie Blake, current c. 1900–c. 1945, very rare since; see also GULLY-LOW, GUT-BUCKET, HONKYTONK] See 1939 and 1960 quots.

1926 *Sweet and Low Down* (tune recorded by Alfredo's New Prince's Orchestra).

1928 *Variety,* Aug. [1962 *Jazz: A History of the New York Scene,* p. 198] Witnesses state that often between two and five A.M. there were as many as 35 or 40 musicians on the stand, kidding around and giving their conception of low-down tunes.

1939 *Jazzmen,* p. 12. From barrel-houses and honkytonks came many of the descriptive words which were applied to the music played in them; hence, "gully-low," meaning, as its name implies, low as a ditch or a "gully," hence, "low-down."

1955 *Hear Me Talkin to Ya,* p. 231. Charlie Irvis could play lowdown on the trombone.

1959 *The Jazz Scene,* p. 290. Terms for emotion were formed by metaphor, e.g., by the widespread practice of equating . . . grief with depth. . . . Thus the quality most desired in the old blues is that it should be *low-down.*

1960 *Dictionary of American Slang,* s.v. *low-down:* in jazz, slow, intense, in the manner of the blues.

lush, *n.* [cf. general slang *lush* (i.e., drunkard); also cf. 1960 *Dictionary of American Slang,* s.v. *lush:* "liquor. 1848: J. S. Farmer. Archaic since c. 1920. Reintroduced by jazzmen in the '30s"; current c. 1930–c. 1945, very rare since; see also JUICE]

1938 *N.Y. Amsterdam News,* 2 Apr., p. 17. The thousands of . . . lushheads and "tea" worms that are being hatched daily . . . are a peril.

1960 *Dictionary of American Slang,* s.v. *lush:* liquor.

1961 *The Sound,* p. 11. I can't make [i.e., use or enjoy] lush at all, baby.

v.i. [cf. 1811 *Dictionary of the Vulgar Tongue:* "to lush: to drink"; current c. 1930–c. 1945, rare since; see also JUICE] To drink liquor.

1950 *Gutbucket and Gossamer,* p. 21. I hate people who don't know when to stop lushing.

1958 *Somewhere There's Music*, p. 174. I lush less and less the longer I'm around town.

lushed, *adj.* [current c. 1935–c. 1945, very rare since; see also BOXED, JUICED, STONED] Drunk.
1959 *The Horn*, p. 213. I got too lushed somewhere.

lying, *participle* [by analogy with verbal communication (see also SAY SOMETHING, TELL A STORY, TRUTH); some currency since c. 1955; see also JIVING, SHUCKING] Playing a lot of musical clichés; hence, playing music insincerely. (According to jazzmen, this is the only meaning; hence, the definitions in the first quot. are somewhat inaccurate).
1957 *N.Y. Times Magazine*, 18 Aug., p. 26. *lying:* playing the notes as written rather than improvising on a hot one; dogging it; playing with a sweet band rather than a hot one.
1970 *Dictionary of Afro-American Slang*, p. 78. *lying:* (1950s) to play music without sincere emotion.

M

M [abbreviation; from underworld and narcotics slang: cf. 1930 *American Tramp and Underworld Slang*, s.v. *M:* "morphine"; some currency among jazzmen since c. 1935] Morphine.

1959 *The Naked Lunch*, p. 221. Your reporter bang thirty grains of M a day and sit eight hours incrustable as a turd.

mad, *adj.* [early synonym for *crazy,* q.v.; some currency since c. 1940; see also INSANE, NUTTY] Exciting, pleasurable, excellent.

1944 *Dan Burley's Original Handbook of Harlem Jive*, p. 15. That's mad, ole man.

1957 *On the Road*, p. 154. We spent a mad day in downtown New Orleans.

main man [prob. popularized by the alliteration; current since c. 1955] See first quot.; also, anyone considered important.

1970 *Dictionary of Afro-American Slang*, p. 79. *main man:* a favorite male friend; one's hero.

1974 *Ladies and Gentlemen—Lenny Bruce!!*, p. 371. He tells me that he's just scored the stuff from his main-man.

mainstream, *adj.* [chiefly a writers' term (see 1961 quot.); some currency since c. 1955] Of music or a musician, characteristic of or belonging to a school or style of jazz that has roots in the swing (q.v.) period (see 1960 quot.)—i.e., occupying an intermediate position between the traditionalists and the modernists.

1959 *Jazz: A Quarterly of American Music*, Spring, p. 161. It's fatuous to assess, currently with its taking place, what is mainstream jazz.

1960 *Swing Swang Swingin': Jackie McLean* (liner notes on LP album Blue Note 4024). Swing with a capital S is a noun and, besides representing an era, is used to describe a segment of jazz which has since been redubbed mainstream.

1961 *Jazz News*, 16 Aug., p. 10. I am often labeled a "mainstream" clarinet player, but the word "mainstream" doesn't mean very much. These labels are normally manufactured by critics to bring some sort of jazz they like to the attention of more poeple.

make it [cf. 1930 *American Tramp and Underworld Slang*, s.v. *make:* "to accomplish. Much the same sense as in standard English, although applied to any object or piece of work"; some earlier use, but widely current among jazzmen only since c. 1948] For the commonest sense, see last two 1959 quots. (a phrase protean in its meanings).

[1927] 1966 *Down Beat*, 20 Oct., p. 18. Do you think I can make it [i.e., succeed] in the big city?

1950 *Neurotica*, Autumn, p. 45. Double lock the door, George. I'm gonna make it [i.e., take narcotics] first.

1953 *This Week Magazine*, 5 Apr., p. 13. It's a kind of music I mostly can't make [i.e., enjoy].

1956 *Sideman*, p. 25. You wanta make it [i.e., go (somewhere) and perform] with me tonight? Bring your ax.

1957 *On the Road*, p. 225. They went to a parking lot in broad daylight . . . and there, he claims, he made it [i.e., had sexual intercourse] with her.

1958 *Somewhere There's Music*, p. 18. Baby and I made [i.e., used] two of those pills. —p. 47. I made it to [i.e., arrived at] Gene's late.

1958 *Down Beat*, 1 May, p. 20. If the drummer doesn't make it [i.e., perform effectively], I don't know what I'm supposed to do at all.

1959 *Toronto Telegram*, 31 Mar., p. 3. *make it:* cope.

1959 *Easy Living*, p. 28. Really? You've never made hash [i.e., smoked hashish]?

1959 *The Holy Barbarians*, p. 78. Just good conversation is often enough to make it for [i.e., satisfy, please] me. —p. 316. *make it:* may be said of anything that succeeds.

1959 *Newport Jazz Festival: 1959*, p. 45. *makes it:* good, acceptable. *make it:* leave, depart.

1960 *Jazz: A Quarterly of American Music*, Winter, p. 50. I print longhand. A typewriter I can't make [i.e., use].

175

1969 *Hip Manual*. *to make it:* to be good. "Trane really makes it, man."

make (one's) love come down [semantic development unknown; some currency esp. among black jazzmen since c. 1925]

1946 *Really the Blues*, p. 35. A woman who really knows how to sing and means it can make your love come down. —p. 372. *make your love come down:* arouse your passion.

make the scene [jazz slang *make* + jazz slang *(the) scene;* current since c. 1950] To join or to participate in the activities of a (particular) milieu or the world at large.

1958 *American Speech*, Oct., pp. 224–225. In *making the scene* one partakes in a larger tableau. (When, on the other hand, he *does the bit,* he is merely part of a short incident.)

1960 *Beat Jokes Bop Humor & Cool Cartoons*, p. 21. I made the academic scene for just a week.

1967 *Down Beat*, 21 Sep., p. 38. You go to New York and make the scene there.

mallets, *n. pl.* [metonymy: term orig. referred to xylophone/vibraphone mallets; according to jazzmen, current since c. 1965] Any percussion instrument (vibes, marimba, triangle, etc.) or an extra set of drums. Oral evidence only.

mammy jamming, see s.v. MOTHER.

man, *n.* [from black slang: see last two quots.; current esp. among black jazzmen since c. 1920, among white jazzmen as well since c. 1940] Initially, a term of address reserved for males; since c. 1955, see first 1959 quot.

1933 *Metronome*, Aug., p. 23. Trum's greeting was in the Negro dialect he usually employed: "Man! How is you?"

1959 *Toronto Telegram*, 31 Mar., p. 3. *man:* omnibus salutation extended to men, women, domestic animals—saves cool cat hang-up [i.e., difficulty] of remembering names.

1959 *N.Y. Age*, 4 Apr. Do you know why we have always called each other "man"? Because we had to confer the mantle of age on ourselves when the white man refused to do so. To the average white person in America, the Negro was always "boy."

my man [current esp. among black jazzmen since c. 1930, among white jazzmen as well since c. 1940] Sometimes, variant of *man,* q.v.; sometimes, my favorite (see 1953 quot.; see also MY BOY).

1953 *Down Beat,* 11 Feb., p. 16-S. That was Frog—Ben Webster! My man!

1966 *New Yorker,* 25 June, p. 36. Red, if you see my man Jelly Roll Morton, tell him hello.

the man [also some general and black slang use, but with esp. currency among black jazzmen since c. 1917]

1928 *The Walls of Jericho,* p. 306. *The man:* designation of abstract authority. He who trespasses where a sign forbids is asked: "Say, biggy, can't you read the man's sign?"

1944 *The New Cab Calloway's Hepsters Dictionary,* s.v. *the man:* the law.

1959 *Jazz for Moderns,* p. 20. *the man:* the person in charge, one of authority (manager, bandleader, headwaiter, bartender, et al). Also any cat who is deserving of great respect, musically or personally. ("Miles is the Man!")

1960 *Esquire,* Dec., p. 72. The latter reflects his listeners' daily experiences with lack of love and cash in a societal context that renews tension each morning in the trip to meet "the man" downtown.

1970 *Shaft,* p. 32. The cat who has the bread is The Man.

mary jane [poss. a pun on "marijuana" or poss. a name translated from Spanish: cf. 1947 *American College Dictionary,* s.v. *marijuana:* "t. Amer. sp.; ? native word, b. with name *Maria Juana,* Mary Jane"; some currency among jazzmen since c. 1950; see also BOO, GAGE, POT, TEA]

1943 *Time,* 19 July, p. 54. Marijuana may be called . . . Mary Jane.

1972 *The Worlds of Jazz,* p. 81. Mary-Jane nourished industrial man and was sown in rows.

master, *n.* [trade term; current since c. 1925; see also TAKE] Of the several recordings made of a particular piece, the one that is deemed most successful and is, therefore, the one offered for sale to the public; also, the original recording from which the pressing is made.

1949 *Music Library Association Notes,* Dec., p. 42. A recording artist *cuts* [i.e., records] a master.

1956 *The Genius of Charlie Parker* (liner notes on LP album Savoy MG-12014). Along with these new versions and short takes, we include some of the original masters to try to give you a more complete musical description of Charlie Parker's recording sessions and also to give you greater insight into his work.

mean, *adj.* [one of several standard terms from which the pejorative connotation has been removed and a favorable one substituted (see also BAD, HARD, TERRIBLE, TOUGH); current since c. 1900] Initially, earthy and primitive; also, by extension, since c. 1950: see 1957 quot.

1922 OKeh Records advertisement [1962 *Jazz: A History of the New York Scene*, p. 95.] And for mean harmony, don't overlook Handy's orchestra.

1931 *Melody Maker*, Dec., p. 1049. (record review in brief) General remarks: Fairly mean.

1954 *Ride Out*, p. 34. Just you play me some more of that mean piano.

1957 *N.Y. Times Magazine*, 18 Aug., p. 26. *mean:* the best, the greatest.

1970 *Roland Kirk: Here Comes the Whistleman* (LP liner notes). Del, I just got a record of a cat who is mean; a cat with that kind of talent deserves everything we can give him.

mellow, *adj.* [standard term used in a somewhat special sense by jazzmen c. 1935–c. 1945, rare since; see also FINE AND MELLOW] Pleasing, excellent.

1938 *Cab Calloway: Hi De Ho*, p. 16. *mellow:* all right, fine.

1946 *Really the Blues*, p. 188. Somebody lays a gentle, mellow phrase on you and it's like your memory crooking its finger.

1948 *Trumpet on the Wing*, p. 185. He thought his mellow chick . . . was dead.

mellow like a cello [from rhyming slang vogue c. 1935–c. 1940, rare since] Beautiful.

1957 *American Speech*, Dec., p. 276. Jazz lingo abounds in similes, e.g., *mellow like a cello.*

member, *n.* [by analogy of the black race with a formal organization; current since c. 1958; see also SOUL-BROTHER]

1962 *N.Y. Times Magazine*, 20 May, p. 45. *member:* a Negro.

mess, *n.* [somewhat varied uses of standard meaning (i.e., a jumble or hodgepodge); some currency among jazzmen since c. 1917; see also GANG, LOT] Many; also, by extension: excellent.

1938 *Cab Calloway: Hi De Ho*, p. 16. *mess:* something good. Example: "That last drink was a mess."

1959 *The Holy Barbarians*, p. 58. I saw . . . a whole mess of old men.

1961 *The Sound*, p. 177. Lot of other cats blow a mess of trumpet, high notes, fast runs, and all, but Red always tells a story.

message, *n.* [prob. from revival meetings (see also RIGHTEOUS, SOUL); also reinforced by analogy with verbal communication (see also SAYING SOMETHING, TELL A STORY, TRUTH); some currency since c. 1950] The feelings and attitudes communicated by music.

1952 *Metronome*, Dec., p. 15. "I got a message from Lester," George explains.

1957 *Down Beat*, 17 Oct., p. 15. But who needs words, man—they'll get the message.

1960 *The Jazz Word*, p. 33. The "message" doesn't always merit the attention.

1961 *Metronome*, Apr., p. 1. The Jazz message has proven itself strong enough to capture the ears and imaginations of peoples all over the world.

mess around, 1. [prob. suggested by sense 2; current during the dance's vogue, c. 1920–c. 1930, obs. since except historical, though parts of the dance survive in other-named dances] A jazz dance.

1962 *Ballroom Dance*, Feb., p. 5. Leon shows it's the same Mess Around he learned years back.

2. [special application of the standard meaning (i.e., to putter around); some currency c. 1925–c. 1940, obs. since]

1935 *His Hi De Highness of Ho De Ho*, p. 35. *messin' around:* to improvise.

1943 *Riverboat Jazz* (Brunswick Records pamphlet), p. 4. A clarinet trio . . . then plays . . . (after the injunction "Oh, mess around!").

mess with [somewhat varied use of its general colloquial sense (i.e., to trifle with); some currency since c. 1900] To trouble (oneself) with; to cheat; to interfere with.

1955 *Solo*, p. 27. And what little lady is going to mess with you?

1955 *Hear Me Talkin to Ya*, p. 374. The really good musicians are too smart to mess with it.

1956 *Sideman*, p. 416. Hell, ordinarily I'd be the last guy to mess with another guy's lovin'.

179

messy, *adj.* [expressive of jazzman's association of the disordered with the complex and his admiration for it (as opposed to the ordered but shallow); current c. 1935–c. 1945, rare since]

1945 *Hepcats Jive Talk Dictionary*, s.v. *messy:* extraordinary.

m.f., see s.v. MOTHER.

mice, *n. pl.* [by analogy with the sounds; according to jazzmen, some currency c. 1917–c. 1930 (obs. since) esp. in Chicago, where violins were commonly part of jazz bands] Violins. Oral evidence only.

mickey, Mickey Mouse, mouse [see 1958 quot. for semantic development; current since c. 1930] See 1947, 1958 quots.

1938 *Down Beat*, Apr., p. 25. A strictly "mickey-mouse" band is still box office.

1947 *The Musical Digest*, July, p. 25. *mickey band:* a type of popular orchestra, which plays commercial, uninspired jazz and/or swing. An orchestra like this represents the most inferior form of jazz. The species inhabits resorts and hotels for the sole purpose of furnishing music for dancing. The term "mickey," for some mysterious reason, is a shortened form of Mickey Mouse.

1958 *American Speech*, Oct., p. 225. A *mickey* or *Mickey Mouse* band is not merely a "pop tune" band . . . but the kind of band that sounds as if it is playing background for an animated cartoon.

1967 *Down Beat*, 5 Oct., p. 22. I don't play mouse music.

1974 *Village Voice*, 2 May, p. 73. In the potted palm/tea dance orchestras of F. Scott Fitzgerald's day, the tenor saxophone was a Mickey Mouse instrument with a cloying, saccharine sound.

moan (low) [special application of standard term; some currency c. 1915–c. 1945, very rare since] To play music or sing soulfully; for its adjective use, see 1922, 1934 quots.

1922 OKeh Records advertisement [1962 *Jazz: A History of the New York Scene*, p. 95.] If you crave those jazz moanin' blues, go get 'em on OKeh.

1929 *Moanin' Low* (tune written by Howard Dietz and Ralph Rainger).

1934 *Metronome*, Jan., p. 31. It was easier to play, easier to sing, and a real moanin' low number.

1941 *Strictly Ding-Dong*, p. 15. I gotta be moaning low before that gate begins to swing.

1954 *Basic Jazz on Long Play*, p. 43. She was the most powerful jazz vocalist that ever moaned the blues.

modern jazz [chiefly a writers' term; current since c. 1950; see also COOL JAZZ, PROGRESSIVE JAZZ] That jazz which embraces some or all of the harmonic and rhythmic developments innovated since c. 1945 (though the earliest period c. 1945–c. 1950 in modern jazz was called *bop,* q.v.: see 1955 quot.).

1955 *Say*, 28 Apr., p. 53. They're calling him [i.e., bop] "Modern Music" now. But he's the same cat who was making crazy sounds back in the '40s—only the critics didn't start cheering until he changed his name.

1961 *Commonweal*, 24 Mar., p. 657. A "cool" reaction to the clawing urgency of much modern jazz began in the late 1940s.

1961 *Metronome*, Apr., p. 12. By the 1950s "modern" jazz, as the more advanced developments were termed, had to free itself both from esoteric tendencies within jazz itself and from over-dependence on Western European classical traditions.

mojo, *n.* [acc. to lexicographer Peter Tamony, term has a complex voodoo origin as a good/bad luck-inducer; currency among black jazzmen c. 1920–c. 1935, rare since; see also JOINT] Penis.

1925 *Mojo Blues* (tune recorded by Lovie Austin's Blue Serenaders).

1930 *New Mojo Blues* (tune recorded by Barbecue Bob). I can't get no action out of this old mojo.

1932 *Keep Your Hand Off My Mojo* (tune recorded by Grant and Wilson).

1972 *Gorilla, My Love*, p. 164. Love charms are temporary things if your mojo ain't total.

moldy fig [by analogy with the shriveled and stale associations; current since c. 1946] See 1952, 1958, and first 1959 quots. (Sometimes shortened to *fig.*)

1947 *Metronome*, Nov., Moldy Figs vs. Moderns (article title).

1948 *Collier's*, 20 Mar., p. 88. The moldy figs . . . are certain that the greatest jazz ever played . . . was played in New Orleans in 1915.

1952 *A History of Jazz in America*, p. 351. *moldy fig:* a modernist's name for an ardent admirer of Dixieland jazz.

181

1958 *Publication of the American Dialect Society*, Nov., p. 46. *moldy fig*: one who likes or plays "traditional" jazz exclusively. . . . (Refers mostly to fans, not musicians.) Often abbr. *fig*.

1959 *The Sound of Surprise*, p. 211. The term "moldy fig," which is one of the aptest derogatory colloquialisms in the language, was first used in jazz to describe those who believe that the music has been in steady decline since around 1930.

1959 *The Collector's Jazz: Modern*, p. 11. But this bickering was nothing compared to the gulf that separated the adherents of bop [q.v.] and those the boppers derisively referred to as "moldy figs" (a term to which the unreconstructed "figs" have now adjusted so completely that they apply it to themselves with pride).

monkey, *n.* [cf. general slang *monkey suit* (i.e., tuxedo): it was customary in most bands for the leader alone to be dressed in a tuxedo; some currency esp. among white jazzmen c. 1925–c. 1940, obs. since]

1942 *The American Thesaurus of Slang*, p. 556. *monkey:* orchestra leader.

monster, *n.* [humorous hyperbole: i.e., an *inordinate* talent; current since c. 1968] A player (or performance) of unproportioned power and beauty.

1970 *Down Beat*, 17 Sep., p. 26. And Harry Carney, he's a monster, too.

1973 *Down Beat*, 29 Mar., p. 14. Charlie Parker was such a monster that we all gave up and switched to tenor.

1973 *Down Beat*, 11 Oct., p. 33. Woody's new album is an absolute MONSTER!!

Mooch, *n.* [cf. 1950 *Dictionary of American Underworld Lingo*, s.v. *mooch:* "to move about stealthily; to skulk"; current c. 1925–c. 1935, obs. since except historical, though the dance survives under other names; for synonymous names, see DRAG, SCRAUNCH] A slow, dragging dance.

1928 *The Mooch* (tune composed by Duke Ellington).

mood (music) [some currency since c. 1930] Initially, brooding, sophisticated music, most frequently associated with the Duke Ellington Orchestra; since c. 1945, most frequently, music that is insipid and pretentious.

182

1947 *Esquire's 1947 Jazz Book*, p. 5. The music America wanted was "mood."

1951 *Jazz* (Hentoff & McCarthy), p. 257. In the "blue" or "mood" category, Duke . . . penned . . . the immortal *Mood Indigo* of 1930.

1961 *Down Beat*, 12 Oct., p. 32. If "mood music" (whatever its style) is some sort of innocuousness, then this is not mood music.

1962 *Down Beat*, 29 Mar., p. 26. This is, in short, no pompous "jazz suite," "concerto," or warmed-over program stuff. Nor is it "mood" jazz.

mootah, mooter, muta, mu, *n.* [etym. unknown; some currency among jazzmen since c. 1930; see also BOO, GAGE, POT, TEA]

1943 *Time*, 19 July, p. 54. Marijuana may be called muggles, mooter, . . . mu.

1946 *Really the Blues*, p. 61. He kept waiting for a big train to pull in with a carload of muta.

1956 *Second Ending*, p. 249. The mootah had snapped the top of his wig.

1959 *The Jazz Scene*, p. 292. *muta:* marijuana.

mop! *interj.* [see 1952 quot. for prob. etym.; prob. reinforced by its assonance with *bop* (q.v.); jazz critic Martin Williams points out that *mop mop* refers to a double staccato drum beat which, when the first beat is lightened and shortened, becomes re-bop (q.v.); current from c. 1942–c. 1960, rare since] *Voila!*

1943 *Mop Mop* (tune recorded by Coleman Hawkins on Commodore C-548).

1952 *A History of Jazz in America*, p. 351. *mop!:* an exclamation of wide currency in the early forties which accurately described a musical device (the final beat in a cadence of triplets, usually bringing the release of a jazz composition to an end).

1959 *The Village Voice*, 28 Oct., p. 13. I wait a while, eyes closed, and I look, mop! I'm in the bathtub, all alone.

more, *adv. & adj.* [one of several terms denoting quantity in standard speech, but used by jazzmen to denote quality (see also GANG, LESS, LOT, THE MOST); some currency since c. 1950] Better.

1959 *The Horn*, p. 51. I can still . . . play more tenor than them.

1962 *Down Beat*, 26 Apr., p. 34. Howard McGhee was quoted recently as saying that Davis used to play "more."

1963 *Down Beat*, 29 Aug., p. 4. Is drummer X, for example, in New York playing more drums now than drummer Y in California?

most, the [one of several quantitative terms given a qualitative meaning by jazzmen (see also LEAST, LESS, LOT, MORE); current since c. 1950] The best.
1954 *Ride Out*, p. 30. "That's the most horn in the world," he said.
1954 *New Yorker*, 18 Sep., p. 30. I'm feeling the most today.
1961 *The Sound*, p. 102. I dig you the most that way.

mother, motheree, mothering, m.f., motherferyer, mother fucker, mother-fouler, mother-grabber, mother-hugger, mother jiver, mother-jumper, mother-lover, mother-sucker, mother superior, mammy jammer [all others are variants of *mother-fucker* and derive from *the dozens*, q.v.; though initially (c. 1900) an insult, the pejorative connotation is not always present since c. 1950 in this very common term; see also POPPA-STOPPA] Initially, an incestuous male; also, since c. 1950, anyone or anything that is formidable or extraordinary; also see first 1969 quot.
1946 *Really the Blues*, p. 10. A motherferyer that would cut your throat for looking. —p. 372. *mammy jamming*: incestuous obscenity.
1948 *Trumpet on the Wing*, p. 70. "I'll be a motheree if I'll wear any damn bedpan intern's suit," I screamed.
1952 *Invisible Man*, p. 469. Let the mother-fouler alone.
1955 *Solo*, p. 42. Hell, this mother never could blow.
1956 *Lady Sings the Blues*, p. 101. A mother-hugger was a mother-hugger.
1959 *The Naked Lunch*, p. 99. "Man, that mother-fucker's hungry," screams one of the Bearers.
1959 *The Jazz Review*, Sep., p. 7. You go and buy me a tenor saxophone and I'll play the m-f.
1959 *Esquire*, Nov., p. 70J. *mother jiver*: someone who cons or fools. Lately has taken on affectionate meaning and even a term of praise. Example: a bad mother jiver is an excellent musician.
1960 *N.Y. Citizen-Call*, 30 July, p. 19. Doctors, lawyers, businessmen and athletes, especially professional baseball players and jazz or cool school musicians, use the term, "M . . . ," as lingual crutches.
1960 *Hiparama of the Classics*, p. 16. Pen in hand, he was a Mother Superior. —p. 27. But The Gasser . . . made himself a connection that shook the whole Mother Peninsula!!

1961 *The Sound*, p. 61. I can remember 'em all, every motherin' one-night stop. —p. 106. That's just too mother much! —p. 285. Red really blew his mother-lovin' soul on that one.

1961 *Metronome*, Nov., pp. 32–33. Make no mistake. Hirt is a talent. A brilliant trumpeter. Not a Miles, not a Clark Terry. Not a jazz trumpeter. But a mother, nevertheless.

1962 *Americanisms.* "Mother-jumping" was reduced to the expurgatory abbreviation of "mother!"

1966 *The Wig*, p. 36. Man. The wind is a mother grabber.

1967 *Down Beat*, 2 Nov., p. 24. A mother superior vibist is Milt Jackson.

1969 *Hip Manual. mother:* friendly form of address. "There you go, mother."

1969 *The Life and Loves of Mr. Jiveass Nigger*, p. 200. He was up on his feet looking the mothersucking nigger in the face.

1974 *Down Beat*, 17 Jan., p. 30. Mutha' Englan'. Now there's a Mutha' fer y'.

mouse, see s.v. MICKEY.

move, *v.i.* [special application of the standard term; some earlier accidental use, but widely current only since c. 1950; see also SWING, *v.i.*] To by dynamic (usually, musically).

1955 *Down Beat*, 6 Apr., p. 15. The only time it does start to move is in the second chorus, with Charlie Shavers.

1958 *Jam Session*, p. 219. "It's got to move," jazzmen say. If it doesn't "swing," it's not jazz.

1960 *The Village Voice*, 20 Jan., p. 2. Norman swung into the obligato. His jacket was off and he was moving.

1961 *Down Beat*, 19 Jan., p. 3. It *moves*—like a Mardi Gras parade.

moving out [current since c. 1955] Starting to play (jazz) dynamically, imaginatively.

1954 *Movin' Out: Sonny Rollins with Thelonius Monk* (LP album Prestige PRL-7058).

1961 *The Sound*, p. 99. The Man's movin' out further than ever.

Mr. B. [not so important in jazz speech as some other nicknames (e.g., BIRD, LADY, PREZ, and SATCHMO), but fairly common since c. 1943] Billy Eckstine, 1914–   , jazz vocalist.

1948 *Mr. B's Blues* (song recorded by Billy Eckstine).
1950 *Life*, 24 Apr., p. 101. But Billy Eckstine, known to his fans as "Mr. B," tried this just once last week.

mu, *n.* See s.v. MOOTAH.

much, *adv.* [one of several terms denoting quantity in standard speech, but used by jazzmen to denote quality (see also GANG, LESS, MORE, THE MOST); current since c. 1935] Well.
1955 *Hear Me Talkin to Ya*, p. 352. I knew Monk when he played ten times as much as he does now.
1960 *Metronome*, Dec., p. 23. He gets a big kick out of playing, but you can never tell how *much* he's going to play.
1961 *The Sound*, p. 142. As for Red Travers' trumpet, there just isn't anyone in the field playing as much as he is right now.

mugging heavy (or **light, lightly**) [special application of vaudeville term *mugging* (i.e., grimacing); some currency c. 1930–c. 1940, obs. since]
1931 *Muggin' Lightly* (tune recorded by the Luis Russell Orchestra).
1936 *Delineator*, Nov., p. 49. *mugging light:* swing with a light beat. *mugging heavy:* swing with a heavy beat.

muggles, *n. pl.* [etym. unknown; some currency among jazzmen from c. 1925–c. 1945, rare since; see also BOO, GAGE, POT, TEA]
1928 *Muggles* (song recorded by Louis Armstrong).
1935 *His Hi De Highness of Ho De Ho*, p. 36. They [i.e., marijuana cigarettes] are also called "muggles."

muta, *n.* See s.v. MOOTAH.

mysterious, *adj.* [special application of the standard term; some currency since c. 1950; see also WEIRD] Profound, imaginative, original (usually applied to music or to a musician). (Note: occasionally the term is used in the sense of *too* imaginative—consequently, unintelligible; this is obviously the sense in which its use in the quots. is to be taken.)
1959 *Down Beat*, 14 May, p. 20. Sonny is no admirer of . . . musicians whose music is "too mysterious."
1963 *Down Beat*, 15 Aug., p. 31. It was interesting . . . but it was mysterious. The average human being who understands jazz, I don't believe, could interpret this.

N

name, *adj. & n.* [chiefly a trade term, taken from entertainment slang; current among jazzmen since c. 1930] (A) well-known (orchestra or musician).

1933 *Metronome,* June, p. 30. The small publishers are often more interested in "name" arrangers than big publishers.

1936 *Stage,* Mar., p. 58. *name bands:* famous orchestras.

1939 *Jazzmen,* p. 25. Robichaux's was for years the class "name band" of New Orleans.

1955 *A Pictorial History of Jazz,* p. 184. Teddy Wilson, a "name" after his Benny Goodman days, led various small units.

nasty, *adj.* [one of several pejorative terms in standard English (see also BAD, MEAN, TERRIBLE, TOUGH) to which a favorable connotation has been given by jazzmen, according to whom the term has been current c. 1917–c. 1945, rare since] Earthy; hence, excellent.

1940 *Swing,* July, p. 17. Very fast semi-boogie blues in Gabriel with nasty, heavy off-beat drumming.

1955 *Hear Me Talkin to Ya,* p. 295. Martha Raye . . . got hung up listening to Lincoln's nasty beat.

1960 *Dictionary of American Slang,* s.v. *nasty:* excellent; "wicked"; "mean."

natural, *adj.* [according to jazzmen, some currency esp. among black jazzmen, since c. 1930] Intensifying word (as in "beat to my natural socks"). Oral evidence only.

New Orleans [after its place of origin; current since c. 1917; see also

DIXIELAND] Jazz (style) from c. 1900, which became somewhat old-fashioned with the advent of swing (c. 1935) and extremely old-fashioned with the advent of bop (c. 1945).

1905 *New Orleans Blues* (tune composed by Jelly Roll Morton, copyright 1927).

1922 *New Orleans Rhythm Kings* (name of jazz band).

1946 *Disc*, Nov. Jazz is improvising in the old New Orleans way, with the kick on the first and third beats.

1947 *The Musical Digest*, July, p. 24. This quality of altering accents, with regard for and in relation to each other, is the essence of the work of New Orleans musicians.

1956 *Guide to Jazz*, p. 195. The New Orleans style is characterized in its rhythm by a very marked accentuation of the beat, though without any heaviness. This regular and supple stress . . . is what gives performances in the New Orleans style an easy, lazy rhythmic quality. Collective improvisation predominates in New Orleans-style playing.

new thing, the [some currency from c. 1960–c. 1968, rare since] The more experimental music of the 1960s, esp. that played by such musicians as Ornette Coleman, Cecil Taylor, Eric Dolphy, and John Coltrane.

1962 *Down Beat*, 12 Apr., p. 20. The anti-jazz term was picked up by Leonard Feather and used as a basis for critical essays of Coltrane, Dolphy, Ornette Coleman, and the "new thing" in general.

1962 *Down Beat*, 5 July, p. 28. It may be that the "new thing"—if such exists—is not so new after all.

1966 *Down Beat*, 2 June, p. 36. It was the public and the critics that put labels on it. Avant garde, "new thing."

nickel (note) [understatement; prob. from gamblers slang; some currency esp. among black jazzmen since c. 1940; see also CENT, DIME]

1944 *Dan Burley's Original Handbook of Harlem Jive*, p. 144. *nickel note:* a five dollar bill.

1946 *Big Book of Swing*, p. 124. *nickel:* $5.

1971 *Bird Lives*, p. 262. I only hit him for a nickel note, man!

nitty gritty [from black slang; prob. formed from *nits* and *grits;* current among jazzmen from c. 1960–c. 1970, when it moved into more general slang use]

1964 *Down Beat*, 4 June, p. 7. The nitty gritty is, and always has been, truth.

1970 *Dictionary of Afro-American Slang*, p. 85. *nitty-gritty:* unvarnished facts, underbelly of a situation; core: the basics.

nod, *n. & v.i.* [cf. standard meaning (i.e., of the head, to fall forward involuntarily because of drowsiness); cf. narcotics slang: 1953 *Junkie*, p. 14. *"On the nod:* full of junk"; current among jazzmen since c. 1930] See 1958 and 1959 quots; by extension, to be inattentive.

1938 *Cab Calloway: Hi De Ho*, p. 16. *nod:* sleep. Example: "I think I'll cop a nod."

1958 *Southern Folklore Quarterly*, Sep., p. 132. *nodding:* succumbing to a drug.

1959 *Esquire*, Nov., p. 70J. *on the nod:* sleeping, usually in a standing or sitting position.

1974 *Down Beat*, 14 Mar., p. 26. Tootie seems to be nodding in spots.

no eyes, see s.v. EYES.

noodle, *v.i.* [etym. unknown: poss. by analogy with a standard noun meaning (i.e., a fool; ergo, v.i., to fool around musically), more prob. by assonance with *doodle;* some currency since c. 1935] To play (music) in a tentative, exploratory, and sometimes desultory manner (see 1942 quot.); also, for its rare noun use, see 1958 quot.

1940 *Noodlin'* (tune recorded by the Willie the Lion Smith Orchestra on General 1712).

1942 *The American Thesaurus of Slang*, p. 565. *noodle:* idle elaboration.

1957 *Nugget*, Dec., p. 5. Every time a jazz musician noodles a passable break these days he is followed by a show of bravura on an open Underwood fingered by a jazz writer.

1958 *The Jazz Review*, Nov., p. 25. My one complaint is that Monk here allows too many of his favorite piano "noodles" (all pianists seem to have them).

1959 *Blow Up a Storm*, p. 8. I noodled around: filling in or playing rhythm figures, and sometimes locking in harmonically with him for a phrase or break.

nothing happens (or shakes) [overstatement; *nothing happening* current

189

since c. 1950; see also HAPPENINGS, SHAKING] Nothing *important* (usually, musically) is happening; whatever is happening is disappointing, unexciting.

1952 *Flee the Angry Strangers*, p. 319. Nothing's happening, Luke.

1960 *The Jazz Word*, p. 109. There's not really a living ass to talk to, and there's nothing shaking.

1960 *Sal Salvador: The Beat for This Generation* (liner notes on LP album Decca DL 74026). No matter how good your sidemen may be individually, nothing will happen if they can't play together.

1961 *The Jazz Review*, Jan., p. 31. Mr. Barnet plays his three saxes serially . . . but otherwise there ain't nothing at all happening.

nowhere, *adj.* [by analogy of a geographic limbo with a spiritual one; widely current since c. 1935] Unhappy, lost, frustrated, undesirable, valueless (see also 1946 quot.).

1942 *American Mercury*, July, p. 86. I ain't nowhere.

1946 *Really the Blues*, p. 373. nowhere: insignificant, broke.

1948 *Trumpet on the Wing*, p. 10. I got to have music or I'm nowhere.

1956 *Jive Jungle*, p. 31. "Aren't they the worst!" "Nowhere!"

1960 *The Jazz Titans*, p. 161. nowhere: the absolute of nothing.

like (Jack) the bear (just ain't nowhere) [part of c. 1935–c. 1940 rhyming slang vogue; some currency c. 1938–c. 1942, very rare since]

1942 *American Mercury*, July, p. 86. Oh, just like de bear—I ain't nowhere.

1946 *Really the Blues*, p. 372. like Jack the Bear: worthless, no-account, broke, insignificant.

nutted out [from general slang *nutty* (i.e., insane) + jazz slang suffix *out;* current since c. 1965] Lost one's rationality.

1966 *Black Music: Four Lives*, p. 93. I just nutted out, and started playing all the things I could think of to the changes without touching the melody.

nutty, *adj. & interj.* [colloquial variant of *crazy,* q.v.; current since c. 1950; see also INSANE, MAD]

1955 *Bop Fables*, p. 12. "Nutty," said the papa bear.

1959 *Newport Jazz Festival: 1959*, p. 45. nutty: excellent.

1963 *Nugget*, Feb., p. 46. She had seen me around and thought that the jazz musician syndrome was kinda nutty.

O

O [abbreviation; from underworld and narcotics slang; some currency among jazzmen since c. 1935]

1934 *A Dictionary of American Slang*, p. 28. *O:* opium.

ofay, *n.* See s.v. FAY.

off beat cymbal [so-called because cymbal was struck on the off beat in traditional jazz; some currency c. 1917–c. 1940, obs. since; see also SOCK CYMBAL] A cymbal struck by the drummer on off beats in much traditional (pre-c. 1935) jazz.

1936 *Metronome*, Feb., p. 61. *off beat cymbal:* sock cymbal.

off note [from its being slightly "off" normal pitch; according to jazzman Eubie Blake, some currency since c. 1900; see also BLUE NOTE]

1955 *The First Book of Jazz*, p. 20. These blue notes are "off notes," just a little bit flat and in between the usual notes. They most often are a somewhat flatted third or seventh note of the scale. They are impossible to show in written music, although they are sometimes indicated as flatted notes.

1964 *New Yorker*, 25 Jan., pp. 99–100. These soon fade into rocky chords, decorated with jarring trills and off-notes.

1966 *New Yorker*, 25 June, p. 33. His solos are full of unexpected off-notes.

oldie, *n.* [formed on colloquial pattern of making a *n.* from an *adj.* by adding *-ie, -y;* according to jazzman Eubie Blake, current since c. 1900]

1942 *The American Thesaurus of Slang*, p. 560. *oldie:* an old tune.

191

1961 *Jazz Journal*, May, p. 35. Another "oldie" is "Four in One," one of his weirdest and most angular themes in the bop idiom.

old lady [cf. its general colloquial meaning (i.e., wife); current among jazzmen in a general slang meaning since c. 1900, in an additional meaning since c. 1935] Initially, see 1960 quot.; also, since c. 1935, a female lover.

1926 *Melody Maker*, Oct., p. 13. He is . . . answered by the words "So does your Old Lady," as his better half, emerging from her concealment, grips him by the ear.

1960 *Dictionary of American Slang*, s.v. *old lady:* a wife, esp. one's own.

old man [cf. its general colloquial meaning (i.e., husband); current among jazzmen in a general slang meaning since c. 1900, in an additional meaning since c. 1935] Initially, see 1960 quot.; also, since c. 1935, a male lover.

1957 *On the Road*, p. 203. Her old man can come in any hour of the night.

1960 *Dictionary of American Slang*, s.v. *old man:* a husband, esp. one's own.

on, *adj.* [prob. from colloquial *to be onto something* (i.e., to be aware of something); according to jazzmen, some currency c. 1945–c. 1950, obs. since; see also DOWN, HIP] Aware, sophisticated.

1970 *Dictionary of Afro-American Slang*, p. 88. *on;* (1940s–50s) informed; sophisticated; "in."

be (or get) on (something) [special application of colloquial use of the *prep.*; widely current since c. 1950] Under the influence of or addicted to liquor, marijuana, or other narcotics.

1955 *Hear Me Talkin to Ya*, p. 372. For an example of a guy who got on, there was Stan Getz.

1960 *The Sound*, p. 20. But let's get on first.

1961 *Swank*, July, p. 58. By the time Bird was 25 he had been on for nearly ten years.

on the scene, see s.v. SCENE.

on top of the beat, see s.v. TOP.

one-night stand, one-nighter [see 1949 quot. for explanation of semantic development; *stand* (i.e., engagement) is borrowed from theater use; current c. 1925–c. 1945, somewhat less since]

1939 *One Night Stand* (tune recorded by the Artie Shaw Orchestra).

1949 *Music Library Association Notes*, Dec., p. 47. *one-nighters:* series of dates or bookings providing for one-night appearances in theatres, nite clubs, or hotel rooms. It's travel all day, perform all night—a grueling schedule. Also known as "one-night" stands.

1961 *Night Song*, p. 100. Sandwiches and one-night stands, blowing before some hicks who won't even know who it is they're listening to.

oo-bla (-dee), oo-bop-she-bam, oo(l)-ya-koo, oo-pa-pa-da (and variant spellings) [from bop singing (see first 1955 quot.); these nonsense-syllable words all reflect bop (q.v.) musicians' impish irreverence for conventional communication (linguistic as well as musical); current c. 1945–c. 1955, rare since; see also EEL-YA-DAH] Nonsense words.

1946 *Oo-Bop-She-Bam* (tune composed and recorded by Dizzy Gillespie).

1949 *In the Land of Oo-Bla-Dee* (tune composed by Mary Lou Williams and Milton Orent).

1949 *Down Beat*, 20 May, p. 16. "Let's jump!" they cried. "Give us a break, will ya!" and "Oo-ya-koo!"

1951 *Ebony*, Oct., p. 34. "You will thank me for hepping [i.e., enlightening] you to this oolyakooing.". . . "Gently ease it out of casing," advises the poobah of oo-bop-she-bam.

1955 *The First Book of Jazz*, p. 55. Sometimes for fun, singers sing "oo-ya-koo" syllables to boppish backgrounds today, as Cab Calloway in the 1930s sang "hi-de-hi-de-ho-de-hey," meaning nothing, or as Lionel Hampton sang "hey-baba-re-bop" in 1940.

1955 *Bob Fables*, p. 17. Once upon a time many years ago, in the land of Oppoppadow, there lived three little pigs.

1956 *Lady Sings the Blues*, p. 207. She told him we couldn't speak the language, she could, and oo-pa-pa-da, we needed someone to help us.

1959 *The Horn*, p. 128. Man, loot is just around the oob-la.

1971 *The Street That Never Slept*, p. 270. Polysyllables like "oolya-koo," "oo-bop-sh-bam," "oo-pappa-da" and "be-bop"—all devices used by the musicians to indicate accents and suggest durations.

oowee (and variant spellings), *interj.* [deliberately childlike exclamation; current since c. 1945] Expression of extreme delight (or excitement).

1955 *Solo*, p. 25. Mahn, but he blows up a storm. . . . Ooooweee.

1960 *Jazz: A Quarterly of American Music*, Winter, p. 47. I was THUNDERSTRUCK. I couldn't say a word. He gasses me. Oooooooo-weeeeee!

1965 *A Drop of Patience*, p. 87. Ooo-eee! If Mama only knew that.

open (horn) [current since c. 1925] Unmuted (trumpet).

1926 *Melody Maker*, Mar., p. 30. For such occasions nothing is better suited to obtain a highly successful result than the beautiful, sweet full tone of the open instrument, and I advise all artistes to try a few "open" solos.

1942 *The American Thesaurus of Slang*, p. 563. *open:* without mechanical mutes.

1955 *Hear Me Talkin to Ya*, p. 234. The Western style was more open . . . open horns and running chords and running changes.

1958 *Shorty Rogers and His Giants: Shorty in Stereo* (liner notes on LP album Atlantic SC 1232). I would just like to point out . . . his jabbing, stabbing open horn solo in "Dickie's Dream."

open (tone) [prob. by analogy with *open (horn)*, (i.e., with its full, unmuted sound); some currency since c. 1930] Full (tone).

1942 *The American Thesaurus of Slang*, p. 563. *open:* without . . . affected tone.

1955 *Hear Me Talkin to Ya*, p. 287. And Knight had such a great big, open tone on alto.

opener, *n.* [special application of its general colloquial meaning (i.e., that which "opens"—i.e., begins—a performance); current since c. 1935] The first chorus of a tune or the first tune of a set (q.v.).

1949 *Down Beat*, 11 Mar., p. 15. "Frost" is a simple but fairly bright arrangement with a good opener.

1961 *Down Beat*, 13 Apr., p. 36. "Orbit," the brisk opener, finds Jones blowing open horn.

organ (chords) [see 1956 quot. for semantic development; according to jazzman Eubie Blake, some currency c. 1900–c. 1945, very rare since] See 1956 quot.

1927 *Melody Maker*, June, p. 533. The sweetness of his sustained notes when playing his part in "organ" harmony is a sheer delight.

1956 *Guide to Jazz*, p. 206. *organ chords:* basic chords of the blues, so called because they're the same harmonies common to most Protestant hymns.

original, *n.* [special application of standard term; current since c. 1935] A tune composed by a member of the performing troupe (as distinguished from a *standard,* q.v.).

1940 *Swing,* Nov., p. 27. The Will Oshborne-Dick Rogers original on the back starts with some superb reed work.

1955 *Hear Me Talkin to Ya,* p. 383. And they're recording more originals now.

other man, (the) [i.e., *not* one of us; prob. from 19th-century black term *other folks;* now general black slang but, according to jazz dancer Leon James, originated by and current among black jazzmen since c. 1945] A white man (frequently a storekeeper, hence the definition offered in the quot.).

1962 *N.Y. Times Magazine,* 20 May, p. 45. *other man:* the liquor dealer.

out, *adj.* [shortened form of *knocked out,* q.v., reinforced by *far out,* q.v.; current since c. 1942] Excellent; also, since c. 1950: imaginative, experimental.

1959 *Jazz for Moderns,* p. 20. *out:* far out.

1965 *Down Beat,* 25 Mar., p. 28. Woody's always had hot saxophone players, but these guys can double [q.v.] out.

1966 *Down Beat,* 24 Feb., p. 26. The rhythm section is just too much. They take it out, out.

1969 *Hip Manual.* "They blow out sounds."

out (chorus) [current since c. 1925; see also ALL-IN, EVERY TUB, LET'S GO HOME, RIDE-OUT] The final (chorus); also, see 1937 quot.

1937 *American Speech,* Feb., p. 47. *out:* to finish a chorus during a jam session. The cry to the player is, "Go on out."

1956 *Sideman,* p. 312. Matt called "Out!" and the band hit the out-chorus.

1961 *Down Beat,* 13 Apr., p. 36. Frameworks for the blowing are in the familiar mold of stated theme, solos in turn, and out chorus.

1963 *Down Beat,* 20 June, p. 31. The brass section struts gloriously in the out chorus.

195

1965 *Down Beat*, 17 June, p. 36. I am sort of waiting till they take it out.

out of it [current since c. 1955] Not included in the activity or in life; not important; not participating.

1961 *Artesian*, Winter, p. 23. I knew that I was a bizarre and unacceptable character when I was a child and that I would always be out of it.

1962 *Down Beat*, 15 Mar., p. 25. And people who say this guy is better than that guy, that this guy is completely out of it—musicians don't even judge like that.

out of sight [extension of *far out, way out,* q.v.; some earlier general slang use: cf. 1924 *All God's Chillun Got Wings*, Act I, Sc. I. "It's purty. Yes, it's—it's purty. It's—outa sight."; current among jazzmen since c. 1958] Extremely advanced; excellent.

1961 *Down Beat*, 5 Jan., p. 23. Frankly, I find some of the musicians I've encountered on the road rather ridiculous. They're like children, the way they dress, the way they talk. It seems everything is "something else" these days. Or is it "out of sight"?

1963 *Down Beat*, 20 June, p. 35. This record is out of sight.

out of (one's) skull [jazz slang variant of general slang *out of (one's) head*; current since c. 1950; see also WIG, LOOSE WIG] Insane, or so intoxicated as to be virtually insane.

1955 *Bop Fables*, p. 9. You're out of your skull.

1961 *Down Beat*, 19 Jan., p. 22. The cat . . . *finds you*, usually out of your skull in Junior's.

1961 *Metronome*, Feb., p. 41. Well, man, we might get out of our skulls now and then.

out of this (or the) **world, out-of-this-world** [see 1959 quot. for semantic explanation; current c. 1925–c. 1945, obs. since except historical; see also GONE, OUT OF SIGHT]

1928 *The Walls of Jericho*, p. 303. *out (of) this world:* beyond mortal experience or belief.

1931 *The Inter-State Tattler*, 17 Dec., p. 12. Alberta Hunter . . . warbles out of this world.

1937 *Mademoiselle*, Mar., p. 68. And Bunny, his eyes closed, is playing out-of-this-world.

1959 *Jazz: A Quarterly of American Music,* Fall, p. 284. The power of musicians of skill to transport is verbalized in *send me.* . . . It is little wonder that swing devotees . . . on the general observations of music as "heavenly" and "melody of the spheres," proclaimed they were sent—propelled by the centrifugal force *out of the world.*

outside [current since c. 1955] Of an instrumentalist, departed from ("outside") the established chord structure of a tune.

1973 *Down Beat,* 15 Mar., p. 16. Today you can go outside, way outside.

over (an instrument), be (or get) (all) [by analogy with the dexterous mobility demanded of the instrumentalist; current since c. 1955; see also GET AROUND ON (ONE'S) HORN, HAVE IT COVERED] To play (an instrument) with great virtuosity.

1960 *The Jazz Review,* Nov., p. 12. You know how the guy got all over that alto.

1961 *Down Beat Record Reviews,* p. 176. Sonny is all over both his horns, communicating directly and deeply.

1961 *The Sound,* p. 47. He gets over the piano and he knows a lot of music.

1962 *Down Beat,* 22 Nov., p. 30. He soon falls into a series of arpeggios, which show how well he can get over his horn, but there are no sustained ideas.

o.z. [standard abbreviation for *ounce,* but not pronounced as an acronym; some currency among jazzmen since c. 1935] Ounce (usually, of marijuana).

1942 *American Thesaurus of Slang,* p. 474. *o.z.:* ounce.

1959 *The Horn,* p. 224. It had been something in his mind that two o.z.'s of ripe Pachuco pot [i.e., marijuana] had brought out.

P

pad, *n.* [the more common meaning was formed by synecdoche: cf. 1811 *Dictionary of the Vulgar Tongue,* s.v. *pad:* "a bed"; widely current since c. 1935; see also CRIB, DOMMY] A room or an apartment; also, rare: a bed.

1938 *Cab Calloway: Hi De Ho,* p. 16. *pad:* bed.

1939 *Fortune,* July, p. 170. There are reefer pads (marijuana dens).

1946 *Really the Blues,* p. 373. *pad:* joint, place to enjoy yourself, bed.

1959 *The Holy Barbarians,* p. 26. Young people . . . hole up in pads in the slums and listen to jazz music.

panatella, panatela, *n.* [by analogy with the expensive cigar; some currency among jazzmen since c. 1935] Top-grade marijuana.

1956 *Lady Sings the Blues,* p. 53. Jimmy's got the best panatella you ever smoked in your life.

1959 *Panatela* (tune recorded by the Woody Herman Orchestra on a Jazzland LP, *The Fourth Herd*).

papa, *n.* See s.v. POPS.

paper, *n.* [according to jazzmen, current c. 1900–c. 1945, rare since; see also CHARTS] Sheet music.

1938 *Down Beat,* July. We don't use paper on a lot of our standards.

1969 *Down Beat,* 26 June, p. 18. But for the rhythm section, the paper is mainly a guide.

paper man [according to jazzman Eubie Blake, current c. 1900–c. 1945, rare since] See 1942 quot. (Note: by jazzmen's standards, a derisive term)

1936 *Metronome*, Feb., p. 21. *paper man:* drummer who plays only what's written.

1942 *The American Thesaurus of Slang*, p. 555. *paper man:* a musician who does not improvise, but reproduces the score faithfully.

1969 *The Story of the Original Dixieland Jazz Band*, p. 13. For the most part New Orleans musicians fell into three categories: (1) the "paper men" who could not play by ear. . . .

paradiddle, *n.* [onomatopoeic; current since c. 1917] A basic drum roll.

1934 *Metronome*, Feb., p. 47. Either the single paradiddle or the flam paradiddle may be used during a march step.

party piano (style) [from origin of the piano style (see RENT PARTY); some currency c. 1920–c. 1940, very rare since; see also BOOGIE-WOOGIE] A boogie-woogie piano style—i.e., eight-to-the-bar rhythm, with a twelve-measure blues pattern for a theme.

1942 *The Jazz Record Book*, p. 81. The "party piano" style, a growth that owes more to oldtime blues playing than to any other one source, was already a flourishing development in the 1930s.

Pasmala, Pasamala, *n.* [see 1968 quot. for etym.; see first quot. for beginning date; very rare since c. 1917] Jazz dance in vogue c. 1898–c. 1917.

1934 *Beale Street: Where the Blues Began*, p. 105. The Pasamala was a ragtime dance which originated, according to Isaac Goldberg, in tin pan alley, at about the same time as the bombershay, in 1898, in which the girls chanted as they danced: "Fust you do a rag, then you bombershay—/Do a sidestep, dip, then you go the other way,/Shoot along the line with a Pasamala,/Back, back, back—don't you go too far!"

1968 *Jazz Dance*, p. 100. A traditional dance-song entitled "La Pas Ma La" (Isaac Goldberg says that the phrase comes from the French *pas mêlé*, or mixed step) was published in 1895—perhaps the dance introduced by Ernest Hogan and his *Georgia Graduates* as the Pasmala.

pay (one's) dues, see S.V. DUES.

peck, the [by analogy with the darting, sporadic movement (see 1955 quot.); some currency since c. 1950]

1955 *Know Your Jazz* (Vol. I), (liner notes on LP album ABC-Para-

199

mount ABC 115). Charlie Rouse plays in a fast, choppy, aggressive style appropriately called "the peck." This is a rhythmic approach that actually amounts to pecking out fast melodic spurts.

1957 *New York Jazz Festival: 1957*, p. 19. "The Peck," a highly abbreviated and syncopated variation of the ideas of Charlie Parker, has been one way of stating music with profundity rather than slickness.

peck horn [according to jazzmen, the term originates from the "oom-pah," pecking-like sound made by the horn; according to jazzman Eubie Blake, some currency since c. 1900]

1942 *The American Thesaurus of Slang*, p. 558. *peck horn:* an alto horn or mellophone.

1966 *New Yorker*, 25 June, p. 46. From the age of eight I played the upright alto—the peck horn—in my father's band.

pecking, peckin', *n.* [from the pecking-like movement of the dance; current c. 1937–c. 1945, rare since] See note above and 1944 quot.

1938 *Pic*, 5 Apr., p. 29. Lindy Hop, Big Apple, Little Peach, Shag, Suzy Q, Peckin', every kind of dance ever invented is seen on the floor of the Savoy Saturday night.

1944 *The New Cab Calloway's Hepsters Dictionary*, s.v. *pecking:* a dance introduced at the Cotton Club in 1937.

adj. See s.v. PECK, THE.

peep, *v.i.* [according to jazzmen, from black slang; current esp. among black jazzmen since c. 1940]

1970 *Dictionary of Afro-American Slang*, p. 90. *peep:* (1940s) in jazz, to read sheet music.

peep on [according to jazzmen, from black slang; some currency esp. among black jazzmen since c. 1930] To look at.

1970 *Dictionary of Afro-American Slang*, p. 90. *peep:* to see, esp. with great understanding.

P.I. [from first two letters of the standard term; cf. 1950 *Slang Today and Yesterday*, p. 454: "P.I.: a pimp (-1900)"; underworld and some general slang use, but also with some currency among jazzmen since c. 1900]

1955 *Hear Me Talkin to Ya*, p. 12. P.I.'s (that's what we called pimps). —p. 117. One night we saw a P.I. (one who lives and makes money from women) stabbed.

piano kid [so called because they were usually young (i.e., in their teens); according to jazzman Eubie Blake, some currency c. 1900–c. 1917, obs. since except historical; see also the more common PROFESSOR] A pianist in any of the cabarets or brothels of New Orleans, New York, Memphis, etc., c. 1900–c. 1917.

1974 *Frontiers of Jazz*, p. 171. His first full-time job was that of "piano kid" at Barron Wilkins' cabaret in New York.

pic, piccolo, *n.* [prob. corruption of *victrola; piccolo* current c. 1930–c. 1945, rare since; *pic* current since c. 1940; see also BOX, sense 3]

1938 *N.Y. Amsterdam News*, 12 Mar., p. 17. The Harlem Hamfats grind out the tune on myriad Harlem piccolos.

1939 *Fortune*, July, p. 170. A piccolo is a nickel-in-the-slot victrola.

1944 *Dan Burley's Original Handbook of Harlem Jive*, p. 145. *piccolo:* juke box, music machine.

pick cherries [from similarity of arm movements; current c. 1920–c. 1930, obs. since] To execute a dance step in vogue c. 1920–c. 1930; also the accompanying drum, guitar or bass solo.

1926 *Nigger Heaven*, p. 242. Pull 'em down! Pick cherries!

picker, *n.* [from the picking movement; according to jazzman Eubie Blake, current since c. 1900] A player or plucker of a stringed instrument (usually bass or guitar).

1944 *Chicago Documentary*, p. 8. That's the bass picker from the jazz band!

pick style [according to jazzmen, some currency since c. 1920] Guitar-playing with a pick or plectrum, as distinguished from "finger-style." Oral evidence only.

pickup, *n.* [cf. standard meaning (i.e., acceleration); current since c. 1930] Musical anacrusis—i.e., the introductory notes leading into the first note of a chorus or tune.

1934 *All About Jazz*, p. 65. After a short passage of one or two bars, as a "pick up," the ensemble will then take the last chorus and coda.

1956 *Sideman*, p. 150. Bernie took pickups into "Laura."

pick-up, *adj.* [a special application of colloquial term; current since c. 1935]

1941 *Gems of Jazz: Vol. 3* (Decca Records pamphlet), p. 3. This unique session features one of the best all-star line-ups ever assembled for a "pick-up" band.

1956 *Guide to Jazz,* s.v. *pick-up band* (or *group*): a group formed of musicians who regularly play elsewhere, but who come together for a special purpose. e.g., a recording date, a broadcast, a concert, a short nightclub engagement.

pick up (on), 1. [correlative of jazz slang *put down,* q.v. (see 1956 quot.) in the sense of taking or being capable (by virtue of intelligence) of taking whatever is available; widely current since c. 1935] See 1959 quot.

1944 *Dan Burley's Original Handbook of Harlem Jive,* p. 15. Let me boot you to my play [i.e., inform you of my plan] and, maybe, you can pick up on the issue.

1956 *Sideman,* p. 291. No, man . . . you're just not picking up what I'm putting down.

1959 *Esquire,* Nov., p. 70J. *to pick up on:* to obtain, to find. To understand, appreciate.

1960 *Hiparama of the Classics,* p. 8. The snakes in the jungle picked up on the beat and came stompin' in.

2. [special application of sense 1; some currency since c. 1935]

1946 *Really the Blues,* p. 373. *pick up on:* smoke marijuana.

1957 *On the Road,* p. 88. The connection came in and . . . said, "Pick up, man, pick up."

piece, *n.* [special application of standard meaning; current since c. 1900; see also AX, HORN] A musical instrument.

1933 *Metronome,* Jan., p. 34. In making stock arrangements I write for the 10-piece combination and then add the extra parts later.

1955 *Hear Me Talkin to Ya,* p. 197. Most of the time the bands in the taxi dance halls had six or seven pieces.

pink, *n.* [from general black slang, but with esp. currency among black jazzmen c. 1900–1940, rare since; see also FAY, GRAY]

1926 *Nigger Heaven,* p. 157. Funny thing about those pink-chasers [i.e., Negroes who deliberately seek out white companions], the ofays [i.e., white people] never seem to have any use for them.

1942 *American Thesaurus of Slang,* p. 358. *pink:* white person.

pipe, *n.* [from the shape; note: *agony pipe* for clarinet and *gobble pipe* for saxophone, both listed in several glossaries of the 1930s are, according to jazzmen, specious; some slight currency esp. among white jazzmen since c. 1935; see also PLUMBING] Any wind or reed instrument.

1936 *Metronome*, Feb., p. 61. *pipe:* sax.

1942 *The American Thesaurus of Slang*, p. 558. *pipe:* clarinet.

1955 *Say*, 28 Apr., p. 53. *pipe:* a trumpet.

big pipe [some currency since c. 1955; see also BARI]

1959 *Jazz for Moderns*, p. 21. *big pipe:* baritone sax.

small pipe [some currency since c. 1955]

1959 *Jazz for Moderns*, p. 21. *small pipe:* alto saxophone.

pitch a ball, see s.v. BALL.

pitch a bitch, see s.v. BITCH.

play, *n.* [from gambling and underworld slang: cf. 1929 *The Dain Curse* (New York: Permabooks reprint, 1961), p. 124. " 'That's the wrong play,' I said"; poss. also reinforced by the football term; current since c. 1930] The plan, scheme, proposal, idea.

1944 *Dan Burley's Original Handbook of Harlem Jive*, p. 15. Let me boot you to my play, and, maybe, you can pick up on the issue.

1946 *Really the Blues*, p. 63. Now-or-never was the play.

play a part [from the standard theater phrase; some general slang use, but esp. current among jazzmen since c. 1935] To assume a personality; to pretend to be a particular social type.

1960 *The Jazz Word*, p. 213. If a man can play the blues from inside himself without straining to play a part, he's a legitimate jazzman.

play (one's) ass off, see s.v. BLOW (ONE'S) ASS OFF.

play (someone) down [current c. 1930–c. 1945, obs. since except historical; see also BLOW (SOMEONE) DOWN, CARVE, CUT] To defeat in musical competition (see CUTTING CONTEST).

1955 *Hear Me Talkin to Ya*, p. 25. Bands in those days . . . play each other down.

play it cool [from jazz slang *play a part* and jazz slang *cool;* some currency since c. 1947]

1954 *Confidential*, Sep., p. 19. "Man, I tried to play it cool," Erskine said.

1959 *The Beat Generation Dictionary*, s.v. *play it cool:* be cautious, be smart.

1959 *Selected Poems*, Langston Hughes, p. 234. I play it cool/And dig all jive.

play on the line [according to jazzmen, some currency c. 1900–c. 1917, obs. since except historical] To play music in the various cafés and/or brothels c. 1900–c. 1916 along New Orleans' main entertainment street, Basin Street.

1947 *Jazz Forum*, Apr., p. 5. The expression "playing on the line" indicates the essentially migrant and transient thrusts of the journeyman rag players.

play that thing [see jazz slang *thing;* current c. 1925–c. 1940, very rare since] Play that music, play that instrument: frequently, hortatory (see first quot.).

1948 *The Record Changer*, June, p. 6. Appeals to "play that thing" might not be necessary then.

1948 *Trumpet on the Wing*, p. 100. Man, he could really play that thing.

plenty, *adj.* [one of several quantitative terms given a qualitative meaning by jazzmen (see also LESS, MORE, MUCH); according to jazzman Eubie Blake, current c. 1900–c. 1940, obs. since] Excellent.

1933 *Fortune*, Aug., p. 47. Mr. Brown plays plenty trombone.

1941 *So It Doesn't Whistle*, p. 53. When they want to say a man's good, they say he plays plenty sax or plenty drums.

plumbing, *n.* [from the shape; some currency esp. among white jazzmen since c. 1930; see also PIPE] See 1942 quot.

1935 *Vanity Fair*, Nov., p. 71. *plumbing:* trumpet.

1942 *The American Thesaurus of Slang*, p. 558. *plumbing:* wind instruments.

1951 *Cosmopolitan*, July, p. 85. Hap said "You with the plumbin', what's your name?"

1955 *Vogue*, 15 Sep., p. 124. Kai Winding and J. J. Johnson . . . pair their spruce, understated trombones ("just plumbing") against a backing of bass, drums, and piano.

pod, *n.* See s.v. POT.

poke, *n.* [prob. by analogy with *hit,* q.v.; some currency among jazzmen since c. 1940; see also TOKE] A puff (of marijuana).

1956 *Sideman,* p. 274. He exhaled, "Sure you don't want a poke?"

pop, *adj. & n.* [from *popular;* chiefly trade term but with some currency among jazzmen since c. 1930; see also STANDARD] See first 1956 quot.

1933 *Metronome,* Dec., p. 31. Pop songs will go along with modern music.

1940 *Swing,* Jan., p. 24. These two pops didn't inspire Benny to any miracles of orchestration.

1956 *Guide to Jazz,* s.v. *pop:* a popular number, a tune enjoying a success with the large public. If it stands the test of time it becomes a "standard."

1956 *Chicago Review,* Autumn-Winter, p. 6. There was a time when jazzmen did not play "pop" tunes.

v.i. [semantic development unknown; current esp. among black jazzmen since c. 1940] To pay someone else's way; to treat.

1960 *The Angry Ones,* p. 179. I'll take the afternoon off and pop to a show.

1961 *The Sound,* p. 188. You pop for all this?

poppa, *n.* See s.v. POPS.

poppa-stoppa, poppa-stopper, poppa-loppa, *n.* [from common practice of insulting someone by characterizing him as incestuous (see THE DOZENS); some currency since c. 1935; see also MOTHER] One who commits sexual acts with (one's) father; also, an intimate term of address.

1944 *Dan Burley's Original Handbook of Harlem Jive,* p. 44. All right, Poppa-Stoppa.

1952 *Invisible Man,* p. 420. "What brand you drinking tonight, Poppa-Stopper?" he said.

1960 *The Jazz Word,* p. 16. You, my audience, are a bunch of poppaloppers.

popping, 1. [prob. from the sense of cracking; current since c. 1920] Especially of brass players, failing to hit a note precisely, or hitting it and then losing it.

1965 *Down Beat*, 6 May, p. 35. We used to play those tunes and have as much finesse in doing it—until you hear popping going on all over it. It's new men breaking in.

2. [by analogy with suddenness and sharpness of the sounds; some currency esp. among black jazzmen since c. 1935] Playing (music) with power and precision.

1935 *His Hi De Highness of Ho De Ho*, p. 35. That brass sure is popping.

1968 *Down Beat*, 22 Feb., p. 19. We wanted guys who could really pop on their horns individually—to see how they would fit together as section men.

1968 *Down Beat*, 21 Mar., p. 32. He does an exceptionally good job of keeping the background popping without getting in the way.

pops, poppa, *n.* [cf. general colloquial use: 1925 *English Words and Their Background*, p. 59: "Expressions circulating in the year 1920 . . . : *Sweet Papa!*"; *according* to jazzmen, Louis Armstrong introduced jazz slang use of *pops* c. 1922; rare since c. 1945; see also BABY, JACK, JIM] Although occasionally used as a nickname for Louis Armstrong (see 1959 quot.) and for Sidney Bechet, for the most common use, see 1938 quot.

1938 *Cab Calloway: Hi De Ho*, p. 16. *pops:* salutation for all males.

1955 *Solo*, p. 187. Too many heroes is nowhere. Right, pops?

1959 *The Jazz Scene*, p. 294. Nobody who plays with Louis Armstrong ever calls him *Satchmo* or *Satchelmouth*, a label much fancied for advertising purposes. He is merely called Pops.

1961 *Metronome*, Feb., p. 60. Jazz is . . . an art in which a musician can become known as "Pops" by the time he is 22 or even at 18.

1961 *The Sound*, p. 25. And you know one thing, Poppa?

pork chop (music) [prob. from jazzmen's approval of both; according to jazzmen, current c. 1900–c. 1917, obs. since; see also BARRELHOUSE, GULLY-LOW, LOWDOWN] Slow, earthy blues music.

1970 *Dictionary of Afro-American Slang*, p. 92. *pork chop: (music):* (1900s) a slow, barrelhouse style of jazz.

pot, pod, *n.* [poss. because frequently grown in window-sill flower pots; widely current since c. 1940; see also BOO, GAGE, MARY JANE, TEA]

1952 *Flee the Angry Strangers*, p. 133. We'll smoke pod and everything.

206

1959 *The Holy Barbarians*, p. 21. Every user I know calls it pot.
1959 *The Jazz Scene*, p. 292. *pot:* marijuana.

potato man [see quot. for semantic explanation; some currency since c. 1900–c. 1917, obs. since except historical]
1961 *Show Business Illustrated*, 5 Sep., p. 133. To plug the gaps, he put together marching bands of ten or twelve men that included three or four nonplaying but horn-carrying stand-ins. They were called "potato men" because the bells of their instruments were stuffed with potatoes to make sure that no disturbing sounds came out of them.

pots (are) on, (put) the [metaphoric extension of *cook*, q.v.; current since c. 1955; see also BURN, POPPING, SMOKE] The music is exciting, thrilling.
1960 *The Paul Horn Quintet: Something Blue* (liner notes on LP album Hifijazz J615). When the quintet drives, it drives hard, and there is hard cooking all the way. Or, as they say in the trade, "All the pots are on."
1961 *N.Y. Times Magazine*, 25 June, p. 39. *the pots are on:* the joint's jumping; all the musicians are cookin'.
1972 *Down Beat*, 25 May, p. 17. I like to put the pots on: it seems happier.

powerful, *adj.* [according to jazzmen, standard term was given special application by and has had some currency esp. among black jazzmen since c. 1900; see also BOSS, HARD, STRONG, TOUGH] Sometimes, possessed of a strong embouchure (see 1946 quot.); usually, formidable as a musician or as a person.
1946 *Jazzways*, p. 31. Joe Oliver was so powerful he blew a horn out of tune every two months.
1959 *A Compendium for the Teaching of Jazz History*, p. 61. All the musicians who heard Bolden play agreed that he "couldn't read a note and he played the most powerful cornet of all time."
1960 *Metronome*, Dec., p. 23. Cootie Williams, he was a powerful man.

Pres, President, *n.* See s.v. PREZ.

press roll [some currency since c. 1917] A kind of drum roll.
1939 *American Jazz Music*, p. 53. . . . . a "press roll," one of the many rhythmic patterns which have been used by jazz drummers for years.

1955 *Hear Me Talkin to Ya*, p. 44. He had a press roll that one very seldom hears nowadays.

pretty, *adj.* [pejorative connotation applied to standard term reflects jazzman's disdain for that which is merely superficially esthetic; some currency since c. 1917; see also COMMERCIAL, SWEET] Ornate, pretentious, deficient in earthiness or simplicity (applies to music only; note: the term may also be used in a neutral or even favorable sense [see 1963 quot.]; the connotation must be determined from the context).

1926 *Jazz* (Whiteman & McBride), p. 242. Nuh, Suh, I jes' can't play that "pretty music" that you all play. And you fellers can't never play blues worth a damn.

1939 *The Kingdom of Swing*, p. 178. There is no member of a prominent swing band who could not if he were asked, or felt the inclination, "play pretty."

1960 *Jazz Scene 2* (liner notes on LP album on Epic LA 16001). Thus, though at times Jamal plays "pretty" piano, he is a real innovator.

1961 *Metronome*, Apr., p. 39. Dig especially . . . Nelson's *pretty* mickey mouse [i.e., saccharine] tone on "The Drive."

1963 *Down Beat*, 26 Sep., p. 24. The album is an extraordinarily pretty one (and the term is used in no way disparagingly).

Prez, Pres/President [see first 1956 quot. for etym.; one of the five or six indispensable jazz nicknames (see also BIRD, LADY, SATCH); current since c. 1942] Lester Young, 1909–1959, tenor saxophonist, acclaimed by musicians and critics as one of the all-time great performers on his instrument.

1949 *Inside Be-Bop*, p. 5. Known today as "Pres," the president of the tenor sax men, Lester was first heard of when he replaced Coleman Hawkins in the Fletcher Henderson band in 1934.

1956 *Lady Sings the Blues*, p. 59. When it came to a name for Lester, I [i.e., Billie Holiday] always felt he was the greatest. . . . So I started calling him the President. It got shortened to Prez.

1956 *Jazz: Its Evolution and Essence*, pp. 116–117. His influence . . . is evident . . . in the work of a whole group of young saxophonists who regard the "President" as their spiritual father.

professor, prof, *n.* [poss. from the fact that they also gave piano lessons, or poss. as term of mock respect; according to jazzmen, current c.

1900–c. 1917, obs. since except historical; see also PIANO KID] A pianist in a brothel or cabaret.

1939 *Jazzmen*, p. 24. "My prof was a Mexican."

1950 *They All Played Ragtime*, p. 270. The spotlight on the "professors" is dimmer and the tips that support them smaller.

1955 *Hear Me Talkin to Ya*, p. 53. The sporting houses needed professors.

progressive jazz [chiefly a writers' term; current c. 1950–c. 1960, rare since; see also COOL JAZZ, MODERN JAZZ] That jazz which embraced some or all of the harmonic and rhythmic developments innovated c. 1945 (though the earliest period c. 1945–c. 1950 in progressive jazz was called *bop*, q.v.).

1948 *Time*, 1 Mar., p. 34. Stan Kenton considers his "progressive jazz" just what the psychiatrist ordered.

1956 *Guide to Jazz*, p. 42. *cool* or *progressive jazz:* a logical development of bop.

1960 *Dictionary of American Slang*, s.v. *progressive jazz:* jazz music based on chord progressions, rather than on a melody.

pull one's coat [common attention-getting device; though now general black slang, the term originated among jazzmen c. 1935]

1962 *N.Y. Times Magazine*, 20 May, p. 45. *pull one's coat:* to bring to someone's attention.

1970 *Roland Kirk: Here Comes the Whistleman* (LP liner notes). Ever alert for jazz developments and new faces on the scene, it was Gus who first "pulled my coat" about Roland Kirk.

punch, *n.* [cf. 1934 *A Dictionary of American Slang*, p. 383: "*punch:* energy, vigor, enthusiasm"; some currency in special sense among jazzmen since c. 1925; see also DRIVE] Musical impact, energy, vigor.

1926 *Melody Maker*, Sep., p. 49. The lyrics in these measures have a particular significance, or what is called "punch."

1940 *Swing*, Jan., p. 24. Everyone, however, seems happy in the rowdy backing, which gives plenty of punch to a good old barroom song.

1961 *Down Beat*, 16 Feb., p. 36. The clear, crisp, punching trumpet of Marsala adds more of this same quality.

push, *n. & v.i.* [according to jazzmen, current c. 1920–c. 1935, rare since]

A strong rhythmic accompaniment; to provide such an accompaniment (usually participial).

1959 *Jazz* (Hentoff & McCarthy), p. 299. It was a drum style that implied . . . a "push" behind the improviser.

1961 *The Jazz Review*, Jan., p. 26. The subtlety of his work is conspicuously absent, and there is a quality of obvious pushing rather reminiscent of Buddy Rich.

1967 *Down Beat*, 21 Sep., p. 31. Carter and Tate continually push Getz and Corea.

v.t. [from underworld slang; current among jazzmen since c. 1935] To sell or promote (something—frequently, narcotics).

1946 *Really the Blues*, p. 373. *push:* sell, handle, purvey.

1959 *The Holy Barbarians*, p. 25. He was pushing heroin to other musicians.

push the beat [according to jazzmen, current c. 1920–c. 1935, rare since] To play with a strong, pulsating beat.

1961 *New Yorker*, 23 Sep., p. 103. But Beiderbecke lacked Young's tricks and simply pushed the beat before him.

pusher, *n.* [narcotics slang, but with some currency among jazzmen since c. 1930] A seller of narcotics.

1943 *Time*, 19 July, p. 54. He is known to his clients as a "pusher."

1959 *The Naked Lunch*, p. 226. In the 1920s a lot of Chinese pushers found The West so unreliable, dishonest and wrong . . . when an Occidental junky came to score [q.v.], they say, "No glot . . . Clom Fliday."

1960 *Beat Jokes Bop Humor & Cool Cartoons*, p. 60. The cat went on the wagon, got rid of his pusher, and even went to church once.

put-down, *n.* [formed from *put down,* sense 2.; current since c. 1942] An adverse criticism, a squelch, an insult.

1959 *The Horn*, p. 215. Anyone makes a hassle this next set, I'll show 'em put-downs if that's all they're after.

put down, 1. [correlative of jazz slang *pick up,* q.v.; from sense of setting something down or presenting it; current since c. 1935; see also *lay down*]

1944 *Dan Burley's Original Handbook of Harlem Jive*, p. 145. *put down:* say, perform, describe, do.

1953 *Down Beat*, 11 Feb., p. 16-S. Those old masters have really put something down, and it'll be a long, long time before those basic sounds change.

1957 *On the Road*, p. 134. Listen will you to this old tenor man blow his top . . . tell the story and put down real relaxation.

1959 *The Holy Barbarians*, p. 67. The party people didn't like me or the ideas that I put down.

2. [from sense of reducing something in status or from setting it down and leaving it there (i.e., discarding it); some 19th century, and poss. earlier, British use; widely current among jazzmen since c. 1940] See 1958 quot.; also, to quit or reject.

1953 *Night Light*, p. 135. You really ought to put school down.

1955 *Hear Me Talkin to Ya*, p. 381. I heard a guy last week . . . putting a musician down.

1958 *American Speech*, Oct., p. 225. When someone puts you down he criticizes you unfavorably.

1959 *The Holy Barbarians*, p. 102. I put that scene [i.e., domesticity] down when I got divorced.

put on [from *put (one) on;* some currency since c. 1955] An act of deception; a joke, a subterfuge.

1961 *The Jazz Life*, p. 18. At the Savoy, I learned, I think, to recognize the "put on."

put (one) on [Early Modern English phrase that survived in dialectal English: cf. 1611 *The Winter's Tale*, II, i, 141–142. "You are abus'd, and by some putter-on/That will be damn'd for't"; widely current since c. 1940] See 1958, 1959 quots.

1948 *Trumpet on the Wing*, p. 119. Eddie Miller and the boys used to put me on for bringing atomizers on these dates.

1958 *American Speech*, Oct., p. 225. When a hipster *puts* someone *on*, he is pulling his leg (perhaps putting him on a stage to be laughed at).

1959 *Esquire*, Nov., p. 70J. *put on:* to make fun of, or ridicule without the victim being aware of it.

1961 *The Jazz Review*, Jan., p. 13. You might be putting yourself on.

1961 *Down Beat*, 5 Jan., p. 43. I think he was putting on [i.e., parodying] the Viennese composers, and it was marvelous.

put (something or **someone) on (someone)** [from the sense of putting someone into contact with something or someone; current since c. 1935;

see also LAY (SOMETHING) ON (SOMEONE)] To present (something or someone) to (someone).

1960 *Hiparama of the Classics*, p. 10. But, I'm gonna put a Cat on you, who was the Sweetest, grooviest . . . Cat that ever Stomped on this Sweet Green Sphere.

1961 *Down Beat*, 5 Jan., p. 16. If any of them who read this think I'm jivin', let 'em look me up, and I'll put some music on 'em.

put the pots on, see S.V. POTS.

put us in the alley! [according to jazzmen, some currency esp. among those blacks who danced to jazz c. 1910–c. 1925, obs. since except historical; see also LET'S DO A SET!, LET'S GO BACK HOME!] A shout of encouragement to jazz musicians c. 1910–c. 1925; to play fast, energetically, and intensely.

1959 *The Jazz Review*, July, p. 12. When they got tired of two-steps and schottisches (which they danced with a lot of spieling), they'd yell: "Now, put us in the alley!"

queen, *n.* [cf. 1960 *Dictionary of American Slang,* s.v. *queen:* "some student use since c. 1915"; not to be confused with its general slang sense (i.e., a male homosexual); current among jazzmen c. 1930–c. 1945, rare since; see also FOX]

1938 *Cab Calloway: Hi De Ho,* p. 16. *queen:* a beautiful girl.

[1944] *Black on Black,* p. 196. Then comes night and you takes out yo' queen.

1952 *Park East,* Dec., p. 30. My queen in her scanties and I in my robe,/Had just fixed our wigs for a long winter's load.

quit the scene [general black slang *quit* (cf. song title "Hit Me But Don't Quit Me" by George Williams and Bessie Brown, listed in *Columbia 1927 Race Catalogue: The Latest Blues by Columbia Race Stars*) + jazz slang *(the) scene;* current since c. 1950; see also CUT OUT, SPLIT, SPLIT THE SCENE] To leave; also, by extension: to die (see also LEFT TOWN, SPLIT THE SCENE).

1955 *Hear Me Talkin to Ya,* p. 248. Ma had quit the scene.

1955 *Babs Gonzales: Babs' Celebrity Party* (lyrics on LP Album Crazy C-0001-A). It was nab [i.e., a policeman] and the super tellin' us we had to quit the scene.

1970 *Dictionary of Afro-American Slang,* p. 95. *quit the scene:* (1950s) to leave or to die.

quote, *v.i. & v.t.* [special application of standard term; current since c. 1945] Of a vocalist or soloing instrumentalist to insert a phrase from another tune into the one being played.

QUOTE

1971 *Down Beat*, 27 May, p. 20. The practice of "quoting," which can become a bore in lesser hands, is something Dexter Gordon is a past master at.

R

race (music or records) [see 1959 quot.: chiefly a trade term, and one which reflects the separateness of white and black jazz markets (see 1960 quot.) during the pre-Swing (i.e., pre-c. 1935) era, a schism which has been gradually closing; some currency among jazzmen c. 1920–c. 1940, obs. since except historical; see also RHYTHM AND BLUES] See 1949, 1960 quots.

1927 *Columbia 1927 Race Catalogue: The Latest Blues by Columbia Race Stars* (title of record company catalogue).

1935 *Vanity Fair*, Nov., p. 71. Negro bands play "race music" (a curious euphemism spread by phonograph companies).

1949 *Music Library Association Notes*, Dec., p. 49. *race:* type of song whose characteristics are difficult to define but which is supposed to appeal particularly to Negro audiences. Such songs are modern derivatives of old *blues* songs in subject matter, harmony, rhythm and form. Trade papers also classify certain performers as race artists, and their recordings are race records. *Billboard* recently substituted "rhythm and blues" for race.

1958 *Jam Session*, p. 275. In the twenties and thirties, rhythm and blues was called "race music."

1959 *The Country Blues*, p. 47. Ralph Peer was trying c. 1920 to think of a catalog title for his new records, and rather than calling them "Negro" records, decided on "Race" records, and the name lasted.

1960 *Dictionary of American Slang*, s.v. *race music:* a simple form of jazz based on the blues, usually with a melancholy or sometimes religious theme, a heavily accented beat, etc. Because such music, during the 1920s and 1930s, was issued by the recording companies on

215

records informally known as "race records," intended primarily for sale to Negroes.

rag, *n. & adj.* [prob. from *ragged:* see note s.v. *ragtime;* see 1956 and 1973 quots. for dates] See 1956, 1960 quots.

[1895] *Harlem Rag* (tune composed c. 1895).

1899 *Maple Leaf Rag* (tune composed by Scott Joplin).

1916 *Variety,* 25 Aug., p. 8. Ash . . . is seen daily on the streets playing rag dance numbers.

1939 *The International Cyclopedia of Music and Musicians,* p. 896. Nearly all the good "rag" composers were pianists.

1956 *Guide to Jazz,* s.v. *rag:* a form of piano piece, generally 16 bars, which flourished in the late 19th century and until c. 1928, and which was, though initially a piano piece, transcribed for bands as well.

1960 *Dictionary of American Slang,* p. 417. Strictly speaking, rag preceded jazz and was distinct from it, being mostly written music.

1973 *Jazz Style in Kansas City,* p. 41. The 1893 Chicago World's Fair. (The word "ragtime" was coined there by a Chicago newspaper man to describe the lively "raggy" style of playing.)

v.i. & v.t. [formed from the n. and contemporaneous with it] See 1939 quot.

1936 *Harper's,* Apr., p. 570. "Ragging," "gut-bucketing," and all the rest are names for the *hot* performance which is the heart and soul of jazz.

1939 *Jazzmen,* p. 43. To "rag" a tune was to syncopate it.

1952 *Music Out of Dixie,* p. 59. They ragged it and rocked it in joyous abandon.

ragman, *n.* [from *rag* and contemporaneous with it] A jazzman, c. 1900–c. 1916.

1947 *Frontiers of Jazz,* p. 107. I used to hear . . . Buddie Cantor, Josky Adams . . . what we call "ragmen" in New Orleans.

rag-time, ragtime, *n. & adj.* [see 1957 and 1963 quots. for prob. etym.; dates are contemporaneous with those of *rag,* q.v.]

1908 *New York Age,* 5 Mar. [1962 *Jazz: A History of the New York Scene,* p. 43]. "The Maple Leaf Rag" . . . was the first ragtime instrumental piece to be generally accepted by the public.

1912 *The Autobiography of an Ex-Coloured Man,* p. 100. [New York: Hill & Wang reprint, 1960]. American musicians, instead of investigating rag-time, attempt to ignore it, or dismiss it with a contemptuous word.

1939 *The International Cyclopedia of Music and Musicians*, p. 896. Though ragtime was sometimes played by larger combinations of instruments, the piano retained a dominant influence over its structure and phraseology.

1950 *They All Played Ragtime*, p. 210. The date was 1896, the place . . . a New York vaudeville theatre. It was "jig-piano" then. Not until a year later was the music christened "ragtime."

1957 *The Book of Jazz*, p. 58. Perhaps this apparently ragged rhythmic imbalance (leading to the spontaneous development of the term "ragtime") . . .

1958 *The Decca Book of Jazz*, p. 29. Ragtime was the hot music of the first ten years of this century. —p. 34. It was not until 1897 that the name "ragtime" was invented to describe the new syncopated piano style that was developing among the Missouri pianists.

1963 *Blues People*, p. 90. Ragtime (which is not to be confused with the verb *rag*, which merely meant *syncopation*) . . . was a music the Negro came to in imitating white imitations of Negro music.

ragtime shuttle [according to jazzman Eubie Blake, current c. 1900–c. 1917, obs. since except historical] A ragtime drum break or figure.

1960 *The Story of the Original Dixieland Jazz Band*, p. 33. Some of his breaks like . . . the "ragtime shuttle" have never been duplicated.

rain on (one) [by analogy of inclement weather with emotional discomfort; some currency since c. 1935] Complain to; bother. Oral evidence only.

raise sand (or cain) [cf. 1934 *A Dictionary of American Slang*, p. 385: "*raise cain*: to create a disturbance; *raise sand*: to make a disturbance"; according to jazzmen, given a special application by them c. 1930–c. 1945, obs. since except historical] See quot. (Note: usually achieved by playing music excitingly.)

1946 *Really the Blues*, p. 374. *raise sand*: make a fuss, create a stir.

rank, *adj.* [prob. from standard meaning (i.e., offensive in smell); also cf. 1930 *American Tramp and Underworld Slang*, s.v. *rank*: "poor; worthless; disagreeable"; current esp. among black jazzmen since c. 1925] Nasty, disagreeable; also, see 1959 quot.

1937 *Metronome*, Aug., p. 7. In my opinion, a great many readers of *Met* are the rankest sort of ickies.

1959 *Esquire*, Nov., p. 70J. *rank:* stupid.

v.t. [prob. from armed forces slang *pull rank on someone* (i.e., to subordinate someone); some currency esp. among black jazzmen since c. 1925; see also PUT DOWN, sense 2]

1938 *Cab Calloway: Hi De Ho*, p. 16. *rank:* to lower.

1945 *Hepcats Jive Talk Dictionary*, s.v. *rank:* to criticize.

1960 *Down Beat*, 7 Jan., p. 29. I'm not ranking either of these two excellent writers.

ratamacue, *n.* [onomatopoeic; some currency since c. 1925] A drum figure.

1934 *Metronome*, Feb., p. 47. The ratamacue is somewhat more difficult than the paradiddle.

ready, *adj.* [prob. by analogy with *hip* and *booted*, q.v.: i.e., if one's hip boots are on, he is ready for any kind of weather, and, by extension, for any eventuality; current since c. 1930]

1935 *His Hi De Highness of Ho De Ho*, p. 35. When an individual or a piece of music is high class or greatly admired, we indicate it by saying,. "He's ready!" or "That's ready!"

1944 *The New Cab Calloway's Hepsters Dictionary*, s.v. *ready:* 100 percent in every way. Example: "That fried chicken was ready."

1958 *Jam Session: An Anthology of Jazz*, p. 91. This time he was *ready*, so to speak, for it was on this second sojourn that he started to impress his musical contemporaries.

1967 *Down Beat*, 2 Nov., p. 23. Miles opened with a medium minor piece that let everyone know he was *ready!*

1973 *Jazz Style in Kansas City*, p. 183. When he came back, several months later, he was a new musician. *He was ready!*

rebop, re-bop, *n.* [see 1957 quot. for etym.; reinforced by popular Lionel Hampton tune recorded 1946, *Hey-Baba-Rebop*; some currency among jazzmen c. 1945–c. 1947, but never so common as and soon completely supplanted by *bebop* and *bop*] Early term for that highly technical and cerebral modern jazz innovated c. 1945, more commonly called *bop*, q.v.

1946 *Disc*, Nov. Re-bop is four-beat music, but it's too complicated.

1956 *Eddie Condon's Treasury of Jazz*, p. 191. The center of attention seemed to be a new kind of jazz, successively known as "Rebop," "Bebop," and finally just plain "bop."

1957 *Giants of Jazz,* p. 188. The word "bop" is a contraction of "bebop" or "rebop." The two-syllable word was merely a way of describing the staccato two-note phrase that became the trademark in its playing.

reefer, *n.* [see 1959 quot. for poss. etym.; some currency among jazzmen c. 1925–c. 1940, obs. since except historical; see also BOO, GAGE, MARY JANE, POT, TEA] See 1938 quot.

1931 *Reefer Man* (tune recorded by Don Redman).

1933 *Chicago Defender,* 2 Dec., p. 5. The humble "reefer," "the weed," the marijuana, or what have you by way of a name for a doped cigarette has moved to Park Ave. from Harlem.

1938 *Cab Calloway: Hi De Ho,* p. 16. *reefer:* marijuana cigaret.

1959 *Jazz: A Quarterly of American Music,* Fall, p. 285. "Smokin' Reefers" was a title in *Flying Colors* produced on Broadway in 1932, where a stick retailed for five cents. . . . The word *reefer* is an Anglicization of *grifo.* . . . Along the border it indicates a drunkard, and by extension one under the influence of any soporific.

reefer man [some currency c. 1925–c. 1940, obs. since except historical]

1931 *Reefer Man* (tune recorded by Don Redman).

1935 *His Hi De Highness of Ho De Ho,* p. 36. A "reefer man" is a peddler who bootlegs these cigarets.

reet, *adv. & adj.* [*all right* corrupted to *all reet,* q.v., then shortened to *reet;* current c. 1935–c. 1945, very rare since] As adv.: all right, yes; as adj.: excellent, nifty.

1942 *American Mercury,* July, p. 85. So Jelly got his zoot suit with the reet pleats.

1944 *Metronome,* Jan., p. 12. Anita O'Day, the gal with the reet beat in her voice.

1956 *Eddie Condon's Treasury of Jazz,* p. 447. "Reet," the trombonist told him.

release, *n.* [prob. in sense of a liberty taken from the major theme; current since c. 1930; see also the more recent CHANNEL] See 1959 quot.

1936 *Hot Jazz: The Guide to Swing Music,* p. 18. Also called, quite poetically, "the release."

1956 *Guide to Jazz*, s.v. *release:* describes the phrase "B" in themes of the A, A, B, A sequence.

1959 *Webster's New World Dictionary*, s.v. *release: in jazz music,* the third group of four measures in a common form of sixteen-bar chorus, which supplies a bridge between repetitions of the melody.

rent party (or stomp, strut), (house) [black general slang, but with esp. currency among black jazzmen c. 1920–c. 1940, obs. since except historical] See first 1955 quot.

1925 *The Inter-State Tattler*, 6 Mar., p. 8. It would be extremely cruel to the South American amateurs if they had to pick up Harlem by the sounds of house rent parties.

1938 *N.Y. Amsterdam News*, 12 Mar., p. 17. The allusion to "peppermint candy" stirs almost primal emotions, hangover from the old "down home house rent strut" days.

1955 *A Pictorial History of Jazz*, p. 127. The music . . . is probably best described by turning to its basic setting during the '20s, the raucous, colorful "rent party." This rather widespread phenomenon . . . originally was literally a device for rounding up the rent money by crowding as many friends as possible into an apartment and having them pay for an evening of food, drink and entertainment. This specific purpose may have been ignored before long, but the parties became a staple item at, seemingly, every flat that boasted a piano in working condition.

1955 *Hear Me Talkin to Ya*, pp. 210–211. Joe . . . would bash at numerous functions and house-rent stomps along Carlisle and John Streets.

1957 *Giants of Jazz*, p. 71. "Rent parties" too became the rage in the early twenties. Admission ranged from thirty-five cents to half a buck, for which the guest received a plate of pig's feet and potato salad or an order of chitlins. But the prime attractions were the piano players.

rest, v.i. [special application of the standard meaning; some currency since c. 1940; see also LAY OUT] To temporarily refrain from playing (music).

1965 *Such Sweet Thunder*, p. 219. "Budd, you rest on this one."

rhythm and blues, rhythm-and-blues, r&b [from its dominant components; current c. 1935–c. 1945, rare since; see also the earlier RACE (MUSIC)]

1955 *The Encyclopedia of Jazz*, p. 347. *rhythm-and-blues* (or *r&b*): a type of harmonically, rhythmically and melodically simple popular music or jazz, originally intended for a Negro audience.

1956 *Guide to Jazz*, s.v. *rhythm-and-blues:* singing style characterized by a very heavy, emphatic boogie bass accompaniment.

1961 *The Jazz Review*, p. 30. At least r&b went back to feeling rather than an idea about feeling.

1968 *Jazz Dance*, pp. 1–2. Originally known as "race" in the 1920s, then "rhythm-and-blues" in the 1930s and 1940s, the tag "rock-and-roll" became popular in the fifties.

rhythm (section) [current in special sense since c. 1925] (Note: since c. 1945, the guitar is frequently omitted).

1937 *American Speech*, Feb., p. 48. In the *rhythm section* are drums, piano, bass, guitar.

1949 *Down Beat*, 11 Mar., p. 15. Allen plays most of his Capitol dance dates with only himself and three rhythm.

1961 *The Sound*, pp. 11–12. The Sultans were six. Three rhythms and three horns.

ricky-tick(y), *adj*. See s.v. TICKY.

ride, *n. & adj.* [by analogy with the rhythmic movement; according to jazzmen, current c. 1922–c. 1945, very rare since; see also CHORUS, SOLO] An improvised solo chorus.

1940 *Swing*, Jan., p. 25. The other side is "Bugle Call Rag" at ride tempo.

1956 *Second Ending*, p. 63. You give him all the hot rides.

v.i. & v.t. [by analogy with the rhythmic movement; cf. 1959 *The Jazz Scene*, p. 16n. " 'Riding,' 'rocking' and 'rolling' are words applied both to the railroad and to coitus"; cf. also its Early Modern English use (i.e., in a sexual sense): c. 1599 *Henry V*, III, vii, 53–54. "You rode . . . your French hose off"; according to jazzmen, current c. 1922–c. 1945, very rare since; see also GROOVE, SWING] See 1938 and 1952 quots.

1933 *Metronome*, July, p. 28. He [i.e., the drummer] "rides" the band.

1938 *Cab Calloway: Hi De Ho*, p. 16. *ride:* to swing, to keep perfect tempo in playing or singing.

1952 *A History of Jazz in America*, p. 352. *ride:* to swing, esp. in the last chorus or section.

221

1956 *Second Ending*, p. 57. They rode into the sock chorus like a storm cloud of marauders.

v.t. [some currency since c. 1930] To play music inspiredly and pulsatingly.

1937 *This Thing Called Swing*, p. 8. *Ride Out*, p. 24. On those passages that belong to you, go right on and ride it out.

ride cymbal [current since c. 1925; see also SOCK CYMBAL] A medium-sized single cymbal, part of a jazz drummer's standard equipment.

1961 *The Sound*, p. 42. And the magic sound he had on the ride cymbal was there.

ride man [from *ride*, *n.*; current c. 1922–c. 1940, obs. since except historical] An improvising soloist.

1935 *Vanity Fair*, Nov., p. 38. *Ride-men* is a term applied to the improvisers of these licks.

1945 *Band Leaders and Record Review*, Mar., p. 20. Within a horn blast of Hollywood and Vine, the crossroads of Glamour-town, can be found many lairs of the hepcats—haunts of gates and ride men.

ride-out, *n. & adj.* [from *ride*, *n.* + *out*, in the sense of exit; current since c. 1925]

1939 *Metronome*, May, p. 19. "Pussy Willow" has a great ride-out.

1958 *Publication of the American Dialect Society*, Nov., p. 46. *ride-out*: the final chorus of an arrangement.

ridiculous, *adj.* [one of several terms reflecting the jazzman's fondness for the bizarre, eccentric, or unconventional (see also CRAZY, INSANE, NUTTY, SOMETHING ELSE); current from c. 1935–c. 1960, rare since]

1959 *Jazz: A Quarterly of American Music*, Summer, p. 209. His technique is ridiculous!

1960 *The Jazz Word*, p. 143. To a jazzman . . . *ridiculous* is wonderful.

riff, *n. & adj.* [etym. unknown: prob. originated in Kansas City; according to jazzmen, some currency since c. 1917, but widely current only since c. 1935] See 1946, 1949 quots.

1936 *Esquire*, June, p. 92. The mutations of musicians' slang are interesting. It was "breaks" originally. Then it became "licks." Today it is "riffs."

1946 *Harvard Dictionary of Music*, p. 378. *riff* technique: short ostinato melodic figures by the band, sometimes against which one of the instruments improvises.

1948 *Down Beat*, 14 July, p. 15. Its final riff chorus spots a repetitive phrase that every small jobbing band from here to Keokuk has used since 1934.

1949 *Music Library Association Notes*, Dec., p. 50. *riff*: musical phrase usually developed by musicians, rather than composers, and taking an identifiable form. Riffs occasionally become the basis of pop songs just as folk motifs serve as symphonic themes.

n. [by analogy with *riff, n. & adj.* (i.e., from the initial sense of a musical phrase that in repetition becomes characteristic, the meaning is extended to anything which through repetition becomes familiar or habitual); current since c. 1940; see also LICK, PLAY]

1944 *Dan Burley's Original Handbook of Harlem Jive*, p. 150. *wrong riff*: the wrong thing—either by words or action.

1952 *Who Walk in Darkness*, p. 90. I've found a new riff. . . . Bicycling.

1959 *Diggeth Thou?*, p. 34. So after he had sounded and she had dug his riff/she cut into his dommy and helped him kill the fifth.

1959 *San Francisco Chronicle*, 4 June, p. 35. None of that trash about how them black rabbits sing and dance all the time and are light on their feet and how they look alike, you know, that old-time riff.

v.i. [according to jazzmen, some currency since c. 1917, but widely current only since c. 1935] To play a riff (see n.).

1936 *Harper's*, Apr., p. 570. "Swing," "riffing" . . . and all the rest are names for the hot performance which is the heart and soul of jazz.

1958 *The Story of Jazz*, p. 199. The repeated phrases which the brass and reed sections threw back and forth became known as "riffs," and "riffing" developed as a fine art.

right, *adj.* [some general slang use, but with esp. currency among jazzmen since c. 1925] In good form, musically.

1928 *The Walls of Jericho*, p. 304. *right*: somewhat in excess of perfection.

1956 *Down Beat Jazz Record Reviews: 1956*, p. 109. She's absorbingly right on these sides.

1958 *After Hours Poetry*, p. 31. When Lester is "right"/All others pale.

right ahead, see s.v. STRAIGHT AHEAD.

righteous, *adj.* [see 1956 quot. for semantic development; according to jazzmen, current esp. among black jazzmen c. 1900–c. 1945, rare since]

1937 *Mademoiselle*, Oct., p. 71. He plays righteous clarinet; no razzle-dazzle, but tremendous warmth and expressiveness.

1944 *The New Cab Calloway's Hepsters Dictionary*, s.v. *righteous:* splendid.

1944 *Dan Burley's Original Handbook of Harlem Jive*, p. 41. Desdemona, the righteous wren, is stashed in her lilywhites.

1956 *The Heart of Jazz*, p. 67. . . . "that righteous New Orleans stuff." This persistent use of an adjective associated with religion, and especially with Judaism and Christianity, can be explained most naturally as a reflection of a conspicuously religious character in the music.

right hand [special application of standard phrase; current since c. 1900, though, for reasons of pianistic technique, less current than *left hand,* q.v.] A pianist's right hand; also: his skill or inventiveness with the right hand.

1940 *New Orleans Jazz*, p. 12. The left hand does (and the right hand knows it!) . . . a New Orleans *hop scop.*

1960 *Jazz: A Quarterly of American Music*, Winter, p. 35. The crowded cult devoted to blinding up-tempo right hand bedazzlement simply holds no allure for him.

1961 *The Jazz Review*, Jan., p. 26. Granted he has a great left hand, but the way he uses it detracts from his right.

1961 *Metronome*, Apr., p. 32. This sensation of tonality is fashioned by the fusion of many wonderful elements: a rich left hand, lagging yet leaping, coupled with a right hand that can seem to do no wrong.

rigor mortis, rig city, rigville [by analogy with the moribund stiffening; according to jazzmen, current since c. 1945] The situation (often, the music or the music business) is bad.

1948 *The Record Changer*, June, p. 6. On the records of the 1920s, one way to loosen things up before rigor mortis sets in completely might be to get out on the floor and "shake that thing."

1961 *Night Song*, p. 47. "B" couldn't record because the war was on. Rigor Mortis.

1970 *Jazz People*, p. 94. All the available women had left with the

224

other musicians before he could finish packing his drums. "Rigor mortis!" —p. 98. When I came back to New York looking for gigs, rigor mortis set in for about eight or nine months.

rimshot, rim-shot, *n.* [from the part of the drum on which it is sounded and its sound; current since 1930]

1937 *American Speech,* Feb., p. 48. *rimshot:* the noise made by striking the rim and head of a snare drum simultaneously.

1959 *The Horn,* p. 34. The drummer for the house band good-naturedly chased Wing's warm-up runs with precise rim-shots.

rip, *n.* [poss. from *ripple* or simply a special application of a standard meaning; current since c. 1925]

1933 *Metronome,* Jan., p. 34. The rip is produced by short and quick glissando up to the tone, attacked sforzando and cut off quickly.

1949 *Music Library Association Notes,* Dec., p. 50. *rip:* modern effect used by reed and brass instruments. Instrumentalist begins on a note, four or five notes below particular note he is shooting for, and leaps quickly up to written note, which he hits hard and staccato.

ripped, *adj.* [hyperbole: emotional analogy with physical fragmentation; some old general slang use but reintroduced by and current esp. among black jazzmen since c. 1958; see also TORE UP]

1970 *Dictionary of Afro-American Slang,* p. 98. *ripped:* (1950s) unhappy; in grief.

roach, *n.* [prob. by analogy with its smallness; current among jazzmen since c. 1930]

1938 *Cab Calloway: Hi De Ho,* p. 16. *roach:* butt of a partially smoked reefer cigaret.

1943 *Time,* 19 July, p. 54. When he has smoked a reefer down to a half-inch butt . . . it is known . . . as a "roach."

rock, *v.i. & v.t.* [see 1927 quot. for semantic explanation; also cf. 1959 *The Jazz Scene,* p. 16n. " 'Riding,' 'rocking' and 'rolling' are words applied both to the railroad and to coitus"; current since c. 1900; see also BOOT, GROOVE, SWING, WAIL] To move or do (something) impressively —usually, applied to dancing, to coition or, in its most common sense since c. 1935, to musical performance; see second 1938 quot.; also, rare, noun: see 1952 quot.

1922 *My Man Rocks Me With One Steady Roll* (tune recorded by Trixie Smith).

1926 *Sugar Foot Stomp* (tune composed by Joe Oliver and Walter Melrose). When they start dancin'/Stompin' and prancin'/the dance called the sugar foot stomp./Let your doggies romp./Rock your mama like a cradle.

1927 *The Journal of Abnormal and Social Psychology*, Apr.–June, p. 15. The majority of the expressions in the blues relating to the sex act are sung from the point of view of women and are mostly concerned with the quality of the movements made by the male during coitus. . . . "My man rocks me with one steady roll." Here the woman boasts of the steady movement with which her man executes the act.

1938 *Metronome*, July, p. 21. Harry James' *Lullaby in Rhythm* really rocks.

1938 *Cab Calloway: Hi De Ho*, p. 16. *rock me:* send me, kill me, move me with rhythm.

1952 *Music Out of Dixie*, p. 245. I want that steady rock.

1961 *Jazz Notes*, Feb.–Mar., p. 39. I don't remember anyone who could "rock" a Kenilworth audience before.

roll, *v.i. & v.t.* [see note s.v. *rolling bass:* also cf. 1959 *The Jazz Scene*, p. 16n. " 'Riding,' 'rocking' and 'rolling' are words applied both to the railroad and to coitus"; according to jazzmen, current c. 1910–c. 1945, rare since] To play a particular pianistic figure with the left hand (see ROLLING BASS).

1925 *Steady Roll Blues* (tune composed by George Bates and Mel Stitzel).

1937 *Roll 'Em* (tune composed by Mary Lou Williams.).

1955 *Hear Me Talkin to Ya*, p. 291. Roll for me—come on, roll 'em, Pete.

rolling bass (or piano) [see 1957 quot. for semantic explanation; according to jazzmen, current c. 1910–c. 1945, rare since] A bass foundation provided by the pianist's left hand (see 1957 quot.).

1940 *New Orleans Jazz*, p. 12. Thus we had, in various places from Pensacola to Dallas and from St. Louis to Chicago, such interesting names for what the left hand does . . . as . . . *rolling bass.*

1946 *Metronome*, Oct., p. 25. Trumpet with modern riffs, and Hodes with that rolling piano.

1957 *Just Jazz*, p. 15. The "rolling" bass was an attempt to recreate the sound of train wheels.

romp, *v.i.* [special applications of standard meaning (i.e., to play or frolic in a lively, boisterous way); according to jazzmen, current c. 1917–c. 1945, rare since] To play jazz or dance (figuratively, see 1946 quot.) to jazz.

1926 *Sugar Foot Stomp* (tune composed by Joe Oliver and Walter Melrose). When they start dancin'/Stompin' and prancin'/the dance called the sugar foot stomp./Let your doggies romp.

1946 *Really the Blues*, p. 73. Romance began to romp all over the Inn.

1961 *Metronome*, Aug., p. 7. We entered as Stan was finishing a set with a romping "52nd Street Theme."

room, *n.* [special application of the standard term; prob. from comparative smallness of modern jazz clubs (i.e., "listening rooms" with no dance floors: cf. earlier *hall*); current since c. 1955] A night club.

1963 *Nugget*, Feb., p. 46. While not as cool [i.e., safe] as blowing jazz in some hip room, I find that monetary rewards are considerably better and more consistent in rolling people.

roost, *n.* [analogical extension of standard meaning; current c. 1945–c. 1955, rare since; see also CRIB, DOMMY, and esp. PAD]

1946 *Really the Blues*, p. 374. *roost:* home.

1974 *Ladies and Gentlemen—Lenny Bruce!!*, p. 479. Lenny had selected as his favorite roost in Frisco the Swiss American, a tiny five-dollar-a-night workingman's hotel.

rubber, *n.* [synecdoche: the rubber of the tires = the automobile; current c. 1935–c. 1950, rare since; see also SHORT, WHEELS]

1944 *Dan Burley's Original Handbook of Harlem Jive*, p. 146. *rubber:* automobile.

rugcutter, rug cutter, *n.* [see 1942 quot. for etym.; current in its initial sense c. 1925–c. 1935, current in its modified sense c. 1935–c. 1945, obs. since except historical] See 1942 quot.

1936 *Cootie Williams and His Rug-Cutters* (name of small performing jazz group).

1938 *N.Y. Amsterdam News*, 2 Apr., p. 17. The thousands of . . . rugcutters . . . that are being hatched daily . . . are a peril."

1942 *American Mercury*, July, p. 96. *rug-cutter:* originally a person frequenting house-rent parties, cutting up the rugs of the host with his feet; a person too cheap or poor to patronize regular dance halls; now means a good dancer.

1944 *Dan Burley's Original Handbook of Harlem Jive*, p. 95. Cop a trot, you rug-cutters.

1946 *Duke Ellington*, p. 181. "Rug Cutter" was one of Harlem's terms for a jitterbug, a technically skillful dancer, fast on his feet and "hip" (in the jazz or swing know).

run away [standard phrase given special application; according to jazzman Eubie Blake, current since c. 1905] To move rhythmically, sometimes harmonically (see last quot.), ahead (of the other players).

1955 *Hear Me Talkin to Ya*, p. 200. Most singers, . . . they're either layin' back or else runnin' away from you.

1961 *The Jazz Review*, Jan., p. 7. Guitarist Freddie Greene, annoyed by Payne's tendency to rush the beat, kept a long stick on the stand with which he poked the drummer when the beat began to run away.

1961 *The Sound*, p. 38. He's a helluva chord man, Red. Even you won't be able to run away from him there.

run down, 1. [cf. entertainment slang *run through* (i.e., to rehearse) and standard phrase *run down* (i.e., to read through rapidly); current since c. 1935] To perform, usually in rehearsal, a piece of written music (for its rare noun form, see 1959 quot.).

1948 *Down Beat*, 1 Dec., p. 10. We ran down three new instrumentals and a vocal for Baubles Buxon!

1959 *Blow Up A Storm*, p. 31. Okay. Let's give it a rundown. Once.

1960 *The Jazz Review*, Nov., p. 12. When we rehearsed an arrangement that no one had seen before, we'd run it down once or twice.

2. **run down** (or **on**) [extension of sense 1. above; current since c. 1955]

1964 *N.Y. Times Magazine*, 23 Aug., p. 64. *run it down:* to elaborate or explain a situation.

1972 *Gorilla, My Love*, pp. 48–49. I tried to figure out the best way to run it down to this girl right quick that they didn't have to live in this town.

1974 *Ladies and Gentlemen—Lenny Bruce!!*, p. 385. Lenny runs this story on the chicks about how you get sweaty, onstage.

running changes [standard term *running* (i.e., successive) + jazz slang *changes;* some currency since c. 1920] See 1971 quot.

1955 *Hear Me Talkin to Ya*, p. 234. The Western style was more open . . . open horns and running chords and running changes.

1971 *The Street That Never Slept*, p. 327. Originally a jazzman . . . improvised by "running changes"—using chord progressions as structures from which to select notes.

running wild [special application of general slang term (i.e., acting with abandon); some currency c. 1920–c. 1940, obs. since] Playing music excitingly, skillfully and uninhibitedly.

1922 *Running Wild* (tune written by A. Harrington Gibbs).

1939 *Jazzmen*, p. 136. Louis, "running wild," regularly tied the show at the Metropolitan Theatre in a knot.

run the changes, see s.v. CHANGES.

rusty dusty [*dusty* prob. from *duster,* q.v., *rusty:* a humorous rhyming modifier; some currency, chiefly sustained by the Count Basie recording (see 1942 quot.), c. 1940–c. 1945, obs. since] The buttocks.

1942 *Harvard Blues* (song recorded by Count Basie Orchestra, vocal by Jimmy Rushing). Mama, get up off your big fat rusty dusty.

1945 *Rusty Dusty Blues* (tune composed by J. Mayo Williams).

salty, *adj.* [poss. by analogy with the brashness of seamen just come ashore, or from the spiciness of salt; cf. *1811 Dictionary of the Vulgar Tongue:* "salt: lecherous; a salt bitch: a proud bitch"; current esp. among black jazzmen since c. 1925]

1938 *Cab Calloway: Hi De Ho,* p. 16. *salty:* angry, ill-tempered.

1946 *Really the Blues,* p. 69. Ray and Fuzzy were salty with our unhip no-playing piano player. —p. 374. *salty:* sour, hostile, unpleasant.

jump salty [jazz slang *jump* (i.e., to be animated) + jazz slang *salty:* current since c. 1930]

1938 *N.Y. Amsterdam News,* 26 Feb., p. 17. Let's sound a high C on the post office man whose Girl Friday is "jumpin' salty."

1946 *Really the Blues,* p. 371. *jump salty:* turn sour or hostile.

Sand, *n. & v.t.* [by analogy with standard meaning (i.e., to sand a piece of wood); orig. a c. 1900 black vaudeville dance step; current c. 1938–c. 1945, rare since] A jazz dance step popular esp. in Harlem.

1946 *Really the Blues,* p. 230. And from the old folks' shuffle to the Suzie Q and Sand, wasn't none of them steps new to grandpa.

sassy, *adj.* [special application of the general colloquial term; according to jazzmen, some currency esp. among black jazzmen c. 1935–c. 1942, obs. since] Lively (esp. as applied to musical performance).

1970 *Dictionary of Afro-American Slang,* p. 100. *sassy:* radiating with youthful energy.

Satch, Satchmo [see 1946 quot. for etym.; one of the five or six indispensable jazz nicknames (see also BIRD, LADY, PREZ); current since c. 1925; see also POPS] Louis Armstrong 1900–1972, trumpeter, generally acclaimed by jazzmen and critics as one of the great figures in jazz history.

1937 *Metronome*, Jan., p. 25. Satchmo, I was only kiddin'. I'll give you your horn back!

1942 *The American Thesaurus of Slang*, p. 557. *Satch:* Louis Armstrong.

1946 *Jazzways*, p. 29. It wasn't long before hangers-on at the Lincoln Gardens bandstand caught on to the fact that Louis answered to "Satchelmouth." The trademark stuck, but it was shortened to "Satchmo," because that was easier to say.

1955 *Hear Me Talkin to Ya*, p. 97. We called him Dippermouth. Satchmo was unheard of then.

sax, *n.* [general colloquial term, but with esp. currency among jazzmen since c. 1920; see also AX, HORN] A saxophone (soprano, alto, tenor, or baritone); see also 1942 quot.

1926 *Melody Maker*, Mar., p. 4. Then, for a certainty, you have heard some bad saxes!

1942 *The American Thesaurus of Slang*, p. 556. *sax:* saxophonist.

sax section [current since c. 1925]

1937 *American Speech*, Feb., p. 48. In the *sax section* are reed instruments.

1942 *The American Thesaurus of Slang*, p. 557. *sax section:* a division of a dance band's instruments.

saying nothing (or something) [by analogy with verbal communication (see also TALK, TELL A STORY); some earlier use of *say* in a jazz sense: cf. 1955 *Hear Me Talkin to Ya*, p. 260. "From those evenings I know what he was trying to say"; nevertheless, widely current only since c. 1958] See first quot. *Saying nothing* is, of course, the antithesis of *saying something*.

1959 *Jazz for Moderns*, p. 21. *saying something:* producing something of value ("That cat is saying something!" This could pertain to a good musician, actor, driver, shoemaker, etc.).

1961 *The Jazz Review*, Jan., p. 6. Basie is also an admirer of Martin Luther King: "Like the cats would put it, he's *saying* something."

1962 *Bird: The Legend of Charlie Parker*, p. 20. It seems that, when he first heard Charlie's music and expressed his opinion to Parker, he said, "You ain't sayin' nothin' on your horn."

scare, *v.t.* [reflecting jazzmen's irreverence for conventional attitudes and modes of feeling (the implication here being that the listeners will be awakened to some terrible—hence, unsettling—aspects of their own natures and/or to the startling possibilities of beauty in the world); reinforced by the group of words which associates impact with negative attributes (i.e., BAD, MEAN, TOUGH, TERRIBLE); current since c. 1948] To impress, to excite, to startle delightfully (by playing music with originality and skill).

1959 *Down Beat*, 5 Mar., p. 19. When Nick settles down on his instrument and begins to find his own personality, he's going to scare everybody to death.

1960 *Playboy*, Aug., p. 109. "I have almost always been able to predict what Miles is going to play. Yet," the musician concedes, "every once in a while, he does scare everybody."

scarf, scoff, *n., v.i. & v.t.* [cf. 1930 *American Tramp and Underworld Slang*, p. 165: "*scoff:* to eat. *scoff:* food . . . Orig. Scottish, 'scaff,' food of any kind, it became English nautical slang as 'scoff,' and the earliest written Am. use appears to be in Flynt's *Tramping with Tramps*, 1893 ('Scoff's always more plenty than money.')"; for earliest use of the verb, 1960 *American Speech*, Dec., p. 310, cites Chapter 15 of Herman Melville's *White Jacket* (1850): "Quick, men, quick; bear a hand and scoff away."; widely current among jazzmen since c. 1935; see also GREASE] See second 1944 and 1959 quots.

1942 *American Mercury*, July, p. 88. Talking about *me* with a beat chick scoffing a hot dog!

1944 *Dan Burley's Original Handbook of Harlem Jive*, p. 102. It's finer than the beans you scarf in the Navy! —p. 146. *scarf, scoff:* food, meat, dinner.

1959 *Newport Jazz Festival: 1959*, p. 46. *scarf:* to eat.

scat, scat-singing, scat-chorusing, *adj. n. & v.i.* [onomatopoeic (i.e., *scat* was one of the more common nonsense sounds made in the early practice of this form); see 1955 and last quots. for further etym.; current since c. 1926] See last quot.

1935 *Metronome*, Apr., p. 54. Cab scats through this pair in his best Harlem manner.

1955 *Hear Me Talkin to Ya*, p. 108. And it's true about the scat-singing story. That's really the way it started. Louis Armstrong forgot the words and just sang sounds.

1956 *Chicago Review*, Autumn-Winter, p. 13. The ultimate in pushing the words away, of course, is "scat" or "bop" talk where the singer produces familiar sounds which don't make words at all.

1956 *Guide to Jazz*, s.v. *scat:* doubletalk; originally a succession of meaningless syllables sung to fill in when a vocalist can't remember the lyrics of a song, or simply "for the hell of it." Innovated accidentally by L. Armstrong in 1926, but since c. 1945, it has become an integral part of jazz, the voices on occasion duplicating the sound of an instrument or imitating instrumental phrasing, though the more traditional jazz use of voice, singing song lyrics, has not been discarded.

scene, (on) the [standard term given special application, and reflecting perhaps the jazzman's sense of the playlike artificiality of life; some currency since c. 1925, but widely current only since c. 1945] See first 1959 quot.

1926 *Melody Maker*, Sep., p. 61. Since "Nelly Kelly's Cabaret" came on the scene, it's put fresh kick into dancing.

1946 *Jazzways*, p. 16. By 1907, Bolden had disappeared from the scene, confined to an insane asylum.

1959 *Jazz for Moderns*, p. 21. *scene:* center of activity for musicians, where they play or gather. ("See anybody on the scene?") A superfluous word to describe further a person, place, thing or happening. ("Have eyes for the Chinese food scene?" Or: "Let's split [i.e., leave], man, I don't dig this scene.")

1959 *The Holy Barbarians*, p. 40. Something was happening on the poetry scene in Venice West.

1960 *Hiparama of the Classics*, p. 7. Everytime India got a little extra Supply in the cupboard, the Lion went ZOOM—snapped it up and swooped the scene [i.e., left].

bad scene [current since c. 1955]

1956 *Somewhere There's Music*, p. 179. It was a bad scene.

1963 *Hiptionary*, p. 18. *bad scenes:* places or situations fraught with danger.

the scene is clean [some currency c. 1948–c. 1955, very rare since] I have a job (i.e., in music).

1955 *Say,* 28 Apr., p. 53. *is the scene clean?:* are you working?

scoobydoo [onomatopoeic, imitating the sound of a musical phrase; current from c. 1945–c. 1955, rare since; see also oo-bla-dee] Nonsense word.

1970 *The World of Duke Ellington,* p. 225. If you create a show, go out and smile, and play scoobydoo solos, the people say, "That's great, that's jazz!"

score, *n. & v.i.* [by analogy with standard use of term in card playing and sports; from underworld slang; cf. 1938 *Dictionary of Slang and Unconventional English,* s.v. *score:* "to gain (a success)"; also cf. 1950 *Dictionary of American Underworld Lingo,* s.v. *score:* "anything secured by skill or craftiness"; current among jazzmen since c. 1935] As noun: that which is obtained or the source from which it is obtained; as v.i.: to obtain something pleasurable or advantageous (most often, a woman, marijuana, or narcotics).

1952 *Flee the Angry Strangers,* p. 368. Who's got [i.e., paying for] the next score, Harry Sticks? Nobody has any gold.

1956 *It's Always Four O'Clock,* p. 8. Wishy-washy babes . . . don't know their own minds; I score big with them.

1958 *Somewhere There's Music,* p. 19. So they went out on the street and scored for some fair pot [i.e., marijuana] and came back.

1960 *Beat Jokes Bop Humor & Cool Cartoons,* p. 23. I scored with an ancient apothecary, and here it is.

1963 *Nugget,* Feb., p. 55. This score I met out here, he got me that job.

scraunch, scrontch, scronch [see 1966 quot. for poss. etym.; current c. 1915–c. 1930, obs. since except historical, though the dance survives under other names; for synonymous names, see drag, mooch] A slow, dragging dance.

1943 *The Jazz Record,* 15 Apr., p. 3. In 1917 . . . there were several dances . . . resembling the rhumba or "scraunch."

1966 *Record Research,* Jan., p. 7. He calls the scrontch a drag or mooch, and that hardly seems to describe the bent-knee and wiggled-rump figure I have seen. (Does *scrontch* derive from "squat" and "hunch"?)

1973 *Jazz Dance.* Plate 11 of Appendix lists "scronch."

scream, *n. & v.i.* [some currency since c. 1930] As noun: the effect produced by such playing; as v.i.: to play a wind instrument (esp. a trumpet) in the upper register and with great volume.

1933 *Metronome*, Jan., p. 34. A scream is produced somewhat the same way as the rip, only in the rip the note is cut off shortly, but in the scream it is held.

1960 *Leisure*, Dec., pp. 40–41. If you remember, the things people liked most about Benny in the old days were the Gene Krupa solos, the screaming-type solos of Harry James.

1961 *Palaver*, Feb., p. 14. Shavers screams, the Hawk honks, and only Bryant and Duvivier show any real sense of proportion.

screamer, *n.* 1. [according to jazzmen, some currency since c. 1935; see also FREAK LIP, IRON CHOPS] A trumpeter who specializes in high notes.

1970 *Dictionary of Afro-American Slang*, p. 101. *screamer:* a jazzman who produces a scream-like effect through his trumpet.

2. [some currency esp. among white jazzmen since c. 1940] An orchestration featuring the brass section, usually very high in volume.

1940 *Swing*, Nov., p. 28. It's another riff tune . . . plus (or minus) a screamer ending featuring the leader's horn.

1948 *Down Beat*, 1 Dec., p. 13. *Minor* is a screamer but not without change of pace.

scuffle, skuffle, 1. [poss. by analogy with the energetic, exaggerated movements of many jazz dances; current from c. 1920–c. 1935, rare since]

1966 *Record Research*, Jan., p. 7. *Skuffle* was a generic term for dancing.

2. *n. & v.i.* [special application of the standard term (i.e., to struggle or fight in rough confusion); current among jazzmen since c. 1935] See 1939, first 1946, and 1959 quots.; also, by extension: any hardship.

1939 *American Jazz Music*, pp. 172–173. At the bottom of the economic pile are those musicians who have nothing which could accurately be called a job but are taking whatever one-night stand happens along; this is called "scuffling."

1946 *Really the Blues*, p. 374. *scuffle:* struggle to get along.

1946 *Jazzways*, p. 26. Often the first jobs were "scuffling"—any sort of work, just to keep going.

1958 *Somewhere There's Music*, p. 136. Three's a scuffle.

1959 *Esquire*, Nov., p. 70J. *to scuffle:* to be down and out.

1960 *Jazz Street*, p. 33. Eddie Condon scuffled through the streets and dives before he became owner of his own club, now on New York's East Side.

1968 *Down Beat*, 22 Feb., p. 18. His charts are not easy to play. We still scuffle occasionally on "Little Pixie."

second ending [so called because it continues beyond the restatement of the theme (which should then be the first ending); current since c. 1925] That passage (after the second eight bars) which leads into the bridge passage.

1956 *Second Ending* (title of novel).

1959 *Blow Up a Storm*, p. 9. A lady gave it to me because she liked my second endings.

second line [cf. standard phrase *front line;* current since c. 1900, though chiefly historical since c. 1915]

1939 *Jazzmen*, p. 27. The funerals and parades always had a "second line" which consisted of the kids who danced along behind.

1955 *Hear Me Talkin to Ya*, p. 30. I was a "second-line" kid. That meant I'd follow the big bands down the streets, and . . . carry their cases while they played.

1955 *The First Book of Jazz*, pp. 30–31. Always following these marching bands on the streets would be a horde of children, dancing along, some playing on their own homemade instruments, keeping time with the music. These youngsters were called the "second line."

section, *n. & adj.* [special application of a standard term; current since c. 1925]

1955 *A Pictorial History of Jazz*, p. 103. Those two men added were both saxophone players; the total of three, instead of a single clarinetist, made a "section." That of course is one of the key words, one of the fundamentals of big-band music.

1959 *The Jazz Scene*, p. 9. *section:* coherent group of instruments in a band, e.g., the brass, reeds, rhythm.

see, *v.i.* [narrowing of general sense; current from c. 1930–c. 1945, rare since]

1958 *Publication of the American Dialect Society*, Nov., p. 47. *see:* to read music.

see around a corner [by analogy with the difficulty and power of doing so; according to jazzmen, some currency c. 1935–c. 1945, rare since] To read music expertly.

1971 *Down Beat*, 15 Apr., p. 19. He only needs to hear it once to play it as if he wrote it! He hides behind the cats with big eyes, the ones who can see around a corner.

send, *v.t.* [see 1959 quot. for an explanation of its semantic development; widely current c. 1933–c. 1948, rare since; see also GAS, KILL, KNOCK (ONE) OUT] See 1938 quot.; also, for a rare *v.i.* use, see 1935 quot.

1935 *Vanity Fair*, Nov., p. 71. Hot artists or bands that can put across their licks successfully are *"senders"*; they *"send."*

1936 *Metronome*, Feb., p. 61. *send me:* inspire me.

1938 *Cab Calloway: Hi De Ho*, p. 16. *send:* to arouse the emotions (joyful).

1947 *Frontiers of Jazz*, p. 64. He has that rare quality of being able to send himself.

1959 *Jazz: A Quarterly of Music*, Fall, p. 284. The power of musicians of skill to transport is verbalized in *send me.*

sender, *n.* [current c. 1934–c. 1944, obs. since; see also KILLER] A musician or, by extension, any person of excellence.

1935 *Vanity Fair*, Nov., p. 71. Hot artists that can put across their licks [i.e., musical phrases] successfully are "senders."

1942 *American Mercury*, July, p. 96. *sender:* he or she who can get you to go, i.e., has what it takes. Used often as a compliment: "He's a solid sender!"

session, *n.* 1. See s.v. JAM SESSION.

2. [special application of standard meaning; current since c. 1940; see also DATE]

1940 *Swing*, Jan., p. 25. "Horn" is from an earlier session.

1959 *The Jazz Scene*, p. 10. *session:* unit of time for recording (e.g., "on the next session six sides were cut"); more generally, any unit of time in which musicians play several pieces.

set, *n.* 1. [special application of standard term; current since c. 1925] See 1956, 1959 quots.; also, since c. 1958, an LP record (since its time length is roughly equal to that of a night club set).

1955 *Solo*, p. 159. Between sets at Fack's, Jaeger found himself alone.

1956 *Guide to Jazz*, s.v. *set:* twenty or thirty minute session in a night club after which the band rests. Between sets either another group will play or the juke box is in operation or there is silence.

1959 *The Jazz Scene*, p. 10. *set:* set of pieces played by musicians followed by a rest or by the end of the session.

1960 *The Jazz Review*, May, p. 22. Everyone, even those who have had reservations about Coltrane, should hear this set.

2. [prob. less from sense 1 than from the old underworld term *set up:* 1960 *Dictionary of American Slang*, s.v. *set up:* "to provide or give someone whisky or food . . . since c. 1870"; current esp. among black jazzmen since c. 1935]

1959 *Newport Jazz Festival: 1959*, p. 46. *set:* a party.

set-ending, *n.* [current since c. 1935] A short musical passage, usually of from four to sixteen bars, played at the end of a set—i.e., a short musical theme or signature.

1958 *Somewhere There's Music*, p. 178. They blew a set-ending.

set up [shortened form of standard phrase (i.e., to set up the music stand, chairs, etc.); according to jazzmen, current since c. 1900] To get things in readiness for a band that is about to perform.

1959 *The Horn*, p. 128. Here, dad, have a brew while I get these boys set up.

1961 *Metronome*, Apr., p. 14. Milt Hinton was snapping pictures, and Gene Krupa was setting up.

shades, *n. pl.* [by analogy with the function (i.e., to keep the sun out); current since c. 1950; see also BEBOP GLASSES]

1958 *American Speech*, Oct., p. 225. *shades:* dark glasses.

1958 *Nugget*, Oct., p. 51. I been thinkin' about these shades (dark glasses), man. Believe I'll get me a pair of contact shades.

1965 *New Yorker*, 2 Jan., p. 41. Sometimes I'd put on shades and play whole shows asleep.

shag, *n.* 1. [cf. 1890 *A Dictionary of Slang, Jargon, and Cant*, s.v. *shag:* "From provincial shake"; also cf. 1937 *A Dictionary of Slang and Unconventional English*, s.v. *shag:* "a copulation . . . v.t. To coit (with a woman)"; some currency c. 1900–c. 1917, obs. since except historical] A crude, earthy type of blues c. 1900–c. 1917.

1939 *Jazzmen*, p. 30. Then there were always the blues, some, such as "the shags," of the meanest sort.

2. [relation, if any, to sense 1 unknown; current c. 1937–c. 1940, obs. since except historical] See 1954 quot.

1938 *N.Y. Amsterdam News*, 26 Feb., p. 17. Let's do the Shag in broad daylight so all can see.

1939 *Fortune*, July, p. 170. The nightly fifty-cent ecstasy of shag and stomp at the Savoy.

1954 *Down Memory Lane*, p. 131. The shag is a fast, nervous, hopping dance, performed in time to a strongly accentuated rhythm.

1955 *Hear Me Talkin to Ya*, p. 266. The jitterbugs are cooling off, and the shag is no more.

shake, *n. & adj.* [from the vibratolike shakiness of the sound; cf. its standard musical sense (i.e., trill); current among jazzmen in an altered sense since c. 1925] See 1956 quot.

1933 *Metronome*, Jan., p. 34. The glissando and the shake may be used in either hot or sweet arrangements.

1956 *Guide to Jazz*, s.v. *shake:* a note executed with particularly pronounced vibrato, almost a trill, esp. by trumpets and trombones, particularly to link one chorus to another or at the beginning of a phrase.

shake, *n. & v.i.* [from body-shaking movements of the dance; according to jazzman Eubie Blake, current c. 1900–c. 1930, obs. since except historical] A jazz dance; as v.i.: to dance the shake; also, as adj., applied to the music (see 1935 quot.) to which the shake was danced, a sensual Oriental style of jazz.

1923 *Sobbin' Blues* (tune composed by Arthur Kassel and Victor Burton). It sure has got 'em shakin' down in Dixieland.

1935 *Vanity Fair*, Nov., p. 71. Negro bands play "race music" (a curious euphemism spread by phonograph companies), and the savagery of their rhythm calls forth the terms "shake music" and "jungle music."

1940 *Jelly Roll Morton's New Orleans Memories*, p. 8. Visitors would propose that one of the girls dance in the nude, or wearing merely stockings and shoes, and the dance—also called "The Shake"—was done on a piece of board about three feet square.

1956 *Lady Sings the Blues*, p. 51. They come to the Cotton Club—a

239

place Negroes never saw inside unless they played music or did the shake or shimmies.

shake it, shake that thing, shake 'em out [see 1927 quot. for explanation of semantic development; according to jazzmen, current c. 1917–c. 1935, rare since] To dance: frequently hortatory.

1926 *Nigger Heaven*, p. 249. Shake 'em out! went the cry.

1926 *Shake That Thing* (tune recorded on Brunswick-Cliftophone 3069).

1927 *The Journal of Abnormal and Social Psychology*, Apr.-June, p. 16. "Shake it," "shake that thing." . . . Ostensibly they refer to dancing, but they are really Negro vulgar expressions relating to coitus.

shake (oneself) apart [hyperbole; according to jazzmen, some currency c. 1917–c. 1940, very rare since] To dance, laugh or cry heartily.

1956 *Lady Sings the Blues*, p. 179. When we got to her car she wheeled around the corner, then stopped and began to shake herself apart.

shake up, *v.t.* [by analogy with the physical act; current since c. 1953] To unsettle, to profoundly trouble. (Note: past participle is always *shook,* never *shaken,* frequently without *up:* see 1955 quot.)

1955 *American Speech*, Dec., p. 304. *shook:* emotionally upset.

1959 *San Francisco Chronicle*, 4 June, p. 35. It might shake up the whole joint and probably lower the real estate values.

1960 *The Village Voice*, 20 Jan., p. 2. "Come on, Norman, say something," Glick exhorted. "Shake up the squares."

1966 *New Yorker*, 25 June, p. 52. It shook me some when I looked at the label.

shaking, *participle* [by analogy of movement with life; current since c. 1953; see also HAPPENING] Happening, esp., of importance.

1958 *Jazz in Hi-Fi*, p. 13. They understand what's shaking.

1971 *Bird Lives*, p. 232. "If something doesn't start shaking pretty quick," he told us, "I'm going over the wall."

sharp, *adj.* [cf. *1811 Dictionary of the Vulgar Tongue:* "sharp: subtle, acute, quick-witted"; also, cf. general and teenage slang *sharpie* (i.e., one who is well-groomed and flashily attired) which derives from this term; current among jazzmen c. 1925–c. 1945, somewhat less since; see also DAP, FLY, HIP] Sophisticated, as reflected by wit or attire, or both.

1928 *The Walls of Jericho*, p. 305. *sharp:* striking; "keen." A beautifully dressed woman is *"sharp out of this world."*

1946 *Really the Blues*, p. 374. *sharp:* alert, dressed well, keen-witted.
1956 *Sideman*, p. 243. You're a pret-ty sharp cat, aren't you?
1957 *On the Road*, p. 61. He liked to dress sharp.

shimmy, shimme-sha-wabble, shim-sham-shimmy, *n. & v.i.* [see 1927 quot. for etym.; see 1917, 1959 quots. for beginning date; obs. since c. 1935 except historical] See 1939, 1959 quots.
1917 *Variety*, 30 Nov. The opening number was programmed as a combination of "Strutter's Ball," "Shimme-Sha-Wabble" and "Walking the Dog."
1919 *I Wish I Could Shimmy Like My Sister Kate* (song).
1927 *The Journal of Abnormal and Social Psychology*, Apr.-June, p. 16n. A note on "shake the shimmy." . . . Chemise is pronounced "shimmy" by most Negroes and a great many whites in the South. In its original meaning it described the effect produced when a woman made a movement or did a dance step which caused her breasts to shake. This caused her "shimmy" to shake.
1938 *Cab Calloway: Hi De Ho*, p. 16. *shim-sham-shimmy:* a dance introduced at the Cotton Club.
1959 *Jazz: A Quarterly of American Music*, Fall, pp. 284–285. The *shimmy* was introduced about the end of World War I. In the Ziegfeld Follies of 1919 vocalists proclaimed that "The World Is Going Shimmy Mad" and "You Can't Shake Your Shimmy on Tea." Ameliorated and no longer a sensation, the Shim-Sham-Shimmy was introduced at the Cotton Club in 1930.

shit, *n.* 1. (occasionally, esp. when used in an exclamatory or other emphatic sense, the vowel is lengthened: see 1961 and 1965 quots.) [scatological analogy in general slang use, but with esp. currency among jazzmen in certain related senses since c. 1900] Stuff (i.e., in the sense either of essence or of nonsense)—frequently, music (concerning which the connotation can be favorable or unfavorable).
1956 *Eddie Condon's Treasury of Jazz*, pp. 238–239. Trumpeter Howard McGhee once said, "Whoever the musician is who plays with him, he feels he's playing shit next to what Bird is putting down [i.e., performing]."
1959 *Jazz: A Quarterly of American Music*, Winter, p. 38. Look, man, if you don't think I can play your shit, you get somebody you think can!
1961 *Night Song*, p. 89. Tell me about jazz and American art and how us niggers did it. Sheeeeeeeeeet!

241

1965 *A Drop of Patience*, p. 40. "Shit!" She drew it out as if it were the last word of a ballad.

1974 *Down Beat*, 31 Jan., p. 16. I just want to keep playing, writing, and experimenting with this shit—because it has unlimited capabilities.

2. [special application of sense 1; some currency among jazzmen since c. 1935; see also BOO, GAGE, POT, TEA] Marijuana or narcotics.

1950 *Neurotica*, Autumn, p. 45. Senor, this shit is the end [i.e., marvelous]!

1956 *Sideman*, p. 282. You oughta smoke some shit.

1959 *The Naked Lunch*, pp. 65–66. Eukodol is like a combination of junk and C [i.e., cocaine]. Trust the Germans to concoct some really evil shit.

shootin' the agate [semantic development unknown; according to jazzmen, current c. 1900–c. 1917, obs. since except historical] A dancelike walk popular in New Orleans and Memphis street parades.

1948 *The Record Changer*, June, p. 10. He would walk with a cake walkish strut and "drive them chicks wild." This was called "shootin' the agate."

short, *n.* [poss. because it was considered the shortest way to get places; current c. 1945; see also RUBBER, WHEELS]

1955 *American Speech*, Dec., p. 305. *short:* automobile.

1960 *Down Beat*, 7 Jan., p. 26. Then when they get there, a corny gig, a cup of coffee, back in the short and on from Roanoke to Tabor City, N.C.

short line [from gambler's slang; some currency since c. 1950] Not much money.

1959 *Lenny Bruce: I Am Not a Nut, Elect Me* (LP record). Listen, man, I'll work it for short line, but you've gotta get me the date.

1969 *Hip Manual*, s.v. *short line:* not enough money. "It's a fun gig, but short line."

shout, *n., adj., v.i., & v.t.* [See 1939, 1950, 1956 quots. for explanation of semantic development; current in various jazz senses since c. 1920] See 1955 and 1956 quots.; initially, where the music was sung and played (see 1928 quot.): obs.

1928 *The Walls of Jericho*, p. 305. *shout:* ball; prom.

1939 *Blues* (Decca Records pamphlet), p. 3. The Fourth chorus is virtually a "shout" vocal with the fire and gusto of a real spiritual.

1950 *They All Played Ragtime*, p. 188. The true "shout" takes place on Sundays or on "praise" nights through the week.

1955 *A Pictorial History of Jazz*, p. 127. Stomping variations of rags, known as "shouts," were the show-pieces most often used in competition; they were ideally suited to be heard over the normal rent party din.

1956 *Guide to Jazz*, s.v. *shout:* a style of singing the blues in a penetrating, shouting tone, usually in the spirit of gospel-singing. "James P. Johnson and Fats Waller are 'shout pianists' and Tommy Ladnier a 'shout trumpet.' "

1973 *Down Beat*, 15 Mar., p. 15. Tiny Kahn could play a 2-bar fill leading to a shout chorus that contained elements you'd heard from the time you were a child.

shouter, *n.* [current since c. 1925] One who sings the blues in shout style (see 1956 quot., s.v. SHOUT).

1955 *Hear Me Talkin to Ya*, p. 245. She was certainly recognized among blues singers—a shouter, they called her.

show out [analogous to general idiom "show off"; current esp. among black jazzmen c. 1895–c. 1935, obs. since except historical]

1968 *Down Beat*, 7 Mar., p. 18. If the newcomer was carrying his saxophone, trombone, or trumpet case, he would be invited to blow some, or, as they said in the argot of the time, "to show out."

1970 *Dictionary of Afro-American Slang*, p. 103. *showing out:* (1890s) to flaunt one's self or one's possessions.

shuck, *n., v.i. & v.t.* [poss. originated as a euphemism for *shit,* or from the general colloquial *shucks* (i.e., something valueless); some currency since c. 1950 esp. in the Midwest and on the West Coast; see also JIVE] See last quot.

1958 *Somewhere There's Music*, p. 91. Mike shucked it up so much that Guy Lombardo might have liked it.

1959 *The Holy Barbarians*, p. 25. I didn't shuck the customers enough to please the crook who was running the car lot. —p. 317. *shuck:* as a noun, a falsehood, deception, fraud; as a verb, to deceive, swindle, or defraud.

shuffle, *adj. & n.* [see 1956 quot. for explanation of semantic development; current from c. 1917–c. 1945, rare since: see BACK BEAT]

1925 *River Boat Shuffle* (tune composed by Hoagy Carmichael, Irving Mills and Dick Voynow).

1940 *Swing,* June, p. 13. The typifying characteristic of the Savitt band is its "shuffle rhythm," which is distinguished . . . by its . . . ¼ jazz time. It gets its shuffle from the piano's push in the treble.

1949 *Music Library Association Notes,* Dec., p. 51. *shuffle rhythm:* mode of playing a popular song, which involves breaking each measure into eighth notes. Four eighth notes in treble of piano follow successively the four eighth notes in bass, which moves step-wise or in arpeggio form. Rhythm is adaptable for orchestra as well as piano, and is used effectively with certain songs.

1956 *Guide to Jazz,* s.v. *shuffle:* a dance created in the South, later applied to a boogie-woogie type rhythm, slow and strongly syncopated.

side, *n.* [from the usual pre-1948 practice of recording one piece of music per side of a record; widely current since c. 1930: see also TRACK] See 1959 quot.; also, since c. 1948, any phonograph record.

1937 *Metronome,* Mar., p. 31. It's the wonder that Victor is issuing so many sides by this band.

1959 *The Jazz Scene,* p. 10. *side:* side of an old 78 rpm record.

1961 *Down Beat,* 19 Jan., p. 40. Four sides. LP? That came later, and you didn't say "track" then.

sideman, *n.* [cf. general slang *front (man),* i.e., leader; current since c. 1930]

1942 *The American Thesaurus of Slang,* p. 555. *side man:* any musician in the band except the leader.

1961 *Jazz Street,* p. 14. There are sidemen as well as leaders in this book.

sing, *v.i.* [analogy to human vocalizing; some slight currency since c. 1925]

1939 *American Jazz Music,* p. 44. The jazz players "sang" with their instruments, played them with personal, expressive inflections variable between robust roughness and pure, bodiless lyricism.

1947 *Frontiers of Jazz,* p. 167. He doesn't make it sing like Bix.

1968 *Down Beat,* 5 Sep., p. 17. Hodges "sang" "Passion Flower" as

244

only he can, replete with the descending moan that can ice your ventricles.

single, *n.* 1. [chiefly entertainment trade (i.e., night clubs and booking agencies) slang, but with some currency among jazzmen since c. 1935] A performer working alone—usually, a singer with only piano accompaniment, or a pianist.

1938 *The American Language,* p. 585. Why don't you air her and do a single?

1961 *Metronome,* Apr., p. 46. Red Allen . . . has disbanded his group and is working as a single.

1970 *Jazz People,* p. 36. "Name" soloists prefer to work as "singles" with a local rhythm section.

2. [chiefly recording trade slang, but with some currency among jazzmen since c. 1935] Initially: a single 78 rpm record (as distinguished from an album containing a set of records); since c. 1950: a 45 rpm record (as distinguished from a 33 rpm LP; in this sense, oral evidence only).

1940 *Mademoiselle,* June, p. 131. The best single of the month is Barney Bigard's "Lost in Two Flats."

single-line, single line [current since c. 1935] Of music, played in a sequence or pattern of single notes (as distinguished from chords).

1958 *Lennie Tristano* (liner notes on LP album Atlantic 1224). In "These Foolish Things," it is the splendidly long line that Lee plays, Lennie's reflective musing, now single-line, now in block chords, and a finish together that puts a glistening coda on both their backs.

1960 *The Jazz Review,* June, p. 23. The fast right-hand single lines are similar.

single-string, single-note, *adj.* [standard musical term, but with esp. currency among jazzmen as a distinguishing term since the innovations of Charlie Christian c. 1940, which had the effect of reestablishing the guitar as a solo instrument instead of merely an accompanying one]

1942 *The American Thesaurus of Slang,* p. 562. *single-string work:* picking melodies on the guitar in addition to rhythmic chords.

1949 *Inside Be-Bop,* p. 6. The single-note solo style was a complete departure from the pattern of solos in chords established by Carl Kress, Dick McDonough and the other conventional jazz guitarists.

sipping [understatement; some currency esp. among black jazzmen since c. 1940; see also TASTE] Drinking (liquor).

1947 *Sipping at Bells* (tune recorded by Miles Davis).

1970 *The World of Duke Ellington*, p. 133. He'd be sipping every now and then, and getting stoned all night long.

sit in [prob. by analogy with card playing slang; also cf. 1934 *A Dictionary of American Slang*, p. 394. "*sit in:* to take part; to be present"; widely current since c. 1930] See 1936 quot. (although it needn't be "by invitation"; i.e., the outside musician, unexpectedly present, may ask or be asked to perform).

1936 *Delineator*, Nov., p. 49. *sitting in:* when an outside musician drops in by invitation to play with a swing band or group.

1959 *Somewhere There's Music*, p. 57. Why not sit in a set or two?

1959 *The Horn*, p. 6. Edgar Pool had been inveigled to sit in with the house group.

sixteens, the [according to jazzman Eubie Blake, some currency c. 1900–c. 1917; obs. since except historical] A pianistic device of rolling sixteenth notes in the bass (quot. is, therefore, inaccurate).

1957 *Just Jazz*, p. 13. At the turn of the century, they called it [i.e., boogie-woogie] . . . "honky tonk" . . . "rolling bass" . . . or "the sixteens."

skiffle (band) [etym. unknown; according to jazzman Eubie Blake, current c. 1900–c. 1914, obs. since except historical] A band consisting primarily of rhythm instruments and playing in a shuffle rhythm style.

1957 *Sing Out!*, Spring, p. 30. In the first decade of the 20th Century, these New Orleans boys called themselves a "Skiffle" band.

1964 *New Yorker*, 25 Jan., p. 8. A sort of skiffle band (three banjoes, a washboard, a tuba, and a trombone) roam the range.

skin, give (or slip) (me) some [synecdoche; current c. 1938–c. 1948, rare since] Slap the palm of my hand with the palm of yours (or vice versa) as a greeting or a farewell or because one of us approves of what the other just said or did.

1939 *Jitterbug Jamboree Song Book*, p. 33. *slip me some skin:* congratulate me.

1944 *The New Cab Calloway's Hepsters Dictionary*, s.v. *gimme some skin:* shake hands.

246

1946 *Big Book of Swing*, p. 125. *skin:* handshake.

1955 *Bop Fables*, p. 38. "Baby," he said, grinning affably, "gimme some skin."

1962 *Down Beat*, 19 July, p. 49. The French horn player tries some very adventurous things, and . . . that's a hard instrument . . . so I've got to give him skin for it.

skins, *n. pl.* [synecdoche; current since c. 1925; see also HIDES, TUBS]

1926 *Melody Maker*, Mar., p. 32. The Skin Game (title of column on drumming instruction).

1942 *The American Thesaurus of Slang*, p. 559. *skins:* drums.

1952 *Music Out of Dixie*, p. 161. He kin sure work them skins.

skin-beater, *n.* [from *skins;* some currency c. 1935–c. 1945, very rare since; see also HIDE BEATER]

1937 *This Thing Called Swing*, p. 9. *skin-beater:* drummer.

1940 *Swing*, Jan., p. 11. How about a bit of Drummer Krupa and the other good "skin-beaters"!

sky (piece) [from its lofty position on the head; some currency since c. 1935]

1944 *The New Cab Calloway's Hepsters Dictionary*, s.v. *sky piece:* hat.

1957 *N.Y. Times Magazine*, 18 Aug., p. 26. *sky:* a hat.

1958 *American Speech*, Oct., p. 224. The cat dons his . . . *skypiece.*

1963 *Hiptionary*, p. 78. The hang up [q.v.] is a tight sky crushing our konks [i.e., heads].

slam, slammer, *n.* [metonymy: by association with the banging shut of the door(s); see 1946 quot. for longer form which is the key to semantic development; also see last quot. for orig. source and dates] For an occasional sense, see 1944 quot.; for the usual sense, see 1959 quot.

1944 *The New Cab Calloway's Hepsters Dictionary*, s.v. *twister to the slammer:* the key to the door.

1946 *Really the Blues*, p. 371. *house of many slammers:* jail.

1952 *Flee the Angry Strangers*, p. 358. I'm hip what you was doin wit Ange while I was in the slammer.

1959 *The Holy Barbarians*, p. 318. *slam, slammer:* jail.

1960 *Dictionary of American Slang*, s.v. *slammer:* a door. Jive use c. 1935. . . . Old underworld use.

247

slap, *v.i. & v.t.* [see 1956 quot. for key to semantic development; according to jazzmen, *slap* has been current since c. 1915, coupled with *doghouse,* q.v., since c. 1922]

1931 *Melody Maker,* Dec., p. 1029. Slapping, too, becomes next to impossible with a high bridge.

1934 *A Dictionary of American Slang,* p. 171. *slap the dog house:* to pluck the strings of a bass viol.

1936 *Esquire,* June, p. 131. What type of people get a thrill out of an orchestra that knows its way to town, out of listening to an expert bass player like Wellman Braud "slap the doghouse."

1956 *Guide to Jazz,* s.v. *slap:* pluck (the bass string so that it hits against the neck of the bass producing a slapping effect).

1959 *The Jazz Scene,* p. 289. *slapping:* pizzicato playing.

slap-tongue, *v.i. & adj.* [some currency since c. 1925] See 1942 quot.

1942 *American Thesaurus of Slang,* p. 563. *slap-tongue:* to strike the tongue against the mouthpiece.

1963 *Down Beat,* 3 Jan., p. 20. Even his first solo with Henderson, a clownlike, slap-tongue effort, presaged important things to come.

1971 *Down Beat,* 18 Feb., p. 28. Harry Carney at 18 was still inventing his baritone style with the slap-tongue sound popular then.

slave, *v.i. & n.* [special application of standard term; widely current c. 1935–c. 1945, somewhat less since; see also DAY GIG, HAME] To work (*not* in music); as noun: a job outside the jazz world.

1938 *Cab Calloway: Hi De Ho,* p. 16. *slave:* to work, whether arduous labor or not.

[1944] *Black on Black,* p. 201. Slip up here and cop this slave . . . I don't care who knows I'm slavin'.

1944 *Esquire,* June, p. 170. *knock a slave:* get a job.

1958 *Jive in Hi-Fi,* p. 15. *to collar a slave:* to get a job.

1966 *Down Beat,* 15 Dec., p. 18. If you have eyes [q.v.], the slave is yours.

slide, *n.* [from sliding effect produced by it; according to jazzmen, some currency since c. 1925; see also GLISS, SMEAR]

1959 *The Jazz Scene,* p. 289. *slide:* glissando.

1961 *The Feeling of Jazz,* p. 29. They're too involved with making sensuous sounds with all those vibratos and slides and slurs.

sliphorn, slip-horn, *n.* [from slipping movements of the slide part of trombone; according to jazzman Eubie Blake, some currency c. 1900–c. 1945, very rare since except to distinguish the slide trombone from the valve trombone (see 1957 quot.); see also BONE, TRAM]

1925 *English Words & Their Background*, p. 45. *sliphorn:* trombone.

1956 *Sideman*, p. 198. Message here for "Tex the sliphorn player!"

1957 *Melody Maker*, 4 May, p. 6. Wilbur himself was somewhat subdued, using both sliphorn and valve, but what he did was pleasant trombone.

slow drag, see S.V. DRAG.

slush pump, *n.* [prob. from the great amount of spittle that collects in the slide part; some currency esp. among white jazzmen c. 1935–c. 1945, obs. since except historical: see also BONE, SLIPHORN, TRAM]

1942 *The American Thesaurus of Slang*, p. 559. *slush pump:* trombone.

1943 *Barefoot Boy with Cheek*, p. 90. Awful fine slush pump . . . you ought to dig that.

small bread, see S.V. BREAD.

smear, *n.* [from the extending or spreading of the sound produced; current since c. 1925; see also GLISS, SLIDE] See 1959 quot.

1933 *Metronome*, Jan., p. 34. A smear is produced by first playing a tone a trifle flat.

1944 *New Yorker*, 1 July, p. 29. Someone may advocate extending a note or cutting it off. The sax section may want to put an additional smear on it.

1958 *N.Y. Daily News*, 4 Mar. Yet, says Father O'Connor, "a conviction has gotten around that a jazz theme supports and girds a seamy tale of human failure, moral or physical. A muted trumpet, a breathy sax, a high trombone smear—these express (in media such as movies and TV) that human area in which a will decides to commit a wrong, a sin, to misuse a freedom."

1959 *The Jazz Scene*, p. 289. *smear:* glissando.

smoke 'em out (or **on 'em**) [by analogy of excitement with heat (see also BURN, COOK); current since c. 1952] To play music excitingly, pulsatingly; also, by extension, to do anything well.

249

1970 *Dictionary of Afro-American Slang*, p. 105. *smoke (them) out:* (1950s) to be really fantastic, esp. in making good music.

smoking (usually *participle*) [by analogy of excitement with heat (see also BURN and COOK); current since c. 1952] Playing (music) with great skill and intensity; by extension, to do anything impressively.

1972 *Gorilla, My Love*, p. 173. "Do you understand?" "You smokin,'" say Gail.

1974 *Down Beat*, 15 Aug., p. 33. That band smokes.

snake hips [from common practice of designating jazz dances by reference to animal movements or parts of the body (see also BUNNY HUG, CAMEL WALK, FOX TROT, TURKEY TROT); some currency esp. in New York City and Baltimore c. 1925–c. 1930, obs. since except historical] Jazz dance.

1931 *Snake Hips* (tune recorded by the Blue Rhythm Boys).

1934 *Beale Street: Where the Blues Began*, p. 105. In the golden days of 1912 . . . brown beauties . . . danced the Pasamala, long before the "cootie crawl," "black bottom" and "snake hips" were thought of.

snakes, blowing [prob. by analogy with snake-charmer's music; some currency since c. 1945] Playing (music) weirdly, disjointedly. Oral evidence only.

snakes, make [by analogy with the quickness of a snake's tongue; current from c. 1920–c. 1940, rare since, prob. because most contemporary jazzmen have great technical facility] Of a hornman, (the ability) to play very fast.

1972 *Down Beat*, 29 Apr., p. 16. He makes snakes, they used to say. That meant he could play fast.

sock chorus [see 1936 quot. for key to its semantic development (i.e., it is the last chorus that generally receives the heaviest emphasis); according to jazzmen, current c. 1920–c. 1945, rare since] Note: phrase generally applies to pre-1945 jazz.

1936 *Delineator*, Nov., p. 49. *sock chorus:* last chorus of an arrangement.

1937 *This Thing Called Swing*, p. 9. *sock:* emphasis, usually referring to the last chorus.

1956 *Second Ending*, p. 57. They rode into the sock chorus like a storm cloud of marauders.

sock cymbal [so called because in much pre-1945 jazz it was the vehicle of the heaviest accents; current since c. 1920] A fairly large single cymbal.

1936 *Metronome*, Feb., p. 61. *off beat cymbal:* sock cymbal.

1944 *Metronome*, July, p. 31. "Dizzy has a phobia about drummers who play sock cymbals," reports drummer Jackie Mills.

sock it (out) [from the sense of giving a heavy accent; some currency c. 1916–c. 1945, very rare since] See 1933, 1935 quots.; frequently hortatory (see 1955 quot.).

1927 *Melody Maker*, July, p. 697. Sock out your last chorus on that, my friends.

1933 *Fortune*, Aug., p. 47. Returning to Trombonist Brown, he can *get off, swing it, sock it* . . . (all of which mean syncopate to beat the band).

1935 *Vanity Fair*, Nov., p. 71. Hot artists or bands that can put across their licks [i.e., musical phrases] successfully . . . can "sock it."

1955 *Hear Me Talkin to Ya*, p. 81. Blow it, kid. Sock it out.

sock rhythm (or style) [from the pronounced rhythmic accents; some currency c. 1920–c. 1945, obs. since except historical] See 1942 quot.: also, that style of playing.

1934 *A Dictionary of American Slang*, p. 171. *sock rhythm:* rhythm that enables special use of drums, tuba, or piano.

1939 *Jazzmen*, p. 50. He had what might be described as a "sock" style, "blowing in" phrases with little bursts of sound and riding the melody.

1942 *The American Thesaurus of Slang*, p. 560. *sock rhythm:* an emphasized syncopated rhythm.

solid, *adj. & adv.* [see 1954 quot. for prob. semantic origin; according to jazzmen, Louis Armstrong was the first to habitually use the term in a jazz sense c. 1920; widely current c. 1935–c. 1945, very rare since; see also CRAZY, GROOVY] See 1938, 1954, 1960 quots.

1928 *Melody Maker*, Dec. He is a complete master, and a "solid" man. A great artist on the cymbal.

1938 *Cab Calloway: Hi De Ho*, p. 16. *solid:* great, swell, okay.

1953 *Night Light*, p. 137. That's all there is to it. Solid?

1954 *Social Forces*, Dec., p. 179. Because of the importance of solid rhythm, the term "solid" came to be applied to anything good or desirable or approved by the jazzmen.

251

1956 *Chicago Review*, Autumn-Winter, pp. 14–15. Appearing suddenly in the song, "Soli-tudy," with its echo of "solid," [it] makes fun of the degraded pseudo-jazz lyrics of a period when everything was "solid."

1960 *Dictionary of American Slang*, s.v. *solid:* . . . often used as a one-word reply to a statement.

solid, do (one) a [from *solid* above; some currency since c. 1965] Do (one) a favor.

1974 *Ladies and Gentlemen—Lenny Bruce!!*, p. 387. The cat who'd invited Lenny to the party knows his way around the political set but, because of all the publicity the case has received, can't do him any solids.

solid sender [jazz slang *solid* + jazz slang *sender,* frequently used in combination c. 1936–c. 1941, obs. since except historical] Someone (often, a musician) or something (often, music) that provides excellent entertainment.

1938 *Metronome*, Apr., p. 26. A really solid sender is the third record from the right in my collection.

something else (or **different**) [see first three quots. for explanation of semantic development; widely current since c. 1957] (Note: usually applied to something or someone in a favorable sense, but also occasionally in an unfavorable sense.)

1959 *Jazz for Moderns*, p. 21. *something else:* a phenomenon so special it defies description.

1959 *Esquire*, Nov., p. 70J. *something else:* so good that it is in a category by itself.

1960 *The Jazz Titans*, p. 109. Musicians say of Earl "Bud" Powell that "he's somethin' else," in the sense that he's in a class by himself.

1961 *Metronome*, Mar., p. 24. Pleasant as this had been, what was to come was something else.

1962 *Downbeat*, 7 June, p. 39. That rhythm section was something different. The band was swinging.

soul, *n.* & *adj.* 1. [see second 1959, 1961 quots. for explanation of semantic development; despite 1946 quot., widely current only since c. 1955; see also FEELING]

1946 *Ebony*, Sep., p. 34. He uses a bewildering technique, and his playing is full of what jazzmen refer to as "soul."

1958 *Down Beat*, 20 Mar., p. 30. Mingus is sensitive, powerful, lyrical, and several other adjectives which make up the feel of the much abused word *soul*.

1959 *Jazz for Moderns*, p. 21. *soul:* an inborn quality of authenticity. The opposite of mechanical. Almost beyond description.

1959 *New York Jazz Festival* (Vol. 3), p. 18. (Most of the critics fifteen years ago were convinced the modernists had sold their blue souls for Mephistophelian technical wizardry and that their music accordingly was "cold, cerebral, and mechanical.") The soul of which Horace Silver speaks is used in a secular sense, but several of the younger jazzmen are happily tracing their music back to such pre-jazz sources as spiritual and gospel singing. . . . "What is 'soul' in jazz? It comes from within; it's what happens when the inner part of you comes out."

1959 *Harper's*, June, p. 75. The frequency with which "soul" has entered into the conversation of young Negro jazzmen is reflected in some of the titles of their works—"Soul Brothers," "Soulville," "Soul-O Blues," "Plenty, Plenty Soul."

1960 *Down Beat*, 24 Nov., p. 18. "Soul" simply means heart and conviction, an unconscious feeling for jazz roots that emerges in a musician's playing and makes it authentic.

1960 *Esquire*, Dec., p. 74. Some of the current "soul fever" being incorporated into the music of musicians who used to be called "hard boppers" is legitimately come by and is yet another way of forcefully reminding white audiences—and themselves—of a basic part of their heritage.

1961 *Commonweal*, 24 Mar., p. 658. It's called "soul music" because its practitioners have incorporated some of the backbeat, rhythms, and exclamatory melodic lines of Negro gospel music.

1963 *Down Beat*, 20 June, p. 21. By the end of 1961, it was evident that "soul" as a movement had been corrupted, suffocated, and killed.

2. *n.* [special application of sense 1; because it is valued highly; current since c. 1957; see also MARY JANE, SHIT]

1959 *Esquire*, Nov., pp. 70H–70I. *soul:* marijuana.

heavy soul, see S.V. HEAVY.

soul brother [special use of *soul* in combination, further reflecting its gospel music origin; current esp. among black jazzmen since c. 1957] A

253

fellow "soul" musician (see SOUL); also, frequently, when used by a black jazzman: another black jazzman or simply another black or any deeply human person, black or white.

1959 *Jazz: A Quarterly of American Music*, Fall, p. 291. It's one of those type LPs. I had all "soul brothers." It's on Riverside. I used "Bags" (Milt Jackson), Percy Heath, Wynton Kelly and Art Blakey.

1970 *Death of a Blue-Eyed Soul Brother* (novel title).

soul food [special use of *soul* in combination; current esp. among black jazzmen since c. 1957]

1964 *N.Y. Times Magazine*, 23 Aug., p. 62. *Soul food:* chitterlings, collard greens, ham hocks, grits, black-eyed peas, and rice, and the like.

1970 *Death of a Blue-Eyed Soul Brother*, p. 31. He and his wife loved soul food.

sound, *n.* 1. [special application of standard term; current since c. 1945] Literally, the "sound" of a performing group—its distinguishing melodic, harmonic and rhythmic qualities, its conceptual approach to music.

1948 *Metronome*, June, p. 15. Woody's new band gets a very fine sound.

1949 *Long Island Sound* (song recorded by Stan Getz on June 21, 1949). [Note: the title is a pun on the word.]

1958 *Jazz: A Quarterly of American Music*, Oct., p. 28. Who else but Basie gets that SOUND, man.

1961 *Metronome*, Apr., p. 13. There was a search for a sound, for a *soul* sound that brought back the "group" feeling, perhaps inspired by gospel music and some aspects of rock and roll.

1971 *Down Beat*, 29 Apr., p. 16. Now Stan and Zoot, they get a beautiful sound.

2. [analogical extension of sense 1; current since c. 1960]

1963 *Hiptionary*, p. 56. *his sound:* his message, his doctrine.

sound (on), *v.t. & v.i.* [cf. c. 1605 *King Lear*, I, ii, "Hath he never before sounded you in this business?"; also cf. general slang phrase *sound (someone) out;* widely current among jazzmen since c. 1950] To speak (to).

1958 *Somewhere There's Music*, p. 82. She probably wants to sound you herself when the scene's cool.

1959 *The Holy Barbarians*, p. 318. *sound:* to voice an opinion, recite a poem, or inquire.

1959 *Esquire*, Nov., p. 70J. *to sound on:* to ask someone for something.

1959 *Diggeth Thou?*, p. 34. So after he had sounded and she had dug his riff,/She cut into his dommy and helped him kill the fifth.

spaces, *n. pl.* [special application of standard meaning; some currency since c. 1950] In music, the silent intervals between notes or between clusters of notes (see last quot. for verb phrase form).

1959 *The Jazz Review*, Sep., p. 10. Always leave some spaces—lay out [q.v.].

1974 *Down Beat*, 14 Mar., p. 13. In the background Mike Mandel is spacing out on keyboards.

spade, *n. & adj.* [by analogy with the black suit in playing cards; very old general slang term (cf. 1934 *A Dictionary of American Slang*, p. 38. "*spade:* a very dark Negro"; also, The Seven Spades, a group formed by Louis Mitchell in 1917); current among white jazzmen since c. 1930; see also SOUL BROTHER] See 1959 quot.

1933 *Metronome*, Aug., p. 16. The blues those spades put in my ear was great stuff for it.

1952 *Who Walk in Darkness*, p. 61. These spade intellectuals really think they've made it.

1959 *The Holy Barbarians*, p. 318. *spade cat:* Negro. The holy barbarians, white and Negro, are so far beyond "racial tolerance" and desegregation that they no longer have to be polite about it with one another.

spasm band [from the fitful nature of the music; current c. 1900–c. 1917, obs. since except historical]

1941 *Observer-Kaleidoscope*, Nov., p. 11. "Stale Bread" Lacoume, white race track tout . . . organized a "spasm" band, playing on instruments made of junk pile material.

1956 *Guide to Jazz*, s.v. *spasm band:* small street band, the instruments of which are objects not usually used for making music, e.g., suitcase for drums, wine jug for tuba, etc. Flourished when jazz was simpler, more primitive.

1959 *The Sound of Surprise*, p. 196. A spasm band (washboard, bones, harmonica, and washtub bass) rattled along with all the force of a quilting bee.

special, *n. & adv.* [limited use of the standard meaning; current c. 1925–c. 1935, when it was largely replaced by *original,* q.v.]

1926 *Melody Maker,* Nov., p. 10. There is a lot of money to be made at this "special arrangement" game.

1937 *American Speech,* Feb., p. 48. *special:* an exclusive arrangement, belonging to one band only.

speed up [special application of standard phrase; some currency since c. 1900] To increase the tempo of the music.

1948 *The Record Changer,* June, p. 6. Jelly Roll Morton's demonstration, on a Library of Congress record, of ragtime "speeding up," is a good example of what happens when the functional controls cease to operate.

spitvalve, *n.* [according to jazzman Eubie Blake, current since c. 1900] The slide part of the trombone, in which the player's saliva collects; also, sometimes: the corresponding part of a trumpet or of a baritone saxophone.

1956 *Sideman,* p. 20. Many of the pages were smeared where drops from spitvalves had fallen and wetted the ink.

split, *v.i.* [prob. derives from the sense of separating self from place; widely current since c. 1950 when it largely supplanted *cut (out),* q.v.]

1956 *Sideman,* p. 294. But that's why the cat split.

1959 *The Real Cool Killers,* p. 15. "Split!" one of the Arabs hissed.

1959 *Swinging Syllables,* s.v. *split:* leave.

split the (or that) scene, [from jazz slang terms *split* and *scene;* widely current since c. 1952; see also LEFT TOWN, QUIT THE SCENE] To remove oneself from a place, circumstance, or situation; by extension; to die (in this sense, oral evidence only).

1956 *Tennessee Folklore Society Bulletin,* Mar., p. 23. *split the scene:* to leave.

1958 *Jive in Hi-Fi,* p. 27. In slang, if you say "split the scene," it means a situation is in progress and your better judgment tells you to leave or stay clear.

1961 *Metronome,* Apr., p. 1. Making a fast buck and splitting the scene is the order of the day.

spot, *n.* 1. [prob. shortened form of colloquial *night spot* (i.e., night club); current among jazzmen since c. 1915; see also JOINT] A night club.

1944 *Metronome,* Nov., p. 18. The Hollywood was quite a spot.

1956 *Enjoyment of Jazz* (EJ410), p. 3. We've proved you can swing and still play commercial spots, like the Statler.

2. [shortened form for "solo spot"; current since c. 1950] Solo chorus.

1967 *Down Beat,* 10 Aug., p. 38. *Bugle Call Rag* had a spot for the band's featured hornman.

spots, *n. pl.* [from the appearance of sheet music; according to jazzmen, some currency since c. 1920; see also DOTS]

1935 *Vanity Fair,* Nov., p. 71. Notes are "spots."

1937 *American Speech,* Feb., p. 48. *spots:* the notes on sheet music.

square. *n, & adj.* [see 1958 and first 1959 quots. for poss. explanation of semantic origin, though more prob. the term stems from colloquial *on the square* and/or the underworld slang *squarejohn* (both taken in the sense of honesty and trustworthiness based solely on innocence or naïveté: see 1945, 1946 quots.); also cf. 1811 *Dictionary of the Vulgar Tongue:* "square: honest, not roguish"; some currency since c. 1935; see also NOWHERE, UNCOOL, UNHIP]

1938 *Cab Calloway: Hi De Ho,* p. 14. *square:* an un-hip person.

1945 *Hepcats Jive Talk Dictionary,* s.v. *square:* a hard-working, unromantic person.

1946 *Really the Blues,* p. 375. *square:* unenlightened person, a working man, an orthodox follower of the rules.

1956 *Sideman,* p. 141. Man, I wanta be *square* . . . settle down some place.

1958 *Publication of the American Dialect Society,* Nov., p. 47. *square:* not in accordance with the jazzman's aesthetic standards. Probably comes from steady 1-2-3-4 rhythm without variation. Many musicians, while saying the word, will make a motion similar to the band director's indication for 4/4 time—the hand moves in a square for the four beats.

1959 *N.Y. Times Magazine,* 5 Apr., p. 81. In the late Nineteen Twenties, an old word acquired a new meaning in the American language. The word was "square," and the world of jazz blew it into everyday usage. . . . A square was someone who did not understand their style of music, . . . a square peg in their musical circles.

1959 *The Horn,* p. 33. The mechanical objections of the square: the man who was captive in a world of regular hours, transportation difficulties and lean thoughts.

squeeze, *n.* [poss. from a double sense: (1) that from which one's artistic style is extracted (i.e. squeezed) and (2) that which makes a powerful *impression* on one's artistic style; according to jazzmen, some currency since c. 1972] The source of one's musical or artistic style; one's influence or inspiration. Oral evidence only.

stand, one-night, see s.v. ONE-NIGHT.

standard, *n.* [from its achieving the status of a fixed part of the jazz repertory; current since c. 1930]

1937 *American Speech,* Oct., p. 184. *standard:* a number whose popularity has withstood the test of time.

1955 *Hear Me Talkin to Ya,* p. 383. You don't have to just hang a tune on the changes of a standard.

1956 *Guide to Jazz,* p. 256. *standard:* a number which has stood the test of time and found a permanent place in the repertory of jazz performers.

stash, stache, *n.* [formed from *v.t.;* current since c. 1925; see also PAD] See first quot.; also: that which is hidden (see last quot.)—frequently, liquor or marijuana.

1946 *Really the Blues,* p. 375. *stash:* house, bed, hiding-place.

1952 *Flee the Angry Strangers,* p. 440. Nobody suppose to know my stash, nobody.

1958 *Somewhere There's Music,* p. 32. I didn't want to bring out the stash while Dog was here.

v.t. [cf. 1959 *Webster's New World Dictionary,* s.v. *stash:* "prob. a blend of *store* and *cache";* also cf. *1811 Dictionary of the Vulgar Tongue:* "stash: e.g., the cove tipped the prosecutor to stash the business"; current among jazzmen since c. 1920]

1944 *The New Cab Calloway's Hepsters Dictionary,* s.v. *stache:* to file, to hide away, to secrete.

1952 *Park East,* Dec., p. 30. The boppers were stashed real cool in their pads.

1959 *The Naked Lunch,* p. 95. The Beagle has stached the heroin in a lottery ticket.

v.i. 1. [special application of *v.t.:* i.e., to put oneself away, to secure oneself (in sleep); current since c. 1935]

1946 *Really the Blues*, p. 375. *stash:* to go to sleep.

2. [prob. extension of sense 1 or of the *n.* (i.e., to assume a place for oneself); current since c. 1940]

1944 *The New Cab Calloway's Hepsters Dictionary*, p. 14. *stashed* [sic]: to stand or remain.

1958 *The Book of Negro Folklore*, p. 487. *stash:* to stand; to stand arrogantly.

1960 *Beat Jokes Bop Humor & Cool Cartoons*, p. 50. He stashes around that battlement until the cock crows, then he splits.

stay inside [in the sense of not going outside of what is essential; according to jazzmen, current since c. 1930] A bandleader's command to the orchestra to dispense with the introduction and the verses and to play only the choruses. Oral evidence only.

stick, *n.* 1. [from its shape (see also BLACK-STICK, LICORICE STICK); according to jazzmen, current c. 1920–c. 1945, very rare since; see also CLARY].

1935 *His Hi De Highness of Ho De Ho*, p. 35. The clarinet player, when he takes a soaring break, is "getting off on a stick."

1936 *Metronome*, Feb., p. 61. *stick:* clarinet.

1948 *Capitol News*, Feb., p. 7. Swedish Stick Star Wins L. A. Acclaim (headline).

2. [from its resemblance to a (very small) stick; current since c. 1935; see also REEFER, TEA]

1938 *Cab Calloway: Hi De Ho*, p. 16. *stick:* a reefer cigaret.

1959 *The Holy Barbarians*, p. 78. Rolling their sticks of tea, they looked like a ring of kindergarteners.

3. [poss. from Yiddish *shtick* (special nature, peculiarity); some currency since c. 1945] Specialty; peculiarity.

1968 *Down Beat*, 11 Jan., p. 17. My music encompasses every kind of mood. That's my stick.

1969 *Sons of Darkness, Sons of Light*, p. 236. They'll make you talk; that's Whitey's stick.

sticking?, are you [jazz critic Martin Williams says question originally meant, "Do you have a stick (i.e., of marijuana)?"; perhaps phrase derives from sense of having the tenacity to continue struggling for

259

subsistence; according to jazzmen, some currency since c. 1925] See 1951 quot.; also: are you working? are you succeeding?

1941 *Are You Sticking?* (tune written by Duke Ellington, recorded by his orchestra on June 5, 1941).

1951 *Esquire*, Dec., p. 210. Then I asked Zoot, "Are you stickin?" (meaning) "Have you any money on you at the moment?"

1952 *Flee the Angry Strangers*, p. 213. How are you, Luke; you sticking?

sticks, *n. pl.* [shortened form of standard *drumsticks;* current since c. 1900] See last quot.

1926 *Melody Maker*, Sep., p. 56. The tambourine is . . . played with the sticks.

1933 *Metronome*, Oct., p. 51. Playing with the sticks widely separated on the head of the snare drum is a common fault.

1942 *The American Thesaurus of Slang*, p. 559. *sticks:* drumsticks.

stiffin' 'n' jivin' [*stiffin'* prob. from general and underworld slang (i.e., failing to pay or tip someone), *jivin'* in the jazz slang sense of deceiving; according to jazzmen, some currency c. 1935–c. 1945, very rare since]

1957 *N.Y. Times Magazine*, 18 Aug., p. 26. *stiffin' 'n' jivin':* showing off or blowing high with lots of sound effects but not much musicianship.

stock, *adj. & n.* [in sense of a (music publisher's) store or supply; current since c. 1925] See 1935 quot.

1933 *Metronome*, Jan., p. 34. In making stock arrangements I write for the 10-piece combination and then add the extra parts later.

1935 *Vanity Fair*, Nov., p. 71. "Stock" arrangements are the conventional ones made by publishers and sold generally.

stomp, *n., adj. & v.* [from a dialectal form: see 1950, 1955, 1956 quots.; current among jazzmen c. 1900–c. 1945, very rare since except historical] As n., see 1940, 1950 quots.; as adj., applied to music: lively and danceable; as v.: to dance to or play jazz in a lively manner.

1906 *King Porter Stomp* (tune composed by Jelly Roll Morton, copyright 1924).

1926 *Sugar Foot Stomp* (tune). When they start dancin'/Stompin and prancin'/the dance called the Sugar Foot Stomp.

1936 *Stomping at the Savoy* (song composed by Chick Webb, Benny Goodman, and Edgar Sampson).

1940 *Swing*, June, p. 24. Fundamentally there are two types of jazz—blues and stomps. . . . Stomp tunes are gay; blues are mournful.

1950 *They All Played Ragtime*, p. 166. The term "stomp," used to designate a hot number of dynamic rhythm, was derived in New Orleans from the stomping of bare feet in the Bamboula and the Congo.

1955 *The Atlantic Monthly*, July, p. 55. The "stomp" grew out of their [i.e., the blacks'] own primitive folk dances.

1956 *Guide to Jazz*, s.v. *stomp:* Originally a synonym for "stamp" . . . and is very nearly synonymous with "swing."

stomp off [variant of *kick off,* q.v.; according to jazzman Eubie Blake, some currency since c. 1910] To kick the floor in rhythm several times with the heel of the shoe as a signal for the musicians to start playing.

1925 *Stomp Off, Let's Go* (tune recorded by the Savoy Orpheans).

1960 *Hiparama of the Classics*, p. 8. Mr. Rabadee, The All Hip Petrillo, stomped off a Leapin' Beat and all these Four Acres of Musicians Began to WAAIL!!

1961 *Artesian*, Winter, p. 33. They stomped off the solid beat/lifted up their horns/and blew it out.

stoned, *adj.* [by analogy with the immobility; some general and teenage use, but esp. common among jazzmen since c. 1945; see also BOXED, HIGH, JUICED, ZONKED] See first quot.; for verbal use, see last quot.

1952 *Life*, 29 Sep., p. 67. *stoned:* drunk, captivated, ecstatic, sent out of this world.

1956 *Sideman*, p. 213. I want to be blind, I want to be stoned, I want to be high.

1959 *Jazz: A Quarterly of American Music*, Fall, p. 290. I heard Phineas Newborn play "I'll Remember April" two Mondays ago at The Five Spot and he completely stoned me.

stone out [variant of *stoned*; some currency since c. 1946] To fall asleep or become unconscious from an excess of a stimulant.

1952 *Flee the Angry Strangers*, p. 139. I don't want to stone out.

stop chorus, stop time (chorus) [from the practice of all but stopping the rhythm accompaniment; current since c. 1920] See 1942 and 1944 quots.

1929 *The Musical Quarterly*, Oct., p. 611. As to what possibilities such free-will tricks as the jazz "break," stop-time, the harmony chorus, an exaggerated syncopation, etc., hold for the development of musical form beyond jazz itself, he would be bold who would predict.

1942 *The American Thesaurus of Slang*, p. 561. *stop chorus:* a chorus in which the orchestra plays only one note in every one or two measures as a background for a tap dancer or other soloists.

1943 *Riverboat Jazz* (Brunswick Records pamphlet), p. 7. Note particularly his trumpet played against "stop time" chords, a familiar Armstrong device.

1944 *This Is Jazz*, p. 24. Another phenomenon peculiar to jazz is the stop-time chorus. This is a solo chorus for any instrument of the band (including rhythm instruments) or even for voice, played with no accompaniment except a periodic pulsing accent by the other instruments generally on the first beat of every measure or alternate measures.

story, *n.* [special application of its colloquial sense (i.e., a lie or a fib); also a special use of an archaic sense (i.e., history); current among jazzmen since c. 1935] One's excuse, explanation, condition, situation, ruling passion, philosophy, or history (note: one of the more protean nouns).

1940 *What's Your Story, Morning Glory?* (tune recorded by the Jimmie Lunceford Orchestra).

1944 *The New Cab Calloway's Hepsters Dictionary*, s.v. *What's your story?:* what do you want, what have you got to say for yourself, how are tricks or what excuse can you offer. Example: "I don't know what his story is."

1952 *Who Walk in Darkness*, p. 66. What's his story? Is he a fruit or something?

1961 *The Sound*, p. 206. It all comes out in what Red plays. It's not just a certain arrangement of notes. It's the way he hears it. His story.

1961 *Jazz News*, 2 Aug., p. 13. But the fact is that Lester was irritated with people like, say, Allen Eager, because, as he put it, they "aren't telling their own story; part of their story is mine."

Storyville, *n.* [cf. 1938 *The French Quarter*, pp. 430, 433. "Alderman Sidney Story's . . . measure set aside an area in the French Quarter wherein prostitution was to be permitted but not actually legalized. . . . By the middle of 1898 the movement had been completed, and the new district, popularly known as Storyville, much to Alderman Story's disgust, was operating full blast under the sheltering shadow of the law"; see 1960 quot. for dates; see also THE DISTRICT]

1946 *Really the Blues*, p. 375. *Storyville:* the old tenderloin district of New Orleans.

1955 *Hear Me Talkin to Ya*, p. 4. I never heard it called Storyville. . . . It was always The District—the red light district.

1960 *Dictionary of American Slang*, s.v. *Storyville:* the famous New Orleans legalized brothel district from 1896–1917, where many of the early jazz musicians first played and introduced jazz music. Some jazz use; not common.

straight, *adj.* 1. [prob. from standard meaning (i.e., undeviating); current since c. 1920; see also COMMERCIAL, LEGITIMATE, SWEET] See 1935, 1956 quots.

1926 *Melody Maker*, Mar., p. 2. "Straight" musicians apparently are piqued because their art is temporarily losing its grip.

1935 *Vanity Fair*, Nov., p. 38. There are two kinds of jazz, *straight* (or *sweet*) and *hot. Straight* jazz, as its name implies, reproduces the composer's score faithfully.

1948 *Trumpet on the Wing*, p. 26. Then we would play it straight.

1956 *Jazz: Its Evolution and Essence*, pp. 129–130. Both "straight" jazz and "sweet" music, which are commercial products, make use of a sonority and a melodic and harmonic language that are exaggeratedly sugar-coated.

1958 *Melody Maker*, 19 Apr., p. 7. Marian Anderson the straight singer?

2. [special application(s) of standard meaning (i.e., properly arranged); current since c. 1935; see also cool] Satisfactorily situated or taken care of—e.g., financially secure, physically comfortable, happy, drunk, sober.

1946 *Really the Blues*, p. 163. We'll be straight with ourselves.

1952 *Flee the Angry Strangers*, p. 190. I want to be straight when I see the kid.

1957 *On the Road*, p. 155. Everything is straight between us at last.

1959 *Easy Living*, p. 90. "You don't want a slug, huh?" "No thanks. I'm straight."

1959 *The Jazz Review*, Sep., p. 7. I was born in Woodville, Mississippi, because my mother went back to the family; so after I was straight, everything was cool, she took me back to New Orleans.

1959 *Esquire*, Nov., p. 70J. *straight:* in good shape.

1960 *The Jazz Review*, Sep.-Oct., p. 14. He was straight at this time—saved his money and everything.

n. [since it arises to distinguish the ordinary cigarette from the marijuana cigarette, the term prob. derives from the once general slang, now standard, adj. connoting legality and conventionality: cf. 1930 *American Tramp and Underworld Slang*, s.v. *straight:* "honest"; current since c. 1937]

1959 *Esquire*, Nov., p. 70J. *a straight:* an ordinary cigarette.

straight (or right) ahead [special application of standard phrases: from sense of moving forward undeviatingly; cf. early instructional use: 1926 *Melody Maker*, Jan., p. 24. "The first time 'have a shot at it'; go straight ahead; don't go back, no matter if it sounds wrong as soon as you have struck the notes"; both current since c. 1955, *straight ahead* much the more common of the two] To play the music in a continuously exciting, unadorned manner: frequently hortatory.

1959 *Jazz: A Quarterly of American Music*, Fall, p. 293. "But Specs is so thorough, he can play in tempo." "Plays right ahead."

1961 *The Sound*, p. 51. Very simple and straight ahead.

1964 *Down Beat*, 17 Dec., p. 30. "McSplivens" is a straight-ahead blues.

straighten, *v.t.* [special application of standard term: cf. jazz slang *straight* (adj., sense 2) and jazz slang *twisted;* current since c. 1935; see also HIP (*v.t.*)] See 1959 quot. (Note: definition in first quot. is accurate but restricted.)

1946 *Really the Blues*, p. 375. *straighten:* pay up, straighten out a debt.

1959 *Esquire*, Nov., p. 70J. *straighten someone:* to give a person the real truth or genuine article. To provide a person with what he needs.

1960 *Hiparama of the Classics*, p. 8. They straightened the nanny goats.

straw (boss) [special application of a standard term; some currency esp. among big band musicians since c. 1935]

1971 *Down Beat*, 15 Apr., p. 19. The band's straw-boss is in charge till the leader gets there. Some straws are liked by the gang and some are not.—*Ibid.* How did it sound, straw?

Street, The/Swing Street (or Alley) [from its importance to jazzmen during the Swing era (i.e., c. 1935–c. 1945); current c. 1937–c. 1949, obs. since except historical] In New York City, 52nd Street between 5th and 7th Avenues (but esp. between 5th and 6th), where small jazz night clubs flourished c. 1935–c. 1948.

1943 *Metronome*, Apr., p. 16. Even today, when you leave a musician and say "See you on The Street tonight," he doesn't have to ask you which street you mean. But soon maybe he will.

1955 *A Pictorial History of Jazz*, p. 185. The year is 1939, a time when Red and Higgy were often to be found on New York's "Swing Street!"—52nd Street in the late thirties and early forties. . . . "Swing Street" they called it.

stretch out [special application of standard phrase; current since c. 1955] To play music over a period of time sufficiently long to permit a thorough exploration of one's theme.

1961 *Down Beat*, 25 May, p. 39. The vibes player really stretched out on that one.

1961 *The Jazz Life*, p. 41. In more and more clubs, the audience expects the experimenting and "stretching" out to be done during working hours for *them*, and not later for musicians only.

1963 *Down Beat*, 29 Aug., p. 30. Some of these things are so short that nobody has a chance to stretch out and blow on it.

stride (piano) [from common practice of designating jazz styles and techniques by kinetic terms (see also MOVE, RIDE, STROLL, WALK): see 1958 and 1974 quots.; current since c. 1925] See 1956, 1958 quots.

1935 *His Hi De Highness of Ho De Ho*, p. 35. But "gut tempo" and "stride tempo" usually are intelligible only to our own musicians.

1956 *Guide to Jazz*, s.v. *stride*: a piano style much in use by soloists about 1930, characterized by a chord on the weak beats alternating with a bass note on the strong beats.

1958 *The Collector's Jazz: Traditional and Swing*, p. 22. A propulsive style which has been labeled "stride piano" because of the striding effect produced by the left hand hitting a single note in the first and third beats and a chord of three or four notes on the second and fourth beats.

1960 *Jazz Scene 2* (liner notes on LP album Epic LA 16001). Bryant's bass, at times, utilizes the "stride" made famous by Fats Waller.

1974 *N.Y. Times*, 12 May, II, p. 15. Kerr fell in love with stride piano playing—named for the "striding" effect of the left hand playing in ten-key stretches.

stroll, *v.i.* [special application of standard meaning (i.e., to wander off); according to jazzmen, term was introduced as an exhortation by Roy Eldridge (see LITTLE JAZZ) c. 1938, current ever since; see also LAY OUT] Of the pianist, to refrain from playing (so that the bass and drums exclusively can play together).

1959 *Jazz: A Quarterly of American Music*, Summer, p. 204. Oh, periodically I like the piano player to stroll. . . . He'll stroll, then he comes back in and he plays a little more.

1966 *Down Beat*, 27 Jan., p. 35. I didn't hear any piano; they just decided to stroll throughout this particular track.

strong, come on, see S.V. COME ON.

struggle, *v.i.* [special application of standard term; according to jazzman Eubie Blake, some currency c. 1900–c. 1935; obs. since] To play music or dance badly.

1965 *A Drop of Patience*, p. 153. The musicians were struggling. They seemed unable to pull their ideas together.

1968 *Black Music*, p. 29. Opening night he was struggling with *all* the tunes.

strung (out) [by analogy with its connotation of immobility (see also HUNG UP), poss. from standard sense of *strung* (i.e., tired), poss. reinforced by *hamstrung* and/or *highstrung*; current since c. 1950] Obsessed with, immobilized by, completely preoccupied with or deprived of something (most often, a woman or narcotics).

1960 *The Jazz Review*, Nov., p. 8. Unfortunately it was at this period he acquired the "monkey" [i.e., narcotics addiction] and frequently was strung out.

1962 *N.Y. Times Magazine*, 20 May, p. 45. *hung-up:* to be quiet, worried, obsessed, addicted ("He's hung up on Matt Dillon always shooting last"). Going out of vogue in favor of *strung out*.

1973 *Jazz Style in Kansas City*, p. 203. It was when Charlie was "strung out," that is, without drugs, that he was in bad shape.

strut, strutter, strut (one's) stuff [see last quot. for explanation of semantic development and for beginning date; obs. since c. 1935 except historical; see also STUFF] To dance: frequently hortatory; *strutter:* one who dances.

1900 *The Blackville Strutters' Ball* (song composed by Bert Williams).

1926 *Nigger Heaven*, p. 242. Some one cried, "Strut your stuff, Lasca!"

1959 *Jazz: A Quarterly of American Music*, Fall, p. 283. The strut of the turkey gobbler was too familiar not to become a figure of speech. The general sense of the metaphor is in earliest English, of course, but here it takes coloration from Bert Williams' 1900 "The Blackville Strutters' Ball," "Strut, Miss Lizzie," the title and song of the 1922 all-Negro revue, and "The Darktown Strutters' Ball." Through the 1920s there were so many "struts" the phrase *strut your stuff* became colloquial.

stud, *n.* [cf. 1960 *American Speech*, Feb., p. 78. "The strong sexual meaning the word *stud* has had cannot fail to suggest *studhorse,* of which it is a shortened form"; current from c. 1938–c. 1945, somewhat less common since; see also DUDE]

1944 *Dan Burley's Original Handbook of Harlem Jive*, p. 148. *stud:* a man, male.

1959 *The Real Cool Killers*, p. 13. "Oh, that's them," the driver said, cooling off as quickly as a showgirl on a broke stud.

stuff, *n.* [also general colloquial use, but with esp. currency in particular senses among jazzmen since c. 1925; cf. 1948 *Shakespeare's Bawdy*, s.v. *stuff:* "marrow or semen"; see also JIVE, SHIT] As in general colloquial usage: anything, but esp. talent or musical style. Also: marijuana (see first 1956 quot.) or strong narcotics (see 1955 quot.).

1928 *The Walls of Jericho*, p. 305. *stuff:* talent.

1929 *The Musical Quarterly*, Oct., p. 606. Indeed, many of its contemporaries there be who execrate the "stuff" [i.e., jazz] as inebriate, doggerel, degenerate, ghoulish, vulturine, etc.

1934 *All About Jazz*, p. 66. The trumpet player is allowed to "do his stuff" [i.e., display his talent].

1955 *Hear Me Talkin to Ya*, p. 374. He had remained off the stuff [i.e., narcotics].

1956 *It's Always Four O'Clock*, p. 48. Have you fellows got any stuff [i.e., marijuana]?

1956 *Sideman*, p. 10. Writes symphonies, you know? Legit stuff.

suitcase, *n.* [because it frequently served as drums in *spasm bands*, q.v.; some currency c. 1935–c. 1945, obs. since except historical]

1937 *This Thing Called Swing*, p. 9. *suitcase:* drums.

Susie Q, Suzie Q, Suzy-Q [see 1944 quot. for beginning date; term obs. since c. 1941, though parts of the dance survive in other dances] A jazz dance.

1939 *Jazzmen*, pp. 27–28. When the big band "went crazy" after the funeral, the kids cut up with their primitive version of the "Susie Q" and danced the "shudders."

1944 *The New Cab Calloway's Hepsters Dictionary*, s.v. *Susie-Q:* a dance introduced at the Cotton Club in 1936.

1946 *Really the Blues*, p. 230. And from the old folks' shuffle to the Suzie Q and Sand, wasn't none of them steps new to grandpa.

sweet, *adj. & n.* [see both 1956 quots. for key to semantic development; largely a writers' term (see MICKEY, TICKY, which are more common among jazzmen); current c. 1928–c. 1945, obs. since except historical; see also HOTEL (STYLE)]

1933 *Fortune*, Aug., p. 47. He is decidedly not a *sweet* trombonist—he doesn't play sentimentally with lots of vibrato.

1944 *Esquire's 1944 Jazz Book*, p. 26. That the popularity of *hot* jazz is not even more widespread may be attributed to the lack of any literature treating of *hot* as a special field, and also to the deadening effect of the shallow emotionalisms of sweet (popular) jazz upon the public ear.

1952 *Mademoiselle*, Dec., p. 120. "Sweet" . . . was the "pop" tune, set in a treacly arrangement, played by a big band loaded with saxophones. And sweet meant *slow*, one of the qualities of the blues—although sweet had no more in common with the blues than swing did with the stomp.

1956 *Guide to Jazz*, s.v. *sweet:* (1) gently played music. (2) commercial music played with a syrupy, insipid sweetness. Pejorative connotation in either case.

1956 *Jazz: Its Evolution and Essence*, pp. 129–130. Both "straight" jazz and "sweet" music, which are commercial products, make use of a sonority and a melodic and harmonic language that are exaggeratedly sugar-coated.

swing, *n. & adj.* [cf. jazz etymologist Peter Tamony's article in 1960 *Jazz:*

268

A Quarterly of American Music, Winter, tracing the semantic development of term to as far back as 1888, since which time the term has had some currency as a property of lively popular and/or jazz music; as a generic term for jazz, current c. 1935–c. 1945] See 1939, 1946, 1956, 1960, 1961 quots.

1899 *In the Hammock: Swing Song* (tune composed by Richard Ferber). With just the right swinging motion [Blurb].

1907 *Georgia Swing* (tune composed by Jelly Roll Morton & Santa Pecora, copyright 1928).

1912 *The Trolley Car Song* (song). It's the cutest little thing/Got the cutest little swing.

1932 *It Don't Mean a Thing, If It Ain't Got That Swing* (song composed by Duke Ellington and Irving Mills).

1934 *Red Norvo and His Swing Septet* (name of a small jazz group).

1936 *Harper's*, Apr., p. 567. The current word "swing" is the latest attempt to name an art.

1939 *Kingdom of Swing*, pp. 174–175. In a word, swing is a *property* of music played in a certain way, rather than a definite kind of music itself.

1946 *Harvard Dictionary of Music*, p. 378. From about 1935 on . . . the term Swing (a word which seems to be of largely subjective import referring to subtle and desirable rubato . . .) comes into use to denote what appears to be a continuation of the Hot Jazz tradition.

1956 *Guide to Jazz*, s.v. *swing:* the rhythmic pulse vital to jazz; but also the dominant jazz mode from c. 1934–c. 1945.

1960 *Jazz: A Quarterly of American Music*, Winter, pp. 6–7. Early in 1935 *swing* was one of several terms used to describe a dynamic of American jazz. . . . By the middle of 1936 *swing* was almost solely employed to characterize a suddenly-appreciated style that was getting daily nationwide publicity as the new sound.

1961 *Metronome*, Apr., p. 12. Though Swing was largely a jazz-oriented popular dance music, peak performances by Basie, Goodman, Lunceford, and a few others transcended popular music entirely and many of these have survived, through recordings, as jazz for listeners.

v.i. & v.t. 1. [see note s.v. *n.:* Tamony traces the *v.t.* to as far back as 1897; however, widely current in a jazz sense only since c. 1935; current with *it* or *out* c. 1925–c. 1935, obs. since except historical] See 1935, 1958, 1972 quots.

1933 *Fortune*, Aug., p. 47. Returning to Trombonist Brown, he can . . . swing it . . . (. . . syncopate to beat the band).

1935 *Stage*, Sep., p. 46. *swing:* play hot and rhythmically.

1946 *Really the Blues*, p. 141. We would say he could swing or he couldn't swing, meaning what kind of effect did he have on the band. This word was cooked up after the unhip public took over the expression "hot" and made it corny by getting up in front of a band and snapping their fingers in a childish way, yelling "Get hot! Yeah, man, get hot!"

1955 *Down Beat*, 5 Oct., p. 13. How can you tell if a man's swinging? When you can pat your feet to what he's playing.

1958 *Publication of the American Dialect Society*, Nov., p. 47. *swing:* to play well in all senses, technically and otherwise, but especially to have the basic feel for jazz rhythms. A man can play well harmonically and rhythmically, but he will not swing without a feel for "the beat."

1972 *The Worlds of Jazz*, p. 109. In order to appraise a musician's swing, a distinction should perhaps be made between quantity and quality, difficult as these are to measure. Milt Jackson may swing *less* than Lionel Hampton (the drive is not so strong) but he swings *better* (his rhythmic sensibility is more developed). Swing may be conventional or vulgar (Roland Kirk, Les McCann); it may be "far out" or wild (Elvin Jones, Charlie Parker).

2. [by analogy with sense 1; widely current since c. 1955] As *v.i.:* see last 1959 quot.; also, by extension: to behave or live in such a way as to have a good time or be at peace with oneself. As *v.t.:* to provide enjoyment (for someone).

1959 *Jazz for Moderns*, p. 21. *swing:* to have a ball—or some 2,000,000 other things.

1959 *The Holy Barbarians*, p. 78. Soon the air was filled with the sweet narcotic smell of pot and everybody was swinging.

1959 *Toronto Telegram*, 31 Mar., p. 3. *swing:* to get the feel of, to comprehend the truth or beauty of anything worth digging; to impart the same truth or beauty to others.

1959 *Esquire*, Nov., p. 70J. *swing:* to have a good time, enjoy oneself.

1961 *Down Beat*, 3 Aug., p. 26. I know groovy chicks swing *me* a lot faster than cute little Scottie dogs.

swinger, *n.* [current among jazzmen from c. 1950–c. 1965, when for the general public it came to mean a sexual libertine; see also SENDER] A person (frequently, a musician) or something (frequently, a piece of music) that provides pleasure or excitement.

1959 *Jazz Poems*, p. 6. If you wish to be a swinger, drink and get high.

1959 *Swinging Syllables,* s.v. *swinger:* hip, like a Satellite.

1960 *Down Beat,* 24 Nov., p. 22. It is fast, furious, thunderous, and has nothing whatever to do with Bill Basie, Kansas City Swinger.

1961 *Down Beat,* 19 Jan., p. 32. "Lover" is handled as a swinger and is one of the better tracks.

1961 *Jazz Journal,* May, p. 31. Suffice it to say that they were a first class group, swingers all the way.

swinging, *adj.* [widely current since c. 1950]

1958 *Publication of the American Dialect Society,* Nov., p. 47. *swinging:* the highest term of approval. May be applied to anything a jazzman likes, or any person.

1959 *The Holy Barbarians,* p. 318. *swinging:* liberated, uninhibited.

swings his ass [according to jazzmen, current since c. 1960] Plays (music) excitingly. Oral evidence only.

Swing Street (or Alley), see s.v. STREET, THE.

T

tag, n. [special application of standard term (i.e., an ornamental or familiar ending to a speech, song, etc.); current since c. 1925] See 1952, 1955 quots.

1932 *Melody Maker*, June, p. 507. The tag . . . implies that this is a band record.

1952 *A History of Jazz in America*, p. 353. *tag:* final ending in a composition, scored or improvised; "coda" in traditional music terminology.

1955 *The Encyclopedia of Jazz*, p. 347. *tag:* musical phrase added to the end of a chorus or performance.

1960 *The Story of the Original Dixieland Jazz Band*, p. 59. The Dixieland Band's stock ending, the "dixieland tag," faithfully concluded every number.

1961 *Metronome*, Apr., p. 18. So many of the comical quotes and tags in jazz come out of different musical experiences, such as being in a little pit band.

tailgate, tail-gate, *adj.* [see 1947, 1957 quots. for explanation of semantic development and 1947 quot. for beginning date; very rare since c. 1945 except historical]

1942 *The American Thesaurus of Slang*, p. 564. *tail gate:* New Orleans style of trombone playing.

1947 *N.Y. Herald-Tribune*, 10 Mar. The term "tail-gate" originated in 1910 when jazz bands rode the streets of New Orleans in wagons. Because the trombone is such a cumbersome instrument its player was always assigned to the tail-gate of the wagon.

1957 *The Book of Jazz*, p. 79. The expression "tailgate" trombone

272

originated when brass bands playing ragtime or early jazz were loaded onto advertising trucks and the trombonist, in order to give free play to the full length of the slide, had to stand near the tailgate of the truck.

take, *n.* [chiefly recording trade term, prob. derived from motion picture camera use, but some currency among jazzmen since c. 1925; see also MASTER] One of the several recordings made of a tune, from which is selected the one "take" (or *master,* q.v.) to be offered to the record-buying public.

1942 *The American Thesaurus of Slang,* p. 569. *take:* phonograph record.

1958 *Playboy,* Nov., p. 66. "The first take, we knew we had it cold," he says.

1960 *The Story of the Original Dixieland Jazz Band,* p. 68. LaRocca attributes this to nervousness on the part of his fellow musicians, who were inclined to play louder on the real "take."

v.t. [special application of a standard meaning (i.e., to perform); according to jazzman Eubie Blake, current since c. 1900] To play (a piece of music); also, a command to an instrumentalist to begin his solo.

1940 *Take It!* (tune composed by Sy Oliver and Calvin Jackson).

1961 *Down Beat,* 19 Jan., p. 31. "Sesame," in particular, is swift-moving and taken up-tempo.

1961 *The Sound,* p. 157. Just flip one hundred of them singles and we'll take it from the top [i.e., play it from the beginning].

1970 *The World of Duke Ellington,* p. 86. So Duke told Tricky, "You take it!"

take charge [special application of a standard (esp. armed forces) phrase; also some sports use; according to jazzmen, some currency since c. 1915] To dominate a musical performance; also, attrib.: capable of giving excitement and coherence to a musical performance (in this sense, oral evidence only).

1955 *Hear Me Talkin to Ya,* p. 220. Come on—let's take charge!

1968 *Down Beat,* 16 May, p. 26. He takes charge with the authority that is the mark of a real player.

1972 *Jazz Masters of the Thirties,* p. 149. Billie motioned to Pres as if to say, "Take charge."

take five [short for *take a five-minute respite:* from theater slang; current since c. 1930]

273

1942 *The American Thesaurus of Slang*, p. 564. *take five:* take a 5-minute rest.

1952 *A History of Jazz in America*, p. 353. *take five:* (said to musicians, usually at rehearsal) you are entitled to a five-minute intermission.

1961 *The Feeling of Jazz*, p. 30. Man, I'm glad they said to take five, because this next arrangement looks rough.

take it from the top, see s.v. TOP.

take it out, [current since c. 1930; see also OUT (CHORUS)] Move into the final chorus; conclude the piece.

1965 *Down Beat*, 17 June, p. 36. I am sort of waiting till they take it out.

1972 *Down Beat*, 7 Dec., p. 24. The solos play [sic] then the vocalist takes it out.

take it slow (also **take it light:** oral evidence only) [cf. general colloquial "take it easy"; widely current c. 1935–c. 1945, very rare since; see also LATER] Used in place of "Farewell!"

1937 *Metronome*, Nov., p. 11. 'Nuff said, Savoy, so take it slow.

1938 *Cab Calloway: Hi De Ho*, p. 16. *take it slow:* be careful.

take-off, takeoff, *n.* [by analogy with flight; some currency c. 1930–c. 1940, very rare since] An improvised solo.

1935 *Vanity Fair*, Nov., p. 71. Breaks [jazz sense] are sometimes known as *get-offs* or *take-offs*.

1959 *Blow Up a Storm*, p. 7. From his first takeoff, I knew that Woody was one of the finest trumpet players I had ever heard.

take off [by analogy with flight; current c. 1925–c. 1945; see also GET OFF, GO TO TOWN, RIDE]

1938 *Cab Calloway: Hi De Ho*, p. 16. *take off:* play a solo.

1945 *Down Beat*, 1 July, p. 2. Johnny Bothwell, star altoist and Raeburn's right hand man, takes off on a solo.

taking care of business [extension of the standard meaning to the jazzman's "business'; current since c. 1955]

1957 *N.Y. Times Magazine*, 18 Aug., p. 26. *Who's takin' care of business?:* Who's on the stand tonight?

1960 *Down Beat*, 22 Dec., p. 42. It is, in fact, a superior, hard-accented session, with all concerned taking care of business in an uncompromising and forthright manner.

1961 *Down Beat*, 5 Jan., p. 16. "There're not enough piano players out here taking care of business," he continued.

1961 *The Jazz Review*, Jan., p. 31. In the notes for Contemporary C-3551, Nat Hentoff tells us that "if a musician is 'taking care of business' he is playing very well." On the back of *Takin' Care of Business* (Jazzland 19), Orrin Keepnews explains that the expression should be reserved "for those no-nonsense occasions on which everything comes out just right and the job at hand is done unusually and excitingly well."

talk, *v.i.* [by analogy with verbal communication: see 1961 quot. (see also LYING, MESSAGE, SAYING SOMETHING, TELL A STORY); some currency since c. 1925] In music, to communicate significantly; also, rare: to attempt to imitate the sounds of the human voice (see 1956, 1961 quots.).

1929 *Heah Me Talkin' to Ya* (tune recorded by the Louis Armstrong Orchestra).

1955 *Hear Me Talkin to Ya*, p. 211. The Box Back Boys used knife blades to keep their whining guitars talking all night long.

1956 *The Heart of Jazz*, p. 36. The disregard of exact pitch is a logical corollary of the effort of New Orleans jazzmen to make their music "talk."

1961 *Down Beat*, 30 Mar., p. 23. The jazz drummer also imitates the cadence of speech, as do other instrumentalists. (It's no accident that the phrases, "Talk to me," "Shout," "Holler," "Now you're talkin'" and other speech references are a large part of jazz argot.)

taped, *participle* [perhaps by analogy with having successfully gotten music onto a tape recorder; also some general slang use; some currency among jazzmen since c. 1950] Mastered, understood, taken care of, under control.

1952 *Who Walk in Darkness*, p. 68. "You really think you have everybody taped, don't you, Max?" I said.

1959 *Blow Up a Storm*, p. 245. Anyway, he had it taped.

taste, a, *n.* [old general slang: shortened form of *a taste of liquor;* current in its initial sense since c. 1945, and in its most general sense since c.

1955] Initially: liquor; also, since c. 1945: see 1951 quot.; also by extension, since c. 1955: see 1959 quot.

1951 *Esquire*, Dec., p. 210. He must have made a nice little "taste" (meaning) the tune made quite a bit of "loot" [i.e., money].

1959 *Esquire*, Nov., p. 70J. *taste:* usually a drink or some money. A portion of anything good.

1961 *The Sound*, p. 89. " 'Bout time I had a little taste," he suggested. "Say a couple of big bills."

1966 *New Yorker*, 25 June, p. 33. Why don't you stop up Wednesday, and we'll have a taste.

tea, tee, *n.* [prob. from the resemblance of the two types of leaves; current since c. 1925; see also BOO, GAGE, MARY JANE, POT]

1930 *Tee Rollers Rub* (tune recorded by Freddie "Redd" Nicholson).

1958 *Southern Folklore Quarterly*, Sep., p. 134. *tea:* marihuana, a plant or weed.

1959 *Mexico City Blues*, p. 61. Powerful Tea you gotta smoke/to believe that.

tea pad [jazz slang *tea* + jazz slang *pad;* some currency c. 1930–c. 1940, obs. since except historical]

1939 *Jitterbug Jamboree Song Book*, p. 33. *teapad:* anyplace where they smoked weed.

1943 *Time*, 19 July, p. 54. Most tea pads are supplied with a juke box.

tear down [hyperbole; current since the advent of the big hotel bands c. 1925; see also its antonym SET UP] To dismantle the music stands, etc., after a performance (also as v.i.: oral evidence only).

1956 *Eddie Condon's Treasury of Jazz*, p. 462. He had no set way of tearing down and setting up a band.

tear (it) up [by analogy with the finality of the effect; some currency since c. 1920; see also BREAK IT UP] To play music excitingly, thrillingly.

1955 *Hear Me Talkin to Ya*, p. 204. He had the first big colored band that hit the road and tore it up.

1962 *Down Beat*, 30 Aug., p. 20. But once I heard Clifford, I wasn't leaving. He was really tearing up.

1972 *Down Beat*, 7 Dec., p. 13. "Man, we tore it up," he says. The glowing reviews in the Continental and English press bear him out.

tear out [special application of its general slang senses (i.e., to fight or to curse), poss. reinforced by *tear out into the streets;* according to jazzman Eubie Blake, current c. 1900–c. 1935, obs. since] To play an exciting improvised solo. Oral evidence only.

tell a (or **one's**) **story** [by analogy with verbal communication (see also LYING, MESSAGE, SAYING SOMETHING, TALK); some currency since c. 1925] In music, to communicate significantly—i.e., what one most profoundly feels.

1934 *All About Jazz*, p. 144. He tells the simple, everyday story . . . to understand and appreciate which requires more than an average musical intelligence.

1956 *Jazz: Its Evolution and Essence*, p. 168. A coherently developed chorus has a much better chance of being musically satisfying than one whose phrases are haphazardly thrown together. Jazz musicians have perfectly well taken into account this necessity; when they compliment an improvisation by saying "It tells a story," don't they show that they recognize the value of good development?

1957 *The Charles Mingus Jazz Workshop: The Clown* (liner notes on LP album Atlantic 1260). "I think," says Porter, "that more jazz groups should tell stories like Mingus does instead of just playing notes and techniques."

1961 *The Sound*, p. 177. Lot of other cats blow a mess of trumpet, high notes, fast runs, and all, but Red always tells a story.

1961 *Jazz News*, 2 Aug., p. 13. But the fact is that Lester was irritated with people like, say, Allen Eager, because, as he put it, they "aren't telling their own story; part of their story is mine."

tell it like it is, see s.v. LIKE.

tenor (man) [shortened form; current since c. 1930] (Note: similar forms exist for most instrumentalists—i.e., an alto saxophonist may be referred to as "an alto," a bassist as "a bass," etc.—but the great importance of the tenor saxophone since c. 1925 has made this form the most common.)

1942 *The American Thesaurus of Slang*, p. 556. *tenor man:* a tenor saxophone player.

1961 *Metronome*, Apr., p. 30. With the release of this album we are given a chance to take a long look at an important tenor.

1961 *The Jazz Life*, p. 34. Like you'd hear about a very good tenor in some night spot, and I'd have to go down there and cut him.

terrible, *adj.* [one of several standard terms in which the connotation has been reversed: see second 1959 quot. for semantic explanation (see also BAD, HARD, MEAN, TOUGH); current since c. 1955]
   1959 *Newport Jazz Festival: 1959*, p. 46. *terrible:* great.
   1959 *Nugget*, Aug., p. 56. Normally cheerful and friendly, he can, when moved, become a regal and awesome figure—a "terrible" man in the jazz sense of the word, which connotes formidability.
   1962 *Down Beat*, 7 June, p. 39. That old man's terrible! Four stars.
   1970 *Jazz People*, p. 95. "It was a *terrible* band!" (Babs, like so many of his contemporaries, often uses a derogatory term as the highest praise).

Texas (piano), (fast) [from its place of origin; current c. 1920–c. 1935, obs. since except historical] Boogie-woogie (q.v.).
   1970 *Down Beat*, 6 Aug., p. 12. Here he heard for the first time the fast Texas or boogie woogie piano player.
   1973 *Jazz Style in Kansas City*, p. 54. Boogie-woogie was called "Texas piano" or "fast Texas piano."

that's what I'm talking about!, that's right! [both are fanciful expressions, since the speaker with premeditated and humorous inaccuracy implies that whatever he is approving of is what he himself had in mind all along; some currency esp. among black musicians since c. 1935 for the longer expression, c. 1958 for the shorter] I approve of that.
   1961 *The Sound*, p. 45. "Yes!" Red cried softly. "That's what I'm talking about!"
   1961 *N.Y. Times Magazine*, 25 June, p. 39. *That's right!:* Bravo! (Improvised by saxophonist Cannonball Adderley after being knocked out [i.e., impressed] by a Miles Davis trumpet coda.)

there you go [by favorable analogy with the kinetic; cf. 1956 *American Speech,* May, "Army Speech and the Future of American English," p. 108: *"There you go!* (Now you're talking sense)"; also some student and teenage use, but with esp. currency among jazzmen c. 1935–c. 1945, somewhat less since; see also SOLID, CRAZY] Expressions of approval or of assent; also, see last quot.

1956 *Sideman*, p. 100. "There you go," he grinned. —p. 296. "There you go!" Bill said happily.

1969 *Hip Manual.* *there you go:* a greeting. "Hello."

thin, *adj.* [special application of standard term; according to jazzmen, some currency since c. 1935] Light (applied to a musician's tone): see last quot.; also, by extension, since c. 1950: superficial (see the antonym HEAVY), not profound.

1960 *Jazz: A Quarterly of American Music*, Winter, p. 20. He's a little thin, you know?

1961 *Metronome*, Sep., p. 7. The thinness of much of his work becomes apparent when contrasted with Miles' deep probing.

1961 *The Jazz Life*, p. 23. Everyone, when he first started, thought: This man, his *tone* is too *thin*, you know?

thing, *n.* [understatement: somewhat special applications of a term which also has many vague general colloquial uses; current in its jazz senses since c. 1945] A musical performance, composition, or conception (see also GET ONE'S THING TOGETHER); also, rapport (see last quot.).

1948 *Down Beat*, 19 May, p. 12. "Sleeps" is an up tempo thing by Norvo.

1960 *The Jazz Review*, May, p. 30. How about we tie up the Latin thing with a college motif?

1961 *Down Beat*, 5 Jan., p. 43. I loved the Ray Nance thing.

1965 *Down Beat*, 6 May, p. 25. The three of us really have a thing, and it's pretty tight (rapport, relationship, intimacy).

(one's) own thing [current since c. 1955; see also GET (ONE'S) SHIT (OR THING) TOGETHER] One's personal musical style or idiom.

1961 *Down Beat*, 2 Mar., p. 43. He's been playing this way 15 years, and he's got his own thing going.

1961 *Jazz Journal*, July, p. 4. I spent two years with him off-and-on, and he was the first one to really push me into my own thing.

third stream, third-stream, thirdstream [see first 1962 quot. for semantic explanation; current since 1960]

1960 *N.Y. Times*, 17 May, p. 44. Gunther Schuller . . . has been heralding the arrival of what he calls a "third stream" of music—a music that is neither jazz nor "classical" but that draws on the techniques of both.

1960 *New Yorker*, 24 Dec., p. 47. The steadily increasing attempts made during the past several years by such composers as Gunther Schuller, John Lewis, George Russell and Charlie Mingus to establish a new music midway between classical forms and jazz have at last been blessed with a new name—"third-stream" music.

1962 *Dinosaurs in the Morning*, p. 214. "What about the third stream?" I asked. "I [Gunther Schuller] coined the term as an *adjective*, not a noun. . . . This music is only *beginning*. I conceive of it as the result of two tributaries—one from the stream of classical music and one from the other stream, jazz—that have recently flowed out toward each other."

1962 *Down Beat*, 10 May, p. 18. Hence the potential growth of a new music that is not in the main stream but is a hybrid: the already familiar Third Stream.

1963 *Nugget,* Feb., p. 7. The other is that curious amalgam of conservatory training and jazz feeling known as "Thirdstream."

threads, *n. pl.* [synecdoche; current since c. 1935; see also DRAPE, TOG, VINES]

1938 *Cab Calloway: Hi De Ho*, p. 16. *threads:* suit, dress or costume.

1959 *Esquire*, Nov., p. 70J. *threads:* clothes. Example: He's wearing a fancy set of threads. He's wearing a good suit.

1961 *The Sound*, p. 46. It's just a shame the way you treat your threads.

ticklers, ivory, see s.v. IVORY.

ticky, ricky-tick(y), tick-tock, *adj.* [onomatopoeic: the longer forms are attempts to render phonetically the monotonous and brittle regularity of the rhythm in such music, poss. reinforced by the tick-tock of a clock; long form current since c. 1930, short form since c. 1935; see also CORNY, MICKEY (MOUSE)]

1937 *American Speech*, Feb., p. 48. *ticky:* the placing of improper stress on some note-values in the music, caused by incorrect phrasing and tonguing.

1942 *The American Thesaurus of Slang*, p. 563. *ricky-tick:* of tempo and tone, gently, softly.

1952 *A History of Jazz in America*, p. 353. *ticky:* corny, spec. applied to a mechanical beat.

1959 *Esquire*, Nov., p. 70J. *ticky:* stale, outmoded.

1966 *Down Beat*, 21 Apr., p. 47. Everybody wants you to play that ticky-ticky-tick stuff.

1972 *Americanisms*, Apr., p. 3. Swing phase, circa 1930, many young white musicians became reluctant to play tick-tock music night after night, preferring to improvise, even lightly, slightly, politely!

tight, *adj.* 1. [according to jazzmen, term developed semantically from an initially sexual use; also some general slang use; current esp. among black jazzmen since c. 1920] Intimate.

1928 *It's Tight Like That* (tune composed by Tommy Dorsey and Hudson Whittaker).

1956 *Lady Sings the Blues*, p. 32. He and Bub were real tight with the cops.

1959 *Esquire*, Nov., p. 70J. *tight:* very friendly.

1960 *Beat Jokes Bop Humor & Cool Cartoons*, p. 50. The Ham's tight ace, Horatio, had brought news of the ghost of The Big Ham.

1961 *Down Beat*, 30 Mar., p. 21. I really got tight with Max and learned great respect for him.

2. [relation, if any, to sense 1 unknown; some currency among jazzmen since c. 1925] Of people, formidable; of things, difficult or dangerous (see 1928 quot.).

1928 *The Walls of Jericho*, p. 306. *tight:* tough; redoubtable; hard.

1956 *Saturday Review*, 17 Mar., p. 30. This is where it's tight, man.

1960 *Hiparama of the Classics*, p. 16. He was a hard, tight, tough Cat.
. . . Naturally Mark has got to put Cleo down [i.e., reject her], this was a tight move for him 'cause this Cleo was an early day Elizabeth Taylor.

time, *n.* [special application of the standard musical term; some earlier use, but with esp. currency only since c. 1945; see also BEAT] See 1959 quot.

1949 *Metronome*, July, p. 17. That cat's blowing, man! His time is good.

1959 *Newport Jazz Festival: 1959*, p. 46. *time:* sense and control of rhythm.

1961 *Metronome*, Apr., p. 15. Little Jimmy Rushing, the man with the greatest time in jazz, came on for "Blue Skies," and Gene settled back into a good groove.

1961 *Down Beat*, 13 Apr., p. 22. Zoot Sims is Mr. Time.

tipple, tiple, *n. & adj.* [relation to any of the standard meanings

281

unknown; according to jazzmen, some currency c. 1920–c. 1930, during which time the instrument was sometimes used in jazz performances, obs. since except historical]

1940 *Swing*, Jan., p. 24. Good tiple solos, solid bass plucking and jive singing.

1953 *The American Thesaurus of Slang*, p. 549. *tipple uke:* a 12-stringed ukulele.

1962 *High Fidelity*, Dec., p. 107. He plays both unamplified guitar and tiple, a ten-string instrument with double and triple strings tuned in octaves.

toddle, *n. & adj.* [from toddling movement of the dance; current c. 1920–c. 1930, obs. since except historical] A slow jazz dance, and the slow tempo of the music to which it was danced.

1926 *So This Is Jazz*, p. 25. A tune played doubly slow for a "toddle" is no less jazz than when performed at its original fox-trot tempo.

1946 *The Jazz Record*, May, p. 10. Just before I left, the boss wanted us to play "toddle time" . . . four beats to the measure.

tog, *v.i.* [old slang and general colloquial term given wide currency by jazzmen since c. 1925] To dress (usually with *out* or some other adverbial modifier).

1932 *The Inter-State Tattler*, 7 Jan., p. 9. Jimmy Ferguson . . . hit the stage togged strictly English.

1938 *Cab Calloway: Hi De Ho*, p. 16. *togged to the bricks:* dressed to kill, from head to foot.

1946 *Big Book of Swing*, p. 125. *togged out:* well-dressed.

1946 *Really the Blues*, p. 29. I togged like a fashion plate.

1961 *The Sound*, p. 109. I mean, that cat can really tog out!

together, get (or have) (one's) self (or shit, thing), be [according to jazzmen, all forms have been current since c. 1955, although the terms are now chiefly black and youth culture slang] To fit all of one's disparate creative and technical elements into a unified whole.

1962 *Down Beat*, 12 Apr., p. 22. I guess I was on my way in '57, when I started to get myself together musically.

1963 *Down Beat*, 29 Aug., p. 30. I guess it's the regular rhythm section behind them because it sounds like everything is together.

1966 *The Wig*, p. 90. In my 14th Street-Saville Row suit (dark, synthetic elegant) that I'd bought from Mr. Fishback—I was truly together.

togs, *n. pl.* [cf. 1925 *English Words & Their Background,* p. 52: "*togs* (Australian slang): clothing"; general colloquial use, but with esp. currency among jazzmen since c. 1925] Clothing.
    1946 *Really the Blues,* p. 41. A busted ragpicker would have given those togs the go-by.

toke, *n. & v.* [prob. by assonance with *poke* (q.v.) and poss. by alliteration with "take"; current since c. 1960] A puff or to puff, esp. on a marijuana cigarette.
    1973 *After Claude,* p. 151. Take a toke, darling.
    1974 *Ladies and Gentlemen—Lenny Bruce!!,* p. 154. Is it hashish that you're toking?

Tom, (Uncle) [from Harriet Beecher Stowe's sympathetic but subservient black in *Uncle Tom's Cabin;* essentially a black slang term, but much in use among jazzmen, black and white, since c. 1945] As n.: see 1959 quot.; as v.i.: for a black to act in a servile manner in the presence of whites; for its gerund form, see last quot.
    1956 *Lady Sings the Blues,* p. 116. He'd bugged me [i.e., persisted] so and practically made me feel like a Tom for not sitting down with him.
    1956 *The Real Jazz Old and New,* p. 147. An *Uncle Tom* is one who caters to white taste.
    1959 *Esquire,* Nov., p. 70J. *Tom* or *Uncle Tom:* a Negro who does not try to maintain his complete dignity before whites.
    1960 *Monthly Review,* May, p. 24. As the late Billie Holiday once said, "Louis Armstrong Toms from the heart."
    1961 *Swank,* July, p. 60. I called Howard a Tom (Uncle) to allow Lennie to talk like that.
    1961 *New Yorker,* 23 Sep., p. 101. The materials include offensive Uncle Tomming.

tonk, *n.* See s.v. HONKYTONK.

too much [hyperbole (see 1946 quot.); widely current c. 1935–c. 1950, somewhat less since; see also OUT OF THIS WORLD, THE MOST] See 1944, 1959 quots.

1937 *Metronome*, Mar., p. 55. That man's too much!

1944 *The New Cab Calloway's Hepsters Dictionary*, s.v. *too much:* term of highest praise.

1946 *Big Book of Swing*, p. 125. *too much:* getting beyond belief.

1954 *Down Beat*, 21 Apr., p. 22. Stan plays too much [i.e., wonderfully] on that!

1955 *Bop Fables*, p. 46. I just dug your nose and it's too much.

1958 *Somewhere There's Music*, p. 155. The City is too much—and that's where I want to be.

1959 *Esquire*, Nov., p. 70J. *too much:* remarkable. Excruciating in its sublimity.

top (down), from the [by analogy with reading sheet music; current since c. 1930] See 1936 quot.; also, by extension, from the beginning of anything (to the end).

1936 *Metronome*, Feb., p. 21. *from the top down:* playing an orchestration right through.

1956 *Eddie Condon's Treasury of Jazz*, p. 219. Let's do this one more time from the top, gentlemen.

top (of the beat), on [according to jazzmen, current since c. 1925; see also the antonyms *drag, lay back*] In musical performance, slightly ahead of the beat or directly on it: as applied to a vocalist or soloist, *sometimes* there is an implication that he is not relaxed, that he is rushing the rhythm.

1964 *Down Beat*, 22 Oct., p. 26. Dawson's top-of-the-beat forward motion and subtle accenting bring out the best in any soloist.

1967 *Down Beat*, 5 Oct., p. 16. Jimmy was tching, tching on the ride cymbal, way on top of the beat.

1971 *Down Beat*, 9 Dec., p. 29. Bucky backs him, always on top but never cutting the beat.

tore up [nonstandard past participle applied in a special way by jazzmen since c. 1950; see also RIPPED] See last quot.

1958 *Jive in Hi-Fi*, p. 27. In slang if you say "tore up," it means something . . . disturbs or upsets you.

1959 *San Francisco Chronicle*, 4 June, p. 35. "Them people down there must be plenty bugged if a book like this can get them so tore up."

1959 *Esquire*, Nov., p. 70J. *tore up:* extremely distressed.

to the nines, dressed (togged) [lexicographer Peter Tamony traces etym. to magical value (trinity of trinities; muses; etc.) placed on the number by classical Greece; cf. 1890 *A Dictionary of Slang, Jargon & Cant*, s.v. *dressed to the nines:* "dressed to kill (American)"; some currency among jazzmen prob. since c. 1900] In the height of fashion.

1971 *Bird Lives*, p. 335. A particularly well-groomed customer approached, "dressed to the nines" in Broadway toggery.

1974 *Ladies and Gentlemen—Lenny Bruce!!*, p. 384. His vines [q.v.] were fine, he was dressed to the nines.

tough, *adj. & adv.* [one of several standard terms in which the connotation has been reversed—i.e., because someone or something that's tough is also formidable, to be reckoned with (see also BAD, HARD, MEAN, TERRIBLE); widely current only since c. 1955] See 1959 quot.; as adv.: much or well.

1959 *Esquire*, Nov., p. 70J. *tough:* great.

1960 *Tough Tenors: Johnny Griffin & Eddie "Lockjaw" Davis* (liner notes on LP album Jazzland J-45703). The big news is that two of the toughest tenors in captivity are working *together.*

1960 *Beat Jokes Bop Humor & Cool Cartoons*, p. 50. Had not the old man shown Little Ham how to make the toughest broads in the kingdom?

1961 *Evergreen Review*, July-Aug., p. 25. You really believe two chicks could dig each other that tough?

1972 *Gorrilla, My Love*, p. 71. I need you right here with me to translate, Violet, cause you know I don't speak Negro too tough. — p. 164. And take a bath too. Incense can't cover funk too tough.

toy band [by analogy with their childlike instruments; some currency c. 1935–c. 1945; see also MICKEY (MOUSE), TICKY]

1946 *Duke Ellington*, p. 126. The field was over-run with "Mickey Mouse" music, "cheese" or "toy" bands, as the jazzman calls orchestras which rely upon synthetic sounds rather than music for popular appeal.

track, *n.* 1. [by analogy with *racetrack:* that around which one moves: also, see 1968 quot.; current from c. 1926–c. 1950, obs. since except historical]

1944 *Dan Burley's Original Handbook of Harlem Jive*, p. 149. *track:* dance hall, a ballroom.

1946 *Really the Blues*, p. 375. *The Track:* Savoy Ballroom in Harlem.

1966 *Down Beat*, 28 July, p. 17. The Track, as the regular patrons called it, sold only beer and wine.

1968 *Jazz Dance*, p. 316. Regular patrons called it "The Track," perhaps because dog races were featured at one time.

2. [from the grooves in a phonograph record; initially a trade term; widely current among jazzmen since c. 1949] Any one of several performances on a long-playing phonograph record.

1949 *Playback*, Oct.-Nov., p. 4. This took the form of a 10" record with two "tracks" or "grooves" impressed on each side.

1960 *Jazz: A Quarterly of American Music*, Winter, p. 19. Sometimes I squeeze a whole LP on one track.

trade fours, see s.v. FOURS.

tram, *n*. [prob. a dialectal corruption of the first syllable of the standard term (cf. 1955 *Atlantic Monthly*, July, p. 55. "There would be no abrupt change in feeling simply because of the acquisition of cornets, clarinets, 'trambones.' ") and a shortened form; current c. 1925–c. 1945, rare since; see also BONE] A trombone.

1948 *Down Beat*, 1 Dec., p. 13. *This* is in a slower vein with good tram, fair tenor, and trumpet, and too much ensemble.

Trane [one of the few indispensables among the many jazz nicknames; widely current since c. 1960] John Coltrane, great, influential tenor and soprano saxophonist, 1926–1966.

1958 *Soultrane*, (liner notes on LP Prestige 7142). Trane is emotional but never baroque.

trick, (turn a) [prob. by analogy with the surprise element in magic; apparently a dialectal survival from Early Modern English: cf. 1948 *Shakespeare's Bawdy*, s.v. *trick*: "a bout of love-making"; prostitutes' slang but some currency among jazzmen since c. 1900] The sexual act or any of its variations (see 1926 quot.); also, see 1960 quot.

1926 *Nigger Heaven*, p. 252. I said, Now daddy, do you know any more tricks?

1946 *Really the Blues*, p. 30. "Turning a trick" was how they described one session with a john.

1959 *Easy Living*, p. 54. You ever have a habit? . . . You ever turn a trick for it?

1960 *Dictionary of American Slang*, s.v. *trick:* a prostitute's customer; a prostitute's "sale" or business transaction.

trim, *n. & v.t.* [relation to standard meaning(s), if any, unknown; cf. c. 1592 *Titus Andronicus*, V, i, 93–95. "They cut thy sister's tongue, and ravish'd her, And cut her hands, and trimm'd her"; rare since c. 1945] A woman sexually; to possess (a woman sexually).

1952 *Flee the Angry Strangers*, p. 429. She was good trimmin', right enough.

1969 *Sons of Darkness, Sons of Light*, pp. 93–94. When that hot Chicago sun started to bear down, all the trim in the world wasn't going to help.

1974 *Ladies and Gentlemen—Lenny Bruce!!*, p. 156. No slatternly, ugly street trim, Sandra was a dead ringer for Sophia Loren.

truck, *v.i.* [see 1945 quot., s.v. 2, for explanation of semantic development; current c. 1900–c. 1945, obs. since except historical] See 1938 and 1942 quots. (Usually with *on* or *on down*.)

1937 *Metronome*, Nov., p. 11. After Louis boots, the cats truck on to their various domiciles.

1938 *Better English*, Nov., p. 51. *truck, truck on down:* to go somewhere.

1942 *American Mercury*, July, p. 96. *trucking:* strolling.

2. *n. & v.i.* [by analogy with sense 1; see 1942, 1945 quots.; see 1944 quot. for beginning date; very rare since c. 1945 except historical]

1937 *N.Y. Amsterdam News*, 4 Sep., p. 12. The new dance sensation [i.e., The Big Apple] . . . has pushed "The Truck" out of the limelight.

1939 *Jitterbug Jamboree Song Book*, p. 33. *truck:* to dance; the dance itself.

1942 *American Mercury*, July, p. 96. *trucking:* dance step from the strolling motif.

1944 *Dan Burley's Original Handbook of Harlem Jive*, p. 149. *trucking:* a dance introduced at Cotton Club in 1933.

1945 *Charm*, Aug., p. 154. The shuffling rhythm which later became a national dance craze called "Truckin'," for instance, was derived from the brass band funeral music played by mourners on the return from the cemetery!

truth, *n.* [one of several terms derived by analogy with verbal

287

communication (see also LYING, MESSAGE, SAY SOMETHING, TELL A STORY); some currency since c. 1945] Music that is authentic, original or soulful.

1959 *The Horn*, p. 27. All who comped with funk . . . and blew the truth. —p. 225. I blew the truth for you sometimes, didn't I?

tub, every, see S.V. EVERY.

tubs, *n.* (occ. *sing.*) & *v.i.* (rare) [poss. from the shape and poss. from the use of it as a homemade instrument in some early jazz; some currency since c. 1935; see also SKINS, HIDES] See 1955 quot.; as v.i., rare: to play drums (see 1944 quot.)

1942 *The American Thesaurus of Slang*, p. 559. *tub:* a drum.

1944 *Down Beat*, 15 Feb., p. 12. Wettling's Solid Tubbing Kicks Any Size Ork (headline).

1955 *Say*, 28 Apr., p. 53. *tubs:* drums.

1961 *The Sound*, p. 99. Yes, it's time that your boy Hass packed his tubs and moved on.

tune, *n.* [analogical extension of standard meaning; some currency since c. 1945] See 1963 quot.; also, by extension: a woman.

1961 *The Village Voice*, 20 Jan., p. 1. I don't dig the tune. [i.e., I don't comprehend what is being said.]

1963 *Hiptionary*, p. 8. *tune:* idea, story.

1970 *Dictionary of Afro-American Slang*, p. 117. *tune:* (very loosely used) an idea or a woman.

tuned in [by analogy with turning on a radio; some currency since c. 1950] See 1970 quot.

1967 *Down Beat*, 2 Nov., p. 23. Wayne Shorter followed with an intense solo to which Herbie Hancock was really tuned in.

1968 *Americanisms*, July, p. 3. Stan Kenton was getting receptive hearings as the 1950s tuned in.

1970 *Dictionary of Afro-American Slang*, p. 117. *tuned in:* in rapport with whatever is going on.

tuned out [by analogy with turning off a radio; some currency since c. 1950; see also TURNED OFF] Uninterested; inattentive.

1970 *Dictionary of Afro-American Slang*, p. 117. *tuned in:* in rapport with whatever is going on; the opposite is tuned out.

288

turkey trot [dance designations frequently refer to animal movements: cf. BUNNY HUG, CAMEL WALK, FOX TROT; term dates from at least mid-19th century, and was current in the jazz milieu c. 1910–c. 1920, obs. since except historical] A jazz dance.

1914 *Modern Dancing* [1962 *Jazz: A History of the New York Scene*, p. 37]. Drop the Turkey Trot, the Grizzly Bear, the Bunny Hug, etc.

1934 *Metronome*, Jan., p. 30. We did create the foxtrot, which has outlasted a flock of other forms such as the Turkey Trot, Charleston, Black Bottom, etc.

turned around [from the sense of disorientation; current since c. 1960] Pleasantly disoriented; amazed.

1966 *Down Beat*, 19 May, p. 20. Getz' starkly beautiful improvisation on the Herman band's record of *Early Autumn* turned listeners around.

1968 *Down Beat*, 27 June, p. 19. Last October Farlow finally came out of the woodshed [q.v.], and when he did, he turned everybody around.

turned off [by analogy with turning off a radio; some currency since c. 1950; see also TUNED OUT] Uninterested; inattentive.

1961 *Metronome*, Feb., p. 30. I am one of those who got turned off a couple of years ago when Brookmeyer started recording albums that sounded like trumped-up dixieland.

turn on, 1. [from sense 2; current since c. 1946] To use marijuana or narcotics.

1956 *Sideman*, p. 274. If everybody starts turning on, you think they'll sell any lush [i.e., liquor]?

1959 *The Holy Barbarians*, pp. 171–172. When the marijuana head (vipers, we called them in the thirties) or the hype [i.e., narcotics addict] turns on, he has the feeling of setting something in motion inside himself.

2. [by analogy of the human being with a machine; current since c. 1945] See 1958 and first 1959 quots.; also, to excite (see 1967 quot.).

1958 *American Speech*, Oct., p. 225. When he [i.e., a hipster] *turns* him [i.e., someone] *on* he supplies him with something—a smoke, a drink, or just a bit of information.

1959 *The Beat Generation Dictionary*, p. 7. *turn on to:* introduce to.

1959 *The Holy Barbarians*, p. 67. It was Richard who turned me on to jazz.

1959 *Jazz Poems*, p. 5. I want you babes to be turned on to the truth.

289

1967 *Down Beat*, 2 Nov., p. 23. Joe Morello's drum feature turned the audience on.

turned the rhythm (or time) around [current since c. 1925] Lost the beat.

1972 *Down Beat*, 9 Nov., p. 22. There are spots where the rhythm gets turned around.

twisted, *adj.* [current since c. 1950]

1949 *Twisted* (tune recorded by Wardell Gray).

1960 *Metronome*, Sep., p. 16. *twisted:* obscure, confused, mentally disturbed.

two-beat, *adj. & n.* [see 1955 quot. for semantic explanation; current c. 1930–c. 1945, rare since except historical] See 1955 quot.

1938 *Metronome,* Oct., p. 23. Just honest-to-goodness, two-beat, driving swing.

1955 *The Encyclopedia of Jazz*, p. 347. *two-beat:* jazz in which two of the four beats in every bar are accented; usually associated with Dixieland jazz.

1962 *The New Jazz Book*, p. 15. The older styles of jazz are grouped together under the heading "two-beat jazz."

1963 *Down Beat*, Feb., p. 37. *Down Beat* came out with the new name back in the '30s, calling it two-beat music.

two cents, see S.V. CENT.

U

uncool, *adj.* [cf. narcotics use: 1953 *Junkie*, p. 13: "*Un-cool:* liable to attract attention from the law"; some currency since c. 1950] Not *cool* (q.v.); i.e., frenetic, needlessly excited, unwise (see 1969 quot.).

1958 *Somewhere There's Music*, p. 175. Like buy my forthcoming book on what's uncool in American education.

1961 *The Sound*, p. 101. I dunno, old man, to the average colored person the average gray acts like he's in a sweat most of the time. Hung up. Uncool.

1962 *Jazz Journal*, June, p. 22. It is uncool to let anybody use your place as a forwarding address for packages from Mexico.

1969 *Hip Manual*, s.v. *uncool:* dangerously incautious.

unhip, unhipped, *adj.* [current since c. 1935; see also SQUARE, NOWHERE]

1938 *American Speech*, Dec., p. 314. *unhipped:* opposite of hipped.

1939 *Jitterbug Jamboree Song Book*, p. 33. *unhip:* not familiar, not wise.

1946 *Really the Blues*, p. 69. Ray and Fuzzy were salty with our unhip no-playing piano player.

1972 *Down Beat*, 9 Nov., p. 19. It was the kind of playing you could use to turn on an unhipped uncle.

untogether, *adj.* [current since c. 1965] Neurotic, confused, obnoxious.

1972 *Gorilla, My Love*, p. 70. That's how untogether Jackson is.

up a breeze, see s.v. BREEZE.

up-tempo, up, [originally prob. shortened form of *speed up; up-tempo:*

291

current since c. 1935, *up* since c. 1945] Of tunes, played at a fast tempo.

1948 *Down Beat*, 19 May, p. 13. "Sleeps" is an up tempo thing by Norvo.

1960 *The Jazz Word*, p. 30. On up tunes, particularly the scat songs, she improvises in a steady flow.

1961 *Down Beat*, 19 Jan., p. 31. "Sesame," in particular, is swift-moving and taken up-tempo.

1961 *The Sound*, p. 37. "Fast or slow?" "Up. 'Way up," Red said.

up tight, uptight, 1. [poss. sexual etym. (see note s.v. *tight,* sense 1); according to jazz dancer Leon James, some currency esp. among black jazzmen since c. 1958] Excellent (usually applies to music).

1962 *Gene Ammons: Up Tight* (LP album on Prestige PRLP7208).

1968 *Esquire*, Apr., p. 160. The expression "uptight," which meant being in financial straits, appeared on the soul scene in the general vicinity of 1953. In the early Sixties when "uptight" was on the move, a younger generation of soul people in the black urban communities regenerated it with a new meaning: "everything is cool, under control, going my way." At present the term has the former meaning for the older generation and the latter construction for those under thirty.

2. [prob. from underworld slang (i.e., impecunious; in difficulty); current among jazzmen since c. 1963] Annoyed; uncomfortable; also see 1968, 1969 quots.

1965 *Village Voice*, 4 Mar., p. 5. I've been uptight for a year because of you!

1968 *Esquire*, Apr., p. 160. The expression "uptight," which meant being in financial straits, appeared on the soul scene in . . . 1953.

1969 *Hip Manual*, s.v. *up tight:* in a difficult position.

1970 *Down Beat*, 3 Sep., p. 16. Miles was a beautiful host. So why am I up tight?

1973 *Target Blue*, p. 542. Lindsay was very uptight with what you said.

uptown, *adj.* [prob. because New York City's largest black neighborhood, Harlem, is "uptown"; current c. 1930–c. 1945, rare since] Harlem; also, see 1959 quot.; also, as applied to music, earthy.

1939 *Uptown Shuffle* (tune recorded by the Erskine Hawkins Orchestra on Bluebird 10506).

1940 *Uptown Blues* (tune recorded by Jimmie Lunceford Orchestra on Vocalion 5362).

1959 *Swinging Syllables*, s.v. *uptown:* an adjective, signifying one who is stylish, quite hip, or important.

1962 *Uptown and Lowdown* (title of LP album of Dick Wellstood and Cliff Jackson on Prestige/Swingville 2026).

1973 *Down Beat*, 25 Oct., p. 15. Let's go uptown, hear some jazz.

vibes, *n. pl.* [see 1954 quot.; current since c. 1937 when these instruments replaced the older xylophone in jazz].

1940 *Swing,* July, p. 17. Lastly, some too-formal ensemble riffing with vibes.

1954 *Esquire,* Nov., p. 82. Contrary to popular belief, the word "vibes" is not the nickname for the instrument; it is the word used to cover all instruments of which the manufacturing company trade names are "Vibraphone," "Vibraharp," "Vibrabells," etc.

-ville, *suffix* [used to represent an extreme degree of the word to which it is appended; jazzman Emmett Berry prob. introduced it into jazz speech c. 1938, but it has been widely current only since c. 1945; see also -CITY]

1949 *Music Library Association Notes,* Dec., p. 41. Addition of the suffix *ville* is a common verbal procedure among song-pluggers. Origin of the device is perhaps Storyville in New Orleans, the area in which jazz reputedly had its birth.

1955 *Bop Fables,* p. 10. "Weirdsville," said the baby bear. —p. 37. Hangoversville, for all I know.

1956 *American Jazz Festival,* p. 55. In fact the whole thing is strictly from Squaresville, U.S.A.

1959 *Swinging Syllables,* s.v. *ville:* a suffix which can be added to any word to emphasize it, i.e., dictionary—wordville.

1959 *The Holy Barbarians,* p. 126. The squares had discovered beatville.

1961 *Down Beat,* 5 Jan., p. 23. Paul Desmond made a parallel observation, commenting wryly, "Diversityville—let a hundred flowers bloom." —19 Jan., p. 22. The telephone rings and the gas and light company informs you that in 24 hours it's "candlesville."

1961 *The Sound*, p. 32. Red had disembarked at the Los Angeles airport, taken one appraising look at Squaresville-on-the-Pacific, and immediately hopped the next plane back to the Apple [i.e., New York City].

1970 *Blue Movie*, p. 59. It's *disasterville.*

vine(s), *n.* (usually *pl.*) [by analogy with the standard meaning—i.e., because it hangs on or clings to one; from underworld slang: cf. 1934 *A Dictionary of American Slang*, s.v. *vine:* "orig. prison use; civilian or nonprison clothes, c. 1930; by c. 1935 in wide jive use and soon changed to 'vines' "; current among jazzmen since c. 1935; see also DRAPE, THREADS, TOG]

1944 *The New Cab Calloway's Hepsters Dictionary*, s.v. *vine:* a suit of clothing.

1955 *Hear Me Talkin to Ya*, p. 106. I . . . brought her a lot of fine vines, a wardrobe with nothing but the finest.

1965 *Down Beat*, 14 Jan., p. 18. I saw this cat on Girard Ave. in a wrinkled, dirty-blue vine.

1971 *Village Voice*, June, p. 1. Another was a sartorially resplendent cat in cool vines.

viper, *n.* [since the term is self-imposed, it is prob., though Biblical in origin, a humorous self-castigation; widely current c. 1920–c. 1942, rare since] See 1940 quot.

1930 *The Viper's Drag* (tune recorded by Cab Calloway Orchestra).

1938 *N.Y. Amsterdam News*, 2 Apr., p. 17. The thousands of . . . vipers . . . that are being hatched daily . . . are a peril."

1940 *American Speech*, Oct., p. 337. *viper:* a marijuana user.

1959 *The Holy Barbarians*, pp. 171–172. When the marijuana head (vipers, we called them in the thirties) or the hype turns on, he has the feeling of setting something in motion inside himself.

1972 *Bessie*, p. 188. Tunes like "Reefer Man," "You'se a Viper," "Kicking the Gong Around," and "Viper's Dream" carried messages about drugs that few whites understood.

vocal, *n.* [from standard phrase *vocal music;* introduced as a distinguishing term c. 1935, somewhat less common since c. 1950] A musical arrangement which includes a part for voice (see last quot.); also, that vocal performance.

1936 *Metronome*, Feb., p. 61. *vocal:* vocal arrangement.

1948 *Down Beat*, 1 Dec., p. 10. We ran down [i.e., rehearsed] three new instrumentals and a vocal for Baubles Buxon!

1950 *Lingo of Tin-Pan Alley*, s.v. *vocal:* contrasts with instrumental. Song is sung.

vocalese, *n.* ["vocal" + generic suffix; current since c. 1955]

1970 *Jazz People*, p. 99. He is always associated with the idiom known as "vocalese" where words are fitted to a previously recorded instrumental line.

voice, *v.t.* [special application of standard meaning (i.e., to harmonize voices); current since c. 1930] See 1961 quot.

1933 *Metronome*, Mar., p. 34. Voicing ensembles should be considered entirely differently from voicing separate sax or brass trios.

1937 *American Speech*, Feb., p. 47. It is voiced peculiarly in that the lead melody is carried lower than the clarinet.

1961 *Down Beat*, 18 Jan., p. 42. The word "voicing" is used—and misused—often enough in record reviews and liner notes. . . . Strictly speaking, voicing is the distribution on the keyboard or in the orchestra of the tones of a chord.

vonce, *n.* [etym. unknown: perhaps from Yiddish and German word for bedbug (hence, anything worthless; hence, anything); some currency esp. among black jazzmen since c. 1942; see also JAZZ, JIVE, SHIT] Thing(s) (may refer to a dance, sex organs—almost anything).

1959 *Esquire*, Nov., pp. 70H–70I. *vonce:* marijuana. —p. 70J. *do the vonce:* make love.

1966 *Black Music: Four Lives.* At the time my head was chock full of "classical vonce."

wah-wah, wa-wa, wow-wow, *adj. & n.* [See 1933, 1956 quots. for etym.; current c. 1925–c. 1945, rare since except historical] See 1942 and 1956 quots.

1926 *Melody Maker*, Mar., p. 30. Secondly, I want to advise musicians of a new wow-wow glass mute modifier for trumpets which has recently been put on the market in this country [i.e., England].

1933 *Fortune*, Aug., p. 47. For example, it is now extremely *corny* to use the once popular wah-wah mutes which make brass instruments sound like crying babies.

1942 *The American Thesaurus of Slang*, p. 561. *wah-wah:* a brass effect obtained by favoring the bell of the horn with a mute. *wah-wah mute:* a rubber mute or plunger used on a trumpet or trombone to produce "wah-wah" effects.

1956 *Guide to Jazz*, s.v. *wa-wa:* a mute placed in the bell of a trumpet or trombone and constantly moved a little in order to produce sounds for which this name is onomatopoeic.

1961 *New Yorker*, 16 Sep., p. 147. In "Dem Blues," Curson played two choruses of muted wa-wa trumpet, an unfashionable skill learned from Rex Stewart at Mingus' behest.

wail, *v.i.* [by analogy with loud lamentation; despite some occasional earlier use, widely current only since c. 1953; see also BURN, COOK, SMOKE] See 1955 and last three quots.; also, by extension: to be superb (see 1958 quot.).

1955 *Vogue*, 15 Sep., p. 125. "Wailing" is the 1955 jazz word for playing superbly; the new equivalent of "really swinging."

1956 *Lady Sings the Blues*, p. 17. If I'd heard Pops and Bessie wailing

297

through the window of some minister's front parlor, I'd have run free errands for him.

1958 *Somewhere There's Music*, p. 32. Those people, man, they had a culture that wailed.

1958 *American Speech*, Oct., p. 224. Just now, the word *wailing* (meaning "playing exceptionally well," and analogically, "Having a very good time") seems destined for longevity.

1959 *Newport Jazz Festival: 1959*, p. 46. *wail:* to do anything very well.

wailer, *n.* [from jazz slang *wail;* some currency since c. 1955] A musician who plays well (see quot.); by extension: anyone who does anything well or simply is a superior person (see 1959 quot., s.v. *wail*).

1958 *Down Beat*, 16 Oct., p. 38. The whole story is right here in eight, eloquent preachments by as fine a quintet of wailers as can be assembled.

wail on him (or 'em), [current esp. among black jazzmen since c. 1955; see also COOK ON 'EM, SMOKE ON 'EM] Best him (musically), play well. Oral evidence only.

wailing, *adj.* [from jazz slang *wail;* widely current since c. 1954] Superb, musically or otherwise.

1956 *Sideman*, p. 98. Coke's a wailing cat.

walk, *v.i.* & *adj.* (& occ. *v.t.*) [from earlier *adj., n.,* and *v.t.* use (see WALKING BASS, CAKE WALK, CAMEL WALK), reinforced by an old analogy—i.e., the 1900 practice of walking rhythmically to the post-funeral march music esp. in New Orleans; some currency since c. 1950] See 1955 and 1957 quots.

1952 *Mademoiselle*, Dec., p. 118. And that's the basic jazz beat, that *walking* beat. Up here in the north all the jazzmen are playing too fast or too slow—nobody walks.

1955 *The Encyclopedia of Jazz*, p. 347. *walk:* establish a lively, four-beats-to-the-bar rhythm (usually said of bass players: "walking rhythm").

1956 *Enjoyment of Jazz* (EJ402), p. 3. In Basie's section . . . the bass and guitar "walk" with even stress on the four beats to the bar.

1957 *N.Y. Times Magazine*, 18 Aug., p. 26. *they really walk:* the rhythm section really swings.

1961 *The Sound*, p. 270. Yes, man, we was *walking!*

1964 *High Fidelity*, Sep., p. 126. Duvivier walks *Chloë* onto the scene in a delightfully sultry manner.

walk (the bass), walking (bass) [prob. by analogy with the progression (see 1950 quot.); current c. 1915–c. 1945, rare since except historical]

1939 *American Jazz Music*, p. 51. *String bass,* more often plucked or slapped than bowed, usually playing two or four notes per bar or a "walking" (melodic) bass.

1950 *Lingo of Tin-Pan Alley*, s.v. *walking bass:* type of bass piano progression in which movement is up or down by semitones, whole tones, or thirds—arranged in broken octaves. Progression may also be used orchestrally.

1957 *The Book of Jazz*, p. 120. In rhythm section work these bass strings are usually "walked"; that is, played continuously, four notes to the bar.

1959 *Selected Poems*, Langston Hughes, p. 229. Down in the bass/That steady beat/Walking walking walking/Like marching feet.

walkin' the dog [dance satirized this act, esp. the haughtiness which frequently characterized it; current c. 1916–c. 1920, obs. since except historical] A jazz dance.

1916 *Walkin' the Dog* (tune).

1943 *The Jazz Record*, 15 Apr., p. 3. In 1917 . . . there were several dances in vogue, namely: "Walkin' the Dog," "Jazz Dance," and "Ballin' the Jack."

washboard, *n.* [some currency c. 1910–c. 1935, obs. since except historical]

1956 *Guide to Jazz*, s.v. *washboard:* literally; used as musical instrument by rubbing thimbles-on-fingers over it.

washboard band [some currency c. 1910–c. 1935, obs. since except historical] A band consisting wholly or partly of washboards.

1955 *Hear Me Talkin to Ya*, p. 50. Even a washboard band was welcome.

waste, *v.t.* [by extension of standard *v.t.;* also some teenage use; current since c. 1955] See first quot.; also: to destroy.

1959 *Esquire*, Nov., p. 70J. *to waste someone:* to do a person bodily harm.

299

1960 *Beat Jokes Bop Humor & Cool Cartoons*, p. 52. One minute you were balling and the next you were stiff. Who wasted you? —p. 53. Claudius stole my kingdom. Revenge me, son. Waste that cat!

1973 *Saint Jack*, p. 193. I'm telling you to get us a table or we'll waste this house.

wasted, *adj.* [see note s.v. *waste;* widely current since c. 1955]

1956 *Tennessee Folklore Society Bulletin*, Mar., p. 22. *wasted:* tired or beat up.

1959 *Esquire*, Nov., p. 70J. *wasted:* in bad physical shape.

1961 *Down Beat*, 19 Jan., p. 22. You wake up at noon, your wig [i.e., head] is aching, your stomach is completely wasted.

1969 *Hip Manual*, s.v. *wasted:* very high.

wax, *n. & v.t.* [from the substance from which records were made; primarily a trade and writers' term, but also with some currency esp. among white jazzmen c. 1925–c. 1950, obs. since except historical] A 78 rpm phonograph record; to make a 78 rpm phonograph record.

1935 *Metronome*, Apr., p. 45. Impressions in Wax (record review column title).

1948 *Down Beat*, 14 July, p. 13. Ventura's doubled up tenoring on "Body" is some of the best that he has set down on wax.

1955 *Hear Me Talkin to Ya*, p. 232. On the second date I remember we waxed "Emigration Blues."

way out, wayout [from its remoteness from the conventional; some earlier use, but in wide currency only since c. 1950; see also FAR OUT, SOMETHING ELSE]

1958 *Publication of the American Dialect Society*, Nov., p. 47. *way out:* departing greatly from the norm; especially said of unusual (or unusually good) treatment of melody or harmony; now of anything that seems especially good—though still used in the original sense too.

1960 *The Jazz Word*, p. 123. How often I painted to wayout sounds.

1965 *Down Beat*, 8 Apr., p. 14. Calling clubowners "hip bartenders who don't know anything except the sound of falling coin" is way-out nonsense.

wear them out [by analogy with the effect; according to jazzmen, some currency c. 1920–c. 1935, obs. since except historical; see also BLOW DOWN, CARVE, CUT] To best another band in musical competition.

1955 *Hear Me Talkin to Ya*, p. 25. Our band really wore them out.

weed, *n.* [metonymy—i.e., marijuana derives from a weed; current c. 1925–c. 1940, very rare since; see also BOO, GAGE, POT, TEA]

1931 *Chant of the Weed* (tune recorded by Don Redman Orchestra on Brunswick 80036).

1933 *Chicago Defender*, 2 Dec., p. 5. The humble "reefer," the "weed," the marijuana, or what have you by way of a name for a doped cigarette has moved to Park Ave. from Harlem.

1938 *Cab Calloway: Hi De Ho*, p. 16. *weed:* marijuana.

weird, *adj.* [see 1958 quot. for explanation of semantic adaptation; current since c. 1945] Imaginative, interesting, delightfully surprising (note: occasionally the term is used in the sense of *too* imaginative—consequently, unintelligible; this is the sense in which its use in the last quot. should be taken).

1948 *Down Beat*, [repr. 3/11/65 p. 32]. I like this. Very weird—marvelous idea.

1958 *Publication of the American Dialect Society*, Nov., pp. 41–42. The adverse criticisms of bop were taken over almost wholesale and made into favorable ones. Such terms as *crazy, weird, wild,* and *nervous,* all used to express favorable responses to music, are adaptations of terms levelled against the bop musicians. Since they knew the music which people called "crazy" was actually good, they took over the word in a good sense.

1965 *Down Beat*, 25 Mar., p. 21. I think my performance was pretty weird but Clark encouraged me again.

weirdbag, *n.* [jazz slang *weird* + jazz slang *bag;* some currency since c. 1959] The source of an unusually experimental musician's (or person's) inspiration or inventiveness. Oral evidence only (see BAG).

weirdie, weird-o, *n.* [from jazz slang *weird;* some currency since c. 1950] An interesting or imaginative musician (or person)—sometimes, too imaginative.

1955 *The Encyclopedia of Jazz*, p. 347. *weird-o:* a weird person.

1959 *The Holy Barbarians*, p. 86. Phil had an arrangement with the weirdie who ran the shop.

1959 *Down Beat*, 14 May, p. 20. Sonny is no admirer of what he calls "weirdies," musicians whose music is "too mysterious."

went down, see s.v. GO DOWN.

West Coast jazz (or school or **sound)** [interchangeable with *cool jazz* (q.v.) as a generic term for a style of playing most of the practitioners of which came from the West Coast; current since c. 1952] The most popular jazz style c. 1950–c. 1957, characterized by restraint, intellectuality and a studied relaxation.

1955 *Hear Me Talkin to Ya*, p. 397. The West Coast restraint can be attributed then, I think, to Mulligan's influence.

1961 *Commonweal*, 24 Mar., pp. 657–658. To the chagrin of those "cool" players who were Negro, a white adaptation of their style began to gain popularity in the comparatively anemic "West Coast" school of the first half of the 1950s.

Western style [named for its place of origin; some currency c. 1925–c. 1935, obs. since except historical; see also its more common synonym CHICAGO (STYLE)] A jazz style differentiated from the earlier New Orleans style (q.v.) on which it was based, though both together constitute "traditional" jazz: see s.v. CHICAGO (STYLE).

1928 *Melody Maker*, Dec., p. 1299. It . . . is known as the Western style, as pioneered in Chicago.

1955 *Hear Me Talkin to Ya*, p. 234. The Western style was more open . . . open horns and running chords and running changes.

wheels, *n. pl.* [synecdoche; current since c. 1930; see also RUBBER, SHORT]

1957 *N.Y. Times Magazine*, 18 Aug., p. 26. *wheels:* an automobile.

1969 *Sons of Darkness, Sons of Light*, p. 169. Hey, baby, I see you got wheels.

1970 *Death of a Blue-Eyed Soul Brother*, p. 18. Your wheels or mine?

where it's (or someone is) at [analogy of a state of being with a place; current since c. 1960] The truth of the matter; the essence of things.

1963 *Down Beat*, 12 Sep., p. 35. I'd say well, you're just an oldtimer—you don't know where it's at.

1964 *Down Beat*, 12 Mar., p. 15. Ethnology ain't where it's at; talent is.

1965 *Down Beat*, 6 May, p. 38. Malcolm X knew better than Whitney Young where it's at.

1970 *Jazz People*, p. 116. I'd like to interview some of the writers as a musician just to find out where they're at!

whip that thing [by analogy with inflicting pain or punishment and/or subduing; according to jazzman Eubie Blake; current since c. 1900; very rare since c. 1940] Frequently hortatory; also *whip it:* oral evidence only.

1939 *Jitterbug Jamboree Song Book*, p. 22. *whip that thing:* play that instrument.

whipped (up) [by analogy with having been literally whipped; some currency with *adv.* from c. 1935–c. 1945, wide currency without *adv.* since c. 1945; see also BEAT, HACKED]

1938 *Cab Calloway: Hi De Ho*, p. 16. *whipped up:* worn out, exhausted.

1969 *Sons of Darkness, Sons of Light*, p. 169. You look really whipped, Daddy.

wig, *n.* 1. [fanciful synecdoche; in its initial sense (hair), current since c. 1935; in its next sense (head), since c. 1938; and in its final sense (mind), since c. 1942]

1944 *Dan Burley's Original Handbook of Harlem Jive*, p. 150. *wig:* head, brain, mentality.

1952 *Park East*, Dec., p. 30. My queen in her scanties and I in my robe,/Had just fixed our wigs for a long winter's load.

1956 *Lady Sings the Blues*, p. 221. I straightened her wig right off [i.e., told her off].

1958 *The Book of Negro Folklore*, p. 488. *wig:* head, hair.

1959 *The Horn*, p. 153. The bandy-legged figure stood, with wild wig that no pomade could subdue.

1960 *Hiparama of the Classics*, p. 11. Take it off you wig, Naz, we've got it covered! —p. 20. Nero's wig went straight up in the air.

1961 *Down Beat*, 19 Jan., p. 22. You wake up at noon, your wig is aching.

2. (also *wigger:* see quot.) [special application of the most recent meaning of sense 1; some currency since c. 1950]

1959 *Jazz for Moderns*, p. 21. *wig:* a person who is very crazy. Sometimes called wigger.

3. [special application of the most recent meaning of sense 1; current since c. 1955] See 1959 quots.

1958 *Saturday Review*, 11 Jan., p. 79. Musicians are now used to witnessing the unfulfilled innovator; they call these musicians "wigs."

1959 *The Horn*, p. 132. Curny was a "wig," as primarily cerebral jazzmen are dubbed.

1959 *Esquire*, Nov., p. 70J. *wig:* a person who is farout [q.v.] intellectually.

v.i. & v.t. 1. [formed from *n.*, sense 1—i.e., as a function or state of mind; current since c. 1950; see also FLIP] As v.i.: see 1952 quot.; as v.t.: to provoke others to exasperation, enthusiasm or insanity (also used with *out*).

1952 *A History of Jazz in America*, p. 350. *wig:* term expressing exasperation, enthusiasm, or insanity; describes the process of losing the hair or skin of the head.

1955 *American Speech*, Dec., p. 305. He wigged out at the prof's gag.

1956 *Sideman*, p. 233. When she found out I was dancing in nightclubs she wigged!

1959 *Toronto Telegram*, 31 Mar., p. 3. *wig;* to make others flip [q.v.].

1959 *San Francisco Chronicle*, 4 June, p. 35. Some real moldy [i.e., old-fashioned] cat in a library in Alabama wigged out when she saw the white rabbits and the black rabbits on the cover of the book together.

1960 *The Jazz Review*, May, p. 30. Baby, there're a hundred car dealers that'd wig for th' opportunity.

2. [formed from *n.*, sense 1—i.e., as a function or state of the mind; current since c. 1955] See 1958 quot.; also, as v.t.: to help someone else's thinking (i.e., to enlighten).

1958 *Publication of the American Dialect Society*, Nov., p. 47. *wig:* to think; to play extremely intellectual music.

1959 *Diggeth Thou?*, p. 43. Let me wig you to the deal that went down.

1959 *Esquire*, Nov., p. 70J. *to wig:* to think, to play. Example: John wigged up this plan.

1960 *Beat Jokes Bop Humor & Cool Cartoons*, p. 22. Don't be brought down 'cause you didn't wig up this plan.

loose wig [*wig, n.*, sense 1, in the sense of the mind, *loose* in sense of relaxed or uninhibited; some currency since c. 1957] An imaginative person (usually, musician). (Note: the phrase sometimes suggests a superfluity of imagination—i.e., unintelligibility: see 1958 quot.)

1958 *Jive in Hi-Fi*, p. 35. In slang, if you say "loose wig" it means a person . . . talking in circles.

1959 *Jazz for Moderns*, p. 20. *loose wig:* a completely uninhibited, really way-out musician.

1959 *Esquire*, Nov., p. 70J. *loose wig:* one who is a very advanced performer.

wiggy, *adj.* [from *v.*, sense 1; current since c. 1955] Bizarre; mind-bending.

1964 *Down Beat,* 27 Feb., p. 22. From the bar it was a pretty wiggy sight.

wild, *adj.* [see 1958 quot. for semantic explanation; current since c. 1948] Imaginative, unusual.

1955 *Bop Fables,* p. 37. I've fixed up a real wild basket of ribs.

1958 *Publication of American Dialect Society,* Nov., pp. 41–42. The adverse criticisms of bop were taken over almost wholesale and made into favorable responses to music. Such terms as *crazy, weird, wild,* and *nervous,* all used to express favorable responses to music, are adaptations of terms levelled against the bop musicians. Since they knew the music which people called "crazy" was actually good, they took over the word in a good sense.

1959 *Swinging Syllables,* s.v. *wild:* the greatest.

1959 *Esquire,* Nov., p. 70J. *wild:* remarkable.

1959 *The Horn,* p. 131. Curn, it's wild, the greatest band you've ever had, but it'll bomb because it's too far out for the average ginmill owner.

1959 *The Holy Barbarians,* p. 111. A maverick architect . . . used it as a hideaway workshop for some wild ideas.

wipe out, *v.t.* [hyperbole; current since c. 1960] To best (in musical competition).

1971 *Bird Lives,* p. 323. Bird wiped them right out.

with it, (be or **get)** [in the sense of unification with life or reality; also some general colloquial use; current among jazzmen since c. 1940; see also DOWN WITH THE ACTION] See 1947, 1959, 1970 quots.; for adj. use, see last quot.

1947 *Jive and Slang,* s.v. *git with it:* enjoy yourself.

1959 *Toronto Telegram,* 31 Mar., p. 3. *with it:* aware, digging [jazz sense].

1960 *Hiparama of the Classics,* p. 10. Now the Naz was the kind of a Cat that came on so cool and so wild and so groovy and so WITH IT, that when he laid it down WHAM! It stayed there!

1961 *The Sound,* p. 38. "Don't seem to be with it on tempo, though," Red commented.

305

1970 *Dictionary of Afro-American Slang*, p. 123. *with it (be or get):* (1940s–50s) to have rapport with whatever is happening.

1971 *Down Beat*, 27 May, p. 12. I'm negotiating right now with a really modern, with-it poet.

won't quit (or stop) [hyperbole; current since c. 1960] Is remarkable.

1973 *Down Beat*, 1 Feb., p. 28. She has a frame that won't quit, reminding one of a younger Julie London.

1974 *Ladies and Gentlemen—Lenny Bruce!!*, p. 383. I make a not-too-subtle zig-zag for the scoff—a buffet that wouldn't quit!

wood pile [from its composition and general shape: the instrument's keys were wooden; current c. 1933–c. 1940 when it was largely replaced as an instrument by the metal-keyed vibraphone and vibrasharp (see VIBES), very rare since except historical]

1936 *Metronome*, Feb., p. 61. *wood pile:* xylophone.

1951 *Time*, 22 Oct., p. 69. Red Norvo kept salting his half-hour stands with such tunes as . . . he used to rap out on his "woodpile" (xylophone) with Paul Whiteman's band 20 years ago.

wood-shed, woodshed, *v.i., v.t. & n.* [cf. 1960 *Dictionary of American Slang, s.v. woodshed:* "From the archaic and rural image of the woodshed where a boy could retire to smoke or otherwise occupy himself without detection"; current since c. 1930] To rehearse or practice (music) privately (see 1936 quot.); a period or a state of privately practicing (music).

1936 *Swing That Music*, p. 71. We used to practice together, "wood-shed" as we say (from the old-time way of going out into the wood-shed to practice a new song).

1946 *Hollywood Note*, June, p. 4. T.D. [i.e., Tommy Dorsey] goes back to the woodshed.

1955 *Hear Me Talkin to Ya*, p. 190. It was here that the term "woodshedding" originated. When one of the gang wanted to rehearse his part, he would go off into the woods and practice.

1959 *The Horn*, p. 59. That harrowing exile in the soul that jazzmen know as "woodshedding."

work, *v.i.* [metonomy; cf. c. 1604 *Othello*, II, i, 116. "You rise to play and go to bed to work"; according to jazzmen, current since c. 1945; see also TRIM]

1959 *The Holy Barbarians*, p. 156. "Work" means sexual intercourse.

1961 *The Jazz Review*, Jan., p. 33. How about a new one called simply *Cojones*, or as the musicians would have it, *Work?*

2. [special application of the standard term; current since c. 1955; see also BLOW, GO, WAIL] To play (music) in earnest, energetically, excitingly.

1956 *Work!* (tune composed by Thelonious Monk).

1956 *Workin': Miles Davis Quintet* (LP album Prestige 7166).

1956 *Saturday Review*, 12 May, p. 34. Sims, along with Stan Getz, is the most exciting of the young tenor saxophonists, and when he is really working ("One to Blow On"), he is irresistible.

work out [special application of its colloquial sense (i.e., to exercise strenuously); current since c. 1958] To play music intensely and energetically.

1961 *Workin' Out with The Barney Kessel Quartet* (title of LP album Contemporary M3585).

worst, the [hyperbole: see also THE END, THE GREATEST, THE LEAST, THE MOST; current since c. 1950] Anyone or anything of poor quality, disappointing.

1958 *Publication of the American Dialect Society*, Nov., p. 47. *the worst:* opposite of *most, end,* etc.

wow, *interj.* [self-consciously childlike expression of wonder; chiefly youth culture slang, but with some currency among jazzmen since c. 1950; see also OOWEE] An expression of surprise or wonder (but in contrast to its standard use, here it is a calculated affectation).

1961 *The Sound*, p. 113. And, wow, I should have thought of this before.

1964 *Down Beat*, 27 Aug., p. 40. You never know if he'll make it, but when he does—WOW!

write, *v.i. & v.t.* [special application of standard meaning; current since c. 1920] See 1958 quot.

1926 *Melody Maker*, Nov., p. 11. Now if you ever come to an instrument you are not sure about, there is only one way to write his part.

1933 *Metronome*, May, p. 39. I prefer to transpose for the instruments as I write.

1958 *Publication of the American Dialect Society*, Nov., p. 47. *write:* to make an arrangement [i.e., musical].

writer, *n.* [current since c. 1935]

1958 *Publication of the American Dialect Society,* Nov., p. 47. *writer:* arranger.

wrong, *adj.* [standard term specially applied (i.e., to the quality of music and, in an altered sense, to people); prob. suggested by earlier underworld use: cf. 1934 *A Dictionary of American Slang,* p. 44. "*wrong:* untrustworthy; unreliable; deceitful"; current since c. 1950; see also NOWHERE, RANK] Of poor quality; nasty.

1959 *The Naked Lunch,* p. 226. In 1920s a lot of Chinese pushers [i.e., narcotics sellers] found The West so unreliable, dishonest and wrong, . . . when an Occidental junky came to score [i.e., buy narcotics], they say, "No glot. . . . Clom Fliday."

1960 *The Jazz Review,* Nov., p. 12. And they were so wrong until it was obnoxious to the average ear.

wrong riff, see S.V. RIFF.

Y

Yard(bird), *n.* [see 1959 quot. for two, contradictory accounts of the origin of the nickname, a less common one than its alternate, *Bird*, q.v.; current in any widespread sense since c. 1945] Charlie Parker, 1920–1955, alto saxophonist; most musicians and critics agree that he was at once the most influential innovator and the greatest instrumentalist in the history of jazz.

1946 *Esquire's 1946 Jazz Book*, p. 43. One is altoist Charlie Parker, familiar to jazzfans as "Yardbird."

1950 *Yardbird Suite* (tune composed by Charlie Parker).

1959 *The Permanent Playboy*, p. 242. One friend says, "When he wasn't allowed in, he would stand outside in the alley with his ear to the wall, fingering his alto and playing—and that's how he got his name, they always found him in an alley or a yard and they called him 'Yardbird.' " (Parker's own version was different: he said people called him first "Charlie," then "Charl," then "Yarl," then "Yard," and finally "Yardbird.").

1961 *Down Beat*, 25 May, p. 21. Yard had brought his horn with him.

yeah!, *interj.* [special use of colloquial term; reintroduced and widely current since c. 1950 after its use in the phrase *Yeah, man!,* q.v., had become passé among jazzmen c. 1940; see also THAT'S RIGHT, THERE YOU GO]

1959 *Newport Jazz Festival: 1959*, p. 46. *yeah:* exclamation of approval.

1961 *Charlie Rouse: Yeah!* (LP album Epic LA 16012).

yeah, man, *interj.* [see note s.v. *yeah;* current c. 1925–c. 1940, very rare

309

since except historical (see 1946 quot.)] Exclamation of approval and/or ebullience.

1932 *The Inter-State Tattler*, 7 Jan., p. 8. Still gatherin' dirt—yeah, man!

1935 *His Hi De Highness of Ho De Ho*, p. 35. Some jazz phrases . . . such as "Yeah, man!" eventually have become part of the everyday language of all Americans.

1938 *Cab Calloway: Hi De Ho*, p. 16. yeah, man: an exclamation of assent.

1946 *Really the Blues*, p. 141. The unhip public took over the expression "hot" and made it corny by getting up in front of a band and snapping their fingers in a childish way, yelling "Get hot! Yeah man, get hot!"

you know? [term has the same vague uses in general colloquial speech, but has been esp. common among jazzmen since c. 1945]

1958 *Publication of the American Dialect Society*, Nov., p. 47. *you know:* means nothing (see "like"), but used as a question at the end of a statement.

1959 *The Horn*, p. 68. Now pull yourself together, pops, you know?

1961 *The Jazz Life*, p. 23. Everyone, when he first started, thought: This man, his *tone* is too *thin*, you know?

1965 *Down Beat*, 20 May, p. 31. He gets a nice full sound in the bottom of his horn, you know?

Z

---

zanzy, *adj.* [shortened form of *Zanzibar,* with whose predominantly black population many black jazzmen identify; some currency esp. among black jazzmen c. 1945–c. 1950, obs. since] Authentic; splendid.

1970 *Dictionary of Afro-American Slang,* p. 126. *zanzy:* (1940s–50s) realistic and excellent.

zonked, *adj.* [cf. comic strip attempt at onomatopoeic rendering of a blow; prob. by analogy with the effect; see also BOXED, HIGH, JUICED, STONED]

1958 *Somewhere There's Music,* p. 85. I think I got zonked on the beer.

1959 *Esquire,* Nov., p. 70J. *zonked:* high, drunk.

1963 *Nugget,* Feb., p. 21. This gentleman was so zonked he didn't remember a thing.

zoot(y), *adj.* [according to jazzman Zutty Singleton, the term was New Orleans patois for "cute" (a suggested etym. differing from the one offered in 1943 quot., q.v.); some currency c. 1925–c. 1945, obs. since except historical; see also the much more widely current DAP, SHARP] Initially: see second 1946 quot.; also, since c. 1935: see 1944 quot.

1943 *New Yorker,* 19 June, p. 14. As for the word "zoot," it is simply a corrupt form of "suit."

1944 *The New Cab Calloway's Hepsters Dictionary,* s.v. *zoot:* overexaggerated as applied to clothes.

1946 *Really the Blues,* p. 311. Colored kids . . . work on their dungarees, pegging the legs till they're real sharp and zooty. —p. 376. *zooty:* stylish, fashionable.

1961 *Down Beat*, 13 Apr., p. 20. After World War II, like the clothing it described, the word *zoot* faded from use, except in satiric context— and as the nickname of a very great tenor player [i.e., Zoot Sims].

zoot suit (with the reet pleat) [from rhyming slang vogue c. 1935–c. 1940 (see also JACK THE BEAR, KILLER-DILLER); though the phrase is originally jazz slang, its currency was short and slight among jazzmen (c. 1938–c. 1940), and it thrived primarily in non-jazz speech] See first (only slightly exaggerated) quot.

1942 *American Mercury*, July, p. 96. *zoot suit with the reet pleat:* Harlem style suit, padded shoulders, 43-inch trousers at the knee with cuff so small it needs a zipper to get into, high waistline, fancy lapels, bushels of buttons, etc.

1959 *The Jazz Scene*, p. 218. Before the vogue of the boppers' costume, it used to be the "zoot suit," with its epaulette shoulders, its frock coat hanging almost to the pavement, and its peg-bottom trousers.

BIBLIOGRAPHY

A List of Works Cited

I. PERIODICALS

Americanisms: Content and Continuum
American Mercury
American Speech
American Weekly
Américas
Aramco World
Artesian
The Atlantic Monthly

Ballroom Dance
Bandleaders
Band Leaders and Record Review
The Billboard
Black Mask

Capitol News
Charm
The Chicago Defender
Chicago Review
Clef
Climax
Coda
Collier's
Commonweal
Confidential
Copper Romance

Cosmopolitan
Current History

Delineator
Different Drummer
Disc
Down Beat

Ebony
Encounter
Escapade
Esquire
Evergreen Review

Flair
Fortune
Frontier

The Griffin

Harper's
Hi Fi & Music Review
High Fidelity
Hollywood Note

The Inter-State Tattler
Intro Bulletin

Jacobs' Orchestra Monthly
Jazz: A Quarterly of American Music

313

BIBLIOGRAPHY

Jazz Forum
Jazz Journal
Jazz Monthly
Jazz News
Jazz Notes
Jazzology
The Jazz Record
The Jazz Review
The Journal of Abnormal and Social
    Psychology
Journal of Negro Education
Journal of Negro History

Leisure
Life
Louisville Courier-Journal
The Lowdown

Mademoiselle
Melody Maker
Metronome
Modern Music
Monsieur
Monthly Review
The Musical Digest
The Music Quarterly
Music Library Association Notes
Music News

Neurotica
The New York Age
The New York Amsterdam News
New York Citizen-Call
New York Daily News
The New Yorker
New York Herald-Tribune
New York Journal-American
New York Post
The New York Times
The New York Times Magazine
The New York Woman
Nugget

Oakland Tribune
Observer-Kaleidoscope

Palaver
Park East
Partisan Review
Philadelphia Afro-American
Philadelphia Afro Magazine Section
Phylon
Pic
Play Back
Playboy
PM
Publications of the American Dialect
    Society

The Realist
The Record Changer
Record Research
Rhythm and Blues

Saga
San Francisco Bulletin
San Francisco Call-Bulletin
San Francisco Chronicle
San Francisco Examiner
Saturday Review
Say
Scribner's Magazine
See
Show Business Illustrated
Sing Out!
Social Forces
Southern Folklore Quarterly
Spotlight
Stage
St. Louis Post-Dispatch
Swank
Swing

Tennessee Folklore Society Bulletin
This Week Magazine

Time

Toledo (Ohio) Blade

Toronto Daily Star

Toronto Telegram

Travel and Leisure

Vanity Fair

Variety

The Village Voice

Vogue

The World

Zit's Theatrical Newspaper

II. BOOKS, MISCELLANEOUS PUBLICATIONS, ETC.

(NOTE: *In order to facilitate reference from the citations to these works, the normal order of listing items has been reversed, the title here preceding the author.*)

After Claude: Iris Owens, New York: Farrar, Straus & Giroux, 1973.

All About Jazz: Stanley R. Nelson. London: Health Cranton, 1934.

All What Jazz: Philip Larkin. New York: St. Martin's Press, 1970.

American College Dictionary: New York: Random House, 1959.

The American Jazz Festival: Louis R. Lawless. New York: International Jazz Associates, 1956.

American Jazz Music: Wilder Hobson. New York: W. W. Norton, 1939.

The American Language: H. L. Mencken. New York: Alfred A. Knopf, 1936–1948.

The American Thesaurus of Slang: A Complete Reference Book of Colloquial Speech: ed. by Lester V. Berrey & Melvin Van Den Bark. New York: Thomas Y. Crowell, 1942; with new appendix, 1947; rev. 1953.

American Tramp and Underworld Slang: ed. by Godfrey Irwin. New York: Sears, 1930.

The Anatomy of Jazz: Leroy Ostransky. Seattle: University of Washington Press, 1960.

The Anatomy of Slang: Gilbert Highet. Book-of-the-Month Club transcript of WNYC radio talk, n.d.

The Angry Ones: John A. Williams. New York: Ace Books, 1960.

The Art of Jazz: ed. by Martin T. Williams. New York: Oxford U. Press, 1959.

The Autobiography of an Ex-Coloured Man: James Weldon Johnson. New York: Hill & Wang reprint, 1960 (New York: Sherman, French, 1912).

Barefoot Boy with Cheek: Max Shulman. New York: Garden City, 1943.

Beale Street: Where the Blues Began: George W. Lee. New York: Robert O. Ballou, 1934.

The Beat Generation Dictionary: ed. by Albert Zugsmith. Hollywood, Calif.: MGM, 1959.

Beat Jokes Bop Humor & Cool Cartoons: ed. by Bob Reisner. New York: Citadel, 1960.

Beneath the Underdog: Charlie Mingus, ed. by Nel King. New York: Alfred A. Knopf, 1971.

315

Bessie: Chris Albertson. New York: Stein & Day, 1972.
Big Bill Blues: William Broonzy & Yannick Bruynoghe. London: Cassell, 1955.
Big Book of Swing: ed. by Bill Treadwell. New York: Cambridge House, 1946.
Bird Lives: The High Life & Hard Times of Charlie (Yardbird) Parker: Ross
  Russell. New York: Charterhouse, 1973.
Black Music: LeRoi Jones. New York: Wm. Morrow, 1967.
Black Music: Four Lives: A. B. Spellman. New York: Schocken 1970 (orig. title
  Four Lives in the Bebop Business. New York: Pantheon, 1966).
Black on Black: Chester Himes. Garden City, New York: Doubleday, 1973.
Blue Movie: Terry Southern. New York: World, 1970.
Blues (Decca Records pamphlet, 1939).
Blues People: LeRoi Jones. New York: Wm. Morrow, 1963.
The Book of Jazz: Leonard Feather. New York: Horizon, 1957.
The Book of Negro Folklore: ed. by Langston Hughes & Arna Bontemps. New
  York: Dodd, Mead, 1958.
Bop Fables: Steve Allen. New York: Simon and Schuster, 1955.
Bourbon Street Black: Jack Buerkle & Danny Barker. New York: Oxford U.
  Press, 1973.
Cab Calloway: Hi De Ho: New York: Mills, 1938.
Call House Madam: Madam Beverly Davis & Serge G. Wolsey. New York:
  Paperback Books, 1963 (1942).
Chicago Documentary: Frederic Ramsey, Jr. London: Jazz Sociological Society,
  1944.
The Collector's Jazz: Modern: John S. Wilson. Philadelphia: J. B. Lippincott,
  1959.
The Collector's Jazz: Traditional and Swing: John S. Wilson. Philadelphia: J. B.
  Lippincott, 1958.
"A Compendium for the Teaching of Jazz History": Robert D. Fisher (unpubl.
  Master of Music thesis: U. of So. Cal., Jan. 1959).
Concerning Jazz: Sinclair Traill. London: Faber, 1957.
The Cool World: Warren Miller. Boston: Little, Brown, 1959.
The Country Blues: Samuel P. Charters. New York: Rinehart, 1959.
A Curtain of Green: Eudora Welty. Garden City, New York: Doubleday, Doran,
  1943.
Dan Burley's Original Handbook of Harlem Jive: Dan Burley. New York, 1944.
The Dead Ringer: Fredric Brown. New York: Bantam, 1949 (E. P. Dutton, 1948).
Death of a Blue-Eyed Soul Brother: B. B. Johnson. New York: Paperback
  Library, 1970.
The Decca Book of Jazz: ed. by Peter Gammond. London: Frederick Muller,
  1958.
Deep Down in the Jungle: Roger D. Abrahams. Hatboro, Pa.: Folklore
  Associates, 1964.
The Dharma Bums: Jack Kerouac. New York: Viking Press, 1958.

Dictionary of Afro-American Slang: ed. by Clarence Major. New York: International Publishing Co., 1970.

A Dictionary of American English on Historical Principles, 4 Vols.: William A. Craigie & James R. Hulbert. Chicago: University of Chicago Press, 1938–1944.

A Dictionary of American Slang: ed. by Maurice Weseen. New York: Thomas Y. Crowell, 1934.

Dictionary of American Slang: ed. by Harold Wentworth & Stuart Berg Flexner. New York: Thomas Y. Crowell, 1960.

Dictionary of American Underworld Lingo: ed. by Hyman E. Goldin, et al. New York: Twayne, 1950.

A Dictionary of Slang and Colloquial English: ed. by John S. Farmer & William Ernest Henley. New York: E. P. Dutton, 1905, rev. 1921.

Dictionary of Slang and Its Analogues, 2 Vols.: John S. Farmer & William Ernest Henley. 1890–1904, reprinted New Hyde Park, New York: University Books, 1965.

A Dictionary of Slang and Unconventional English: Eric Partridge. New York: Macmillan, 1937.

A Dictionary of Slang, Jargon and Cant, 2 Vols.: ed. by Albert Barrers, ed. by Charles G. Leland. London: Ballantyne, 1889.

Diggeth Thou?: Dan Burley. Chicago: Burley, Cross, 1959.

Dinosaurs in the Morning: Whitney Balliett. Philadelphia: J. B. Lippincott, 1962.

Down Beat Jazz Record Reviews 1956: Chicago: Maher, 1957.

Down Beat Jazz Record Reviews 1959: Chicago: Maher, 1960.

Down Beat Jazz Record Reviews 1961: Chicago: Maher, 1962.

Down Beat's Yearbook of Swing: ed. by Paul Eduard Miller. Chicago: Down Beat, 1939.

Down Memory Lane: Arthur Murray's Picture Story of Social Dancing: Sylvia G. L. Dannett & Frank R. Rachel. New York: Greenberg, 1954.

A Drop of Patience: William Melvin Kelley. New York: Doubleday, 1965.

Duke Ellington: Barry Ulanov. New York: Creative Age, 1946.

Easy Living: Maitland Zane. New York: Dial Press, 1956.

Eddie Condon's Treasury of Jazz: ed. by Eddie Condon & Richard Gehman. New York: Dial Press, 1956.

1811 Dictionary of the Vulgar Tongue: Reprinted Chicago: Follett Publishing Co., 1971.

The Encyclopedia of Jazz: Leonard Feather. New York: Horizon Press, 1955.

The Essential Lenny Bruce: ed. by John Cohen. New York: Ballantine, 1967.

English Words & Their Background: George McKnight. New York: D. Appleton, 1925.

Enjoyment of Jazz (EJ 401, 402, 410): New York: American Recording Society [1956].

Esquire's 1944 Jazz Book: New York: Smith & Durrell, 1944.

Esquire's 1945 Jazz Book: New York: Smith & Durrell, 1945.

BIBLIOGRAPHY

Esquire's 1946 Jazz Book: New York: Smith & Durrell, 1946.
Esquire's 1947 Jazz Book: New York: Smith & Durrell, 1947.
Father of the Blues: An Autobiography: W. C. Handy. New York: Macmillan, 1941.
The Feeling of Jazz: George T. Simon. New York: Simon and Schuster, 1961.
The Female Eunuch: Germaine Greer. New York: McGraw-Hill, 1971.
Find a Victim: Ross Macdonald. New York: Bantam, 1955.
Finnley Wren: Philip Wylie. New York: New American Library, 1949 (Rinehart, 1934).
The First Book of Jazz: Langston Hughes. New York: Franklin Watts, 1955.
Flee the Angry Strangers: George Mandel. Indianapolis: Bobbs-Merrill, 1952.
The French Quarter: Herbert Asbury. New York: Garden City, 1938.
From Spirituals to Swing: (Carnegie Hall program: December 23, 1938).
Frontiers of Jazz: ed. by Ralph de Toledano. New York: Oliver Durrell Co., 1947.
Funk & Wagnalls New "Standard" Dictionary of the English Language: 1913, rev. 1960.
Gems of Jazz: Vol. I (Decca Records pamphlet, 1941).
Gems of Jazz: Vol. III (Decca Records pamphlet, 1941).
Gems of Jazz: Vol. IV (Decca Records pamphlet, 1942).
Giants of Jazz: Studs Turkel. New York: Thomas Y. Crowell, 1957.
Go: John Clellon Holmes. New York: Charles Scribner's Sons, 1952.
Gorilla, My Love: Toni Cade Bambara. New York: Random House, 1972.
Guide to Jazz: Madeleine Gautier & Hugues Panassie. Boston: Houghton Mifflin, 1956.
Gutbucket and Gossamer: Fred Miller. Yonkers, N.Y.: Alicat, 1950.
Harlem Jazz 1930 (Brunswick pamphlet, 1943).
The Harder They Fall: Budd Schulberg. New York: Random House, 1947.
Harvard Dictionary of Music: Willi Apel. Cambridge, Mass.: Harvard University Press, 1946.
Hear Me Talkin to Ya: ed. by Nat Shapiro & Nat Hentoff. New York: Rinehart, 1955.
The Heart of Jazz: William L. Grossman & Jack W. Farrell. New York: New York University Press, 1956.
Hepcats Jive Talk Dictionary: ed. by Lou Shelly. Derby, Conn.: T. W. O. Charles, 1945.
Hip Manual: no author. SR62145 Mercury Records brochure: 1969.
The Hiparama of the Classics: Lord Buckley. San Francisco: City Lights, 1960.
Hiptionary: Elliot Horne. New York: Simon and Schuster, 1963.
His Hi De Highness of Ho De Ho: Ned E. Williams. New York: Laurel, n.d.
A History of Jazz in America: Barry Ulanov. New York: Viking Press, 1952.
Hoagy Carmichael Songs (Decca Records pamphlet, 1939).
The Holy Barbarians: Lawrence Lipton. New York: Julian Messner, 1959.
The Horn: John Clellon Holmes. New York: Random House, 1958.

The Hot and the Cool: Edwin Gilbert. New York: Doubleday, 1953.
The Hot Jazz of Jelly Roll Morton: Charles Edward Smith. Camden, N.J.: R.C.A. Victor, n.d.
Inside Be-Bop: Leonard Feather. New York: J. J. Robbins, 1949.
The International Cyclopedia of Music and Musicians: ed. by Oscar Thompson. New York: Dodd, Mead, 1939.
Invisible Man: Ralph Ellison. New York: Signet reprint, 1960 (Random House, 1952).
It's Always Four O'Clock: James Updyke. New York: Random House, 1956.
I Want It Now: Kingsley Amis. New York: Harcourt, Brace & World, 1968.
Jam Session: An Anthology of Jazz: ed. by Ralph J. Gleason. New York: G. P. Putnam's, 1958.
Jazz: Paul Whiteman & M. M. McBride. New York: Sears, 1926.
Jazz: ed. by Nat Hentoff & Albert J. McCarthy. New York: Rinehart, 1959.
Jazzbook 1947: London: PL Editions, 1947.
Jazz Dance: Marshall & Jean Stearns. New York: Macmillan, 1968.
Jazz for Moderns: New York: Associated Booking, n.d.
Jazz: A History of the New York Scene: Samuel B. Charters & Leonard Kunstadt. Garden City, N.Y.: Doubleday, 1962.
Jazz: Hot and Hybrid: Winthrop Sargent. New York: E. P. Dutton, 1946.
Jazz: Its Evolution and Essence: André Hodeir. New York: Grove, 1956.
The Jazz Life: Nat Hentoff. New York: Dial Press, 1961.
Jazz Masters of the Thirties: Rex Stewart. New York: Macmillan, 1972.
Jazzmen: ed. by Frederic Ramsey, Jr., & Charles Edward Smith. New York: Harcourt, Brace, 1939.
Jazz People: Valerie Wilmer. Indianapolis: Bobbs-Merrill, 1970.
Jazz Poems: Ted Joans. New York: Rhino Review, 1959.
The Jazz Record Book: Charles Edward Smith. New York: Smith & Durrell, 1942.
The Jazz Scene: Francis Newton. London: MacGibbon & Kee, 1959.
Jazz Street: Nat Hentoff. Garden City, N.Y.: Doubleday, 1960.
Jazz Style in Kansas City and the Southwest: Ross Russell. Berkeley: U. of California Press, 1971.
The Jazz Titans: Robert George Reisner. Garden City, N.Y.: Doubleday, 1960.
Jazzways: ed. by George S. Rosenthal & Frank Zachery. New York: Greenberg, 1946.
The Jazz Word: ed. by Dom Cerulli, Burt Korall, & Mort Nasatir. New York: Ballantine Books, 1960.
Jelly Roll Morton's New Orleans Memories: Jelly Roll Morton. New York: Consolidated Records, n.d.
Jitterbug Jamboree Song Book: Jean Herbert & Otis Spencer. New York: Marks Music Corp., 1939.
Jive and Slang: ed. by Marcus H. Boulware. Hampton, Va.: M. Boulware, 1947.

BIBLIOGRAPHY

Jive in Hi-Fi: Willie Bryant. Los Angeles: Wilfern, 1958.
Junkie: William Lee (pseud., William Burroughs?). New York: Ace, 1953.
Just Jazz: Sinclair Traill & Gerald Lascelles. London: Peter Davies, 1957.
The Kingdom of Swing: Benny Goodman & Irving Kolodin. New York: Stackpole Sons, 1939.
Ladies and Gentlemen—Lenny Bruce!!: Albert Goldman. New York: Random House, 1974.
Lady Sings the Blues: Billie Holiday. New York: Doubleday, 1956.
The Life and Loves of Mr. Jiveass Nigger: Cecil Brown. New York: Farrar, Straus & Giroux, 1970.
Lingo of Tin-Pan Alley: Arnold Shaw. New York: Broadcast Music, 1950.
Location Shots: J. F. Burke. New York: Harper & Row, 1974.
Louis Armstrong: Hugues Panassie. New York: Charles Scribner's Sons, 1971.
Mexico City Blues: Jack Kerouac. New York: Grove, 1959.
A Mind to Murder: P. D. James. New York: Charles Scribner's Sons, 1963.
Mister Jelly Roll: Alan Lomax. New York: Duell, Sloan & Pearce, 1950.
Modern Dancing: Vernon & Irene Castle. New York: Harper & Bros., 1914 [as cited in *Jazz: A History of the New York Scene,* q.v.].
Murder on the Downbeat: Robert Avery. New York: Mystery House, 1943.
Music Out of Dixie: Harold Sinclair. New York: Rinehart, 1952.
The Naked Lunch: William Burroughs. Paris: Olympia Press, 1959.
The New Cab Calloway's Cat-ologue: New York: C. Calloway, 1938.
The New Cab Calloway's Hepsters Dictionary: Language of Jive: Cab Calloway. New York: C. Calloway, 1944.
The New Edition of the Encyclopedia of Jazz: Leonard Feather. New York: Horizon, 1960.
The New Jazz Book: Joachim Berendt. New York: Hill and Wang, 1962.
Newport Jazz Festival: 1959 (program). Chicago: Down Beat, 1959.
New Short Novels: ed. by Mary Louise Aswell. New York: Ballantine, 1954.
New York Jazz Festival 1957: New York: n.p., 1957.
New York Jazz Festival: Vol. 3: New York: n.p., n.d.
New York Panorama: Federal Writer's Project. New York: Random House, 1938.
Nigger Heaven: Carl Van Vechten. New York: Knopf, 1926.
Night Light: Douglass Wallop. New York: W. W. Norton, 1953.
Night Song: John A. Williams. New York: Farrar, Straus and Cudahy, 1961.
The Night the Old Nostalgia Burned Down: Frank Sullivan. Boston: Little, Brown, 1953.
Nobody Knows My Name: James Baldwin. New York: Dial, 1961.
On the Road: Jack Kerouac. New York: Viking, 1957.
Oxford English Dictionary: 1884–1928; rev. ed., 1933.
Paris Blues: Harold Flender. New York: Ballantine, 1957.
The Permanent Playboy: ed. by Ray Russell. Chicago: Playboy, 1959.

A Pictorial History of Jazz: Orrin Keepnews & Bill Grauer, Jr. New York: Crown, 1955.

The PL Yearbook of Jazz: ed. by Albert McCarthy. London: PL Editions, 1946.

Raise Up Off Me: Hampton Hawes & Don Asher. New York: Coward, McCann & Geoghegan, 1974.

The Real Cool Killers: Chester Himes, New York: Avon, 1959.

The Real Jazz Old and New: Stephen Longstreet. Baton Rouge, La.: L. S. U. Press, 1956.

Really the Blues: Milton Mezzrow & Bernard Wolfe. New York: Random House, 1946.

Ride Out: Shelby Foote, in *New Short Novels* (ed. by Mary Louise Aswell). New York: Ballatine, 1954.

Riverboat Jazz (Brunswick Records pamphlet, 1943).

Saint Jack: Paul Theroux. Boston: Houghton Mifflin, 1973.

Salute to Fats Waller (Carnegie Hall program: April 2, 1944).

Satchmo: Louis Armstrong. New York: Prentice-Hall, 1954.

Second Ending: Evan Hunter. New York: Simon and Schuster, 1956.

Selected Poems: Langston Hughes. New York: Knopf, 1959.

Shakespeare's Bawdy: Eric Partridge. New York: E. P. Dutton, 1948.

Shaft: Ernest Tidyman. New York: Macmillan, 1970.

Shroud for a Nightingale: P. D. James. New York: Charles Scribner's Sons, 1971.

Sideman: Osborn Duke. New York: Criterion, 1956.

Smaller Slang Dictionary: Eric Partridge. New York: Philosophical Library, 1961.

So It Doesn't Whistle: Robert Paul Smith. New York: Harcourt, Brace, 1941.

Solo: Stanford Witmore. New York: Harcourt, Brace, 1955.

Somewhere There's Music: George Lea. Philadelphia: J. B. Lippincott, 1958.

Sons of Darkness, Sons of Light: John A. Williams. Boston: Little, Brown, 1969.

So This Is Jazz: Henry O. Osgood. Boston: Little, Brown, 1926.

The Sound: Ross Russell. New York: E. P. Dutton, 1961.

The Sound of Surprise: Whitney Balliett. New York: E. P. Dutton, 1959.

The Story of Jazz: Marshall Stearns. New York: Oxford U. Press, 1956.

The Story of the Original Dixieland Jazz Band: H. O. Brunn. Baton Rouge, La.: L. S. U. Press, 1960.

The Street That Never Slept: Arnold Shaw. New York: Coward, McCann & Geoghegan, 1971.

Strictly Ding-Dong: Richard English. Garden City, N.Y.: Doubleday, 1941.

The Subterraneans: Jack Kerouac. New York: Grove Press, 1958.

Such Sweet Thunder: Whitney Balliett. Indianapolis/New York: Bobbs-Merrill, 1966.

Swinging Syllables: Memphis, Tenn.: Kimbrough, 1959.

Swing That Music: Louis Armstrong. London: Longmans, Green, 1936.

Target Blue: Robert Daley. New York: Delacorte Press, 1973.

BIBLIOGRAPHY

They All Played Ragtime: Rudi Blesh & Harriet Janis. New York: Alfred A. Knopf, 1950.

The Thin Man: Dashiell Hammett. New York: Permabooks reprint, 1961 (Knopf, 1934).

This Is Jazz: Rudi Blesh. San Francisco: n.p., 1943.

This Thing Called Swing: ed. by Benny Goodman. Winston-Salem, N.C.: R. J. Reynolds, n.d.

Toward Jazz: Andre Hodeir. New York: Grove, 1962.

Transatlantic Jazz: Peter Noble. London: Citizen Press, n.d.

A Treasury of the Blues: ed. by W. C. Handy. New York: Simon and Schuster, 1949.

Treat It Gentle: Sidney Bechet. New York: Hill & Wang, 1960.

Tremolo: Ernest Borneman. New York: Harper & Brothers, 1948.

The Trouble with Cinderella: Artie Shaw. New York: Farrar, Straus & Young, 1952.

Trumpet on the Wing: Wingy Manone & Paul Vandervoort. Garden City, N.Y.: Doubleday & Co., 1948.

The Two Worlds of Johnny Truro: George Sklar. Boston: Little, Brown, 1947.

The Walls of Jericho: Rudolph Fisher. New York: Alfred A. Knopf, 1928.

Webster's New World Dictionary of the American Language: College Edition: Cleveland: World, 1959.

The Wig: Charles Wright. New York: Farrar, Straus & Giroux, 1966.

Who Walk in Darkness: Chandler Brossard. New York: New Directions, 1952.

The World of Duke Ellington: Stanley Dance. New York: Chas. Scribner's Sons, 1970.

The Worlds of Jazz: André Hodeir, translated by Noel Burch. New York: Grove, 1972.

A Wreath for Rivera: Ngaio Marsh. Boston: Little, Brown, 1949.

Various song titles and lyrics, and various LP album titles and liner notes—as indicated in the lexicon citations.